EZ Does It:

The Journey of a Lifetime

by
Edward Smith

ISBN: 0-9749701-3-1

Library of Congress Control Number: 2005920409

Published by
Inkwell Productions
6962 E. First Avenue, Ste.102
Scottsdale, AZ 85251
Phone (480) 481-6036
Fax (480) 481-6042
Toll Free 888-324-BOOK (2665)
Email: info@inkwellproductions.com
Web site: www.inkwellproductions.com

Angels Watching Over Me

In Loving Memory of my grandparents:

Edward M. Smith Sr.

Catherine Smith

Wheeler Miles

Amelia Miles

My Best Friend, Eric Dickson

and

Biggest Fan, Dianne Lewis

Acknowledgements

First, and foremost, I want to thank God Almighty. Without His guidance and forgiveness, through the longest of days and darkest of nights, there would be no story to tell.

To Mom and Pop, thank you for loving me unconditionally! You taught me how to be a man and never stopped believing in me, even when I sometimes didn't believe in myself. And through it all, "We never gave up". I love you both!

To Irv, you'll always be my baby brother, but I couldn't be more proud of the man you've become. You forced me to set the bar high because I knew you were destined for greatness. Let's continue to do it like the Smith Brothers know how to do it.

To ALL my family and friends, thanks for all the love, inspiration and support through the years. You will never know how much a shared laugh in the middle of the night, most times from a different time zone, can lift one's spirits. Special shouts to Ms. Edith and Monika (Moni).

To Nick Ligidakis and Inkwell Productions, thank you for your ongoing support and direction in the production of this book. It was sitting in a closet when we first met, now look what we've done!

To Debbie Moyer, editor extraordinaire, thank you for all the hours of hard work. You turn good stories into great books. More importantly, I appreciate you becoming a friend for life. Let's do this again.

To Ronny Cromwell at Graphix Out West Today, a big thanks to you. Your cover tells a story without saying a word.

To Madalyn Johnson at Type 'N Graphics, a special thank you. Not only did you *set* this book up with precision and skill, you are an absolute joy and pleasure to work with.

To Ed Ford and Al Goldis, thank you for believing in my athletic gift and never turning your backs on me as I tried to climb the ladder.

To Don Wolfe, Super-Agent, I would have traveled a much different road if not for all of your efforts. You Da Man!

To Pat, Amy and Bill at Pro-Files Sports Management, thank you for believing in a well-traveled minor league baseball player. Who said you can't teach old dogs new tricks?

To all of my people back in Browns Mills/Pemberton, New Jersey, thank you to EVERY neighbor, teacher, administrator and coach for your part in raising me. I wouldn't be who I am today without you. Too many to name individually, I love each of you as if you were a part of my family, especially you, Mrs. Pierce!

To Amanda, thank you for not allowing me to give up on my dream. Whenever I thought I was fighting an uphill battle, ready to give up, you were that inspirational voice. This wouldn't have gotten done without you!

To each and every fan that paid the price of admission, cheered me in victory or defeat, waited for an autograph or showed a simple gesture of kindness during my roller coaster journey, thank you. You are a big part of the reason why the whole ride was worthwhile!

To every teammate, as well as all opposing players I faced, thank you for ACCOMPANYING me along and through my incredible voyage. Some joined me on crammed buses, while others lounged across aisles on comfortable chartered flights. Some shared truck-stop snacks in the middle of the night, while others ate with me at the finest restaurants. Some waited in long lines to get into the club, while I walked with others straight to the front and enjoyed V.I.P. status. This book is soaked in the blood, sweat and tears left on sports fields all across the land. Regardless of where we are now, we will ALWAYS be brothers; Nate Miller, Calvin Collins, Kinnis Pledger, Doug Glanville, Mike Farrell, Mike Carter, Don Reynolds, Rodney McCray, Ray Payton, Bobby Benjamin, Caesar Bernhardt, Al Lewis, Andrew Monaco, Nandi Cruz, Stephon Gamlin, Paul Torres, Benny Castilla and countless others!

TABLE OF CONTENTS

THE
EARLY YEARS

CHAPTER ONE

In The Beginning

"Full many a flower is born to blush unseen and waste its sweetness on the desert air."

Thomas Gray

Susan Sarandon quoted this when she played the character Annie Savoy in the movie *Bull Durham*. The same could be an epitaph for my fifteen-year sports career. Besides being the best baseball movie ever made, *Bull Durham* perfectly depicts the life I led for almost a decade before moving on to greener pastures. While I struggled with many things along the road, nearly giving up on several occasions because the fight just didn't seem worth the reward, I learned valuable life lessons and "whatever didn't kill me only made me stronger". Today I plan to tell you how I resemble that blushing, unseen flower in the sweet desert air.

My life has been played out as if I were living it through the dreams of the millions of little boys drifting off to sleep the night before their big games, visions of hitting winning homeruns dancing around in their heads. It hasn't, however, been the fairytale life in which many believe all athletes exist. Along with success, I have also experienced incredible feelings of pressure and loneliness as well as lack of personal and emotional fulfillment (which come with trying to be what everyone expects one to be). In some cases, the pressure of my own seemingly unreachable standards lay heavily on my head.

Overshadowed by the huge salaries and inflated egos of

today's athlete is the fact that beneath it all we are all still human, of flesh and blood. The general public seems to feel that every athlete is pulling in the million-dollar paycheck, living in the huge mansion, wearing the expensive jewelry, or driving the fancy car. That is not the truth and those particular things don't make the man anyway. Behind every fast-running, high-jumping, homerun-hitting or football-throwing face seen on the television there is a heart and soul that can love, hate, hurt and ache just like the next person. I am not trying to paint athletes as saints totally misunderstood and misrepresented by the media and general public because that is not the case either. There are immoral human beings entertaining millions each and every week of the year. They dance in the end zone or fly through the air en route to a spectacular dunk wanting the spotlight totally focused on them while team goals are secondary. Those are seen and heard about most often, but should not serve as the standard of judgment for all. We all travel our own roads and follow different destinies. Each is an individual who has been blessed with and fortunate enough to get the most out of God-given talents. What we do with that talent and how we live our lives is what makes us, both good and bad.

Living my professional life under the radar has been both easy and satisfying for me because of the strong family foundation in which I was born and raised. By no stretch of the imagination have I lived a charmed life, as you will come to see. But I also have never had an ego that couldn't be contained mostly because of the struggles and uphill battles that have kept me grounded throughout my life and career. That is why Thomas Gray's quote has such meaning to me. We are not all here to shine like the brightest star in the darkest of night. Many of us have been put on this earth to be the light for only a chosen few to see, to brighten another's light or in some cases never to shine at all but simply to make sure your brother or sister in spirit does not fall from the sky.

My first breath on this earth was taken on the 5th day of June 1969 in Trenton, New Jersey. Born to Patricia and Edward Smith Junior, I was the next in line to carry the name proudly as Edward Martin Smith III. My brother Irvin showed up a little over two years later in October 1971. He tells anyone who will listen that he is not only the younger but the more handsome of the two boys that my parents produced. With two hardheaded sons to raise in the early 1970's my parents probably decided that was enough, and so, our family unit was set.

My father met my mother just weeks after his return from a navy stint post high school graduation. It was the late 1960's. Lucky for him, the bar he was coming out of (in the middle of the afternoon) was conveniently located next to a corner grocery store. Pop would be the first to admit that my mother more than likely would have passed him by had she known he had only stopped in the grocery store minutes prior to her walking in that direction, having spent nearly the entire day on a bar stool next door. Furthermore, it was not merely a one-day drinking binge for him.

At the tender age of 23, having served his country abroad for four hell-bent-for-leather years, my father was a full-blown alcoholic. Many factors worked against him at that time and it is evident there wasn't much defense against the disease. Besides the fact that alcoholism runs rampant through that side of the family was the lifestyle my father led while overseas. Plenty of stories exist about the drunken nights, almost being killed in the streets fighting and being thrown in the brig numerous times. In an ironic way my father's early years run parallel to my own once I started playing professional baseball at a very young and immature age. Minus the street fighting and being thrown in the stockade, I also experienced plenty of drinking and teetering on the edge of losing all for which I had worked so hard.

As luck would have it for my father and mother, a spark swept the two up and a courtship evolved from that corner store meeting that ended in my father walking the pretty young lady home. And against some odds (the number one being my grandfather's disapproval of the relationship because he thought my father was too experienced for his eighteen-year-old daughter) the two were married in September of 1968.

To support a new wife, and later his two boys, my father used the trade he learned in the navy as a boiler operator to make ends meet. He did quite well. Shortly after I was born, my mother and father purchased their first home in Trenton, not far from where he ran two 50-story boilers, which generated electricity for a major portion of the eastern seaboard. But the inner city was not where they wanted to attempt raising two boys. The confines of the concrete playgrounds and the traps that lie in the belly of some of our major cities, the same problems we see today on a much larger scale, motivated my parents to make life better for all of us.

So, at the age of four and a half years, I was heading to the suburbs of south Jersey. The Smith family was 'movin on up' like the Jeffersons! The major difference: we were not moving to a deluxe apartment in the sky but to the pastures where cows and chickens roamed free and one truly gets the full picture as to why New Jersey is known as the Garden State. It was quite the contrast from the city life of Trenton only about twenty-five miles away. It was also the only move our family has ever made together; my parents live in that house in Browns Mills to this day!

The city has grown a bit over the thirty years since I laid eyes on my first deer leaping across one of the back roads.

Around the time I was creeping into teenage-hood in the early Eighties we got our first fast food chains, a McDonalds to go along with our Dairy Queen. And, just a few years ago a Burger King was added, so it is really 'booming in the big city' now. I look back now and see the many sacrifices made were mostly for the benefit of my brother and me. My father worked a swing shift which included many doubles and the commute was not an easy one after working sixteen-hour days. Then too, there was the financial struggle that resulted, primarily because the bread-winner of the family was a functioning alcoholic on his good days and an extreme alcoholic on the bad ones.

Still, growing up in Browns Mills was the very best thing that could happen for me for one particular reason; the city would have chewed me up and devoured me. Either that or I would have had to develop a toughness that I simply did not possess at that early stage of my life. I was a big kid who looked like I could handle myself on the outside but my shy, reserved and quiet nature was something that ran deep to the core. From all the stories I have heard, my character traits all go back to my namesake, my grandfather, Edward Sr., who was lost to cancer just before my fourth birthday. Everything from the way Pop Pop carried himself to his nickname on the streets, Live-Easy, was who I was and who I would become. I was well into my teens before I realized my full potential for expressing myself in any other way than sports, but I was EZ from birth.

Now, if this story were to be told by my father, I would have come out of the womb with a basketball in one hand and a baseball glove on the other. I would have already had the ability to shoot the three or hit the long ball before I was more than five minutes old. Pop has always been my biggest fan and while his version would be stretching things, it would be safe to say that it was evident very early in my life that I was born to be an athlete, another attribute passed on by the patriarch of the family. Similar to child prodigies who, laying their hands on a piano, barely of the age to speak, play beautiful music as if they had been receiving lessons while in the womb, all forms of sports equipment were my musical 'instruments' and I was destined to do great things if I could stay the course and overcome the obstacles.

On the whole, life was good in the sticks of South Jersey. Gone was the row house on South Walter Avenue with the backyard the size of a big box. Replacing it was the three bedroom split-level with a full size backyard. For two young boys armed with bicycles and Big Wheels, the still-developing neighborhood was like a jungle just waiting to be explored. Irv and I spent many a summer afternoon that year wandering through our future neighbors' basements and family rooms- then simply holes in the ground with foundations recently-poured. At that time our only concern was making sure we were heading in the direction of the house by the time the streetlights came on. That was a rule you didn't want to break.

It was a different time and parents did not have the concerns of today. While I am very thankful for that, in the same breath I feel remorse concerning the situations and conditions in which children of today have to attempt to grow up. Many of them are being robbed of their innocence and are dealing with adult situations far too early in life. Back in our day, we were allowed to simply be kids.

Irv and I grew up in a house filled with love but ruled with an iron fist. I mean that in the most positive of terms. There was no such thing as 'time out' in our day and an offense that was worthy of the belt got just that. We hoped it was Mom who was dishing out the punishment before Pop got home but even then, depending on what the infraction was, we might get a second helping. And unlike the many current voices against spanking, I am here to tell you that the prescription the doctor ordered for the Smith Brothers was exactly what was needed.

Irv and I did not get into a lot of serious trouble but we *were* hardheaded boys who sometimes did things that made our parents shake their heads. For instance, one day during a summer afternoon when I was about seven and Irv five, we looked up on the fireplace mantle in the house and found a wad of money. Instead of leaving alone something that we knew was there for a reason, all it took was for us to hear that beautiful sound of the ice cream truck playing its melodic music and we were running out the door cash in hand. And, as if it wasn't enough to get just us a treat, all of our friends shared in our new-found treasure as well! A day or so later, when it was time to put that money to use to pay an electric bill, my mother hit the roof when the truth finally came out and the mystery of the missing money was solved. Initially trying to lie and say we had no idea where the money went was a big mistake and only added to the thumping we received. I usually got the more severe punishment because I was the ring leader, the eldest, being watched at all times by a little brother who idolized me, and I should have known better!

There were some tough lessons learned up until we got our last whipping around the time I turned twelve but each and every one of them was not only well-deserved, but necessary to teach us the difference between right and wrong. Many would argue that we were abused children because our parents put their hands on us, but I thank God they loved us enough to raise us in the manner in which they did.

A vicious cycle reared its ugly head in our household and the cloud hung over our domain even after it was time for me to spread my wings and leave the comforts of the nest. For the millions of families dealing with the disease of alcoholism, the pain of watching someone you love live their life in such a reckless and careless fashion can be an excruciating experience which in most cases, brings the strongest of families to its knees. And for a young boy who idolized his father and wanted nothing more than to be able to respect him as well, it was twice as hard. It was apparent to me even as a little boy that, although seemingly normal on the outside, there was something different going on behind our closed doors. My father was making very good money working for Public Service but we always seemed to be struggling to make ends meet. And that was with my mother taking work in the library at the local community college. With my father's disease though, there was no telling how much of his paycheck would actually make it home each week. Pop worked six days straight and then had the next two off so his off days fluctuated. If payday happened to fall on an off day there was no telling where the mortgage, utilities or grocery money might end up. And when he finally got home my father was usually in such a state that it was pointless for my mother to argue with him because he wouldn't remember any of it in the morning anyway. My mother was unsinkable and truly the glue that held our ship together through some difficult times. I give her all the credit in the world for loving a man determined to drink his life away at one point because he just could not control the monster that had a grip on his soul.

One thing I can be appreciative about is that my father rarely took the form of an abusive alcoholic. I've heard stories of mean drunks who want to fight everyone and usually take out their anger on innocent and undeserving children or their spouses. Instead, Pop was the type to come stumbling through the door, eyes as red as a fire truck, breath reeking of the foul stench of cheap beer, and calling for his boys because it was playtime. When we were little, my brother and I ended up wrestling with my 'big-kid intoxicated father'. It was actually fun. But as we got older and realized it was no laughing matter, we dreaded him coming home in that condition. This was partially due to the rare times that things got physically violent between my parents. On these tumultuous occasions my brother and I would retreat to a back room and sometimes cry in each other's arms hoping he would pass out before anyone got hurt.

This was the way we lived for years. There were periods mixed in between all of the chaos when my father tried to take control of his addiction, cleaning up his act and finding sobriety, but there was always something that pulled him back in and he'd fall off the wagon again. It was usually overconfidence, his mind telling him he was bigger than the disease itself, that allowed him to take that one drink and then the whole vicious cycle would start all over again.

I was always proud of the fact that even during his worst times my father rarely missed anything my brother or I were involved in, even coaching us and leading us to a championship during one magical basketball season when I was about ten. It didn't matter if he worked a double shift, getting off in the afternoon after sixteen hours on the job, my father was front and center in the stands cheering and rooting for one of his future stars. That is something that amazed me about him. While other parents took the easy way out, dropping kids off and picking them up after the game or hoping another parent could transport them home, he made an effort to always be there for us as well as for any other kid who needed a cheerleader.

That being said, it was still mortifying when he got out of hand and sometimes nearly fell out of the stands because he was under the influence. It was something we had to deal with because he didn't have control of his life at that time. There were to be many hard times waiting ahead before he finally hit 'rock bottom' with nowhere to go but up.

Both my brother and I gave my parents plenty to cheer about early in our lives. My first shot at organized sports came on the baseball field in the Police Athletic League (P.A.L.) of Pemberton, New Jersey, a neighboring township to Browns Mills. It was the summer I turned seven. The year prior, my brother and me in the backseat as we passed the overflowing fields, my father promised to have us signed up the following year. He was true to his word and my journey into the sporting world was about to take off.

I really was a natural athlete almost directly from the womb. Again, if my father were telling this story I was both more powerful than a locomotive and able to leap tall buildings in a single bound. I simply say I was truly God-blessed with athleticism! By the time I reached ten years of age I had logged three seasons in the P.A.L. And Pemberton was slowly gaining recognition as a contender. Then, it was time to take the show on the road and outside the little community bubble. Each year after crowning regular season champions in both the minor division (ages 7-10) and the majors (ages 11 and 12), the traveling all-stars were selected by the leagues' coaches. I was a member of that team every season and my brother followed in my footsteps when he began playing at the age of seven as well.

In the traveling all-star tournaments Pemberton Little League had been consistent over the years for first day eliminations, two quick losses and we were sent home. We were considered to be a little backwoods community happy to just be on the playing field with the larger and more affluent surrounding areas. In my adolescent years I was now leading from atop the mound, in the field at shortstop or wielding my big bat in the cleanup position of the lineup. By the age of twelve I was playing with very familiar teammates, some since my first year in P.A.L. at age seven as a member of the Cubs. Because we all went to school together and played together on and off the field, friendly rivalries grew between opposing teams resulting in increased competition and better games.

I didn't stop with baseball either; I was multi-tasking at an early age. The fall after my first baseball season I began with basketball, then attempted to add football as well when I was eight years old. That first go-around was incredibly unsuccessful and discouraging. Although I was big for my age and looked intimidating, I didn't have the killer instinct needed to play football, even on the peewee level. Weighing in at 130lbs already, actually struggling to get down and maintain that weight, I was forced to play with the bigger kids who were a lot tougher. After a couple of practices I actually wanted to quit, but my mother and father, teachers of many valuable lessons, would not even hear it. If I started something, I was going to finish it, end of story!

I spent that fall playing on the offensive line as a fifth quarter player. The fifth quarter was designated for the kids that did not play in the game, the scrubs, of which I was one. And that was not because I didn't have the talent but because I did not put the effort in. If I didn't play to my full potential, expectations for success would not be high and failure would be easier to accept. And because I didn't like it, I didn't want to do it. The experience was so demoralizing that I put football on the back burner, choosing instead soccer to fill that time slot of the calendar year. This pattern continued the following five seasons all the way up until I entered high school. And if not for a good friend talking me into it, I don't think I would have ever put a helmet or shoulder pads on again.

The little boy away from the sport fields didn't quite match the one that walked through the hallways of the elementary school. Inward and shy would be understatements as to how I was perceived for years to come. While I stood tall and confident on any field and in any uniform I ever put on, I walked with slumped shoulders and made very little eye contact away from the sports environment. I spoke with a soft voice to grownups and especially the little girls. Amazingly, my little brother was the sibling that walked tall, spoke loud, had all of the friends, and was involved in every activity. A brotherly rivalry brewed early on between us because of the two roles we were almost forced into playing.

As the big brother it was my duty to lead the way in all achievements and my brother had to walk in the shadow I created. Whenever I thought he was closing the gap the pressure was on me to take things to the next level. If I moved too far ahead of him, it was his job to try and keep pace because I wasn't going to slow down for him. We pushed each other and sometimes lost sight of the fact that we were actually on the same team, being brothers. Every now and again my brother and I argued and fought and it sometimes became physical between us. When it got out of hand and I dished out too much punishment, my mother evened things out by taking up for my brother.

Looking back, it was the course my brother and I had to walk as we established our identities. I had to be bigger and better because I was the oldest but Irv wasn't going to settle as second fiddle just because of that fact. We constantly pushed each other to be better and loved each other deeply even though we didn't show it much back then. One rule though, if you were not me and you put your hands on my baby brother you were going to have to answer to me because that was not tolerated. Irv got good use out of that rule. More than one time he came home crying about something someone had done to him and we took a walk to find that person so things could be set straight. Isn't that what big brothers are for, though?

If my brother and I were not on the field playing an organized sport we had some type of pickup game going somewhere. The video games and computers that hypnotize today's kids were not even a thought back in the day. In the late Seventies and early Eighties we were responsible for half of our upbringing, with both parents working. And only people with money to throw away bothered with Daycare or babysitters. I was my brother's keeper when my parents were away. To stay out of trouble we played baseball in the backyard, two hand-touch football in the streets during the summer, tackle on the sidelines when the snow was piled high enough after the plows did their job and basketball anywhere and anytime we could find a court.

I was gaining recognition as an all-around athlete a few years before entering high school. No longer a pushover, the Pemberton Sporting world began to earn notice from people both far and near. And the two athletes repeatedly mentioned when talking about the newfound respect were Eddie and Irvin Smith. Local and tournament championship trophies in three sports, accompanied by Most Valuable Player awards, decorated the mantle in the house and a wall at the front door was being transformed into a virtual plaque collage. At the age of twelve I threw my first no hitter striking out seventeen out of eighteen batters in a tournament in Willingboro, New Jersey. I hit home runs and set new records every summer all the way through the Babe Ruth League, threw up game-winning shots on the basketball court and developed all sorts of useful skills as a center and goalie on the soccer field.

The one blemish on my resume came in junior high school, my seventh grade year at Isaiah Haines. It was my one and only year attending that particular school. Though I felt I did well in the tryouts, I guess I didn't make a significant enough impression on the basketball coach. He promptly cut me from the team, opting for more familiar faces. My father, always wanting to stand up for me, was irate after hearing the news and went to school the next afternoon and informed the coach that he had just made a big mistake that he'd someday come to regret. I used that setback to remind me for a long time to never take anything for granted. You are only as good as what you have done today, yesterday means nothing and you have to be ready to repeat it all tomorrow in order to be near the top. In eighth grade I was shifted across town to attend Newcomb Middle School, made the basketball team as a starter, and had two twenty-five point games against the coach that cut me and the team I was not good enough to play for the previous year. And my father received both a handshake and an apology from the man who had let me go.

In the midst of many good things happening, there were internal struggles within our family. These situations presented themselves mainly because of my father's alcoholism, and the poor judgment while he was under the influence. It sometimes took great effort, pulling together as a family, just to make it from one day to the next. Money was tight, not always there, and even my mother's broad shoulders threatened to succumb to the pressure from time to time. Even during these tough trials, I never stopped loving my father because I knew how good a man he was when he was not under the incredible grip and influence of his addiction. At an early age though, I became very protective of my mother. I would do anything in my power to keep her out of harm's way.

Aside from abusing alcohol, my father also abused his body in other ways, compiling irrevocable damage. An auto accident shortly after returning home from the navy was his first stroke of bad luck. After that it was just lack of common sense, mostly when intoxicated, which impaired his judgment. For example, Pop once saw a blown-over tree at the side of the road and attempted to single-handedly bring the whole thing back to the house for the cheap firewood. By the time I graduated from high school in the summer of 1987 my father had had four major back operations, including two disk removals. Number seven in the year 2003 was hopefully his last time under the knife. Due to his injuries, my father lost some valuable chunks of time, once spending an entire year on bed rest due to the severity of his back ailment. His day then consisted of gathering enough energy to make it from the bedroom to a foam mat that was laid on the living room floor of the house. He would then spend the entire day lying on cushions while watching television. When I returned home late in the evening I found him in the same position as when I left. His lack of mobility was its own form of sobriety but when the internal demons were speaking loud enough even that severe pain couldn't stop him from getting off the floor to get that next drink. Amazingly, my father's attendance at baseball and basketball games was not severely diminished either. Armed with a pillow to combat the hard bleachers, he still regularly supported his two sons.

By the time I entered high school my body had gone though a transformation comparable to the caterpillar to butterfly conversion. I traversed the early, awkward stages of pudginess and baby fat as a little boy, eventually sprouting upward and fighting to stay coordinated while my body tried to keep pace with my ever-growing feet. From nine to fourteen my shoe size matched my age and when it came time to go to high school, I was a lanky, 14-year old shy, pimple-faced young man standing 6'3" and weighing in at 185lbs. I was also a high school coach's dream and my reputation had justly preceded me. I would definitely have my chance to take things to the next level over the next four years.

Every high school has the pecking order and the last time I looked freshmen were still at the bottom of it. It was no different back in the fall of 1983 when I first entered the halls of Pemberton Township High School (PTHS). I was still the same shy kid in a much bigger package now. The success I enjoyed while playing sports did not translate likewise into my personal life. I still had not had my first girlfriend by the time I was in the ninth grade (although I had plenty of girls who liked me and did not make it a mystery that they did). I had managed my first kiss at the end of eighth grade but had no clue as to what I was supposed to say to a girl to show interest or eventually make her my girlfriend. I was actually petrified of the whole thing. Regardless of how socially far-behind I was of my classmates, it wasn't like I was uninformed of the do's, don'ts and what to do if's. Another role accepted completely and done thoroughly by my father was making sure his boys got the abc's about the birds and the bees from the right source. While my brother and I were coming of age we got periodical rap sessions about what it truly meant to be a young man going through life's changes. He slowly spoon-fed us, trying not to stuff the whole cow down our throat at one time. He also taught us that there was more to sex than the physical nature of it. We learned what it meant to be a real man and how to treat a woman. I can't say that every one of them in my life has been the beneficiary of those lessons but I have never *intentionally* strayed too far away from that model.

A very significant thing took place on my second day in high school. My boycott on football had lasted from the age of eight all the way up to that morning. It was somewhere in the middle of that day and I was sitting on the bleachers during my gym period going through an orientation when an announcement was made: The freshman football team was short on numbers and needed players. My first taste of the game all those years ago left a bad taste in my mouth and I had no desire to give it another try. For the first time in a long time, though, I was not scheduled to be involved in a sporting activity. I was content to sit that first part of the year out and wait for basketball season in the winter because playing soccer in high school was not considered the macho thing to do. But that all changed as I sat in the bleachers that day. My best friend, Andre, equally as awkward with the girls but not quite as shy, pointed out the fact that girls loved football players. If we went out for the team, we could wear our football jerseys during the week as advertisement and become instant 'chick magnets'. At that point I was willing to do anything I could to try and give me an edge when it came to the girls. I was one big, raging hormone that was about to pop if I didn't do something about it soon and that was as good a reason as I needed to sign up to play football. Two weeks later I was the starting tight end and Andre had already put in his last practice and returned his uniform. Andre wanted to wear the uniform without suffering the pain that came with it. He also wasn't that athletically inclined either.

If I could change one thing though, it would be to eliminate the little pockets of inconsistency that plagued my work in the classroom. I was an advanced student even at the elementary level and my curriculum of classes once I got to high school were all of the college prep standard. However, when I got lazy or didn't see eye-to-eye with a particular teacher I lost my focus and resisted putting the proper effort into soaking up the knowledge. The end results were a few more C's rather than those A's and B's that seemed to come with such ease when I inserted the least little effort. I was a very good student and still have a great relationship with many of my former teachers.

I have always been told that I was a cute kid that turned

into a handsome young man but physically I struggled through the ugly duckling stages that plague the majority of teenagers. And while I was a little slow to learn about and experience certain things for the first time, some of my classmates were picking up the slack for me. I was very naïve and although I was considered a jock I was not one of the most popular kids at Pemberton High because I wasn't very outgoing or 'cool'. The first time I sat through a lunch table conversation about marijuana in my freshman year I went into a narrative about why drugs were bad and was asked to mind my own business. Sadly, several of my classmates sitting in that group never made it past their sophomore year educationally, having developed drug dependencies and dropping out of school. A few can still be found on the streets of Browns Mills today, strung out on today's drug of choice all because of a little harmless marijuana in the mid-Eighties. Because of what I had seen in my personal life already, the danger of drugs and alcohol was one issue I did not have to be convinced of as a young man growing up. The Smith side of the family was both a constant reminder of how close I was to the edge and of how hard the fall would have been. In addition to my father's addiction, the disease was prevalent with his younger siblings and other family members. Pop was the eldest of five children, three boys and two girls. About the time I entered high school we had to bury the youngest, Uncle Billy, due to a drug overdose. His was a sad case because of the talent he never realized, having been one of the best baseball players Trenton High had ever seen and full of future potential. And that was a path down which I did not want to venture. Later, in young adulthood, I would have to confront myself and look my own demons face-to-face in the mirror, but I was not ready to throw my life away at such an early stage.

One 'thing' I was very curious about was girls. Girls, girls and more girls! But once again, I was behind on the learning curve. If there was one class that had my full attention it was sex education in the first semester of my freshman year. My father had been a great teacher of the subject, having warned me of the pitfalls of becoming sexually active too early. I however, was a hormonally charged young man that could not wait to see what all the excitement was about.

Every school has both the girl that will 'put out' and the guys who say they are 'getting it'. Everyone seemed to assume I was one of those guys, but I was certainly not. I stood out as an athlete but lacked the confidence that was supposed to go along with being a blossoming "Big Man on Campus". Girls both enticed and confused me from the very start of puberty, evidenced by the usual form of uncontrollable erections, wet dreams and mid-class daydreams about the girl of the day. That girl could come in any form, color, shape or size. The age of the liberated woman was still pretty far off, but that didn't stop the girls of PTHS! I caught the eye of many but approached few at first. It was only a matter of time before the overwhelming desire and curiosity would take charge, though.

By the end of my freshman year I had conquered the obstacle of both petting and serious necking, eventually leading to the momentous occasion of losing my virginity. I eventually popped the proverbial cherry at the tender age of sixteen, just a week before the end of my second year of high school. My first and only girlfriend (before entering the real world post high school) turned out to be my first love and lover. In retrospect, it was a comical experience because it was the first time for both of us and it couldn't have been any more awkward. I didn't know what I was doing, my heart was about to jump out of my chest and I fumbled all the way through it. We dated all the way from the end of my sophomore year and into my junior year until I felt the need to spread my wings in my senior year. Still, we remained friends for several years after I graduated. I'll always remember her and hold her in a special place in my heart and, conversely, I hope I'm thought of fondly when she reminisces.

My list of sports accomplishments and accolades started piling up from Day One in high school. I played as a starter for the football, basketball, and baseball teams, earning great praise from the varsity coaches who were waiting to get their hands on me. I also accomplished something that was not heard of in our neck of the woods at that time. As a freshman I finished two seasons, football and baseball, at the varsity level. While at the start of that year I didn't even have a desire to play football, by the end of it I was asked to join the varsity team for the final game of the season! I never made it on the field of play that brisk Saturday November afternoon but made sure I looked as though I had been in the heat of battle by rubbing handfuls of mud on my white pants. For the final five games or so in the Spring I joined the baseball team as a reserve, showing that I was already able to handle myself at that high level. I made no major impact on either field but it was an honor to be singled out like that and a hint that I was headed for great things in the future!

When my sophomore year rolled around I began an unprecedented three-year march toward the top of the South Jersey Scholastic Sports World. I was a triple threat on the football field as the starting tight end, a defensive end on the other side of the ball and I took care of all of the kicking duties. The five years of soccer, from age 9-13, were not lost as I developed a very powerful leg swing that could boot forty-yard punts with ease and split the uprights from 45-yards away. On the basketball court I was the only sophomore both to dress and to contribute on a team that compiled the best record in school history, 20-5. No great matter that this was en route to a loss in the South

Jersey Group IV finals against national powerhouse, Camden High. And in my senior year I led the 19-6 team that again lost to Camden in the finals.

While these many accomplishments brought much attention, it was my love for the game of baseball that made me the happiest. Yes, the least glamorous of the three sports was truly home to my heart. I was born to play the game of baseball. Unlike the other sports where I was simply out to have a good time, I had a passion for this game. I was at peace whenever ball and glove were involved and each game I played was like stepping on the field for the first time.

Leading up to my senior year I was the star pitcher and shortstop on every team I had played on. It was just before the start of that last year that both college recruiters and professional scouts encouraged me to begin playing third base as my primary position and to give up pitching to concentrate solely on hitting the ball and playing the field. I attended invitation-only scouting combines at various big league stadiums including Shea and Yankee Stadiums during the summer break between my junior and senior year. That was just the start of the parade of suitors that would come calling in hopes that my future would coincide with their particular institution or organization.

Life rolled on as it has a tendency to do and through the mid 80's I began to build a reputation that would accompany me through life. As an athlete I felt greatly respected and admired by everyone who saw me. More importantly though, I was seen simply as a good human being, which was the bigger compliment to me. I never saw my accomplishments as anything spectacular; I was well-rounded and playing for the love of all the games rather than the adulation. I racked up countless awards, trophies and newspaper articles but none of those were my personal goals. Yet when all was said and done I had put together a very impressive high school resume.

Football
1st Team All-County Tight End 1985
1st Team All-County Tight End & Punter1986
1st Team All-South Jersey Tight End 1986
1st Team All-State Tight End 1986
Honorable Mention All-American 1986
Baseball
1st Team All-County Shortstop 1986
1st Team All-County Third Base 1987
1st Team All-State Third Base 1987
Basketball
1st Team All-County Forward 1986-87
2nd Team All-South Jersey 1986-87

Philadelphia Inquirer Offensive Player of the Year 1986
Tri-State Athlete of the Year 1987
(New Jersey, Pennsylvania & Delaware)

"With great power comes great responsibility."
Those words, spoken by Peter Parker's Uncle Ben in Spider Man hold strong meaning and rang true for me during the whirlwind courtship that took place during the closing months of my stellar high school athletic career. Mine was a different era compared to the media coverage barrage surrounding today's high school athletes. Years before Kevin Garnett and LeBron James, I was staring my future directly in the face, hit from every angle and all sides, and I had no clue as to the direction I was supposed to go or where the next jolt was coming from.

Every major college in the country was recruiting me as a tight end and there wasn't enough time in the day to accommodate them all. The middle of my senior year, post football, became a never-ending college interview session. There were times when I spent as little as two periods of a school day actually in class and it didn't stop there. At home the phone rang and I conversed with one school just to hang up and start the whole thing over. I used an early period study hall to get homework done and to try to keep up with the rest of my class. The legendary Joe Paterno, head football coach at Penn State University, even made a special trip to visit me at my school and later sat with my parents and me in our living room. The media joined the circus calling for interviews both at school and at home. My previously quiet life was now in chaos.

To make it a more complicated situation I was not interested in playing football at the collegiate level. I was a baseball player and I thought that was where my heart would forever be. I explained this over and over again to deaf ears. The ruling opinion was that football was the route I was supposed to take. It got to the point where every school that called not only *assured* me but also *guaranteed* me that I would also be able to play on the baseball team but even that did not attract my attention. There were times when I began to seriously regret that I had ever taken up the game of football.

My only refuge from the onslaught of callers was my senior year on the basketball court where I had my best year. Though I still commonly saw football recruiters in the stands during games awaiting an opportunity to talk to me, I felt free running up and down the court, mostly away from all the worries about my future. My parents did their best to shield me, but were actually as confused as I was. Everything sounded attractive and the only advice my parents could give me was to follow my heart in whatever decision I made, that they would do their best to help me along the way.

Unlike most athletes, debating where to go, I also had to figure out what sport I was going in search of. The best thing I could have done from the very beginning was tell schools (crazy as it sounds) like Oklahoma, Nebraska, UCLA and others, that I was not interested. I didn't, however. Smaller schools, such as Rutgers and Temple, held out hope that I would want to stay near home. I allowed many others to continue to call as well, clouding the entire picture even more. I soon became tired of the whole ordeal and wanted it all to stop. There was a lot of unnecessary communication before I finally drastically cut down the number of schools under consideration and began avoiding the telephone whenever possible.

When it came time to set up my five official recruiting visits I was still in turmoil. I had already decided that baseball held my future destiny in hand, but considering that football might be something I could also do on the side to appease a lot of people. It was not what I wanted to do, but I felt like I would be disappointing many if I did anything else. My head football coach as well as others on the staff, most notably Coach Pete Brower who had been my tight end coach all the way through high school, had become not just whistle blowers, but family to me. And I knew how much it would mean for the program as far as recognition in the county and state if I went to a major school and played at the next level. I would be the next in a prestigious line to put Pemberton on the map in the world of big-time college football and there was no telling how far I could carry that torch.

The first trip I took was to the University of Florida at the end of December. Octavious Gould, an all-American running back and new owner of the freshman running record for the Gators was both an old friend and PTHS graduate of the class of 1986. Octavious and I went all the way back to the very first time

I played P.A.L. football. "O" was a gifted running back even in the early days and, had it not been for the fact that I played so many sports exceptionally well, I would have been following in his footsteps instead of creating my own legacy. Reunited for the weekend with Octavious as guide and myself as recruit, my head spun from the time I got off the plane. I was away from my parents and the friendly confines of home for the first time. And nothing was spared in trying to convince me that Gator Country was where I was supposed to spend my next four years. Minus a few hours to see the beautiful facility and talk to coaches and staff, the bulk of the trip was spent showing me all that awaited if I chose to make this my college home. I ate barbecue and rode horses at a ranch, hit every party on campus Friday and Saturday nights and met some of the famous Gator Getters. The Getters were lovely young ladies who showed loyalty to the program by paying new recruits as much attention as they could handle. Both innocent and seductive in their approach, the pretty college co-eds made it clear that whatever one wanted one could have if one returned in the fall. They so inflated my ego that, had I been a fish, I more than likely would have jumped in the boat; no need for pole or hook to reel me in.

Weekend wooing complete, I flew back to Jersey to inform my parents that I had made my decision: I was Florida-bound with a bang. My nose was wide open and I had been sold. The coaching staff looked for me to be a full-time starter by my sophomore year, allowing me to play baseball as well. This was exactly what I was trying to avoid because I had an idea of how that system would work. Football would eventually take full precedence over baseball with that side of the program buttering my bread and I didn't think it would be possible to pull both sports off for four years. The recruiters used enough smoke and mirrors to cloud my vision, however. This included some illegal activity according to the strict NCAA. While no money ever changed hands directly to me, current scholarship players and 'friends of the program' (alumni), made sure I needed nothing while I was in town. And I departed with a suitcase filled with more than what I had arrived with two short days prior.

One thing the University of Florida did not count on was my mother back in Jersey awaiting a full report of the weekend's activities. Her red flag went up the second I told her my search was over. As much as I felt I had agonized over the entire ordeal, it just didn't sit well with her. And when the coaching staff called from 'down in the swamp' with their used car salesmen approach she became even more leery. I was ready to cancel every trip I had but my mother urged me to follow through with my original plans to make a sensible decision rather than rushing to judgment. My father was as caught in the excitement as I was so my mother had to work doubly hard to convince both of us that there was no need to run through this process. After all, we were talking about a decision which would affect the rest of my life. When all of the hoopla died down and I had a chance to put my feet back on the ground I realized she was right and went about the business of being sensible once again.

Noteworthy

Because my visit to Florida needed to be squeezed in between some important basketball games, the best time to take it was not when the majority of out-of-state recruits came into town but the bigger group of in-state recruits. Florida is saturated with quality athletes and the three major powers, the University of Florida, University of Miami, and Florida State University are in fierce competition for the talent. For this reason, visiting the campus during that particular week made it more imperative for the University to impress and pull out all of the stops. During my tour through Florida's football facility, we ventured through the locker room where hung every recruit's Gator jersey with name and number boldly displayed on the back. My E. Smith Number 88 jersey was in a locker right next to an E. Smith Number 22. That Number 22 belonged to the future all-time NFL rushing yardage leader Emmitt Smith. He would attend the university the following year, then resetting the freshman rushing record held by Octavious. "O" lost his job due to an early injury his sophomore year and never recovered enough to reclaim it from Emmitt, who went on to become one of the best running backs ever. A year later Octavious transferred to the University of Minnesota but failed to recapture any of the magic he once possessed in Florida.

The university also took a huge hit a couple of years later as the NCAA uncovered major recruiting and other violations. The school was placed on probation and not allowed to participate in Bowl games, scholarships were lost, and coaches were fired. All of this happened right in the middle of what would have been the most critical stages of my collegiate career.

After the Florida trip, my parents decided to take a more active approach in helping me through the decision process. This was welcomed. I had tried to do it on my own but was not quite prepared for what was being thrown at me. I scheduled three trips for January, one football school and two baseball schools. I was entitled to five visits total but wanted to hold off on scheduling the last one because I felt it might be good to have an ace in the hole. If I was still undecided by the second week of February, the official football signing date for all letters of intent, that visit might come in handy. After two lackluster visits, the third would be the charm. A national contender full of rich baseball history with a football team that was at least competitive and a basketball team coached by the great Dean Smith, the University of North Carolina turned out to be my final destination. I made this trip with my family by my side, opting to drive down together rather than flying in on my own. And from the moment we arrived on the beautiful campus, I knew I was close to ending the long search.

Head Baseball Coach Mike Roberts had put in a great deal of time pursuing me early on but had backed off because of the football competition. When I expressed interest in coming down he was both surprised and excited, but didn't try to over-sell me. The tranquil atmosphere of the campus, friendliness of the entire college community and a full baseball scholarship with the option to play football if I wanted were exactly what I was looking for. The full scholarship was not a normal practice in baseball because of the limited number allowed. Most athletes on a baseball ride were given partial scholarships supplemented by some type of aid. Before leaving the campus I informed Coach Roberts that I was verbally committing to him and the deal was done. The only things left then were making my announcement back home (something I knew was going to shock and surprise a few) and awaiting the April signing date when baseball players put ink to their actual letters of intent. On the ride home my family heaved a collective sigh of relief, my brother's due to the fact that he could now have the phone back to himself. With the knowledge that the hard part was seemingly over, I felt a huge weight off my shoulders and couldn't have been happier than with the very road I had chosen to pursue. I had no idea that a tougher decision was waiting only months ahead.

On the national football-signing day in early February a huge press conference took place in our high school auditorium. This type of coverage was unparalleled during that time. ESPN was in its infancy as a legitimate news source and it was unheard of for a high school athlete to receive the type of attention that swirled around the speculation about where I was going to spend the next few years of my life.

Alongside me several of my football teammates were also making announcements as to their intentions. My best friend, Andrew Ward, was headed to East Carolina as a quarterback. Jason Lucas was going to Rice as an offensive lineman. And Tim Williams was committing to West Virginia to help the Mountaineers' ground attack as a running back. Once the preliminaries were done it was time to inform the large crowd of our plans. I confidently approached the podium and gave a brief statement, stating North Carolina as my school of choice. The ordeal was now over and it was time to get back to the business of living a normal life as a carefree teenager.

Things quieted down for a few weeks – a very welcome break from the past months' madness. I helped lead the basketball team back into the state playoffs and took my usual one day off before joining the baseball team, which was already into the first week of practice. With all of the distractions behind me, it was easy to relax and have a good season, enjoying both the last few months of my high school experience and my newfound celebrity status. For a very brief period I had much less to worry about. My concerns shifted from what to do with my future to the simpler things that face the average high school senior – taking the SAT's to secure my college eligibility, who I was going to ask to go to the prom and how I was to get my face to clear up!

Peace and serenity didn't last very long. Coach Roberts, who kept close contact with me as I progressed through my senior year on the baseball field, alerted me that the professional baseball scouts were bound to be showing up soon. When they arrived they brought all of the commotion back with them. First, a few folding chairs appeared, off to the side, occupied by old men scratching notes and talking into mini recorders. Toward the end of our twenty game season they were no longer as inconspicuous. At one game in particular a representative from every major league team was present, each sporting their particular team logo on a shirt or hat. And once again, the barrage of phone calls began from both the teams and the media, everyone curious about what my decision might be in regards to turning pro right out of high school.

By the end of my senior year, the lanky 6'3" 185 pound frame I entered high school with as a freshman had blossomed into a robust 6'4" 215 pound casing. I had a commanding presence at an early age. On the field I used all of my attributes impressively to put together another great season: a .459 batting average and an on base percentage of .566 plus only six strikeouts all season. Unfortunately, our high school baseball field did not have a fence to keep the opposing outfielders from standing 400 feet away from home plate. If not for that fact I would have hit a ton of homeruns and it wouldn't have been necessary to sprint around the bases at full speed to record the ones I did get. It wasn't uncommon to hit a ball a country mile only for it to be recorded as a routine fly-out but all of that was taken into account by the drooling scouts. I was near the top of the list of a lot of teams' wish lists.

I maintained a bit of normalcy in the home stretch before my mid-June graduation by going to my senior prom, passing my finals and the SAT, and enjoying the yearly ritual of Senior Skip Day (I spent it deep sea fishing 40 miles off the coast of the Jersey Shore). But when, three days before my eighteenth birthday, the Chicago White Sox drafted me in the seventh round, I was confronted with yet another major decision. This one would be even tougher because of the new element involved, money.

The decision to forego college and turn pro early was an

excruciating one. In February when I made the choice to attend North Carolina I thought I had everything I wanted. Now this. The pressure was twice as intense because of the pace of everything from the limited amount of time to cycle through all of the information to the negotiations. The calls from the head scout and White Sox front office came in a blitz as they tried to sweeten the offer each time we communicated. My mother and father opted for college at first but as the purse increased to $70,000 (a huge number for that time) and a paid education, it became increasingly difficult to say no. To show the disparity of today's standards wherein high school athletes receive millions of dollars to sign professional contracts, the first round pick for the White Sox in 1987 received a whopping $250,000. All of this was thrown at me over a seven-day period. The White Sox pointed out that playing professionally should be my ultimate goal anyway and that the three or four college years would only postpone that. Coach Roberts continued to present opposing arguments and I became more confused as the two scenarios swirled around in my head. I didn't sleep well for days after the draft and even at school, which should have been my refuge now that I had completed the task of finals, I had a tough time escaping the constant questioning. What should have been on my mind was what party I was going to attend after walking across the stage on graduation night. Instead I was contemplating another major life-altering decision. There were quite a few sleepless nights leading up to the tenth of June, the day I made the decision to follow my heart and begin chasing my baseball dream as a professional. I was going to take the early shot at becoming a major league baseball player.

The 'no-school' harsh winter and snow days that had to be made up pushed my graduation walk to the 22nd of June. All newly-drafted players were scheduled to report to rookie ball on the twelfth of the month but the White Sox agreed to allow me to graduate with my classmates and report on the 24th. The two weeks that preceded my departure moved in double time. My existence in the quiet and comfortable surroundings that I had called home was quickly coming to an end. I would no longer be the big fish in the small pond as I ventured out to test my abilities against men. Yes, it would take a lot of work to turn my raw talent and natural ability into big league material but I felt I was up for the challenge. While I did not fear the road ahead, I definitely had no idea what might be hiding in the dark night or the bright lights of the unknown.

For tax purposes it was best to have my signing bonus split into two payments, one half when I signed and the other to be paid in January of the following year. The first thing I did was purchase a 1987 white Chevy Camaro to replace the 1973 Plymouth Fury (a gift from my grandfather Wheeler Miles early in my senior year). A big step up from the vehicle known around school as the Banana Boat because of its size and yellowish color. My Camaro showed I was now driving in style. Placing some of what was left in a CD, I used the remainder to open a small checking account. Though Uncle Sam got his huge cut, I considered myself rich since I had never had a meaningful job before and still relied on my parents for lunch money!

It wasn't until graduation night that the full blow of what I was about to encounter hit me. I was less than forty-eight hours away from jumping on a plane, heading for Sarasota, Florida, to begin life as a man. For all intents and purposes my childhood was over. While many of my classmates would spend the summer preparing for college, working at Six Flags and enjoying an extended period of youth, I would be jumping out of a plane without a safety net.

As typical, we found ourselves late heading to the

Philadelphia Airport my departure morning. By the time we reached the gate, having run through the airport like we were filming a Hertz car rental commercial, the final boarding call was being issued and there was literally no time for the appropriate good-byes. The finality of the moment right on top of us, all emotions exploded. Mom burst into tears and headed for a bathroom to compose herself. Pops, Irv and I all embraced one last time, weeping like little girls. Reluctantly, I pulled away and boarded the plane. As I slowly walked down the tarmac it hit me what I was leaving behind:

My mother. She was an epitome of strength and the role model by which every woman in my life would be measured. She loved her two sons, made sacrifices, disciplined and showed tough love in all the right places while trying to keep our family together through some of the most difficult times when my father was at his weakest.

My father. He still struggled to gain control over his life, but through his darkest days he was always there for me, supporting me even when he could barely stand on his own two feet. He too was my role model and in the coming years he would become my hero.

My brother. He idolized me. We would become the driving forces behind each other's life successes. As the older brother it was my duty to help in raising Irv by showing him the way. And as the older brother I had sometimes taken the lumps, but he had always been there, a sponge, taking notice. Our love and support for each other had blossomed and would so continue as we began to develop our own identities.

I sat on the plane awaiting takeoff. The door to the big bird closed. There was no turning back now. Already missing my family, I was wiping away my tears when I noticed a flight attendant walking slowly down the aisle looking, apparently seeking someone. When she finally saw me nestled in my seat she asked my name to assure my identity and then extended her hand with a twenty-dollar bill in it. My father wanted to make sure I had some pocket money for the journey! This act of love provided more evidence that when I needed someone in this life my family would be there forever. The time would come when I needed them more than ever because, unbeknownst to me, the road ahead was to be filled with trial and tribulation. For now though, it was time to begin "Chasing the Dream"!

*High School Football at
Pemberton Township High School*

Sophomore year
◀

Senior year ▼

High School

*Senior Class
Picture*
◀

*Graduation
1987*
▶

Family Home - Browns Hills, New Jersey

Camaro - Graduation Night (1987)

Granddad and Dad - Senior Graduation Night

Ed - Age 10

Ed and Irv - Age 16 and 14

Edward Sr. and Jr.

Eddie, Dad and Irv

Ed and Aunt Barbara

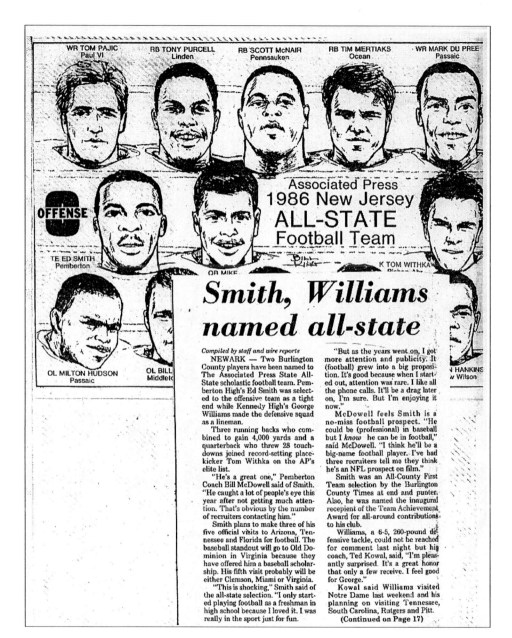

WR TOM PAJIC
Paul VI

RB TONY PURCELL
Linden

RB SCOTT McNAIR
Pennsauken

RB TIM MERTIAKS
Ocean

WR MARK DU PREE
Passaic

OFFENSE

Associated Press
1986 New Jersey
ALL-STATE
Football Team

TE ED SMITH
Pemberton

QB MIKE

K TOM WITHKA

OL MILTON HUDSON
Passaic

OL BILL
Middlet[

HANKINS
Wilson

Smith, Williams named all-state

Compiled by staff and wire reports

NEWARK — Two Burlington County players have been named to The Associated Press State All-State scholastic football team. Pemberton High's Ed Smith was selected to the offensive team as a tight end while Kennedy High's George Williams made the defensive squad as a lineman.

Three running backs who combined to gain 4,000 yards and a quarterback who threw 28 touchdowns joined record-setting placekicker Tom Withka on the AP's elite list.

"He's a great one," Pemberton Coach Bill McDowell said of Smith. "He caught a lot of people's eye this year after not getting much attention. That's obvious by the number of recruiters contacting him."

Smith plans to make three of his five official visits to Arizona, Tennessee and Florida for football. The baseball standout will go to Old Dominion in Virginia because they have offered him a baseball scholarship. His fifth visit probably will be either Clemson, Miami or Virginia.

"This is shocking," Smith said of the all-state selection. "I only started playing football as a freshman in high school because I loved it. I was really in the sport just for fun.

"But as the years went on, I got more attention and publicity. It (football) grew into a big proposition. It's good because when I started out, attention was rare. I like all the phone calls. It'll be a drag later on, I'm sure. But I'm enjoying it now."

McDowell feels Smith is a no-miss football prospect. "He could be (professional) in baseball but I *know* he can be in football," said McDowell. "I think he'll be a big-name football player. I've had three recruiters tell me they think he's an NFL prospect on film."

Smith was an All-County First Team selection by the Burlington County Times at end and punter. Also, he was named the inaugural recepient of the Team Achievement Award for all-around contributions to his club.

Williams, a 6-5, 260-pound defensive tackle, could not be reached for comment last night but his coach, Ted Kowal, said, "I'm pleasantly surprised. It's a great honor that only a few receive. I feel good for George."

Kowal said Williams visited Notre Dame last weekend and his planning on visiting Tennessee, South Carolina, Rutgers and Pitt.

(Continued on Page 17)

Eddie Smith:

By Don McKee
Inquirer Staff Writer

With the large number of outstanding athletes competing in boys' sports all across South Jersey, it usually is impossible to call one player dominant. But in the case of Pemberton's Eddie Smith, such high praise may not be excessive.

Consider:

• Smith was The Inquirer's offensive player of the year for the 1986 football season. He caught 20 passes for 509 yards and five touchdowns on a 7-3 team that made the NJSIAA playoffs for the second straight year. He was equally outstanding at defensive end, intercepting passes for two more touchdowns.

• He averaged 18.2 points and 10 rebounds a game for a basketball team that ended the season ranked No. 5 in South Jersey by The Inquirer.

• This spring he played third base and batted .459 with a .566 on-base percentage, went 4-0 as a pitcher, and led Pemberton to its first winning baseball season in 21 years.

• After turning down the entreaties of defending national football champion Penn State in February, he announced he would attend the University of North Carolina on a baseball scholarship.

• Earlier this month, he was chosen in the fifth round of the major-league baseball draft by the Chicago White Sox.

• After signing two weeks ago, Smith left Wednesday for the White Sox' rookie-league team in Sarasota, Fla.

Today, after dominating three sports, earning major-college recognition and a professional baseball contract, Eddie Smith is honored as The Inquirer's South Jersey Male Athlete of the Year.

"Signing a baseball contract wasn't really a goal all along," he said the other day. "I didn't really think about it until it happened.

"Then, it was something I felt in my heart."

Smith, probably the first player in recent years who could legitimately have earned a college scholarship in all three major sports, said baseball always was his first love.

"Basketball was something I played for fun," he said. "Football was something I never played until ninth grade, when one of my best friends got me to go out with him.

"For me, it was always baseball, all along."

Dominant may be the word to describe him

Smith, who lives in Browns Mills with his father, Ed, and mother, Pat, obviously had talent.

But, said Pemberton baseball coach Gary Schafer, he worked to hone his natural gifts and skills.

"Eddie brings a lot of dedication and hard work to his sports," Schafer said. "For example, when he was told he might go in the draft, he began bringing wooden bats to practice, so he could get used to them for the future."

(High schools use unbreakable aluminum bats to save money. Wooden bats exclusively are used in the pros.)

"Eddie has a strong arm — a cannon," Schafer said. "He has a good glove. But the big thing is, he has unlimited power."

Swinging from a tight end's 6-foot-4½, 222-pound frame, Smith could drive balls major-league distances.

"We don't have a home-run fence at our field," Schafer said. "If we did, he would have hit 20 home runs.

"He would hit balls well over 400 feet and they'd be outs. The major-league scouts saw that all year. The other teams would conceede anything in front of them

and play back, under the trees."

The sight of Eddie Smith knocking down branches with 400-foot fly balls was funny to everyone but Pemberton players and fans.

"At times he could have gotten frustrated," Schafer said, "but he never did. He's got a real good, all-round personality."

Smith's personality is such that he said his strongest memories from high school will be of people, not sports or honors.

"What I'll remember most are my teammates," he said. "A lot of teams just go out and play. We were good companions on and off the field. Some of the guys from my freshman team ended up playing together all the way through school."

"There were no jealousies on that team," Schafer said. "Any time Eddie talked to the press, he'd mention a teammate. That's the thing I'll remember about him."

Meanwhile, Smith has joined the Sarasota White Sox, bringing with him the attitude that enabled him to excel in high school.

"It's like anything else," he said. "You've got to earn it."

Powerful Pem

Smith receives accolades from all sides

By Wayne Richardson
Assistant sports editor

PENNSAUKEN — There have been some outstanding football players to wear the green and white of Pemberton High School. Octavius Gould comes to mind quickly. And there were the Meyers brothers, Charlie and Eddie.

Now meet Eddie Smith. He may be the best of all.

"Mr. America, isn't he," was the way Pemberton Coach Bill McDowell described him. "He's probably the greatest football player we've ever had. He's very talented. I think it was pretty obvious today."

Anyone who witnessed yesterday's 40-21 victory by Pennsauken in the South Jersey Group IV playoffs had to come away impressed. Smith was awesome, catching four passes for 104 yards and two touchdowns. That, by the way, computes to 26 yards per catch, which also happens to be his season average. Not your average statistics for a high school tight end.

Oh yes, those touchdowns of 13 and 25 yards came despite perfect coverage from a pretty fair Pennsauken defense. South Jersey's top-ranked team had only given up 25 points all year going into the game.

"He's a great player," said Pennsauken Coach Vince McAneney. "We had him covered real well.

He's 6-4 playing against Tim Phillips who is 5-9. I just told Tim that he had to jump five feet.

"We concentrated on stopping him at halftime," McAneney added. "We played a sandwich, using a linebacker and defensive end to bump him coming off the line."

The Pennsauken defense never really did stop Smith and Co. However, the Indians offense did as they held the ball for nearly three quarters of the game.

"If I didn't catch a pass and we had won, it would have meant more," said Smith, who also played quite a bit on defense. "They were able to shut down our wishbone and we went to the pass.

"Andrew Ward (quarterback) deserves a lot of credit," Smith added. "Without him, it just wouldn't have happened. We've worked hard together. He can read where I'm going and it's up to me to get there.

"Last year I would just stand around if there was coverage. Now I know how to get to the open spot. Andrew and I have worked pretty hard. We have good eye contact."

The Hornets battled strength vs. strength and it wasn't enough. When Pennsauken completely shut down the Pemberton offense, the Hornets went to the air. Ward ended the day 15-for-25 for 241 yards and two touchdowns.

"They have a good team and deserved it," said Smith. "We went strength against strength, their offense against our defense and we came came out on the losing end. We worked hard. Sometimes it just doesn't work out.

"This has been our goal since August," added Smith, who seems to have a strong interest in following Gould to the University of Florida. "There were a lot of teams in South Jersey not playing today. There was a lot of hard work put into this, we have a great coaching staff and have a lot of support from family and friends. It just wasn't meant to be."

Smith, who has 16 receptions on the year for 477 yards and five touchdowns, praised Pennsauken. "I think at halftime they knew they were in a dogfight," he said. "Their interior line was very strong. A mark of a good team is to come out and do what you have to do. They did it a little better.

"We really haven't faced a team that strong before," Smith added. "Our guys hung tough. I still feel our line is the best. We played to the best of our ability and they executed a little better. I knew our offense would score. The offense had to pick up the defense today and we didn't."

FOOTBALL

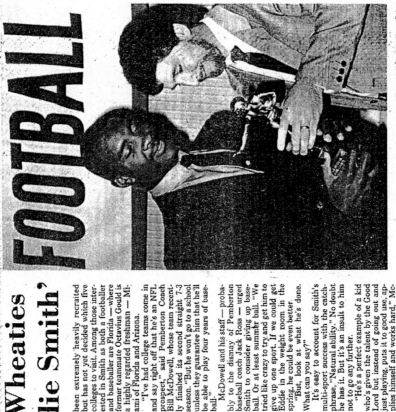

Times staff photo by Nancy Rokos

Pemberton's Ed Smith receives the Team Achievement award from Jeff Pettit.

'You don't just eat Wheaties and end up like Eddie Smith'

By Reuben Frank
Times sports writer

PENNSAUKEN — Ed Smith sat patiently and listened as statistics for candidates for the Burlington County Football Club's Team Achievement Award were listed.

"This guy had 1,000 yards of this," that guy had 1,000 yards of that," the Pemberton High senior said, after becoming the inaugural winner of the award, sponsored by All-Star Sports of Medford and selected by the Times' sports staff.

"Quarterbacks and running backs — those are the glory positions. I didn't think I had a chance."

Smith, a tight end and defensive back for the Hornets, was honored last night at the 16th Annual BCFC Awards Banquet at the Woodbine Inn.

"I didn't expect this at all," the 6-foot-4, 215-pound Smith said. "It's probably one of my greatest honors. I didn't even know about the award — I thought they just had an offensive player and a defensive player.

"I was happy with my season, although I did start off slowly," he said. "But I feel an honor like this should go to the whole team. It takes a group effort and that's what we had this year.

"It didn't hit me 'til they started reading the stats that I had won it."

Stats. Smith has reams of 'em. How about 20 catches for 509 yards and five touchdowns. How about a punting average near 40 yards per kick. Looking back to the winter, how about 15.2 points per game on the basketball court? In the spring, how about a .355 batting average in baseball?

The grand total is two selections to the All-County Football First Team (three if you include his selection as first-team punter this year) and one to the All-County Baseball Team. Plus first-team mention to the Associated Press' all-state football team, scheduled to be announced next week.

"Earlier, I wanted to be a quarterback," Smith said. "But after I saw what our offense was like, I knew I was built for tight end."

In basketball, he's built to play forward. And in baseball, he's built to pitch and play outfield. "It's hard to be totally dedicated to one sport when you play all three," Smith said.

"When I play baseball, for instance, I can't lift for football. But I enjoy all three sports. You get a blend of things — each season is different and you're not stuck to the same thing. But I like baseball the most."

Smith has a built-in training partner for all three sports. That is younger brother Irvin Smith, a Pemberton High sophomore who is 6-4, 220 pounds. "I still have maybe an inch on him," Smith said. "But he's gaining on me. He'll be as good as me, if not better."

Smith's future is the source of considerable speculation. He has been extremely heavily recruited but has not yet decided which five colleges to visit. Among those interested in Smith as both a footballer and baseballer are Florida — where former teammate Octavius Gould is a highly regarded freshman — Miami of Florida and Arizona.

"I've had college teams come in and say right off that he's an NFL prospect," said Pemberton Coach Bill McDowell, whose team recently finished its second straight 7-3 season. "But he won't go to a school unless they guarantee him that he'll be able to play four years of baseball."

McDowell and his staff — probably to the dismay of Pemberton baseball coach Jack Ross — urged Smith to consider giving up baseball. Or at least summber ball. "We tried like crazy to try and get him to give up one sport. If we could get Eddie in the weight room in the spring, he could be even better.

"But, look at what he's done. What can you say?"

It's easy to account for Smith's multi-sport success with the catch-phrase, "Natural ability." No doubt he has it. But it's an insult to him not to go any further.

"He's a perfect example of a kid who's given the talent by the Good Lord but instead of going out and just playing, puts it to good use, applies himself and works hard," McDowell said.

"You don't just eat Wheaties and end up like Eddie Smith."

CHASING
THE DREAM

CHAPTER TWO

Chicago White Sox

The misconceptions surrounding the glamorous life I was supposedly going to lead were far from reality of playing minor league baseball in the late 1980's. First, many thought I was already a millionaire or close to it, collecting a huge salary as I climbed up the ladder to the big leagues. In actuality, the first contract I signed was for a miniscule $700 a month, the standard rookie issue. And I was fortunate to receive the signing bonus that I had. Many of the young men starting out at the rookie ball level were late round picks who had put their name on the dotted line for as little as a couple of thousand dollars as a signing bonus. At the bottom of the totem pole were the Latin players seeking any possible escape from the squalor of poverty in their homeland. The majority of those fortunate enough to possibly use baseball to support families back home and search for a better life abroad literally signed for the plane ride alone.

Secondly, I was not going to be living a pampered life as long as I was in the lower levels of minor league baseball. Arriving in Sarasota, fresh off the farm, I was housed in a hotel free of charge for two days. After that it was up to me to find my own living quarters. This wasn't college and there was no dorm room replete with free meals, compliments of the athletic department. And I wasn't going to live in the lap of luxury overlooking the pristine beaches of the gulf of Florida on $700 a month. I quickly realized the exaggeration of the picture painted by the convincing parties.

Most importantly, the game I was getting paid to play was now a job. The baseball-playing environment I was accustomed to included a twenty game schedule during the school year and scattered play throughout the summer in leagues and on traveling all-star teams. In that first professional summer alone I saw more balls hit and thrown at me than I had cumulatively in my entire life to that point. Up at the crack of dawn, my day didn't end until the sun set in the early evening.

To understand how the system works, one must first get the true feel for what rookie ball is all about. At the lowest levels there are no roster restrictions. Rookie ball is both the breeding ground for new talent and the dumping ground for leftover products not well-enough developed to send into the real world. My rookie ball team had over a hundred and thirty players on it, which meant overcrowding at every position. A typical day consisted of a pre-dawn wakeup call at the extended stay hotel where the majority of players resided, two to a room. As if it wasn't bad enough that we spent entire days around one another, the necessity of being roommates forced spending evenings together as well. And the personality diversities made for both comical and tense moments. Player ages ranged from eighteen to the mid-twenties, so maturity levels were also at issue. Few players had individual transportation so we were cattle-transported in vans. Those were some of the most uncomfortable fifteen-minute trips in the world. Imagine twenty grown men trying to squeeze into a non-air conditioned vehicle with max occupancy somewhere around ten. It was not very comfortable! Fortunately, my parents made a road trip down a couple of weeks after I left home to drop off my Camaro. For obvious reasons, I soon became one of the more popular players.

Our facility's locker room at the decrepit stadium in the

heart of downtown Sarasota was nowhere near big enough for our huge number of players, so we were also forced to co-exist in lockers. Once our day started on the field it consisted of fundamental work all morning. The breakdown of player activity was as follows:

Pitchers did their own thing most of the day. They threw off the mounds on the side, went through fielding drills, and got their daily dose of running in. The majority of them were the best athletes on the team in high school and college but some type of transformation took place once they got to the professional level. They looked so uncoordinated doing the simplest things; bending down to pick up a ground ball or running to cover a base was sometimes comical.

Group one took live batting practice on the main field.

Group two worked in the field either fielding live balls off the bat, infield and outfield, or received ground balls from a fungo hitter near the batting cages. Players had to have split vision if they wanted to keep their lips intact. If the timing was off one might have two balls screeching at him at the same time, one from the hitter in the cage and the other from the fungo man.

Group three had individual fielding position work on a side field or the half diamond. It was intense work that everyone hated because they were at the mercy of whichever coach they had. Some were like drill sergeants while others made it into more of a game, rewarding for working hard by allowing one to catch one's breath. In a half hour a player might easily take a couple hundred balls with no escape until it was thought that enough work had been put in for the day.

Group four hit in the cages and did every hitting drill

known to man.

This was the day's course until lunch, which consisted of soup and a sandwich every single day. After lunch it was game time against one of the other ten or so teams located in the central Florida vicinity. There was no sitting around- whether in the lineup or not. If the game was at our facility players did individual work while awaiting game insertion or after exiting the starting lineup. On the days the team played away it was the same scenario. If you were not on the list to travel, you stayed behind until the coaching staff felt they had tortured you enough for the day and you were allowed to go home, dog-tired and exhausted. As always, I was extremely receptive to coaches and instructors and my work ethic placed me as a favorite in the large group of Big Time hopefuls.

Away from my parents and the security of home for the first time, I had a lot of growing to do both on and off the field. I had yet to discover the future chef within myself, so preparing a meal for myself consisted of pouring spaghetti sauce out of the jar and onto plain, boiled pasta. Having never taken care of bills or managed a checking account, my concept of money was a little distorted. I had never had the responsibility of totally caring for myself. That was what my parents were for. Therefore, the simplest tasks turned into tricky situations with no help to be found in Florida. It was all trial and error. It would be some time before I realized that the grocery store had more to offer than cold cuts, frozen dinners, chips and snacks. It was around that time that I wished I had paid more attention to what my mother was doing as she dragged my brother and me from aisle to aisle doing the weekly shopping. There was going to be time enough for the metamorphosis from boy to man though, as weeks and months turned into years on the road, fending for myself.

From the very start of our intertwined individual journeys I forged lifelong friendships with a number of teammates. Each and everyone of us had a different story and circumstance but in many ways we were similar, with the same goal in mind: make the big leagues. Kinnis Pledger was a big, strong, left-hand-hitting outfielder. Tall and lanky, he could cover a lot of ground and run like the wind. At nineteen Kinnis was also right out of high school but his personality was the exact opposite of mine. Loud and abrasive, he initially rubbed many coaches and fellow teammates, including me, the wrong way. It would take years for Kinnis and me to come full circle and become the best of friends, but he would be in my life watching one episode after another, even as I was there to see his drama unfold.

Ray Payton was from the backwoods of Sorrento, Louisiana. Poochie, as he was affectionately called, spent four years at Southern University as an outfielder and was then drafted by the White Sox. It looked like a stiff breeze might blow Ray's 6'5" frame over, but when it came to hitting fastballs, he had the power of ten men at the plate. Throw him something off speed, though, and he'd twist himself into a knot trying to make contact. He was a product of playing in an all-black college conference where pitchers who threw good breaking stuff were at a premium. The bread and butter was the hard heat and if one could catch up to it he would make a killing. Ray's jumbled talk and funny anecdotes made him a favorite with all of the fellas. I still quote him to this day. He had such a way with words that we often laughed to the point of tears when he got on a roll.

Nandi Cruz was from a small town in mid-Ohio. Also a gifted basketball player, Nandi had an opportunity to play either of the two sports at a high level. Drafted in the eighth round, right behind me, he was pegged as the shortstop of the future, and the two of us played side by side for the next few years.

Nandi was the big fish in the small pond back in Ohio and carried that attitude with him to Sarasota and beyond for a while. Still, he was a great athlete and good friend for many years to come.

While I could go on forever about the different personalities, the bottom line is that a good crop of talented comrades surrounded me. These are the people with whom I experienced many firsts. Growing together through the years, we also encountered all facets of life through each others' experiences.

That first summer away from home was a learning experience in so many ways. On the field I worked harder than I ever thought imaginable. And I earned the title of 'prospect' within the organization. That one, simple word meant that I was one of the chosen few into which the organization put stock into. It was no guarantee that I was going to make it to the big leagues, but the Sox were definitely going to do all they could to promote me. Kinnis, Ray and Nandi also carried the 'chosen' designation and we envisioned making our grand debut together.

In regards to hitting at the professional level I discovered I had much on which to work. I now performed against men with much more experience than I had. Factors working against me were the switch from aluminum bat to wooden model and my lack of coaching up to the point of being drafted. As a prospect, I was daily both reminded of these things and encouraged to give myself time. The White Sox knew the talent was within me and wanted to make sure I knew I was under no pressure to succeed right away. I was a piece of clay to be molded and sculpted. I, on the other hand, had never known anything but success for so long, so it was tough for me to accept anything else.

Because of the number of players in camp and the logjam at each position, it was tough to be consistent in everyday play.

No one played a full game, so it was actually more important to get one's work in on the side, demonstrating development, then implementing the skills in real action when one had the chance. After a slow start, I finished the 1987 season strong by batting .296 in the month of August. My final numbers:

Rookie Ball 1987:

Games	At Bats	Runs	Hits	HR	RBI	Average
32	114	10	27	2	18	.237

These weren't outstanding numbers, but a great deal had been accomplished. The foundation for a great career was developing. All I needed to do was stay the course.

I greatly missed home and my friends that first summer away and the phone bill proved it. Only weeks removed from high school, I was still the shy, reserved and humble kid from Browns Mills. My new teammates picked up on that and utilized the nickname I had been branded with back in the halls of PTHS; I was known by one and all as EZ. We had commandeered the hotel and made into our own little community. The drinking and loud music there sometimes got out of hand but I was never close enough to it to get sucked in. At that time I kept a safe distance mostly because of the reminder I had in my father; alcohol could destroy a life, family and career. I was not a drinking virgin, having participated in the traditional rituals of having quite a few too many on both prom and graduation nights in high school, but that was the extent of my drinking experience. It was easy to stay away from it all at that time because the evil streets had not yet lured me out.

With rookie ball coming to an end the last day of August I took a ten-day break before reporting back to Sarasota for another month of work in the Instructional Ball Program. At every level in the organization, Instructional Ball was the equivalent of Spring Training in the fall for all of the prospects. This period was used to build up on successes or to correct problems which may have occurred during the season. These six weeks of work were more personalized due to smaller player numbers and I flourished in them. The competition level was especially beneficial because of the experience that joined me both on the field and in the clubhouse. And, I held my ground, impressing my teammates as well as the competition during actual games.

At eighteen years of age I stood tall in the batter's box and went head to head against pitchers who had already had big league experience. I took a great deal of confidence back to New Jersey to enjoy a long and well-deserved off-season at the end of October. My first season of professional baseball had now come to an end and the reward was rest and relaxation. My body was worn out, my mind was beat down, but my spirits were high. My debut into the professional world was a success!

I spent an uneventful but peaceful winter season at the house in Browns Mills. The majority of friends I had left behind had moved on to college or away from our small community in search of bigger and better opportunities. That left me with a lot of time to sit back and do a lot of nothing until it was time to head out the following spring.

In the family at this time, I remember well that Pops was making a valiant effort to pull himself away from the grip that his addiction had over him. It's not an easy thing to conquer, though. On and off the wagon my father went for the next few years until he hit what he called 'rock bottom'. And when that day comes it is a total realization for everyone in that person's life, not just the addict. My father never even had an excuse as to why he drank; it was just in his blood. And although I was coming of age, I still considered it disrespectful to question my father no matter how reckless he was living his life. My mother constantly begged and pleaded with him to get clean but it fell on deaf ears. That winter I spent an awful lot of time around the house, witnessing my father's demise and telling myself that I would never allow that to happen to me. I had no idea how untrue that statement would prove to be. When March rolled around it was time to head back to Sarasota for Spring Training and to begin the next chapter of my quest. Little did I know that troubled times loomed ahead. I was about to find out that I, too, had my own set of demons with which to deal.

South Bend White Sox 1988

If I were to climb every ring of the ladder up the White Sox farm system I would have to go through several cities to do so. The list included:

South Bend- Low A
Tampa- High A
Birmingham- Double A
Vancouver- Triple A

I was informed from the very start of camp that rookie ball was behind me but not to expect to jump too fast. I was also penciled in as the everyday starting third baseman for the first-year-franchise South Bend White Sox. The organization felt it was the perfect level for all of the prospects drafted the previous June. Our Director of Minor League Operations, Al Goldis, was very hands-on and communicated with his young talent often. He felt the level of competition in the Midwest League was about par for where we each were in our developmental stages. I began that Spring Training working with the Double A team before players in big league camp were sent down to their rightful spots and the trickle down effect began. After a solid month of preparation I was convinced that it would not be long before I impressed the organization enough to warrant a promotion out of the Midwest League; all I had to do was put up numbers. That was my goal before I left Florida.

South Bend, Indiana is home to quite possibly the most famous football-college campus in the country. If you do not immediately think of Notre Dame and the Fighting Irish by mere mention of the city, it may be safe to assume that you don't follow college football. Rich with tradition including the legendary "Four Horseman" and "Touchdown Jesus", Notre Dame is one of the most recognizable names in all levels of sports.

Even knowing this did not prepare me for the amazing welcome awaiting the new South Bend White Sox before we made our first appearance into town! Television and radio promos started hitting the airwaves while we were still in Florida, media crews following our every move the last few days of Spring Training and relaying it all back. It was like being in the big leagues already. When our inaugural team arrived the first week of April, 1988, everything was new to the city, the downtown stadium walls still practically wet with paint. The largest crowd in front of which I had ever played a baseball game couldn't have been more than a couple of hundred and that included my first rookie ball season. That summer in South Bend there weren't more than a couple of nights that the 6000 capacity stadium wasn't packed to the gills.

Young prospects littered our opening day roster but the front office in Sarasota knew a hint of leadership was needed so a couple of veterans were mixed in to help the young talent find its way through the long and grueling season ahead. The average age on our team was 20 years old. I hadn't even celebrated my nineteenth birthday yet, while the rest of the league was more experienced; average age 22. Nandi, 18, and Ray, 22, were roommates that first season, sharing rent on a three-bedroom apartment minutes away from the stadium. Kinnis, also along for the ride, roomed with the oldest players on the squad, Rodney McRay and Larry Allen, both 24. They were sent to keep us in check but we all became partners in crime. With 142 regular season games on the menu we were in for a long, winding and bumpy road.

I'll never forget taking the field on that first, frozen Midwest night in April, 1988. The capacity crowd cheered our every move and we put on a show for the fans, winning the very first game played at Coveleski Stadium. We hit the ball all over the field, played sparkling defense and executed the fundamentals of baseball, playing the game exactly as it was meant to be played. Incredibly excited that first post-game night in the clubhouse, I remember Kinnis making a joke that we might not lose a game the entire season. As it was, we were lucky to win even a few more the rest of the way through that trying season!

All hell broke loose in South Bend shortly after settling in and finding out what being out on our own truly meant. Unsupervised and left to make decisions as men we all failed miserably in our first true test, but I blame myself for not being stronger-willed when I knew better. Things were quiet on the Notre Dame campus as spring gave way to summer vacation. The only show in town at the time, we enjoyed unprecedented celebrity status and took full advantage. It wasn't long before our first year manager, a devout Christian man who wouldn't step on an ant, lost control of his young group of prospects.

Kinnis, Nandi and I began our walk on the dark side by innocently venturing out with our older teammates, Ray, Rodney and Larry, after a home game one night. The three of us weren't even old enough to walk through the door of the bar but this was a college town. Half of the people in the establishment weren't old enough to actually be in there but nobody cared. I spent the first part of the night holding up a wall as a bystander. I was still very inexperienced when it came to dealing with the opposite sex. Though sexually active, my list of women all came from Browns Mills or PTHS and could be counted on one hand. My reluctance and inhibitions headed for the exit when someone handed me a beer, followed by another and then another and so on. The next thing I knew I was in the middle of the party along with my teammates, having the time of my life. And when I went home early the next morning after shutting the club down, I was not alone!

That was the first night of a string that would last through the rest of the season in and out of town. As a group we lost our focus, as an individual I went off the deep end. And by the time that season ended I had evolved into the stereotypical athlete seen in the news and read about every day in scandalous cover stories.

Through the season we spent six out of seven nights in South Bend in the clubs. Monday was the only evening you might find us around the house and that was just to recharge our batteries after running ourselves ragged. Nandi, Ray and I were in our apartment so infrequently after games and up so late in the morning (if we even rose before noon) that we cancelled our cable television subscription. TV-watching consisted of three local channels and three video-taped movies: *Friday The 13th Part I*, *Friday The 13th Part II* and *The Color Purple*, the latter reserved for those rare nights when we didn't have female companionship. It got to the point that *The Color Purple*, my all-time favorite movie, could be acted out by the three of us from start to finish. We watched it that much.

Our play on the field suffered. Without a strong voice to step in and put us back on the right path, an entire season was virtually lost. I was like a kid in a candy store and everything was free; the girls of South Bend couldn't get enough of us and the drinks were always on the house and I just wouldn't say no to any of it. One night I actually had three women in game attendance to see me. One might think that impossible to pull off but I was learning this wrong type of game all too well.

When the final out of the game was recorded I looked up in the vicinity of all three girls, strategically placed according to my wishes on the guest pass list, and gave a wave. I enlisted the services of one of our batboys to make sure I had a way out of my situation. He delivered two discreet messages upstairs in the family waiting area, instructing one young lady that I would call her at home later that evening, the other was to meet me at the club that night. I greeted the last girl in the waiting area and talked to her for a while before dismissing myself so I could continue on with the rest of the night. In such a short time I had lost my way and all of my morals were being replaced by unscrupulous living.

Old Milwaukee Day

Minor league seasons are broken down into two separate halves; at the halfway point a first-half division champion is crowned and a second season begins. We had performed miserably in that first portion of the season and our optimism on a second-half resurgence was short-lived. We were once again at the bottom of our division and would eventually stagger to an overall 59-81 season record.

Late in the season on one of those dog days of August we took things to a new low. Before heading to the park for batting practice Nandi, Ray and I went over to our other three amigos' apartment. Sitting around trying to figure out how we had put together such an abysmal season, we thrived on denial and placed the blame on our manager and his lack of aggressiveness. With Rodney in the kitchen cooking lunch, someone suggested a beer to go with the meal. Then, before we knew it, we had put away almost a case of Old Milwaukee. And we didn't stop there. A beer run to the liquor store around the corner resulted in each of us having a buzz and being nearly drunk, before we packed ourselves into the car and scurried to the stadium to begin our day.

During batting practice we were all out of control, laughing and running all over the place. Incredibly, that day turned out to be one of the most productive of our entire season. The six of us, spread out through the heart of the lineup, collected a minimum of 2 to 3 hits apiece by the seventh inning; total team output 21 hits and 15 runs. Coming down from our high by the end of the contest, we sat side-by side on the bench holding our heads in our hands, feeling the booze. Still, we were the first group out of the clubhouse that night after our victory, headed to the club to celebrate and finish off the evening in the same manner in which we had started the day. Looking back, I thank God for watching over all of us during this period. I spent countless nights in a drunken state that year and there were many more to come. Actually, I should not be here to tell you my story today because I drove under the influence countless times carelessly handling my life as well as those of other innocent motorists sharing the road. I might have wrapped my car around a tree or driven into a ditch but the good Lord had plans for me.

Our actions during that wild summer did not pass without consequence. While each of us had our fair share of groupies (most of the stories you hear about such are true) we also attempted to find "nice girls". I began spending time with one young lady, Lee, on the quiet nights. We liked to sit on swings, holding hands and talking. Lee was my "quality girl"; still a virgin when I left after that season and attending college that fall. We really liked each other.

Kinnis also had his quality girl. Their relationship was a little more advanced though, and the end result was a mid-season pregnancy. In the coming years that became a recurring event; the law of averages just seemed to dictate this. We played with fire enough and it was inevitable; we were bound to get burned every now and then.

Reviewing that horrible game season, our one bright spot was Ray's first half at the plate. He was our lone All-Star selection. Fading a bit in the second half, most likely due to fatigue, he finished the season hitting somewhere in the vicinity of .270. The front office in Chicago was understandably livid about our evident lack of respect for our trade and the game. I'm sure we weren't the first crop of young talent to fall prey to temptation, but we were all going to have to answer the obvious questions when we once again reported to Instructional Ball just a couple of weeks after the end of our first full regular season. The final totals on my first campaign:

South Bend White Sox 1988:

Average	Games	At Bats	Runs	Hits	HR	RBI
.237	130	462	51	107	3	46

Defensively, I led all third baseman in the Midwest League in games played (130), total chances (419), assists (272) and double plays (37).

The biggest topic of discussion in Sarasota during Instructional Ball, we took our well-deserved lumps from instructors, coaches and front-office personnel. That was not a fun fall for any of us down in Florida with our antics widely known throughout the organization. It was up to each of us to decide how we would take the criticism. I decided from the first day that my goal to make it to the big leagues outweighed the lure of the fast life. I rededicated myself to working hard to get back on track and spent six quality weeks demonstrating that to those who had my professional life in their hands.

To demonstrate my recommitted attitude, I spent very little time in New Jersey during the off-season months. The White Sox offered me an opportunity to get back into good graces by choosing me as one of four players to occupy an apartment located directly next to our practice facility in Florida. Through hitting, fielding, putting time in the weight room five days a week, and working with instructors within the organization I was able to hone my skills.

My biggest contribution back home in New Jersey was advice to Irv, who had moved out of my shadow since my departure from PTHS. My little brother had picked up the torch, using the momentum I had created. Stepping in to fill my shoes as the next tight end for the Hornets, Irv earned 1st Team All-American Honors and had every college in the country recruiting him. His post-high-school decision was a lot less complicated because it was well known that Irv's best sport was football. He played the other sports decently, but did not have the success or impact that I had. In mid-basketball season late January of 1989, in his senior year, Irv debated where he might spend the next four years of his life. After visits to Florida State, University of Southern California and Clemson, respectively, Irv had decided to verbally commit to becoming a University of Clemson Tiger. He had one scheduled visit left and wasn't interested in going because he did not want to waste anyone's time. That was to be to the University of Notre Dame in South Bend, Indiana.

As the big brother who only wanted to give good advice,

I reminded Irv via phone that he would lose absolutely nothing by taking that last recruiting trip. At the very least he was in for a good time and if anyone could attest to what the University and city had to offer, it was me. He took my advice, went on the trip the next week and called me the second he returned to New Jersey to inform me that he had changed his mind and was going to accept the scholarship to play for the Irish football team! That would be one of his biggest and best life decisions as well as the start to his own incredible journey.

Knowing what was at stake, I intensely prepared for my second full season of professional baseball. I was only going to be a prospect for so many years and all the potential in the world would mean nothing if I didn't show that I was worthy of the title. Taking full advantage of the resources provided to me by the White Sox, I got into the best shape of my young career, physically and mentally. I was ready to get back on the right track. The coming year, though, would prove a travesty, marking both the 'beginning of the end' of my dream and the start-point for a two and a half year nightmare.

South Bend White Sox 1989

Two steps forward and five steps backward. After my second full season my baseball career would never fully recover. I, along with innumerable others, would be left to suffer the irreparable consequences of an organization gone mad.

Somewhere in the middle of the winter season the White Sox hired a big league hitting instructor, Walter Hreniak, who was given total power of the entire organizational hitting philosophy. After a grueling off-season of work, I had gotten all of the chinks out of my armor and was in the best shape of my nineteen years. I was ready to go. Entering the 1989 season I was completely unaware that all of that work would be rendered a useless waste of time. On the first day of minor league training camp over two hundred players were gathered and informed that we all had a new way of hitting. (We were going to be the guinea pigs for a mad hitting scientist).

Hreniak was a teacher of the Charlie Lowe approach to hitting; a front foot style that put hitters in an awkward and vulnerable position. The theory involved lunging forward to meet the ball, thrusting your head down to the point of contact and finishing with a high one-handed swing. It contradicted every rule that I had ever learned about a good, sound approach to hitting a baseball; weight back, short stride with good balance, hands back before committing, and good, two-handed follow-through. When first explained, everyone thought the approach a sick joke, but we quickly found out it was not. Nobody was laughing, especially the group's older veterans. And all thoughts of rebellion were thwarted when we were instructed that it was the ONLY way one was permitted to hit as long as sporting a White Sox uniform. Whether taking batting practice on the field, hitting in a cage, on a tee or taking soft toss, if one converted back to old style, instructors demanded compliance or ended the hitting session.

The first few days of Spring Training players tried to make the best out of a bad situation. But it was evident that this style of hitting was not for everyone. It is a known fact that each hitter is as unique as a fingerprint. What works for one hitter does not necessarily work for the next. Body styles, hand-eye coordination level and swing starting triggers are some attributes which make every hitter distinct. Yet, we were all being forced to do it one way, like it or not, end of story, no questions asked. An entire crop of big, strong and athletic mashers was going to be transformed into a bunch of front-foot hitting Punch and Judies.

As camp wore on several revelations dawned. This decision

came directly from the top, the general manager of the Sox, and he was the only one buying into it; players were not the only ones mumbling under their breath. Our hitting instructors, having put in equal amounts of time with us on the field trying to help us develop as hitters, were equally frustrated but they had no choice as to what to teach. They hated what was being done, but their hands were tied. Sharing our disbelief and aggravation in the matter, they conveyed to us privately that their jobs were at stake if they failed to tutor us in this new manner. One known fact was that once Spring Training was over and we were away from Hreniak's watchful regular season eye, some hitters would be allowed to go about their duties in their own fashion. I, however, would not be so lucky that year or any other for the rest of my days in a Chicago White Sox uniform.

I was headed back to South Bend for a second tour of duty in the Midwest League. Along for the ride were Kinnis and Nandi. The front office in charge of bringing the young talent along felt that we needed to return to have some success at that level before making the jump. Ray had earned a promotion to the High-A ball team, which had been relocated from Tampa to the new facility in Sarasota. He would become a victim of the Hreniak hitting style a month or so into the season and be sent back to South Bend due to lack of success. Larry Allen was not re-signed by the organization and Rodney had made the jump to AA in Birmingham. Along with those changes, new leadership was hired to guide those prospects who had lost their way the previous season.

Rick Patterson, aka 'Rick the Ruler', new captain of the ship, would bring conflict and chaos to an already tumultuous situation. With a very intense personality, it appeared his goal was to transform those around him to be the same. A few days before we even left Spring Training Rick and I had a conversation in which he informed me that his goal was to pull me out of my shell. That wasn't my personality, and I explained that all the problems of the previous season were behind me, that he would not have any trouble from me, and that I simply wanted to play ball for him, develop, and get to the next level. That entire season in South Bend was spent pushing and pulling against one another, rather than working together. Several times he singled me out and pulled me aside during the summer, even confronting me about my nickname, EZ. He tried every single angle to get into my head and I did everything in my power to keep him out. My miserable existence in South Bend that year only further complicated as the season progressed.

My hands were tied behind my back and my growth and maturity as a hitter were stunted from the first pitch of the 1989 season. Our hitting instructor, new to the organization, was a brainwashed, Hreniak-influenced zombie who ate, slept and breathed the 'head down, finish high' style of hitting. The plan to use my own approach at the plate once away from Sarasota was not going to work. From the day we arrived we learned that nothing had changed; if you didn't do it the way you were told, you weren't going to do it at all! I had made an honest attempt to use the new technique; it simply did not work for me. In a man-to-man, behind closed doors conversation with Rick a month into the season I made a request (I found this necessary.), "Could I go back to what worked for me?" My plea fell on deaf ears.

From that day forward a huge tug of war developed. I was young and still trying to find my way, but I was not going to be a puppet. While I was not alone in the struggle for individuality, I was one of the few who voiced an opinion and tried to stand up against the system. The sacrifice for my 'insubordination' was lost time in the batting cages before games and verbal reprimands during games. What was funny was the support I got from outside my organization. I had many conversations with opposing players and managers before and during games, all of whom wanted to know what we were being taught and from whence it came! They had never seen anything like it and the most common phrase I heard was that we all looked like robots at the plate. It was a known fact as well that the easiest way to get us out as hitters was a steady dose of high inside heat; we were giving up valuable real estate by lunging forward. Another tactic was off-speed breaking pitches because the lunge already had us out in front of everything. The end result was a lot of broken bats and ground balls.

Things went from bad to worse for me in a flash. On the field I struggled with mediocrity, but still held out hope that someone would come to his senses and put an end to the talent destruction. My goal was to weather the storm and simply try to survive, but a life-altering event off the field lay just ahead.

My quality girl, Lee, was attending college at a small university in southern Indiana on a softball scholarship when I returned to South Bend in early April. Spending the majority of the winter season in Florida got in the way of any plans to head to the Midwest. We had kept in contact during the seven months I had not seen her, so I was a little hurt to learn that she was no longer a virgin. Still, I was anxious to see her when she said she would make the four-hour trip up to visit the second week into the season. Like a hurricane, she blew into town to watch a game, joined me at my apartment where we had protected sex, and was back on the road headed for school before the sun came up. That blew my mind. It was in total contrast to the girl I had spent time with the year before. She seemed so innocent the previous summer.

The next time I saw her was a month later at the end of

her school year. Her return coincided with the increasingly rough co-existence between Rick and me. Then, while sitting in a Denny's restaurant after a game, she announced being pregnant with my baby. Having thought I knew what pressure was before, I was in for a taste of what the word truly meant.

In retrospect, I noted that Lee had been testing me for several days before dropping the bomb. Kinnis was a new daddy and Lee knew of his situation. I fielded a few questions from her about what I would do if I were ever in his position. How would I handle things? I gave honest answers about stepping up to the plate and taking care of my responsibilities. Because that was how I was raised, I naturally made myself the perfect candidate to be a daddy. And, after my initial shock, I realized I really had a new life coming into this world; I was going to have to support him/her and try to build a stronger relationship with Lee.

In the first several weeks I only told a couple of my closest teammates as I carried the heavy burden of what to do next. The conversation with Lee's parents had gone over like a ton of bricks, but that was expected. I didn't even know the family and there I was, sitting in their living room, explaining how I had gotten their daughter pregnant. They didn't believe in abortion, which was out of the question for the two of us anyway. They did state adoption might be the answer, but Lee and I were adamant in our conviction that we could make this all work out. Donating reluctant support, they welcomed me into the family. It was a tense beginning to our relationship.

Word travels fast inside the small circle of pro sports so it wasn't long before Rick got word about my predicament. He respected my privacy and didn't mention a word to me until the end of May when I assume he figured I wasn't going to say anything to him. In yet another closed-door meeting, he brought things out in the open and was actually very sympathetic to my situation. He had gone through the same thing early in his career, many years ago, and understood what I was carrying. The first time he showed any compassion, his response meant a lot. I told him I could not bear to inform my parents via phone. After my explanation Rick even made a call to the front office in Chicago, arranging that I take a leave of absence for three days to return home at the end of the first half of the season. I would then have the opportunity to fill my parents in on the fact that we had an upcoming addition to the family.

The mid-season break was perfectly timed. I explained to my parents that I was returning for Irv's high school graduation. Because I had only a couple of days to work up the nerve to break the news, it wasn't until my last day in town, graduation night, that I actually found the time to sit with them. Never more nervous in my life, I felt like I was going to let them down and that they would be very disappointed in me. The house was finally clear of the last celebrating family member. Even Irv had headed out to join his fellow classmates at a party. I asked my mother to turn the television off because I had something to tell her and my father and I could see a look of trepidation cross her face. I composed myself enough to finally get the words out, but not without a great deal of fumbling. Highly underestimating them, I couldn't have been more wrong. When it was finally all out in the open my mother looked at me and sighed in relief. My parents thought I was coming home to tell them I had reached the end of my rope in attempting to achieve my goal of playing in the big leagues. That would have been a big disappointment to them because it would have demonstrated that I was giving up.

Becoming a father was not the end of the world, they reassured me. It was not how they would have written the script for me, but it was something that we, as a family, could deal with together. I was not going to have to go through this new chapter in my life by myself and I had not disappointed or let them down. The only advice my mother gave was to be true to my feelings. I didn't know what she meant by that, but didn't let on; I'd find out what that meant in due time. Unconditional love, they showed me again, means that you accept the good as well as the bad. That is what they offered me.

The remainder of the season was a mixed bag of highs and lows. On the field I struggled to find some form of consistency but never found quite the right formula to make it a successful year. I tried to fight the system, but eventually wore down. I got tired of being beaten down day in and day out and succumbed to the pressure applied by Hreniak's minions. The realities of not making a move upward that year and fighting Rick each day were more than I could handle. While I made an attempt at being the good soldier, not trying to make waves in the water, and keeping my employers happy, I did not do much for myself.

My season then came to an abrupt end at the beginning of August. Behind in the count, no balls and two strikes, I was expecting the pitcher to throw something off-speed. Right in the path of a 95mph high and tight fastball, already committed to the pitch, and lunging out on my front foot, I had no escape route. The end result was my right hand being crushed between the speeding fastball and the bat. I remained in the game for another inning before the throbbing became too much to bear. The pain was excruciating so I had a feeling something was wrong even though the x-rays showed negative on any damage. I missed the following game but showed some grit over the next ten days, playing in a makeshift soft cast in the field and at the plate. A week and half later, still in the same amount of pain and discomfort, an MRI was performed. It turns out I was playing with a broken hand! I was immediately shut down for the year, put in a cast and ordered to Instructional Ball once again. Still a prospect in the organization, I knew that title wouldn't last forever. My second full season of baseball came to an end and the final numbers were nowhere near spectacular. In my defense, I had not been allowed to use all of the tools with which I had been blessed.

South Bend White Sox 1989:

Average	Games	At Bats	Runs	Hits	HR	RBI
.246	115	382	52	94	8	49

Throughout that summer Lee and I developed our relationship. Young and full of optimism, we envisioned the happily-ever-after scenario. As I struggled through the season Lee became a source of strength. At first this was very strange because, for the short time I had been out on my own, I had lived for no one but myself. Now I was dating and planning a life with a young lady that I had just gotten to know speedily due to necessity. That fast I was in an adult, committed relationship, cutting off all outside communication from other women. I was happy. For a while, Lee still living with her parents, spent most of her nights with me while I was in town. When I was on the road we talked like a happy couple for hours on the phone. In the beginning, that house with the white picket fence seemed inevitable, but life was preparing to throw us a whole bunch of curveballs.

When the season came to an end it was time for me to get on the road back to Florida. The plan was set. I was to return to the Midwest when Instructional Ball was over, hopefully with my career heading up the positive slope again.

Heading back to Sarasota, away from the woman I

thought I loved and my unborn child expected in the middle of January 1990, was tough. The White Sox did not make it any easier to be away. Nothing had changed within the organization.

I had held out hope that the experiment to mold us all into one hitter would be considered a failure and the nightmare of 1989 would be put behind us. Instead they were stronger in their convictions, moving ahead swiftly with Hreniak's plan. The fact that players from the top to the bottom of the organization were all in disagreement was of no consequence. I watched averages and power numbers drop but very little was said or done because we were, in fact, nothing but a bunch of cattle. Our job was to be quiet and do our job. Otherwise, we could kiss any advancement good-bye. And at the tender age of nineteen I had very little voice. The experienced veterans knew the game and if they weren't going to open their mouths what place did I have to do it for them?

The name of the game now was survival. Wait out your time here to become a six-year minor league free agent and move on if things remained the same. The only problem was that I had an eternity of time before that even be an option, but what could I do? Biting my tongue, I did everything the Sox asked of me. I played the part that fall because I had no choice.

In the first week of October I returned to South Bend. Lee and I, moving full steam ahead, decided we should live together, so we got our first apartment, a small one-bedroom not too far from Notre Dame University. It was an exciting time for me for a couple of reasons. First, when I returned Lee's physique showed evidence that she really was going to have a baby. I almost cried the first time I put my hands on her belly and felt movement. Secondly, I now had a new connection to the Fighting Irish of Notre Dame. Irv was on the sideline in his freshman year and sitting in the stands made my chest swell with pride.

He didn't see much action that year (playing behind two upper-classmen) but his moment would come. And I was going to be there as much as time would permit over the next four years!

The initial rush of excitement after returning to South Bend was replaced by serious anxiety in the following weeks. While I had been frugal with the money I had put away, there were already times when I had to dip into the cookie jar simply to take care of life's bare essentials. Still in the baby stages of my career, the $700 dollar a month salary was now up to a whopping $850. And we were not paid throughout the year, only during the months we were in season. The medical expenses leading up to the birth were already starting to mount and there was no relief in the form of medical coverage afforded me under my minor league contract. I could not sit around this off-season without getting a job so I worked through the cold Midwest winter moving furniture for a small company. I hadn't anticipated anything like this for my career. And while everyone thought I was living the high life, footloose and carefree, the pressure to keep my head above water was increasing.

By November Lee and I had become a couple, living and planning a life together, but I knew I was in way over my head. Things had moved and happened too fast. My daily routine now consisted of moving furniture all day, then returning home about the same time as Lee (who had picked up a part-time job herself). I wasn't ready for the whole package. I had deep feelings for Lee, but I don't think I truly knew what love was at that time. Nonetheless, I told myself I was in it.

I also felt the constant pressure from Lee's parents, whom we saw on a weekly basis. They reminded us we were living in sin and should be married before living together. I wanted to honor my commitment in the respectable way, so when I flew home to New Jersey for the Thanksgiving holiday I asked my mother to help me pick out a wedding ring. I intended to ask Lee to marry me once I got back home. Mom asked the important questions to find out if this was something I wanted to do and I gave her standard answers which I knew were not true. Satisfied, but obviously not convinced by my lack of conviction, my mother helped me pick out a ring and I asked Lee to be my wife on bended knee the day I returned to South Bend. She tearfully accepted, her parents expressed relief, and I was supposed to be happy. But I was not. The façade I displayed masked the fear I hid. I was doing what I thought everyone expected from me, not what I felt in my heart. It was going to be tough to live the rest of my life like this, but I had made my bed and now it was time for me to sleep in it. That's also what I thought.

Early in the morning on December 29th, a few weeks before the actual due date, Lee went into labor. No class or any book had prepared me for the actual moment. I was petrified. Fourteen hours later, after rubbing her back, feeding her ice chips, hearing her call me everything but a child of God, and walking the halls for what seemed like an eternity Lee gave birth to a healthy baby. When son, Edward Smith IV, came into this world, I cried like a baby myself. And that is when I realized why I was willing to make the sacrifices I had. I wanted to love him and always be there for him like my father had for me. At that moment nothing was more important; he was going to be the reason for everything I did in my life.

I held the notion that fatherhood was going to perfect everything! What it actually did was turn the swirling storm into a raging hurricane. Lee and I couldn't have been any less prepared for the disarray and disorder a baby brings into a young couple's life. The pressure built from the beginning. Morning feedings, crying, diaper changes and constant demand of time were all part of the package, but our combined patience ran thin and we were at each other constantly. It had looked so much easier on television and in the movies.

The one saving grace I enjoyed in South Bend was Irv. Right around the corner from each other, in the Hoosier State, we were enjoying two entirely different lives. Having completed a successful freshman season on the field, Irv was reaping the fruits from all of his hard work. In between his busy college schedule and my hectic life we squeezed in some much-needed brotherly love time. I put on the happy face for him but he could tell things were not right. We reversed roles and for a while he became the crutch that I leaned on for support. Not one time did I tell Irv I was unhappy; he just knew it. My release was spending time with him, laughing and reminiscing about the good old days growing up, hoping for better days to come.

I was preparing for the biggest Spring Training of my short career, less than two months away. It was tough keeping my focus on baseball, but I had no choice. I didn't have the luxury of falling back on a college education and at this stage I had to find a way to make things work on the baseball field or everything was lost. I began to wonder seriously whether I had made the right decision about a lot of things in my life, number one turning pro at such an early age. I believed that God had a plan for me though, and that everything in this life happens for a reason. We don't have all the answers when life happens and that is frustrating. But I knew all would be revealed, not according to my time but His.

When it came time to pack my bags and head off to Spring Training toward the end of February, I knew I was going to miss my son though it would only be a few weeks before we were reunited. It seemed like he accomplished something new almost every day. Being away from Lee was also going to be tough, but I have to be honest in saying that I was looking forward to getting away for a while. Our constant arguing, the strain of living together, and raising a child while still trying to get to know each other were damaging our relationship. Another contributing factor was the upcoming date of September 15th. That day had been selected by Lee and her mother for us to walk down the aisle. I was like a deer caught in the headlights, awaiting the moment of impact.

For now, though, the smell of fresh cut grass, the chatter and banter of a crowded locker room, and the glorious sounds of the ballpark were calling me. I would take one more shot at pulling my troubled career off the mat.

1990 Sarasota White Sox

If the wheels were wobbly in 1989, they were about to fall off in 1990. I realized exactly how dispirited I was once I had gotten back with the familiar sounds and commotion of Spring Training. As a new head-of-household, playing role of both *impending* husband and *present* father, I felt my entire future was mapped and planned out. The passage from boy to young man and the eventual blossom into true manhood is the process that every male should go through. Mine was wild to the extreme. I didn't handle things well starting out and I knew it. But my biggest fear was that my system wasn't clean. It was clogged with prematurely held responsibilities. I still had so much I wanted to do in discovering the man I was meant to be *down the road*. At nineteen I was not ready; it was too early.

I felt I was selfish in having these negative thoughts, but I knew I wasn't being fair to myself. How was I going to make someone else happy if I was living my life as a lie? I was torn because my conscience wouldn't allow me to do anything other than what I was supposed to do. Wedding plans had been made and my son deserved a father in his life. The fact that I wasn't ready or prepared to sacrifice the rest of my life to a still-developing relationship could not stand in the way of that. Or so I reasoned. I tried to push feelings to the back of my mind. That would become increasingly tough as the negative season wore on and I sat through one story after another, living my life vicariously through the same teammates with which I had once been partners in crime.

Spring Training 1990 was a mirror image of the last two. The Hreniak experiment continued. When the final rosters were set for the upcoming season I was designated to start the year at the next level: High-A in the Florida State League. It was a small jump, but anything was better than returning to the Midwest for a third go around. The Florida State League was unique in the sense that it was mostly a commuter league; we didn't have many overnight road trips. The ten league teams were scattered throughout central Florida, close enough to return home at the conclusion of each game. The only two cities we didn't return from were Miami and Fort Lauderdale. This meant that each and every night I would return to a small studio apartment where son and fiancée would be waiting.

Once Lee and little Eddie arrived in Florida a few days after the start of the season, the happy reunion only lasted a few weeks, mostly my fault. Eddie had grown unbelievably since I last saw him. I loved seeing him every day, playing with him before Lee dropped me off at the ballpark, and seeing him when the day was over whether it was a good or bad one 'at the office'. The problem was that I was simply not ready to be *both* a father and a <u>husband</u>. Don't get me wrong, I did love Lee; she was as beautiful on the inside as she was on the outside. And as the mother of my son I couldn't have asked for a better mother. But I wasn't *in* love with her.

As the summer progressed I experienced as much frustration on the field as I did at home. My daily routine consisted of waking up and playing with my son. Lee and I had quickly turned into one of those couples with little to say to each other. In the early afternoon she dropped me at the stadium. I was making enough to support us during the season, so she didn't work. Most times she brought Eddie to watch me play, but not always. The similar level of futility at the plate sank to a new low as well. I was being dominated by pitchers that, as a high school junior, I would have hit all over the field. As a so-called professional athlete I couldn't hit water falling out of a boat if I were in the middle of the Atlantic Ocean. The Chicago White Sox were destroying my chance of ever making it to the big leagues as well as my spirit and love for the game! Things got so discouraging by the end of May that I seriously thought about packing my bags, walking away from the game and never looking back. Two events were right around the corner in June, though. One would reset the course of my professional life with a soft blow. The other would rock my personal life like ten sticks of dynamite.

Just when things seemed hopeless and I was going under for the third time I was thrown a raft; someone came to my rescue. My mother and father came to visit and see me play. It was the first time they would lay eyes on their first grandbaby so the last thing I wanted them to note was how bleak things actually were at this time. Sometimes, while sitting on a bus heading back to Sarasota, I fought back tears. My career was going nowhere, I felt like a failure and my personal life was in shambles. It wasn't long ago that I had been sitting on top of the world. Now I struggled under the weight of it. I couldn't allow the two people who had sacrificed and hoped for so much for me to see that.

My reasonable masquerade during their four-day visit probably fooled my father. But I was fooling myself to think that I was pulling one over on my mother. Nobody in this world knows me like her, primarily because I am so much like her. When something bothers either of us, we don't wear it on our sleeves but the encrypted signs are there to be read; one just has to know for what to look. And my mother could read me like the back of her hand.

My family watched me play, and they spent time bonding with Eddie during the day, and we ate dinner together every evening, but Mom never said a word to me while they were in town. For that matter, it was nearly a week before she could no longer hold her tongue, admitting that she had wrestled with the idea of meddling in my personal life. I'm very happy that she loved me enough to butt in.

Just days before my twenty-first birthday, in an evening phone conversation, Mom asked me to do her a favor: call her when I was alone and had some time to talk. I didn't think much of the request; I had a feeling she knew the picture wasn't as rosy as I had tried to portray it the week prior. I figured she just wanted to make sure everything was okay with me.

A day later, when the typical central Florida summer rain cut our batting practice short, I called her from the middle of a crowded locker room. I had some time to kill right when Mom would be getting comfortable at home after her day at the college. Nobody I knew had cell phones back in that day so I was forced to make the call from a payphone right in the middle of chaos. With one ear plugged by a finger and the other firmly pressed against the phone, I listened as my mother reached out with words of wisdom. She didn't waste a second getting to the point: Was I happy in my decision to get married? I gave her the politically correct answer and then it was her turn to talk. I might as well have been the only person in that crowded room when she started speaking to me because I couldn't hear anything but her words, "If you are getting married for any reason other than the fact that you are in love, you are not doing the right thing. Your father and I know you want to do the right thing and we are proud of you for the way you have handled everything. You have options; you can still be a father to your son without being a husband if you are not ready. You have not and will not disappoint us. Just make sure you are living your life to be happy and not to make others happy!"

The floodgates opened when she stopped talking. I confessed that I was not ready for everything that I had taken on but felt that I had gone too far to turn back. Things had moved way too fast. The most important thing was that I didn't want to ever feel like I was letting my parents down, not taking care of my responsibility as a man. Before the talk with my mother I felt that was exactly what I would be doing. After, I realized that I still loved Eddie, even if I wasn't ready to marry his mother. I didn't want to hang up with Mom. I had much to say because I had been keeping it all bottled up for so long. Meanwhile, the tarp on the field had been removed and I did have a game to play in that night, so I promised my mother I would call her once I had a talk with Lee. That was going to be one tough conversation and I rehearsed it even as I stood on the field that evening, baseball the last thing on my mind. I was about to reclaim control of my life and *that* was the most important thing.

As scheduling would have it, an off day was upcoming in two days. I deemed that to be the perfect day to sit down with Lee. This was definitely going to be an all-day affair because I expected all hell to break loose with my announcement. I was right. My plan of attack was to be honest with Lee. It wasn't that I didn't love her; I was just worried about the rush. Neither of us was happy and we were going through the motions at this point. Why not slow things down, take some more time to get to know each other and see what the future might hold?

Arranging for a day-long baby sitter, I proceeded to stall for time all afternoon, taking Lee to a movie and then some dinner. I sat in the dark theater in a daze and offered idle chitchat over our meal, but time was running out. When we got back to our apartment it was 'now or never'. Eddie was down for a nap when I finally worked up the courage to voice my concerns. All turned out to be as bad as I had anticipated; Lee went ballistic. Before she ran out of the apartment she screamed, hollered and yelled at me. I took it all, with thick skin and sympathy for her feelings, because I knew the shock she had to be in.

When she finally came back, an hour later, she pushed her way past me and barricaded herself in the bedroom where Eddie was still sleeping. I tried to talk to her through the door, but she was on the phone with her mother, with whom my next conversation occurred when Lee tossed the phone into the living room and relocked the door. The mother-in-law conversation became semi-confrontational because she hit some nerves. The point she stressed was that if I didn't marry her daughter someone else would; she wasn't going to wait for me. That struck me the wrong way because, as I explained to her, I wasn't in competition to be the first one to marry her. We had a child together and I did want to make things work but I also wanted to make sure we were doing the right thing for the right reasons, not because we were supposed to do it. That conversation, my last of the evening, didn't end well. I slept on the couch and drove myself to the ballpark the next afternoon without so much as a word from my now estranged fiancée.

At the ballpark something was transpiring. From the second I arrived at the stadium to put in my day of work, it was no mere game; I was receiving special attention. Director of Minor League Operations, Al Goldis, was in town and he specifically requested spending time with me. As the biggest opponent to the organization's chosen direction, he claimed he could no longer sit on his hands allowing those players he had drafted to be destroyed.

Therefore, I spent a two-hour crash course in the cages before we took batting practice out on the field. Al tried to deprogram me. My swing infected, it was tougher than one might imagine trying to revert to swinging the bat like a man with authority. After two and a half years as a front foot, head-jamming, high-finishing singles hitter, Al wanted me to sit back, keep my head up and finish strong with two hands on the bat. Things went well in the cage and carried over to the field that evening to a small degree. Five hits later, all singles, I had apparently shown Al enough of what he came to see.

I was informed after the game that I was to be promoted to the next level, Double-A. I had one night to pack my things before flying out to Birmingham. The fact that I was hitting less than .200 for the season was of no consequence. Things had happened so fast that I didn't even have a chance to be in shock. By the end of the night I was saying goodbye to Ray, Nandi, Kinnis, leaving our close-knit group as the first to make it to the next level.

There wasn't much to cheer about in my apartment, though, that evening as I prepared to head out of town. I was hooking up with my new team on the road in Memphis, TN, where they were in the middle of a three-game series against the Kansas City Royals Double-A team in the Southern League. Lee was still barely talking to me and we had serious issues before us. We agreed that she would stay behind for a couple of days in Florida to close up matters in Sarasota and by the time I laid my head on the pillow, she had allowed me to at least sleep in my own bed. Once I completed the last few days of the road trip I was to get an apartment set up. Then she would make the drive up. What happened after that was anybody's guess.

"Hell hath no fury like a woman scorned."
"The Mourning Bride"
by William Congreve

The few days we were apart, undoubtedly filled with conversations between Lee and her mother, allowed her anger to simmer. She was understandably bitter and angry and generally didn't want much to do with me. For that reason it was no surprise to hear that she was not going to stay with me for the remainder of the season. If I were not willing to marry her in September, she was not going to stay under the same roof.

I knew there was a significant Indiana influence present. I tried to reiterate that postponing the wedding did not mean that we were never going to get married; it meant that we were just going to take some time to slow things down. She was not willing to wait. She let me know that I had hurt her and that it was going to take a great deal to ever make things right between us again. Two days later she was gone like a thief in the night, along with my son and any hopes of being the father I had always wanted to be.

Over the course of the summer my relationship with Lee further deteriorated. She went to stay with her parents who had relocated to Terre Haute, Indiana, from South Bend. While I took advantage of my fresh start in Birmingham, her resentment was obvious in every phone conversation. That felt somewhat unfair. I had not asked her to leave, but her take on our situation was that I was choosing the easy way out. That was far from the truth as I struggled daily recalling the silence that surrounded me every night I returned to my small studio apartment in Birmingham. The only contact I now had with my son was listening to him breathe on the phone as I talked to him remotely. Even that was used as a punishment, a daily verbal reminder of what I was giving up. I had to put that all to the side though, as I had a very important summer task before me.

Back To The Roots

Both my mother's parents were born and raised in Alabama (Granddad in Mobile, Grandma in Birmingham), before marrying many years ago and relocating to New Jersey. So heading to Birmingham was a homecoming of sorts for me. More family followed them up north in search of a different lifestyle, but the majority remained in the South. My Grandfather worked as a porter for Amtrak for over thirty years and retired shortly after turning 65. Soon after I graduated from high school and started my professional career, he told the family he was tired of living in New Jersey and wanted to return to Birmingham to be closer to the family. When my Grandmother refused to accompany him he didn't put up a fuss. He simply packed his bags and jumped on an Alabama-bound train. As much as Grandma loved him she wasn't leaving the family she had nurtured and surrounded herself with to go back to the South.

Watching me play professional baseball was my Grandfather's dream come true. Diagnosed with diabetes some years ago past, he still got around on his own. In fact, I met most of the family down there through him. Because I had only been to Birmingham one time in my life (when I was six) I wasn't familiar with most of my distant relatives. Now I usually had a few of them cheering me on each game and enjoyed quite a few southern meals. Having those *roots* took away some of the sting of being alone.

I had a lot to prove at the next level and not just to the many eyes in the organization; I had begun doubting my own abilities over the last two and a half disappointing seasons. I knew I had been handicapped but the level to which I had sunk was demoralizing. I was once considered one of the best high school athletes the Northeast had ever seen. Most who had seen or heard about me had expected great things. And even those expectations paled in comparison to what I had envisioned for my career. So, I now put an incredible amount of pressure on myself. I was supposed to be in the big leagues by now. Instead, I was merely trying to justify my promotion out of the lowest level. Time was of the essence and I had to make a move now!

Only a couple of weeks removed from my twenty-first birthday I was considered a youngster again at the AA level. And everything I had seen playing side by side with the experienced players in Instructional Ball and heard about playing in the higher levels was true. The pace of the game was accelerated; ground balls that found their way through an A-ball infield were gobbled up with routine effort while outfielders covered the territory as if they sported a set of concealed wings. Hitting was not merely physical battle now but mental war against the pitchers on the mound. Being ahead in the count at the plate did not dictate one would get the ever-predictable fastball. Weaknesses were exploited and strengths were avoided; there was no need to look for anything straight if mashing the fastball in a particular game or series.

As the everyday third baseman I held an important position on the Birmingham team and I wasn't being cut any slack for age or lack of experience. Because we were in a dogfight pennant race all the way through the second half of the season after a second place finish in the first half, it was especially intense. This team, loaded with talent, was led by young Frank Thomas, aka "The Big Hurt", playing first base. The two of us made imposing bookends on the baseball diamond, manning both corners, and by the end of the season I was referred to as "The Big Pain". Trying to correct my swing on the fly while facing big league-caliber pitching prospects was not the ideal situation. I put in extensive work at home and on the road, sometimes arriving at the ballpark hours before batting practice. I didn't have much of a reason to be around my empty apartment and had turned over a new leaf, alcohol and nightclub free, since beginning my relationship with Lee. I took full advantage of this chance to resurrect my career. Al Goldis had stuck his neck out for me and I was not going to let him down.

I quickly earned the respect of my teammates by playing the best third base of my career. My batting was slower coming around, but I was removing a lot of garbage from my system. At 6'4" and a robust 220lbs I was a line drive hitter in search of his power stroke. I should have been leaving the yard on a consistent basis rather than spraying the ball in the gaps but this is to what I had been reduced to. A great deal of damage had been done and trying to correct it was no small task. I played in all 72 games of the second half and when the dust settled we had won both the second half title and a spot in the playoffs. During that momentous last game of the season I was also given my first award as a professional athlete. After only half a season with the team I was selected as the Gem Defensive Player of the Year, an honor sponsored by a local jewelry store. I received a gold watch and plaque for my standout performance.

Unfortunately, our post-season aspirations took a big hit when Big Frank was recognized that night as well; he got the call for which every young player hopes. He would make his big league White Sox debut September 1. Spots were also made available on the Triple-A roster by call-ups so we lost two or three other valuable players in our quest to win the league championship. The holes left in our depleted lineup were too much to overcome and we lost the Division Series two games to one. The season was now over and I had taken a pretty substantial step in re-establishing myself as a prospect in the organization. My numbers were not staggering, a mediocre average to go with my sub-par power numbers, but considering the past, I had done the job well.

Sarasota White Sox 1990:

Average	Games	At Bats	Runs	Hits	HR	RBI
.192	63	239	22	46	4	23

Birmingham Barons 1990:

Average	Games	At Bats	Runs	Hits	HR	RBI
.247	72	247	22	61	1	23

The season over, it was now time to go see if there was anything to salvage in my relationship with Lee. That was going to be a lot tougher than anything I had come up against during the summer.

My reception in Terre Haute was more than chilly. The same family that had accepted me into their bosom as one of their own now could not stand the very sight of me; I had become the enemy! I couldn't understand how they felt justified in making me out to be such a bad person. The only thing I may have been guilty of was having cold feet about a marriage that would occur more for their family image than because two people were in love and knew they wanted to spend the rest of their lives together. Aside from that, what had I done? I treated their daughter with nothing but respect, never cheated on her, called her out of her name or raised my hand toward her. I was a good father to my son. I supported them when they lived with me and sent money while they were away. I wasn't due a medal for any of that because they are the duties of a true man, but they should have counted for at least a small credit. And I was busting my hump trying to overcome the obstacles in front of me so I could be successful in making a better life for, hopefully, the three of us. Yet, I was now Public Enemy Number One. With Instructional Ball once again on the menu, I only had a few days to spend in Indiana before hitting the road. Treated as though I was deserting or walking out on my son, what was I to do? I had business (baseball) to tend to elsewhere. Their feeling was unless there was a wedding I was no longer considered a welcome member to the family. I am not sure if that's exactly how Lee felt, but she was ultimately delivering the message. Unfortunately, I knew I was not ready to be a husband, so we arrived at a crossroad. Lee was still wearing my engagement ring the day I left, but I knew, as bitter as she was, that that could change any day.

Players in any major sport will tell you that we are the LAST to hear about ANYTHING. In this case it would be no different. The tide had one more shift in it, a devastating professional blow that would ultimately lead to my last days in a Chicago White Sox uniform. While we went about our business on the field during Instructional Ball, a power struggle came to a nasty ending behind closed doors in the front office. Al Goldis, the Director of Minor League Operations, had no voice in the manner in which his talent was being destroyed. He had stepped in on my behalf as well as others' and had walked across the tips of some toes in doing so. A few weeks after the conclusion of Instructional Ball, Mr. Goldis, my biggest supporter, was fired. The day he left the organization effectively ended any realistic hope I had in making it to the big leagues with the team that had drafted me.

I knew I was going to be an outcast when I returned to

Spring Training next season. I had bucked the system and made some waves over the last three years and that was not a popular position. I knew what faced me and that I would now be virtually alone in the fight. Fate stepped in half way through the winter off-season period though, with contact from a young and upcoming agent from the West Coast, Don Wolfe. 'The Wolf', as I like to call him, had never met me, but had heard good things from an inside White Sox. He sought young talent to represent and aid in the climb to the big leagues. From all reports, I was a viable candidate for his new flock. Despite the lackluster performances of my sputtering career, my talent was described as untapped and limitless. Beginning with Don's winter call and his desire to help me up the ladder, we developed a relationship. No pressure on either side, we agreed simply to keep in contact and see if our paths eventually crossed. No contract was signed; we had a gentleman's agreement to be honest with one another and see how things developed. By the end of my winter hibernation away from baseball we realized there was some reason we had been put in contact and I signed a contract with my first agent. Don had never met me and I wouldn't know who he was if I passed him on the street. But I now had an agent and new partner in my mission to make it to the big leagues. Ironically, it would be another year before we even met and I wasn't going to be wearing a White Sox uniform when that happened.

My life was in a state of turmoil at this time. The uncertainty in my professional life ran parallel to that in my personal life. In Indiana I met harsh resistance from Lee and our relationship continued to crumble. The bitterness she felt toward me was apparently insurmountable. She felt that while she was doing the hard part of raising our son on her own, living with her parents, I was living the high life. She didn't want to hear anything I said in my defense. I wanted nothing more than to be in my son's life, but she made it very clear that I was losing that right. While I recognized that was unfair play, I respected the fact that Lee was hurt, so I set out to get back in her good graces. Constantly I reminded her that even if things did not work out between the two of us I still wanted to be a father to my son. He was almost one year old and I had seen him only a fraction of his young life. I desperately wanted to correct that. Driving from Florida to Indiana after Instructional Ball, I hoped for some type of reconciliation. That was not forthcoming.

Lee insisted we meet in South Bend instead of me making the trip to Terre Haute. She explained that she wanted to see some friends in town and that the visit would work better that way. I felt there was more to the story than that. Her parents probably didn't want me to visit in their home. Mom and Pops were making a road trip to watch my brother in his sophomore season on the football field as Penn State was in town to take on the Irish, so I made it into town on a Thursday night and was holding my son in my arms in my parents' hotel room Friday afternoon. That great reunion was one of the last I would have that felt that good.

Little Eddie had grown so fast I almost didn't recognize him. Realizing exactly how much I was missing out on, I felt compelled to rectify the situation between Lee and myself. I didn't relish the thought of spending chunks of time away from him. After dinner I suggested that Lee and I take a drive so we could talk while my mother and father look after our sleeping son. Our drive took us around the city that I had called home for two summers, so it was only fitting that we park the car at the stadium. That place held a lot of memories, both good and bad.

By the time we shut off the engine and got out to walk in the bitter winter wind I had fully relaxed my guard; Lee had been opening up all night. Having laughed like we hadn't in a long time, there was no tension between us. Her smile was more evident in that one night than it had been the entire last year. So when she dropped the bomb on me I was less than ready. Handing back the engagement ring, Lee announced that she was moving on. I was devastated. According to her, returning the ring did not mean that we were splitting for good but we obviously weren't getting married any time soon, so she wanted me to hold the ring. Should we ever head in that direction again, she would again wear it.

I definitely hadn't expected this. With tears in my eyes, I took the ring back. There was nothing I could say to make her change her mind. For the time being we would go our separate ways. I would have the task of being a part-time father on the road and out of the picture. I understood her rationale that I was simply not there for her, but in my defense I was trying to do a job. She knew what I was going through and what I was trying to accomplish. My gut feeling was that there was more to the story, but I wasn't going to get any of it that night. Minutes after returning to the hotel she packed up my son and made her get-away.

The next afternoon I sat in a stadium crowded with over 60,000 cheering fans. The Fighting Irish and Nittany Lions fought to the last whistle of the afternoon while my thoughts were everywhere but on the game being played on the field. And on Sunday it was time to pick a direction in which to drive off into the sunset.

After a couple of weeks break in New Jersey it was decision time again. For three years I had lived and supported myself and then a family while working for peanuts. The prior season, even with a slight increase due to my promotion, I still had not made $1,000 a month. And the money from my signing bonus was slowly being drained, a large bulk having gone toward paying the huge medical bills that coincide with having a baby. Almost broke now, I had to find a way to support myself and to send money to help raise my son. Beside my family, there was not much for me to do in New Jersey so I went to the only place that seemed logical at the time, Sarasota, Florida. Al Goldis' departure from the organization left me on an island. Unlike previous years, the White Sox were not inviting me down or accommodating me in any way. Even without their backing, or *any* sign of support, I was dead set on trying to make things work with the organization. They had my rights for the next three years until I was a six-year minor league free agent so my options were limited. For the next three and a half months I worked a full time job moving furniture during the day and baseball became my second occupation while I simply tried to survive. Very depressed during this stretch, I spent many nights in my small apartment wondering how things had gone from so good to so bad so quickly.

1991 Sarasota White Sox

Near the point of giving it all up by the time Spring Training rolled around the first week of March, I knew I was not in good graces with the Sox now that Al had moved on. A new director of Minor League Operations was brought in from another organization and I was simply statistics on a sheet of paper. When we reported there were a lot of new faces on the field as well. When staff moves to another team they bring as much of their talent with them as possible. The first week of camp I learned that Al Goldis had wanted to do the same exact thing after being hired in his new position with the Milwaukee Brewers, but had been stopped. In contact with his former employer during both the off-season and training camp, Al tried to orchestrate some minor league trades.

The new staff vetoed all deals and then informed me that I would return back to Single-A to make room on the Double-A roster for a player from their old team. The day I was taken aside and given that news, I called Don out in California. I had been so upset that I left camp that day ready to give up baseball altogether. I was that frustrated and ready to give it all up and end the 'so called' dream. If not for Don's urging, I would have packed my bags and gone home. Instead, I returned the next day determined to show the new front office that they were making a mistake; I deserved a better look than they were giving me.

We've all heard the old saying, "When it rains it pours". In my case I was standing in the middle of monsoon season and was in for another treat just a couple of days after deciding to continue with my baseball career. I had kept in touch with Lee up in Indiana two or three times a week, always trying to call early enough in the evening to hear Eddie rustling around on the other end when she placed the phone to his ear. Very important to me that he heard my voice, I wanted him to know who I was even if I could not be there.

When a strange male voice answered the phone this particular night and informed me that everyone was out and he was caring for Eddie, I asked the obvious question: "Who was he and what was he doing looking after my son?" I didn't get much out of him other than he was "a friend". His name was Teddy and the rest, he said, would have to be taken up with Lee. Two days later she finally got around to returning my call and I posed the same questions to her. Her reply slapped me in the face: It wasn't my business who she kept company with while I was away. He was a friend. That was as much information as I deserved or needed. From that night on our conversations occurred less frequently and I became increasingly estranged from both my ex-fiancée and son.

Instead of rallying the troops and coming out fighting I lost the will to succeed and gave up! I adopted a self-destructive lifestyle that bordered on professional suicide.

I convinced myself everyone, personally and professionally, was out to get me and I couldn't do a thing about it so why put in any effort? Both aspects of my life were equally in shambles. Besides dealing with Lee, the White Sox made it clear: There would be no trade, I would have to stick it out in the organization at the Single-A level and there was nothing I could say or do about it. They were right about two of those things; I was their 'property' and they could play me wherever they wanted to, but I could do whatever the heck I wanted to do. I chose to run the streets of Sarasota with some of my old teammates, all still looking to climb above the level in which we seemed destined to rot. I drank and partied all night, chased women until the sun came up and played on the field like I just couldn't possibly care less. I was, subconsciously, on a mission to see how low I could sink and how quickly.

Feeling sorry for myself and blaming everything in the world for my misfortune, I assumed zero responsibility for my actions. My new best friend and confidante came in the form of any alcoholic beverage, preferably a frosty cold beer, and I was heading toward the same fork in the road my father had undoubtedly faced in his early years. If I didn't choose to regain control of my life, there was no telling how bad things could end up. I was lost at this time and didn't want be saved, so I kept my behavior from my parents as much as I could. They knew I was having a tough season on the field but I kept them thinking I was one good game from turning it all around. All I wanted to do was get to the clubs so I could drown my sorrows and feel better by the end of the night. I knew in my heart that I was walking down a path of destruction but couldn't see pulling myself up to do anything about it. I was angry with a lot of things but repressed all. Drinking allowed me to forget and let go. The problem is that when I sobered up nothing had changed, it was just a different day and I had to go out and do it all over again to keep from having to deal with life.

If the White Sox had been, in fact, punishing me, they apparently felt like I'd had enough around the beginning of June, right after my 22nd birthday. For the first half of the season Don had been in contact with Al in Milwaukee while I had given up hope of anything positive happening. In my mind I was giving the Sox exactly what they had given me, nothing. It was the immature way to go about things, but I wasn't thinking clearly at that time. On June 13th, between the first and second game of a double header, I was called into Rick's office and he gave me good news. I had been rescued! A single player trade had been worked out and I was heading to the Milwaukee Brewers organization. In an instant all despair and hopelessness was washed away.

Granted, a portion of that was replaced by uncertainty. I had been issued a Get-Out-Of-Jail-Free card but still didn't know if that meant I was headed for greener pastures. Had I fallen too far off track to recover? The last three years of my career had been filled with much darkness – both of my own doing and that of the powers that be. Could I still possibly make it to the big leagues? *Somebody* evidently thought I had what it took, but the person who should have felt it the most, myself, was in doubt. The million swirling questions would be asked and answered over the next few years. And I'd definitely have enough time to think about them soon, during the two days of travel I had in front of me before meeting my new team. I packed my locker belongings, said my good-byes to teammates that had become like family to me, and pulled out of the parking lot as the first inning of the second game got underway. It was time to begin the next chapter of my life.

Sarasota White Sox 1991:

Average	Games	At Bats	Runs	Hits	HR	RBI
.217	54	198	27	43	3	27

South Bend Sox, 1988

South Bend Sox, 1988

South Bend Sox, 1989

*South Bend
White Sox, 1988*

*South Bend
White Sox, 1989*

*Kinnis Pledger
Ed
Ray Payton
1990*

CHAPTER THREE

Milwaukee Brewers

The first leg of my new course took me back to the Midwest League in Beloit, Wisconsin. Initially, I felt that I was taking yet another step back in my already-faltering career, but my new employers explained it otherwise. Al Goldis and the Brewers knew how much difficulty I had experienced and what I now had to overcome. They desired as little pressure as possible in transitioning and trying to correct the years of physical and mental damage at the plate. Providing a chance to begin again and to work the kinks out at the lower level was what they felt best suited the situation.

By the time I exited my car after 30 hours on the road, meeting the team on the last day of a road trip in Kane County, Wisconsin, I didn't care *where* they were sending me as long as I could stop driving. After having packed my entire life into my Camaro and burning up the highway to put my past behind me, I hadn't slept in two days, coffee and No-Doze acting as my traveling companions. I arrived at the stadium two minutes before the team bus and when I went into the locker room most of my teammates thought I was a new coach. At twenty-two, sporting a beard that made me look even older, I was surrounded by young Brewers prospects. A few short years ago I was in their position, but my role now was reversed. In my fifth season I was going to be the veteran in charge of keeping the young talent in line. I had some re-growing up to do myself as I guided them, though.

First Impression

The opportunity to make a *first impression* with my new team arose soon enough. Still wobbly from my 30 hours on the road, I put on my new uniform and went straight to batting practice. During the game my eyes felt like they had ten-pound weights pulling them down as I fought the almost-overpowering urge to sleep. In the top half of the last inning my new manager asked if I wanted to bat; I wasn't about to refuse. Stepping up to the plate, I hit a line drive double off the left center field wall. Then, in the field, I made the last out of the game! Making a diving play to my right, I scrambled off the ground and threw a bullet across the field to spoil a late rally by the home team. Two hours later I was again on the road, in my Camaro, following the team bus three hours back to Beloit, Wisconsin. Life couldn't have been better when my head finally touched the pillows. Sleep, how sweet the sound.

The plan in Beloit was very simple: in order to find my way back from the dead as a hitter I had to return to the beginning and start again. It was a tough road ahead because I was facing a major disadvantage: the coaching staff was minus a hitting instructor. Only a pitching coach assisted our young manager, Rob Dirkson, and neither of them had swung a bat in their professional career. That meant that I was on my own for as long as I was in Beloit.

Dirk obviously lacked all knowledge about hitting, exemplified by the first piece of advice he ever gave me: "Just swing hard in case you hit it." He only knew he did not want to see me swinging mechanically or timidly. We all knew it would be a while before I erased all of the front foot from my swing as it was tough not resorting to bad habits of the last few brainwashed years. Both Razor, our pitching coach, and Dirk offered their arms to me for the rest of the season. Their support made it easy to again want to work as hard as I ever had. We arrived hours before scheduled to be at the stadium, both home and away, taking batting practice on the field, just the three of us. They'd throw, I'd hit, and we'd pick up bucket after bucket of balls, scattered across the whole field, while I took the constructive criticism they offered. I took full advantage of this fabulous second chance. The result of all of the hard work I put in trying to resurrect my career was an above-average finish to the second half of my season. With this, I was pleased.

In the beginning of my new campaign I neglected to regain control of my life off the field. Still angry about the last three years and the demise of my deteriorated relationship with Lee, I continued on the same destructive path. I was still trying to run from life rather than embrace it. What hurt most was the forced absence from my son's life. One of the first things I did when I returned to the Midwest was contact Lee in Indiana. Things had gotten so frigid between us that she felt I was imposing when I asked her to make a trip to Beloit so I could see my son. While I was resolved not to entertain fantasies about us getting back together at that time, I was frustrated by her vindictiveness in keeping me from my own flesh and blood. I had rights too. I was well aware that she was moving on with her life but she did not have the right to exclude me in the way that she had set out.

So what did I do to ease the pain? You guessed it; I drank and ran the streets of the small Wisconsin town as the president and founder of a new organization I had founded. I called it "The He-Man Woman Haters Club" and although I was the only member, I was going to spread the word: get them before they get you! Due to my experience with Lee I vowed to never again allow myself to care about a woman if I could help it. It would be nice to hang out with them and have a good time but that was it. I wasn't disrespectful to any woman I encountered but letting any past the brick wall that I had put up around my heart was out of the question. And if I felt like any caught a feeling it was time to move on as fast as I possibly could.

With the help of two of my teammates I picked right back up where I had left off in Florida. I moved in with Bobby when I got into town and Mike joined the club a week or so after me. Engaged and loyal to his future wife, Bobby almost never left home; he left the carousing and womanizing to Mike and me. What the three of us did for beer sales in Beloit was amazing, though. Time spent out of uniform that summer was spent drinking beer and playing Madden Football on Sega Genesis. Late nights and early afternoon wakeup calls. The level of competition in the league, playing at the low level, allowed me to get away with what I was doing: working as hard off the field, like a vampire in the night, as I was on.

I soon found myself looking in the mirror trying to figure out who I was during the sober hours of my day, usually right before I went to the park early in the afternoon. There were instances when I'd wake up and find a strange woman in my bed, sometimes not even remembering her name. I was depositing most of the little money I did earn at whichever bar or club we frequented. While I didn't like who I was, I also failed to see anything wrong with what I was doing. I was just having fun and enjoying my freedom, right? At least that is what I told myself. The road I was on didn't have an end to it considering the direction I was taking. The only way to get off was to change course, but I felt I didn't have the will to do it. It was going to take something big to show me a new way. As in my father's case I was going to have to eventually hit my own form of rock bottom, nowhere to go but up.

Rock Bottom: Part 1

I love my father and know he would never do anything to hurt me – his job is to protect me. As his son I share the same duty. Never would I intentionally harm my father in any way. Nevertheless, I failed him miserably that summer. In late August he made a solo visit from New Jersey to spend a week watching me play. Mom couldn't get away from work to make the trip so Pops flew in and stayed with my two roommates and me, sleeping on our sofa.

The first night Pops was in town he watched me play from the stands and I watched him drink one beer after another from the field. He was totally drunk well before the end of the game. Where I failed him was by joining in on the fun, taking him to one of our local drinking holes after the game, to party with some of my teammates. I eventually ended up as drunk as he. My father had been off the wagon for some time now but I was spending less time at home these days so I had not witnessed the everyday destruction he was doing to himself. My mother was now the lone prisoner in captivity dealing with the daily effects of life with an alcoholic. And here I was, helping him fuel his addiction.

The week my father spent with me was the lowest point of my life to that date. We spent that whole visit drinking as if we were old navy buddies, not father and son. I was so far gone that I thought this interaction was actually a good thing. Sitting at a bar or in a restaurant after a game having a meal with a few beers and then finishing it off sitting around our apartment before we all passed out, it was like hanging out with a good buddy, not a man who had raised me and with whom I should act like I had some sense. And my teammates thought he was the life of the party – the coolest father on the earth. Had it not been for the last day he was in town I probably never would have ultimately seen the light.

I woke up around eleven that morning and came out of my room to find my father absent from the couch where he had passed out the night before. I thought it slightly odd that he was gone but didn't dwell on it. The area in which we lived was spread out and there was very little within walking distance. Because of that, when Pop had not returned after almost three hours I became alarmed. I had no idea where he had gone or where he was now and it was getting close to two o'clock, when I'd have to be heading to work. He had been riding to the stadium with us each day and watching batting practice as I was the only one with transportation. He knew we couldn't come back to get him. None of us had cell phones at the time so contact would be impossible. We decided to look for him on our way to the stadium, leaving the apartment door unlocked in case he made his way back.

Fortunately, we found him five minutes into our search. Walking on the side of the road a few miles from our apartment, he was carrying a case of beer and sweating profusely. And of course, he was fully drunk. When I saw him, eyes red and speech already slurred on a day that hadn't even started for us, I was ashamed. Not so much of him, as of myself. How was I ever going to help my father in finding the strength to overcome his addiction and regain control of his life when I didn't have control of my own? We loaded Pop in the car, and when he gave us his account of the day, I was sick. My father had awakened at ten to finish the beer in the refrigerator. Then he needed more beer. Walking the unfamiliar streets of Beloit, Wisconsin, in search of a liquor store he found a bar, had some drinks there and picked up some more to bring back to the house. Problem was he had lost his way and didn't know how to get back to our apartment. He didn't remember the number or address so his only course of action had been to walk until he found something familiar to lead him back in the right direction. Fortunately, we found him. He had been walking and carrying that case of beer for over an hour and a half.

In the locker room I took a long look in the mirror and saw where I might be heading if I didn't make a change in my life now! I thought about my father the entire day, on the field, in the dugout and at dinner as I drank lemonade while watching him have yet another beer. I didn't say a word about the incident that night or the next day when I dropped him off at the airport, but I felt like a failure and a fraud. I wasn't being truthful or fair to myself, my father and family, or anybody else in my life. I was living the lie that I was in control of my life. Putting my father on that plane, I realized I had a choice to make: "Get busy living or get busy dying". I didn't want to see how low I could actually sink; I knew the depths could be bottomless. I had descended as far as I wanted to go and it was time to start moving in the right direction: up. The final two weeks of that season were spent in a much more sober state, not totally clean as old habits are hard to break. But it would soon be time to give it all up for at least a while.

The Beloit Brewers of 1991 were a mirror image of my 1987 South Bend White Sox club. It was like déjà vu. This time around I played the part of the experienced vet leading the stable of young prospects. The end result was similar to my former experience; a load of talent did their best work off the field in the clubs and chasing the women. We won more games than we lost but never reached our full potential and finished in the middle of the pack. There were no playoffs for this team.

When the regular season came to an end it was time for

my teammates to go home while I headed to California. Despite my former attempt to sabotage my future, the half-season of work in Beloit paid off. My recovery was initially slow, but the turnaround was evident and the organization promoted me at the end of our regular season to help the playoff bound high-A team. Next stop would be in the California League as a member of the Stockton Ports. And when I arrived it wasn't as a spectator; I stepped in immediately as starting third baseman and hit right in the heart of the order. In the first series I led the assault as we won a best of five series. Unfortunately, we were not destined to win the league crown, losing in four games in the League Championship Series. In the mix, though, I headed slowly but surely back up the ladder.

Mid-September brought time for rest. I had started my year all the way across the country in Florida and ended it in northern California with stops all through the Midwest. With no Instructional Ball ahead of me, I would have an extended period of off-season for the first time. My immediate plan was to return to the Midwest, pick up my car in Beloit, then head to Indiana and move my personal life in the positive direction that my professional life seemed to be heading.

Old Home

I made two trips back to South Bend to sit in the visitors' dugout and play against my old team/organization. Having been a fan favorite I received a huge standing ovation even as an opposing player. With a vendetta against the White Sox, I was on a mission to do everything in my power to show them that through all of their efforts they still had not destroyed me; I had some of my best games against my old team!

Beloit Brewers 1991:

Games	At Bats	Runs	Hits	HR	RBI	Average
61	218	31	57	4	37	.261

The Play

Irv was starting his junior year at the University of Notre Dame as the backup tight end for the Fighting Irish just as my season was coming to an end on the West Coast. Though he played in the first two seasons, a logjam of upperclassmen had impeded his march to the top. At the start of his third season he was playing nearly half the game, sharing time with the last remaining senior who was an All-American in his own right. It was time for Irv to take center stage though, and he did so during a game I watched on television from my hotel room in California.

Notre Dame was to play its second game of the year against the Indiana Hoosiers on the road. The game was televised nationally and I was up at nine Pacific Coast Time to watch my little brother in action though I was still half asleep as the opening kickoff soared through the air. Each time I saw Irv head into the game I sat up to pay extra attention. He had been in and out and it was exciting to see his number 84. Plus, I didn't want to miss anything he did.

The Irish, a national contender all four years Irv wore the Blue and Gold, were handling the Hoosiers and nothing really exciting happened until late in the third quarter. In a double tight end set my brother ran out for a pass. The quarterback, Rick Mirer, looked his way and hit Irv for a fifteen-yard gain at about the twenty-five yard line of the opposing team. Turning upfield quickly in search of more yardage, he was surrounded by defenders, so it looked like the play was about to come to an end. Irv had a different idea in mind!

At about the twenty a small defensive back made the first contact with him but couldn't bring him down. With the goal line in distant sight Irv proceeded to carry one defender after another as they piled on for the ride. By the time he reached the end zone he was carrying what looked like the entire Indiana defense. One was on his back, another tugging on the ball trying to pull it away, he had one of his own teammates pushing him from behind and they were hitting him from every side but he just wouldn't go down. When his legs finally gave out and they got him down there was a pile of six or seven, all laying on top of my brother across the line: touchdown! Without even realizing it, I had lost my mind. I went from lying under the covers to running and jumping in my bed right along with him, almost hitting my head on the ceiling as the play came to an end. I probably woke half the hotel yelling and screaming, arms upheld to emulate the referee's signal that Irv had scored. Everyone saw the play, including my new teammates in California; I was a celebrity by association. With that one play Irv moved to the top of 'Players to Watch'. The play itself was considered one of the best ever. To further prove that fact, the following year, during his senior season, the play was re-enacted at the pep rally the night before the big Penn State rivalry game. Irv was then introduced and spoke to the crowd of nearly 15,000 who thanked him with a standing ovation. I was a proud big brother!

I had been trying to contact Lee in Terre Haute for days because I wanted to plan a visit to see my son. I had been in the Midwest for two and a half months before heading to California, hours from my own flesh and blood, and Lee had not made one attempt to bring him out to see me. The simple task of catching her on the phone became increasingly tough. Eddie was creeping towards two years of age and I knew it was important for me to maintain some presence in his life. The one-sided phone conversations did not satisfy the need. But I was now the enemy. Having built up a great deal of animosity over the situation, I kept trying to be civil toward Lee and her family.

My first choice, upon arrival back in the Midwest, was to head to Terre Haute and then up to South Bend to see my brother but the plan would have to be done in reverse since I couldn't get in touch with anyone in Lee's household. I thought it was strange that all had seemingly disappeared, but for all I knew they might have just been avoiding me. It was Thursday night when I got back into South Bend. Irv had a home game coming up on Saturday and I was going to stay with him in his dorm room, sleeping on the bottom bunk bed through the weekend.

Friday night he had to report to the team hotel, so after dropping him off I went for a bite to eat. Upon returning to the dorm I heard a female voice calling my name from across the parking lot; it was Lee's best friend, Shelly. No coincidence that she was there, she had purposely come looking for me at my brother's place as she didn't have a number to contact either of us. It was pure luck that I pulled in as she came down from knocking on the dorm door. After a few pleasantries it came to mind that she might know both where Lee and her family were and why I had not been able to contact them. The puzzled look on her face when I asked immediately made me wonder what bit of information she had that I was missing. Lee, her family and Eddie were all in Vegas where Lee and Teddy, her 'friend', were getting married the very next day. The honeymoon would be a family vacation. Oh. Shelly felt bad being the one to break this news to me, but I thanked her. If not for her, when was I going to find out? Finishing our good-byes, we parted.

Alone again, the news hit me from the blind side; Lee had not once mentioned wedding plans. Whenever I had mentioned her 'friend' she went so far as to say that he wasn't even in the picture any more. I guess when it all came to a head though, her mother's statement came true: "If you won't marry her, someone else will". Almost exactly one year from the day we had set to walk down the aisle, she did so with someone else.

I spent that night alone, wondering what all of this meant for my relationship with my son. Another man now filled my place in Eddie's everyday life. That would make it tougher to develop a relationship with him as his father figure. I watched my brother play on Saturday afternoon, then left one last message for Lee to give me a call when she returned from Vegas. In it I informed her of my new awareness. On Sunday I loaded up and headed for the one place I always knew I could call home, Browns Mills, New Jersey. I had a lot to think about during my twelve-hour drive.

I had been settled in Jersey for over a week before hearing from Lee. When I did, the conversation was heated and nasty. According to her, it was none of my business what she did with her personal life. I argued that her life affected my son's life and in turn mine, so I had every right. The more we talked, the more we yelled and it got pretty ugly. When she blurted that she didn't think it was a good idea that I keep appearing in my son's life, conversation came to a halt. Lee felt that I would only confuse my son as he began to understand things. Eddie knew Teddy as his daddy and she didn't want me to try to play a part-time role. It would be more beneficial to both him and her new relationship if I just didn't come around any more. As angry and hurt as I was at that moment I had a hard time arguing with her after those words. I really had to think about what she said.

What good was I going to do popping in and out of my son's life?

Would he be better off without me?

Would I be doing an injustice by forcing my way into

their supposedly happy family?

There was a man already taking my place; what role would I even have?

Lee had hit some deep nerves because although I had not spent a lot of time with my son it wasn't because I didn't love him or want to be there. To a certain degree I was a victim of circumstance; at least in my mind I thought I was. By the end of the conversation I forced myself to think about things from her side. In a gut-wrenching, emotionally-charged decision I told her I would make an effort to allow her and Teddy to raise my son without interference from me. In my mind at that moment I was doing what was best for him. I didn't want to do anything to hurt my son and the way she explained it that would be all I was doing by coming and going. Lee stated she didn't want me to continue sending money; she and Teddy were doing fine all by themselves and they didn't want anything from me. The second I hung up the phone I regretted ever letting the words come out of my mouth. I felt I had made a mistake. The decision was made though, and I suppose I had to live with its consequences.

I did not know what to do next. For the following several weeks I wandered listlessly around Browns Mills with no plan. I knew spending my whole off-season in this fashion was out of the question because the little money I had managed to put away from the season was going fast and I would soon be flat broke. My signing bonus was long gone, thanks to the huge medical bills and the fact that I still wasn't making any real money in the bus leagues. Everyone thought I was living the life, but my little secret was that I was just another minor league player working for peanuts during the season and living paycheck-to-paycheck. The task ahead? Survive the long cold winter by any means necessary. The best place to make that happen was not in the cold Northeast. After several weeks in limbo I decided to load the

Camaro once again. The one place to which I thought I would never return was the only place that seemed logical; I headed for Sarasota, Florida for one more go-around.

Rock Bottom: Part 2

My getaway set for the first week of November gave me one more opportunity to see my brother play in his junior season on the football field as my mother and father planned a road trip out to South Bend. On this trip Pops would come as close as possible to losing all respect from his family; it was his time to hit rock bottom.

My father's visit to Beloit in August had been enough for me to see the light and where I was heading if I did not make a decision to eliminate alcohol from my life until I was truly able to handle it responsibly. I am incredibly fortunate not to have the addictive gene carried on my father's side of the family. If I did I possibly never would have been able to walk away from the hold that drinking had on me. I took my last drink the day I headed from Beloit to California to finish my season in Stockton and it would be two years before I felt comfortable enough to include alcohol in my life as a mature adult. My father, on the other hand, was still a slave to his compulsion and the problem was about to reach an all-time low.

Pops was up to his old tricks. Through the years he had made serious attempts to release alcohol's death grip. More than once it almost seemed like he had finally beaten the evil force; once he was clean and sober for over two years! His biggest downfall was thinking that he could pick up a drink and not abuse it; he made himself believe he was not an alcoholic. But all it took was that first drink and he was right back where he had left off the time before and taking it to a new subterranean level from there. The years of struggle put incredible pressure on my mother. While my brother and I were out of the house she was left to bear the brunt of the heartache that came with living with an alcoholic. I think at a certain point she resolved herself to the possibility that this was the way the rest of her life with my father was going to be; nothing could be done. And yet, she stayed- a true indicator of her love for him. All of the talking, the tears, and pleading with my father did not penetrate.

On this particular trip, a group intervention brought on by the last drunken episode that we could tolerate as a family, turned out the be the eye-opening medicine for my father; he was going to lose everything if he didn't make a change.

We pulled out of the driveway early on a Friday morning heading to South Bend. Half-way into the twelve-hour trip my father purchased some beer during a stop to gas up the car in Pennsylvania, nothing out of the ordinary. By the time we met Irv on campus that night, after our long drive, he had succeeded in getting drunk and it was just one more night that we all had to deal with it. Nothing was said, however confrontation was right around the corner.

On Saturday, November 2, 1991, my father pushed the limits to the very end. By the time we headed for the stadium for the three o'clock kickoff my father was well on his way to drunkenness. In fact, when we arrived at the stadium I had to help him into the stands and escort him to and from the bathroom. This included pit stops to beer vendors before returning to our seats. By the third quarter of the game, in a crowd of over 60,000 fans, my father sat passed out and my continuing, unenviable task for the rest of the contest became making sure he didn't fall out of his seat. He was oblivious to all around him and it was embarrassing. Had I not caught him a few times he would have plunged head first into the person in front of him.

The game over, it became my responsibility to get him out

of the crowded stadium. I half-walked, half-carried him from the upper levels of the bleachers; my mother was so disgusted she just went ahead of us. We finally caught up with her in the crowded area behind the players' locker room, where she waited for Irv's exit. The look on Irv's face when he saw Pop's condition mimicked how I felt inside; my father was dangerously close to crossing the family line. With bloodshot eyes, slurred speech and the inability to stand without assistance, my father faced the family for the last time in this manner; by the end of the night this issue would be addressed and *finally* confronted.

From the stadium we went directly to dinner; Pop fell asleep in the car and the three of us talked as if he was not present. In the restaurant, seated and waiting for dinner to arrive, the frustration of the day began to spill out. First to pour was Irv. Speaking to my father with as much respect as he could muster, his point was both direct and straightforward: Pop had truly embarrassed him; never again would this type of behavior be accepted or tolerated. My brother further expressed that he would rather our father never come support him again if it meant seeing him like this.

When Irv was done I took the opportunity to convey to him that watching him drink his life away resulted in intensifying pain for all who loved him. It was like talking to a child as he looked at me through glazed eyes and I actually felt sorry for him for the first time in my life. It was at that moment that I realized how difficult it had to be to actually have so little control over something that exerted such power over one's life. Sympathetically, I pleaded with him to search for the strength to overcome because if he did not we might lose all respect for him. And, I reminded, there was no telling where he might end up without the love and support of the three people that believed in him the most.

No defense to his actions, it was unclear if my father had heard a single word any of us had said. Somewhere, deep in the pit of my father's soul, we had struck a nerve, though we would not see the effect immediately.

For the remainder of that night and the drive back to New Jersey the following day my father grappled internally with what he saw in the mirror; I could see in his eyes how much he hated the image looking back at him. He was in danger of losing the one thing he could count on in this life, the respect of his wife and two sons. And that scared him. The lifelong battle with alcoholism was threatening to take it all away from him if he was prepared to surrender to it. Thankfully, and fortunately, he was *not* willing to give up without one last fight. A few days of denial remained but on November 14th of 1991 my father went to an Alcoholics Anonymous meeting with the intent of making that the date he would celebrate for the rest of his life as the anniversary of his start to a life of "Total Sobriety". He would later confess to me that it was the fear of losing the respect of my brother and myself that played a major role in pulling him out of the clutches of his disease. He might as well not even be alive if he didn't have that. Actually, I would love and respect my father no matter what he did but if it took him believing I would turn my back on him, I'm glad the thought crossed his mind.

On *November 14, 2003,* my father celebrated his twelfth year of sobriety. He lives his life by one very important motto, "One Day At a Time," because an alcoholic cannot afford to look one minute past the last one he has lived. According to the serenity prayer by which he also lives and counsels others, God has thus far granted him the wisdom and knowledge to be victorious. Lord willing, tomorrow will bring one more triumph; that's all we can ask for!

Just a couple of days after returning to New Jersey I

loaded the Camaro and headed south on Interstate 95. After all these years I could do this drive with my eyes closed and hands tied behind my back. Fourteen hours from the driveway in Browns Mills got me to Jacksonville, Florida; I drank coffee and took No-Doze like they were tic tacs. After a couple hour power nap at the same chosen truck stop every trip, I'd finish the remaining three-hour drive as soon as the sun came up. I had it down to a science, including State Highway Patrol Officers' all the way down the Eastern Seaboard.

Just a little over two months into my off-season I arrived in Sarasota with barely enough money to get settled and some lean months ahead. I had no further working relationship with the Sox the second I was traded and pride wouldn't allow me to ask for help from the organization that had turned its back on me. If I were going to make it to March I'd have to swallow some of that pride to make ends meet. Good news at this time: I didn't have much overhead as Lee had cut off all contact with me and expressed wishes that I do the same. Her knight in shining armor had rescued her and my services were no longer necessary or needed, as father or boyfriend.

I called a small efficiency apartment (a glorified hotel room) home for the remainder of the winter months. As for employment, the professional athlete that everyone knew on weekends was moonlighting during the week as a car washer. I had fallen on serious hard times. Things got so bad one week I was forced to take drastic measures just to put groceries in the refrigerator; I pawned the wedding ring set that had once symbolized the love I thought I felt for Lee. Walking into the shop feeling that desperate was a very humbling experience. Pride was not something I could *afford* right now though.

Breaking ties with the White Sox also meant I was without a facility to prepare for the upcoming season. I was forced to use one of the last contacts I had in the city, a good friend turned high school coach. From time to time I worked out with his young group in exchange for knowledge I shared. When that wasn't available I went to a local batting cage and hit off machines. There were days when I felt I had signed my soul to the devil and I wished I could take it all back, but I had to continue to push if I was going to make it out. I had been through way too much to give up now. In late February I dried my last car at the Sarasota carwash and headed to New Jersey to see my family before flying out to Phoenix, Arizona, my new Spring Training home. Not living the life I had envisioned when I signed my name on the dotted line a few years ago, this is where I was and what I had to go through right now. I kept telling myself that better days were ahead and hoping they really were.

1992 Stockton Ports/El Paso Diablos

Set to further impress my new organization by demonstrating that I was making a full recovery ready to unleash the full potential that had been both stifled and locked away, I was maturing as a hitter and learning the mental aspect at the plate. More to it than simply getting into the box and having a good swing or approach, one must use one's head to stay a step ahead of the man on the mound. I started going to the plate with a plan and taking advantage of my years of experience. Now considered a veteran, I should treat the game with more respect. My goal to improve every day, I was well on my way until an experiment went horribly bad. Tough luck was about to step in my path one more time.

I was showcasing myself in front of most of the organization for the first time in the spring. According to the buzz around camp I was exceeding all expectations too! Management had heard I was a big strong kid with great potential but damaged goods because of what the Sox had done to me. I countered this by utilizing my 6′4″ 225 lb. physique, imitating a cat-like creature on the field, playing third base as if I had my glove on autopilot and reaching everything in and out of my range. Through my entire career most scouts estimated that I would eventually grow too big to play third base the way I did. They thought I'd have to move to first base one day. Quick feet, incredible athleticism and a cannon for an arm made believers out of them every year though! And now that I was hitting the ball all over the field with power, I was becoming a total package. All I needed was to get away from the prison wherein I had been captive for the last four years.

I was on the fast track again heading back to the top in a hurry, when one of the organization's roving instructors asked if I had ever played in the outfield. I hadn't but knew I could pick it up so I accepted the offer to begin working out in the pasture as well as in the infield. The Brewers recognized increased player value of my raising the number of positions I could play. Third base was my everyday position. I played first as well. If outfield was added to my repertoire, I could become invaluable. I had no problem with the concept of increasing my worth so I started hanging out in the outfield a bit.

For five days I took fly balls off instructors' bats, live ones during batting practice on the field. On the sixth day I got my first chance to play in a late Spring Training game against the Triple-A team for the Seattle Mariners. Taking tips during the game, I cruised along noting that the coaching staff watching were pleased with what they saw. Complete smooth sailing was not in the picture for me, however. In the eighth inning a fly ball was hit deep and over my head in left field. The ball dancing high in the air, I managed to find my way directly underneath it, but that was not the proper position in which to be with a runner tagging on third and heading home as soon as I caught the ball. Aware that the runner would score easily, I still had to attempt a throw toward home plate in case he fell down or something else occurred.

Using the proper footwork to get into long throw position meant taking up valuable time, so from a flatfooted position I made a mighty heave toward the infield. The runner scored without incident at the plate but something even worse happened when I released the ball; I felt a snap and heard a slight popping sound which came from my shoulder and resulted in immediate pain. I thought I might have pinched a nerve; I remained on the field and tried to shake it off. By the time the inning ended I could barely lift my arm to shoulder height and my trainers shut me down for the day. Neither alarmed or considering this a big deal, I agreed with our head trainer that a day or two of rest would see me good as new. Unfortunately, reality meant my right shoulder would never be the same and my first full year with the Brewers would be a "season of pain".

In addition, I was about to learn another eye-opening, important lesson: "The grass is *not* always greener on the other side". Though I was having a great Spring, I was not a 'product' of the organization. That meant I was now more of a suspect than a prospect. Had this injury happened during the early part of my White Sox career, I would have been pampered and nursed back to health. Rather, I was encouraged to get back on the field as fast as possible and at all costs. Then, when it became obvious the problem was more serious than first diagnosed, I was tossed quickly to the side. No courtesy of x-ray or MRI, the trainers insisted I had just pulled or strained a muscle and should take mere days to regain arm strength.

It was decision time with just over a week to go before we broke camp and my shoulder had suddenly reduced me to a designated hitter. I fought through the pain of swinging a bat to continue my assault at the plate. It was not enough to prevent my tumble down the ladder, putting another climb out of A-ball on hold. I would start the year where I had left off in the playoffs at the end of last year, Stockton. Told that as soon as I recovered I would be called to a higher level where I deserved to be, I would learn that would be a long time coming.

"The Wolf"

The previous year Don had been instrumental in helping me depart the White Sox. I had developed a very good relationship with him, a friendship stronger than our business tie- very strange in the world of sports. He had represented me a full calendar year now, helping negotiate my minor league contract over the winter and getting me a little more money. Present to help turn my professional life around, he also leant a much-needed ear, no matter what the topic of discussion. Still I hadn't met the man.

Half way through Spring Training, 1992, we met for the first time when he made the trip out from Fresno to Chandler, Arizona. The picture of him I had designed was way off. I had envisioned an older gentleman, possibly sporting the proverbial stomach-over-belt bulge, and the receding hairline. In truth, Don was in his mid-thirties and probably in better shape than I was. He had a full, flowing mane of hair and you could tell he was no stranger to the gym. I saw in his eyes the same integrity that had originally invited relationship via the telephone. Instantly, I knew that I had made a wise decision in allowing Mr. Wolfe to represent me. It was so nice to finally match face to voice and our meeting strengthened our bond. Destined to travel a long and winding road with me over the next few years as I tried and failed to fulfill my dream, his commitment and who he is as a person would make him a very important player in helping me make things happen down the line. And my gratitude to him would know no bounds.

Like a bird with wounded wing, I sat grounded at the start of the 1992 season. It didn't take a rocket scientist to figure out that I wasn't going anywhere unless I got back on the field. After two weeks in Stockton my trainer began pressuring me to do something that I was initially totally against. The request had more than likely come from way above him but he was the messenger. Rather than sending me to a specialist or taking internal pictures to determine my shoulder's problem, they wanted me to agree to a cortisone shot to get me back on the field. In retrospect, proper diagnosis and surgery, if necessary, would have rendered me useless to the organization because I definitely would have been out for an extended period of time. The Brewers were trying to take the easy way out and get whatever they could out of me.

And I couldn't see the whole picture. Submitting to the Brewer's persuasive urging, I eventually agreed to my first shot near the end of April. All the promises offered moved me to think I would be rewarded as a good soldier for sucking it up and playing through the pain. They wouldn't keep me in Stockton a second longer than I had to be, they promised. The cortisone would have me feeling as good as new, they assured. Both statements turned out to be untruths, and that's putting it lightly.

Cortisone, like alcohol, does nothing to correct a problem; it only fools one into thinking the problem is absent or not as bad as it really is. A masking agent, cortisone is similar to novocaine before a root canal. The second the drug wears off, you feel as if someone has been digging in your mouth with a jackhammer. I had a demonic little man inside my shoulder going at it with that jackhammer every day from that first shot in April, into October well after the conclusion of the season.

The first shot I got burned like hell. I was told that was normal. Missing two days in the lineup to allow the drug to settle and take effect, on the third day I was on the field playing third base. The outfield experiment was off for the time being because I did not have enough arm strength. Actually, every throw I made from third base felt like someone was stabbing me with a pitchfork but I didn't complain. Biting my lip, I played through the excruciating pain day after day after day; I was in so much pain I couldn't lift a drink to my mouth or drive with my right hand. This was all for 'The Cause,' though.

The Brewers left me in Stockton until late in the summer. I wasn't promoted to the El Paso, Texas league, Double-A, until August. And the entire time that I suffered through the California bus league I was taking shots of cortisone for my damaged shoulder like Advil for a migraine headache. Like clockwork, about every three weeks, the pain in my shoulder became so severe that I couldn't go on without another injection. So, shoot me up, sit me down for a couple of days, and then plunk me back in. Had I been a horse, they might have just put me out of my misery rather than watch me suffer in the manner that I was.

For the first time in my professional career I was putting up numbers that didn't stink. Injured and playing in a cavernous pitcher's ballpark notorious for swallowing up and knocking down balls, I regained respect where it most counted: from opposing pitchers who could no longer consider me an easy out. Considered for a spot on the all-star team at the halfway point, I hit more consistently for power and raised my average considerably. In less than a year I again successfully headed in a positive direction. It was a shame that I had to waste the bulk of this season at the lower level while dealing with an inhumane amount of pain, but that wasn't my call. The Brewers called all the shots; I was just a lowly worker bee looking for a little honey.

My on-the-field success was no doubt directly related to my renewed self-discipline off the field. Last year's free-for-all would NOT be repeated. As easily as I had fallen into the bad habits of drinking and running the streets, I pulled the reins back in and inserted positive elements. That is where I was different from my father. I looked in the mirror and told myself, "I shouldn't be drinking now," and followed my own advice. For the most part, a cold beer after a game is like a toothpick after a meat-filled meal, just something that you supposedly have to have, so my teammates thought there was something wrong with me. In the beginning I had to actually explain my transformation. The last time anybody had been out with me I was the life of the party, just getting started when I hit beer number ten. Over a single off-season I had transformed into a lemonade-drinking hippie who was very comfortable with what he was doing. I still went out with teammates at home and on the road and I still had my share of women to chase and be chased by. Difference: I was alcohol-free and responsible for my actions. Good or bad I had to deal with what life was going to throw me and I intended to do that with a clear mind. I treated the ladies with a little more respect, still tough on them, but not thinking they were all out to get me. I didn't put a drink to my lips that entire season, and I knew the name of every young lady I happened to wake up to the following morning.

The Brewers took their sweet time calling me up to El Paso. And when they did take me, we were right in the middle of attempting to win the second-half division title. Fortunately, I was jumping out of one race and right into another, called up because the Diablos needed some help in the middle of their lineup in the Texas League as they made a second half push for a shot at the playoffs as well. That month in El Paso turned out to be the icing on top of the cake of an already good season. Inserted into the starting lineup from the first day, I led a charge that resulted in us winning the division on the second to last day of the season. Then heralded in the paper almost every day as 'the spark that turned things around', I was most frequently asked by fans and reporters, "What took you so long to get here?" This type of attention and respect was something I could really get used to!

The Texas League was my first real taste of what life in the big leagues might be like if I was ever fortunate enough to make it. The cities in the league were so spread out across the Southwest Region that we did all of our travel by plane. The fourteen-hour bus rides I had endured in the Midwest and Southern Leagues were gone. No more six a.m. arrivals, dragging laundry off the bus and eating the majority of meals at convenience stores because everything else was closed. Double-A baseball was not the ultimate goal but it was welcome after all the suffering I had put up with to this point.

Success did not come without consequence in El Paso. Joining my new team I downplayed my torn shoulder because I did not want to admit any weaknesses. I had fought through too much to make it there and felt I couldn't afford any discovered flaws. The Diablo trainer knew my year's trouble, but I told him I didn't need any shots to make it through the last month. For no reason other than stupidity, I spent the season's last segment in an unspeakable amount of pain. And, I paid the price for that lack of common sense every night. On the field I felt like I had been shot every time I threw a ball or swung a bat and away from the ballpark the simplest tasks had to be done with my left arm, my right appendage ripped to shreds internally, dangling from my right shoulder.

Al Goldis' new title with the Brewers was consultant to

the General Manager versus Director of Minor League Operations, but it seemed he had made another smart baseball move by pushing the Brewers to go after me. Far out of the picture and off the charts one short year ago, I was now doing the things I always knew I could. Meanwhile, my resentment toward the White Sox and their decisions grew more intense whenever they crossed my mind. I was one of the lucky who happened to get out; others were not so fortunate. Both Ray Payton and Nandi Cruz were already out of baseball. Two of my best pals, they had grown discouraged and walked away from professional baseball altogether. The thought of existing in that organization under those playing conditions simply wasn't worth it to them. And I could feel their pain.

After winning the division championship against the Padres' double-A affiliate in Wichita, Kansas we fell short in the league title series. Therefore, no celebration on the field in El Paso. My old Stockton teammates did bring home the ring though, winning the California League title. I would get my ring next year in Spring Training. For now, over 120 games played, my shoulder was literally hanging by a thread and ready for a cooling down period. I couldn't have continued even if the Brewers had asked me to their Fall Ball (Instructional Ball with a different name) in Arizona. Never mind that they offered neither the invitation or much enthusiasm over what I had accomplished. But I didn't let that rain on my parade. The most important thing for me was to take some time off and get healthy; I was tired of hurting every day.

A look at the season's numbers evidences that the White Sox had robbed me of some valuable developmental years. The time I lost was invaluable and my professional growth would forever be stunted as I continually played catch up.

Stockton Ports 1992:

Games	At Bats	Runs	Hits	HR	RBI	Average	2B	3B
99	355	57	93	11	57	.262	21	4

El Paso Diablos 1992:

Games	At Bats	Runs	Hits	HR	RBI	Average
22	86	11	25	2	15	.291

Diablo Dollars

There was a tradition in El Paso that I consider one of the best in all of professional sports: "Diablo Dollars". If a Diablos member hit a homerun at home the fans rewarded him by showering him with tokens of appreciation. Those tokens came in the form of money. After congratulations from teammates it was time to go receive one's loot. Long lines formed in the stands, ending at the lower level next to home and visitor dugouts. One by one, the fans shook the player's hand and stuffed money into his helmet- ones, fives, and the occasional ten. To help out, if players were short on time due to the end of that half inning or if the lines were extremely long, the batboys helped out by taking one the sides or standing when one had to go out on the field. If you were lucky and happened to be the designated hitter, you had all the time in the world to gather your prize. As far as I was concerned this was the greatest thing in the history of baseball!

You wanted to save your best efforts for nights when the stadium was crowded to the gills as you could bring home a few hundred dollars with one swing of the bat. Still, there was nothing to frown at on a slow night. After all the money was taken in, the batboys sat in a corner of the dugout counting and stacking currency for a small fee. Then they put the stash away until the end of the game.

One night as I stood in the on-deck circle, a fan that had

taken to me quickly came out of the stands to provide an incentive late in a crucial game; he offered to start the Diablo Dollar pot off with a crisp $100 bill if I hit a homerun. I scorched a ball, a line drive that missed going over the twenty-foot high left center field wall by less than two feet! Missed it by that much.

Fiancés & Finances

Abiding by Lee's wishes I had had no contact with her or my son since the day we had our heated conversation on the phone one year ago. That was the toughest thing I ever dealt with in my life. I don't know when I started doing it, but I began blocking my son out of my mind as a method of coping. It hurt too much to think about him, so 'forgetting' seemed the only way to ease the pain. If I didn't think about him I couldn't miss him, wonder how much he was growing, or imagine what new activities he was enjoying. The most painful part was pondering whether he knew who I was or had any memory of me at all; I knew in my heart he didn't. I was in and out of his life so early that I was sure he had no recollection; Teddy had taken my role as father long ago.

The $1500 a month I made during the season was not going to go far in holding me over until next season. With Don working on my behalf I was creeping up the pay scale but there was still no real money being made. For that reason, surviving meant having roommates. It was nothing out of the ordinary for a two-bedroom apartment to have four or five players crammed into it, the more the merrier as long as rent was paid on time. We ate cheap, fast food restaurants being favored, and Denny's seeming like a night on the town. About the only thing that could cause a player to throw money around was alcohol. It was an expensive habit not only because of the drinks bought for self but the added constant trade-off of buying rounds. And on the

particularly bad nights when one treated the entire bar population, total strangers included, it wasn't unusual the next day to
find only a few crumpled singles in one's jeans pockets after
starting with a fat wad the evening before.

Though I saved a little penny from the split season of
1992, it would not be enough to live comfortably for an extended
period of time. I didn't want to spend the entire off-season struggling, so I decided to spend at least the first couple of months at
home in New Jersey. That would give me time with my family
while I caught my breath and figured out the next move. The
slow pace of Browns Mills was welcome and the miraculous
changes in my father were a true delight. Pops was coming up
on his first year anniversary of sobriety that November. Not the
first time I had seen him try to beat his disease, something was
definitely different this time around. He was living his life with
purpose. Instead of merely attending Alcoholics Anonymous
meetings, sitting in the back barely participating, he was now
chairing them and sponsoring others on their road to recovery.
He was truly living one day at a time with the goal now of finding himself sober at the end of each. Always my hero, Pops was
again justifying the reason for holding that title since I was a little boy. Watching him face and overcome the monster inside was
an amazing event. His triumph demonstrated that if he could
conquer that I could prevail against *anything* in my life as well.
I'd soon have the chance to test that theory.

After a month of walking around dragging my useless
right arm it was apparent that time was *not* going to heal my
shoulder. Something needed to be done. The season over, the
Brewers showed an extreme lack of concern by not even suggesting that I have the arm examined. Rather, they told me to
contact them a few weeks after the season ended if I wasn't
feeling any relief. So, in early October I went to see a shoulder

specialist in Philadelphia. A few days after the MRI my doctor informed me that: A – I was in need of surgery and B – The prognosis was grim. The inside of my shoulder looked like shredded lettuce. Arthroscopic surgery was one option to cutting me wide open to fix the problem. If that was successful I was looking at four to six months recovery. If he got inside, however, and felt that he could not do the job properly, he'd have to give me 'The Big Cut'. If that was the case I was looking at missing an entire year. The scary part was that I wouldn't know the outcome until *after* I woke up from my surgery. Nevertheless, the event was scheduled a few short days away, on October 15, 1992.

While I was pretty calm heading up to Jefferson Hospital, located in the heart of downtown Philadelphia, Pennsylvania, the morning I was to go under the knife, Mom was a nervous wreck. We had all been through my dad's surgeries but my mom was going through the mother hen syndrome; she didn't want anything happening to her firstborn. I assured her I'd be fine though I wasn't really sure myself. In a few short hours I could wake up to the fact of no baseball for a year, if ever. Saying my prayers as the anesthesia was administered, I put my fate in the hands of The Man Upstairs; it was all according to His will now.

I woke up to my mom holding and rubbing my hand, my right shoulder strapped in a sling and throbbing. Exiting the mental fog I was relieved to hear that I only had two holes in my arm and not the 'big zipper cut'. My doctor told me it had been touch-and-go all the way through and I that I had come very close to the big knife. With a long road ahead, I had no assurance that I would be ready for Spring Training but that was much better than the other possible alternative. I started rehabilitation a few days later, commuting 35 minutes to Philadelphia three times a week. My recovery was slow and very painful, replete with times I wished I had never had the surgery, as I had experienced less pain before it. For a long time I lacked improvement, no matter what I did. That was the scariest part. Four and a half months later, in March, as I prepared to head to Spring Training, I still couldn't throw a baseball hard enough to bust a grape up against a brick wall. Struggling to rehabilitate my shoulder had set me back in every aspect of season preparation. When it was time to set out on the road again I did so with little optimism. I believe that everything happens in life for a reason, but I spent quite a while trying to surmise why I was yet again being derailed when I had just gotten back on track!

Family Matters

As a family it seemed as if we had finally hit the upswing. My father was working his program, one day at a time, and my parents had survived the toughest years they would face together in their remarkable married life. My mother maintained her role as the glue that kept us all together whether near or far, through the good times and bad. My family was a constant source of strength for me through all the ups and downs of my turbulent on and off field life. When I beat myself up about affairs with my son my mother was there in support, not to criticize but assure me that God had a plan and it would be revealed in His time, not mine. We loved one another unconditionally and did not judge so I was never alone when things seemed to be crashing on all sides.

Out in South Bend, Irv was in his senior year at Notre Dame. He had patiently waited his turn for three years but was now the featured tight end. At the end of that season he played in his fourth major bowl (the team was nationally ranked in the top ten every year). Recognized as one of the top tight ends in the country after his junior year, great things were expected at the next level. More importantly he was on schedule to graduate the following spring with his degree in Business, more impressive than anything he was doing on a football field.

Before my shoulder surgery it seemed that I was back on the fast track to jumpstarting my seemingly stalled career, but this latest setback was devastating. I knew in my heart that God hadn't brought me all this way for nothing but I was beginning to have my doubts. It seemed like each time I got up off the mat I was knocked back down. I knew I had to keep going though. I had come too far to give up easily.

Uncle Eddie

In December I got a call from Mike, my best friend and teammate with the Brewers. Settling down and getting married in March, right before Spring Training, he requested I be his Best Man. The wedding would take place in Indianapolis, Indiana, a couple hours drive from Terre Haute. Since it would be convenient to have my car with me during the season (it had spent the entire last summer sitting in front of the house in New Jersey), I decided to make the cross country drive in segments. My first stop was to South Bend to spend a couple of days with Irv before continuing to Indy where he would rejoin me for the wedding.

The Saturday wedding went off without a hitch and Mike and his lovely bride, Nikki, departed for their one-day honeymoon. Day after next the three of us, Mike, Nikki, and I would exit the state, taking two cars all the way to Arizona for Spring Training. Since the plan left Irv and me with a little time to kill, I called Lee, hoping she'd let me see my son, who had turned three in December. After talking it over with Teddy she felt it was all right so Irv and I made the trip on Sunday morning to see little Eddie. I hadn't laid eyes on him in over a year and a half. It was a very strange and unusual reunion.

I was meeting Teddy for the first time. I didn't have

anything against him though, and as long as he was being a good father to my son there would be no trouble. He was. I didn't know it until we arrived at their home but Eddie was already a big brother; Lee and Teddy were the parents of a baby girl. And they all seemed so happy that it made it hard to hold on to the anger that I sometimes felt over the decisions that were made. I was in no position to offer Lee the stability that she craved, so I couldn't be mad that another man was doing what I could not. What did hurt was being introduced to my own son as an uncle – Lee's idea.

I stood face to face with my own flesh and blood, hiding my identity. Desiring no trouble, Irv and I went along with the plan and I became Uncle Eddie; from which side of the family I didn't know, but that would be up to her to one day explain. Lee was cooking Sunday dinner for her family but I didn't want to intrude on that so I didn't intend for our visit to take up the bulk of their day. She surprised me by suggesting that Irv and I take Eddie over to his favorite place, the McDonald's Playland. It was bittersweet to watch him as he ran and played, running back and forth to our table to munch on his cheeseburger. Realizing all I was missing in his life, and knowing I'd never have the opportunity to reclaim any of this lost time, the toughest part of the visit was dropping him off, once again to fade off into the sunset. I knew I might not see him again for a very long time, maybe never. Before I left I asked Lee if there was anything I could do for him. She insisted there was not: I wanted what was best for my son and it seemed that he had all he needed, two loving parents under the same roof. So, I walked out of the door and out of his life again; hoping this was not the last time I'd see my son but not knowing for sure.

Rudy

By the time he completed his senior year on the football field Irv had become very popular on the Notre Dame campus. Ever the social butterfly, he was constantly meeting new people and I was introduced to all of his friends whenever I came into town. On this latest visit to South Bend, before going to Indianapolis, Irv took me to the townhouse of one of his favorite people associated with the university; he told me I just had to meet this individual. The first thing that struck me about this gentleman when I walked in his front door was that he was an absolute Notre Dame fanatic; there wasn't one thing in the entire place that wasn't monogrammed with the Notre Dame insignia, all the way down to the bathroom tissue dispenser. We spent about an hour talking and I got the condensed version of a very interesting life story about to be turned movie according to him. That man was Rudy Ruettiger and the name of his truly inspirational and true story? *Rudy!* After later witnessing his life on the big screen, overcoming all obstacles to fulfill his dream of playing for the Fighting Irish, the message was very clear: You can't let ANYTHING stand in your way!

1993 El Paso Diablos

Though well-liked as a person and player, I was never a fully welcomed member of the Brewers organization. I was considered an outsider because of the way I had been brought to the organization. Al Goldis, in bringing me on, had stepped on some toes and ruffled some feathers by making his presence felt in such a big way on the field. Mainly a consultant to the big league club, his expertise was in player personnel and development and it was hard for him not to want to be involved with the talent. Al wanted nothing more than to see me succeed and did everything in his power to try and make that happen; after all, he was responsible for drafting me in the first place.

When I returned for duty in the spring I was still hampered by the fact that I could not throw a baseball across the field. Under the watchful eyes of my training staff my rehabilitation was accelerated and before we broke camp I was at least functional. It was my steady work at the plate that allowed me to leave Arizona with my team and avoid staying behind to further strengthen my repaired arm. Just as I had before, I would start this season as a designated hitter until I was well enough to join my team on the field.

It took the better part of the first month of the season to regain full form on the playing field and I knew my arm would never be the same. Even at 80% I was still better than most players in the field. A good athlete, I realized as I matured, must know how to adapt throughout his career if he is going to exhibit staying power. With more range in the field than any average third baseman, I would rely on a new, quick release now that I lacked some of the old gun's fire.

I played in 118 games that year and, still durable, I showed great versatility by moving around – playing both corners of the infield and outfield. If the Brewers had had any plans for me I would have been at the top of their prospect chart. Unfortunately, I was now just a face in their crowd. Al Goldis had worn out his welcome as far as the minor league directors were concerned. They had apparently passed word to the top brass that they would feel more comfortable with less input from the man whom I consider a baseball guru. And, even with the impressive numbers I was putting up, playing multiple positions in the field and never complaining about a thing, I could tell there was also very little love for me in the organization. I could have been promoted easily to the next level during the season but don't think I ever came into consideration. I was looking at the bigger picture this year though, so I remained focused and fought my discouragement. I was in my sixth season of minor league baseball, after which I would become a free agent; the Brewers would no longer hold sole rights. Each time I took the field I considered myself auditioning for anyone paying interest in my displayed talents. If the Brewers did not pay attention or care, someone else would.

First Round Pick

My little brother was all grown up after four years of college football and in April, 1993, I watched the NFL Draft with increased interest. Irv was projected as a first round selection, the first tight end to be taken off the board, so he was invited to New York to attend the draft live, my mother and father joining him. I watched from El Paso, anticipating my brother's name being called, which it finally was as the 21st pick of the day.

Irv would begin his professional football career a member of the New Orleans Saints. I couldn't have been any prouder of him, but I couldn't ignore the thought swimming around in the back of my mind: "Where would I be and what might I be doing if I had gone the route of football?" It was quite possible that I would have been on that stage a couple of years prior. Neither here nor there, it was pointless to entertain such thought. I was living in the 'here and now' and there are no do-overs in life. It was time to be happy for Irv because of all he had accomplished. And besides that, it was a family victory; we were all in this together.

Happily Ever After

Earning $2500 a month in my second full season with the Brewers (no money considering the fact I was only getting paid during the season) gave me freedom to live comfortably in El

Paso during the season. My roommate, Al Lewis, a utility infielder who, at times, shared third base with me, was the perfect person with whom to share an apartment. Joining the Brewers from the Dodgers as a six-year free agent in the last off-season, Al was equally as reserved and quiet natured as I. And, he was just a good person! We hit it off rooming together in Spring Training and didn't have to think twice about sharing a place during the season.

Life does imitate art. Half way through the season Al asked me to be the best man in his wedding in a scene right out of the film *Bull Durham*. He and his fiancé, Michelle, who was living back in Illinois, didn't want to wait until the end of the season to be wed, so the two came up with the idea to marry on the field, just like in the movie. The wedding was set for July before one of our home games as over 2,000 fans arrived early to help in the celebration. A beautiful ceremony, it was one of the most special and remembered events in my professional career. Al and I stood at home in our baseball uniforms as a white stretch limo transported his wife-to-be through an open gate out in right field. The rest of our teammates stood in two lines facing each other, bats in hand to create an archway for the bride to walk down from the pitcher's mound toward Al. Vows exchanged, Al and his new bride got back into the limousine for a victory lap around the warning track of the field, standing together and waving to the crowd through the sunroof of the vehicle.

Al wasn't done for the day though; he was in the starting lineup and had a game to play that night! He didn't get a hit during the game but I took up the cause for him and collected Diablo Dollars every time he came to the plate. The spirit in the ballpark on that day is what minor league baseball is all about. That certain connection between players and fans cannot be found at the big league level. I miss that more than anything else.

(After bouncing around the minors for a couple more years Al retired. He and Michelle are still happily married and living in Illinois.)

Nineteen Ninety Three should have been the year that sent me back up the ladder instead of beginning my slide across the board. The better I played, it seemed, the less attention I got from within the organization. I didn't know it until after the season, but Al Goldis was being forced out of another front office position; at the end of the big league season he broke ties with Milwaukee. My biggest supporter, he was obviously the only reason I was in the organization. His imminent departure unbeknownst to me, my best full season as a professional was wasted because nobody cared. I felt like that proverbial tree falling in the forest with no one around: Does it make a sound? And would anybody hear it if it did?

I flirted with hitting .300 all the way into the last week of the season on a winning team but got no respect; my breakout season went unrewarded. Players with seasons much inferior to mine were patted on the back and encouraged and I was shown the door. All part of the business of the game, I had been around the block enough times to not take it personally. Once residing on the other side of the fence as a prospect, now I was a suspect. When the year was over and it was time to leave El Paso I didn't know my days as a Brewer were numbered, but they were. Don's request of the Brewers to help me in finding a winter ball job in one of the Latin countries during the off-season was virtually ignored.

Now a six-year free agent, I was in a sense, a man without a team a month after the season. Milwaukee's stance on resigning me was a 'wait and see'. Unfazed by the turn of events I was becoming callous to my cold baseball world. Still, I was determined to not allow it to break me down. The only way to succeed was through maintaining my strength and convictions. I knew I had been blessed with all this God-given talent for a reason and after all I'd been through it would take more than a bumpy road to stop me from continuing my journey.

El Paso Diablo's 1993

Games	At Bats	Runs	Hits	HR	RBI	Average	2B	3B
118	419	64	123	8	69	.294	23	6

The beginning of the off-season brought silence from the Milwaukee Brewers in regards to my future. It was a tough pill to swallow after all my pain and commitment level to them. With little support I had managed to find some resemblance of the athlete I once was, but the Brewers treated me like Cinderella, unworthy of attending the ball. I found it hard to believe that I was washed up at only 24 years of age. And I refused to even allow the thought to more than briefly enter my mind. If I had to move on, that is what I would do; and that is what it came to. On November 5, 1993, three days after Minor League Free Agency officially opened, the Chicago Cubs contacted Don in hopes of signing me to a minor league contract. The main man behind the inquiry was, yet again, none other than my dear friend and greatest supporter, Mr. Al Goldis. He had taken a minor league consulting position with the Cubs and was eager to bring me aboard. A no-brainer as far as Don and I were concerned, we felt the dream was back in motion. I was now becoming a journeyman; this was my third organization and I was already seven seasons into my quest to make it to the big leagues. The fire burning deep inside of me yet, and I was not going to be satisfied until one of two things took place: I would either make it to the big leagues or get all of this out of my system so I could move on.

1991 Beloit Bewers vs. South Bend Sox

1991 Beloit Brewers

Best Man 1993
Ed and Mike Farrell

Ed and Irv
Wedding

CHAPTER FOUR

Chicago Cubs & Cleveland Indians

A week after signing with the Cubs I received a phone call from Arizona and an invitation to join the club during the winter off-season program. This was the perfect opportunity to work with my new instructors, get a head start on getting in shape for next year and get away from the cold Northeast. The Cubs Spring Training facility was located in Mesa, Arizona and the city had everything I would need to make it through the lean winter months. Every day was 70 degrees and sunny and I was minutes from the Arizona State University campus with all the lovely young coeds. I set out to earn some money to help make ends meet until it was time to go back to playing baseball full time. With a fresh start ahead I was optimistic that good times were not far off. And I was going to take advantage of them while they lasted because nothing was a guarantee or sure thing in my eyes.

I broke my cross-country trip into tiny little bites to make it more tolerable since I was doing it all by myself this time. From New Jersey I went down to see Irv in New Orleans in the home-stretch of his rookie season with the Saints. After five days down in the bayou I drove across the state of Texas through New Mexico and into Arizona.

My first off-season in Arizona was a welcome treat. I wasn't sure of what to expect initially, not knowing anyone in the area and starting all over in my third organization. Any reservations

I had were quickly put to rest as I saw what the Valley of the Sun had to offer; the winter weather was incredible, the women were beautiful, and the laid-back nature of the city fit my style.

The first few days in town I took up residence in a small hotel room. Fortunately, that stay didn't last long. After a couple of days of getting settled I contacted a young lady I had met during the previous Spring Training. I was invited over to the house in which she was living with her two female roommates. All three girls, nineteen years of age, had been friends in high school and they had a party going on in the house. I felt like an old man, surrounded by drinking teenagers but I was certainly a hit! The four-bedroom home belonged to the parents of one of the young ladies, Jennifer, to whom they were renting it. When she learned of my living situation she offered the remaining bedroom to me. I seriously doubted how that would all work out and silently questioned what her parents would say, but accepted the offer on a trial basis. If her parents, she, or anybody else had a problem with me staying there, I'd move out.

The next day I gathered my belongings and moved in. Ironically, the friend who introduced me in the first place had a falling out with the other two girls a couple of weeks later and moved out. I was then left living like Jack Tripper in *Three's Company*. It turned out to be a great living arrangement. I met Jen's parents; they approved of my staying in the house and looked at me as an overseer to a certain degree. Had I not been in the right frame of mind, the situation could have been more like leaving the wolf in charge of the sheep but it wasn't like that. The girls became like little sisters to me and I was the protector of the house.

Even though the rent I was paying was minimal, I had to get a job to make it through the off-season. Money, or lack thereof, was becoming a constant problem for me when the off-season months came around. Without a lot of job skills other than being an athlete, there wasn't a great deal that I was qualified to do. My imposing physique and intimidating look did make me a good candidate as a bouncer at one of the hottest nightclubs in the area, though. That job turned out to be a gold mine.

I worked out with my new team five days a week from morning until early afternoon. While a few instructors occasionally came in, most of our training was left up to us, a group of about ten players. We started the day by hitting on the field live, then worked at our individual positions. Next, it was into the weight room before finishing off the day with conditioning. We were normally done with the day shortly after lunch because we got such an early start, trying to beat the desert heat. The work was intense but fun and we all helped one another in honing our skills. I made some good friends in a hurry and became comfortable with my new surroundings immediately. The end result of all of the hard work was the best shape I had ever been in. At 6'4" and 218lbs. I was as quick and agile as I had ever been and the intense weights unmasked hidden muscle I had taken for granted.

Three nights a week, I bounced over at the nightclub in Scottsdale, Arizona. I got more attention and dates standing around the dance floor, making sure there weren't any drinks in hand and watching for fights than I would have had I frequented the club every night as a patron. I don't know what it was, but it was as though I had a red bull's eye on my back. On a typical night I'd spend half my time turning down drinks offered to me despite the fact I sported a tee shirt obviously labeling me 'employee'. Yes, I turned down those drinks, but easily accepted the many phone numbers slid in my hand and pocket during the evening! The women's boldness grew as their consumption of alcohol increased and their approaches had me pinching myself sometimes to see if I was dreaming! I thought there was no way I could be this popular or desirable as a bouncer. I had never experienced this type of 'reverence' as a professional athlete. Women of all ages, occupations and social standing practically threw themselves at me and I gallantly attempted to catch every one of them!

My failed relationship was the furthest thing from my mind, which meant that my son was as well. I began to repress the fact that I was a father and at one time almost a husband. I had no communication with Lee or Eddie for another full year by the time Spring Training rolled around again. As far as I knew she was living happily ever after. The pain over the circumstances of my absence from my son's life was easiest dealt with through denial. And to cover the void I filled my life with women looking simply to enjoy my company. It was all mutual consent, so I didn't feel guilty about anything I was doing. I told the truth and nothing was promised; both sides were in it for the good time. It was another form of running from something that I would some day have to face but it would be a long time before I ever did that.

A few weeks before the start of Spring Training I quit my bouncing job; it was time to completely focus on the upcoming season. I had put in a great deal of work on the field and it was time to put that all to good use. The long climb up the ladder was about to resume and I was about as optimistic as I had ever been. This year would show me exactly where I was and how far I had to go or how far I was away to making it to the big leagues.

1994 Orlando Cubs

I got a taste of what it would truly feel like to be a big leaguer during the spring. For the first time in my career I participated with the big team during the exhibition games. The

Cubs had almost outright invited me to camp but I didn't get that call even though I was told by many that I should have. I'm convinced that was all about not having to pay me big league money during Spring Training. Instead I worked every day in minor league camp and received spot calls to dress with the big league club. This mostly occurred on the days that there were split squad games going on; two games one day. One game was at home while the other was on the road. The veterans didn't like to travel during the spring so they usually played in the home game and left the travel to the younger players. That wasn't the way it always worked, but it was pretty consistently so.

On the days that I joined the big league club they sent for me early so I could take batting practice on the big field. I was in heaven. I got to experience what I had sought all along. Every ball we hit or threw was sparkling white. Crowds gathered just to watch us hit or take infield practice and reacted to every ball hit. And the food in the clubhouse was catered; there was no such thing in our minor league clubhouse as we ate bagged lunches.

I had developed a renewed confidence in my abilities and it showed at the highest level of competition whenever I was given the chance to shine. A realist, I knew I was not fighting for a spot on the big league club, but I also knew that I was being given the opportunity to show what I was capable of doing at this level of play. I took the time to soak up as much knowledge as possible. Standing near the batting cage while someone like Mark Grace took batting practice or talked about his hitting philosophy was like gold, and I was greedy for it. I had come a very long way in a short period of time and I was trying to do everything I could to make sure I stayed pointed in the right direction. I played in about ten games that spring, mostly late inning duty, but what I gained and accomplished in those interludes was invaluable. That's why I was so disappointed the last week of minor league camp when I got word that I was being designated to play for the double-A team in Orlando, Florida. The excuse was the same as it always had been with the same promises made: the organization already had a prospect to play third base in Triple-A. They assured me that I was not going to spend a lot of time at the Double-A level as they wanted me in Iowa with the Triple-A team. They just wanted me to be patient while I had a good season; the call would come soon. Being the obedient soldier, I didn't complain. I did exactly what they wanted me to do. It's just a shame they didn't behave likewise.

As a member of the Orlando Cubs I was returning to the Southern League where I had spent half a season with the Birmingham Barons in 1990. Placed again on the bus and in the worst travel city in the league made this a tough year to swallow. Orlando was scorching hot and humid, making it a rough place to spend a baseball season, but that was only the half of it. The other teams in the league were all clustered in Alabama, Tennessee and North Carolina. The average length of their trips from one city to the next was about three and a half hours, while our shortest trip was seven hours. Because of this, we had to take off on all of our road trips almost immediately after the last game of a home stand, our bus departing around midnight and us sleeping through the night crammed next to each other or lying on the floor or in the luggage racks above. We'd wake to the sun peering through the windows of our carriage as we pulled into our hotel and then have to play a game that night. No team was more tired than ours and we were notorious for getting beat pretty bad, manhandled, on travel days; we were like the walking dead on the field sometimes. Each day I spent in Orlando that year I felt like I was serving a jail sentence for a crime I did not commit. And, there was nothing I could do about it. I deserved better than I was getting but, once again, what could I do?

The Orlando team was the typical mix of veterans and young prospects. I knew my role because my manager constantly approached me, urging me to help the youngsters' development. The rough schedule, extreme road travel and intense heat and humidity of Orlando would wear down the fragile group the Cubs had put together. Because I had been through everything I was supposed to be that glue that kept us together when times inevitably got tough. I didn't have a problem helping keep the waves to a minimum during the choppy summer, but the Cubs had it wrong; my sole intention was not to be present as club babysitter. I wanted out of Orlando and expected just that due to the promises previously made. It turned into a long Central Florida summer and one in which I never got 'the call'.

I lived alone during this long and disappointing season. Having turned twenty-four during the summer, I had tired of the whole roommate thing; it was time to start doing life on my own. This was a little easier now that I was making decent money according to minor league standards: $3,000 a month. If not for two teammates, Doug Glanville (DMG) and Paul Torres (PDT), each dealing with their own Cub drama, I might have gone crazy dealing with this team. Doug was a high prospect but wasn't getting the respect he deserved and Paul was being ignored by the organization that drafted him and was now apparently unconcerned as they buried him behind younger talent. The three of us bonded. Paul and Doug were roommates at home and Doug and I roomed together on the road. I rarely hung out with anyone, opting to spend most of my free time around my one bedroom apartment learning how to cook and perfecting the art of efficiently taking care of myself; I was finally growing up.

MJ

The Southern League was the focus of a great deal of attention in 1994 because of a very special guest taking his own shot at making it to the big leagues, Michael Jordan. MJ, six-time NBA champion and the greatest player ever to play the game of basketball (in my opinion), had stepped away from the NBA after his father's death. He had signed with the Chicago White Sox and was playing for my old Double-A team, the Birmingham Barons. Michael and the Barons were the talk of the league and all games he played in that year, at home and on the road, were sellouts. This was unheard of for minor league baseball, but how many times does something of this nature happen? We played three separate three game series against the Barons in Orlando that year and those nine games were sold out a week into the season. The atmosphere? CIRCUS!!

I have never been in awe of anyone but even I have to admit that I stayed in our dugout to watch MJ take a round of batting practice the first time they were in town to play us. What he had walked away from and what he was trying to do amazed me. The funny thing is, after that he became just another player to me and I made it a point to treat him as such. While everyone marveled over him (our team even sending items to the visiting clubhouse for his autograph) I talked to and treated MJ like he was just another minor league baseball player because, in my eyes, he was. And he respected that.

After just one game we were on a nickname basis, I was Big E and he was, of course, MJ. Because I was a former member of the White Sox I already had a relationship with the manager and half the players on their squad that year so I wasn't one of the enemies. In that first game MJ made it to third base, which was followed by a game-break for a pitching change. He, their manager, Terry Francona (who was coaching third base) and I started a conversation. The next thing I knew the three of us were laughing like we were in a bar somewhere having a couple of drinks. As play resumed MJ mentioned to me that he was going to get a ball past me during the game. From there, it was ON!

Every time he came to the plate he gave me a big grin and took his shot at lacing a ball by me; he didn't succeed that first night, but for the rest of the year that was his goal when he saw me standing down the line. A few times during the year he even tried to drop a drag bunt down on me to draw me in and put that thought in my mind. The closer I stood to him, the easier it would be to get one by me. We played a serious game of cat and mouse and laughed about it whenever he was on second, made it to third base, or he was close enough to get into my ear from his dugout. I joked that he must be getting desperate, resorting to those tactics. I wish I could say I shut him out for the season, but he finally accomplished his goal with a one hop double down the third base line late in the season. I looked over at him, standing tall and proud with his chest all puffed out, on second base, and he smiled this huge grin; I tipped my hat and laughed as he flashed that winning smile that millions adore.

Michael is not only a great athlete, but one of the best people I've ever met. He did much for his teammates. They traveled around the Southern League in style on the bus that Michael bought and customized specifically for them, replete with sofas, card tables and televisions throughout. And the Barons were the best-fed team in the league, also courtesy of their benefactor. Another little known fact was what MJ did at the end of the Barons' season. A Most Valuable Player was named and Michael thought the selection was unfair because there was a more deserving player. So what did he do? The player who had been passed over became the recipient of a brand new Nissan truck, courtesy of the owner of the dealership: Michael Jordan! And his generosity didn't stop there; I, too, was the beneficiary of a very nice gesture at the tail end of our season when, in August, we played the Barons for the last time of the season, the game in Orlando.

Late in the game MJ was on third. We talked and wished each other well for the remainder of the season. In the clubhouse after the contest, I was getting undressed in front of my locker when one of our batboys came up to me holding two gifts sent over from the visiting clubhouse: two pair of Michael Jordan cleats. The shoes were exact replicas of his famous basketball sneakers, transformed by NIKE for him to use during his days on the baseball diamond. The shoes had his baseball number 45 on the back and were in excellent condition. It took less than five seconds for a crowd of my teammates to gather around me. Everyone wanted to know what I had done for him to send me something like this. The only thing I could think was that I treated him as I do everybody else, an equal. I sent a thank you note to Michael, via batboy, before they departed and took the shoes home that night. To this day they are one of my most prized pieces of memorabilia.

Michael finished his season with the Barons hitting .200 and returned to basketball the following year, going on to win the last three of his six total championships with the Bulls. An honor and pleasure to play on the same field with him, I respect what he did during that season with the Barons. I give him a great deal of credit because there aren't many people that could come close to doing what he did. He didn't light the league on fire at the plate but was never overmatched and that is saying a lot considering hitting a moving object coming at one in speeds excess of 90mph is considered one of the toughest feats in all of sports. Michael was also a very competent outfielder with good range. He definitely took a hit or two away from me during that season. That said, I was happy to hear the announcement that he would return to the NBA the following year. He performed okay as a baseball player but is the greatest basketball player to ever play the game as far as I'm concerned. It was more than good to see him flying high above the rim again.

Second Homecoming

Returning to the Southern League and traveling to play my old team, the Barons, also meant I was able to see the family in Birmingham. Granddad's health was seriously deteriorating at that time. I hadn't seen him since leaving Birmingham at the end of the 1990 season and his diabetes was beginning to get the best of him. On the first trip into Birmingham I had my second cousin, John Gice, pick me up at the team hotel so I could go see the man who had given me my first car way back when I was in high school. When I had last seen him he was driving himself around and still taking care of himself. Now he was confined to bed with an around-the-clock nurse tending to his needs. I'd heard he wasn't doing well, but had no idea his condition was such; his eyes were open and he looked at me, but I don't think he knew who I was. I saw him again, later in the season. Little had changed. He was still holding on, but not with a firm grip. I said good-bye to him on our last visit to Birmingham that summer, not knowing if I'd ever see him alive again. My only hope was that he did not suffer too long.

Frustration beginning its build at the halfway point of the season, it became apparent I would spend the year right where I was- no promotion. I was leading a team full of their prospects in almost every offensive category, but all seemed to go unnoticed. More aggravating were the players with whom I shared the field. Spoiled Cubs prospects, they were some of the worst I had ever played with as far as approach to the game. All about individual statistics, they did some of the most blatantly selfish things trying to pad and protect those during the season. If a particular pitcher was on the mound and a certain player did not hit well against him he'd come up with a phantom injury that mysteriously kept him out of the lineup just for that one day; blister on the hand, tight hamstring and migraine headache were just some of the lame excuses used. On the field every day, I played iron man on a team that could never put it all together because some of its members just didn't care enough. While travel, heat, and our schedule may have prove too much for any to overcome now and then, there was no excuse for what went on otherwise. Select players knew that as did our manager. From time to time he actually called me into his office or sat with me on the bus discussing the problem as we drove through the night. I suggested being tougher on the group, but he didn't want to offend the precious prospects under his guidance so I washed my hands of trying to baby sit. I should have been looking out for myself the rest of the way out, since nobody else apparently had my best interests in mind. That may have saved me a lot of pain. It is not, however, in my nature to turn my back or to ignore cries for help.

Not having missed a game all the way through the later part of the season, I played third base and did spot duty at first base daily. My manager rode me like a horse, but I didn't mind because I figured it was the only way I could prove my worth. It was almost inevitable that I break down somewhere on that grueling road though, and I did hit what should have been a small roadblock in the middle of July. I pulled my right hamstring running out a ground ball. The injury was going to put me on the bench for at least a few days.

After a week of rehab and rest I was still hobbling around. I could jog lightly, but anything above that still brought a degree of discomfort and pain. I had apparently done more than just stretch the muscle and it was going to take a little more time before I got back on the field. Instead of allowing me the time that would have no doubt been afforded one of the prospects, my manager was in my ear each day letting me know that the front office was urging him to get me back in the lineup as soon as possible. No one even knew how serious my injury was because we never took an inside look. I was as frustrated sitting on the bench watching my team struggle as my manager was; we were in the middle of one of our patented losing streaks.

The following week I doubled up on my rehab and fought to get back as soon as possible, but it came along slowly. My trainer, a good man whose first concern was the health of his players, was against throwing me back on the field before I was closer to full recovery. He knew I was attempting to get back too soon. Exactly two weeks after the injury we had a double header at home in Orlando and my manager wanted me to play in the second game. I went out on the field and took a running test during batting practice in the afternoon while my trainer emphatically urged my manager to give me more time, about a week. I knew I shouldn't be cleared to play, still feeling the tight knot in the hamstring. My manager desperately wanted me back in the lineup. We'd lost twelve of the fourteen games I spent on the bench and he was feeling the pressure himself; he wasn't supposed to be losing this many games with the amount of talent he had on the roster. After game one of the double-header, another loss, he put me in the lineup in the middle of the batting order playing first base to limit my movement in the field.

In my first at bat I hit a deep fly ball to right center field. It missed leaving the 'yard' by about two feet. The ball was hit on a line and bounced right to the outfielder, so I had to kick it into second gear to collect my double. When I did that, I felt the first grab; I had pulled the hamstring again. My trainer looked on from the top step of the dugout, knowing I had re-injured myself, but I played the pain off.

In my very next plate appearance I hit the same exact fly ball to deep right center field and the ball hit almost the precise spot as the time before. This time, rounding first base, the pain was more severe and I had to pull immediately. Halfway between first and second base I put the brakes on, came to an easy stop, turned around, and trotted back to first base. By the time I made it to the bag, a pinch runner was up and off the bench, heading into the game for me. This second pull was equally as bad, if now worse than the first. I knew I would be out at least as much time as I already had.

In that one night I had regressed to the beginning. While I hold myself accountable for jumping the gun in that situation, I never felt my manager or even the Cubs shared any responsibility for how the matter was handled. When all was said and done, that hurt. I realized I was about as significant as crumbs at the bottom of a potato chip bag when it came to the Chicago Cubs. They refused to put me on the disabled list and I traveled with the team for the next two weeks, still without a professional diagnosis. What I did next was drastic but my options seemed limited.

One of my teammates told me he had some DMSO, a product used on horses for muscle problems. I've heard it described as a steroid, but I am not sure if that is true. It is neither injected nor ingested, but rubbed on the outside of the animal. Absorbed through the skin, it goes directly to the muscle on which it is applied. The biggest problem with DMSO is that it also absorbs anything else it comes into contact with through the skin as well. For instance, if a person put DMSO on his leg and wore a pair of blue jeans, the dye from the jeans would also go right into the system. That was of no consequence to me when I learned that my teammate had some that he would let me use. I had no alternative at this point. At least, I thought I didn't. Against the objections of my trainer I started rubbing myself down with DMSO, hoping for a miracle.

In a matter of days I could feel the difference; this stuff was strong and it really did work. A long road trip coincided with my day and night application of the clear liquid to my injured hamstring. The trick to using it was to wear plastic gloves and to wrap the leg in clear plastic to keep anything from coming into contact with my skin. That way I could keep my system from absorbing anything other than the DMSO. On the long bus rides I wore shorts and kept the leg propped up, out of harm's way.

The DMSO worked its magic and two weeks later I was well enough to take a second shot at getting back into the lineup. I was still rushing it, but we were into August now and I didn't have a lot of time to waste if I was going to finish my season as I had started it. This was just another example of what I was willing to endure and sacrifice- all for The Cause.

The problem with missing that many games in succession as a hitter is timing disruption. During the second recovery I necessarily scaled back batting practice, so I was lost by the time I got back to swinging. My averaged dipped 25 points in the first two weeks back on the field. I was hitless in the first six games back and it just got uglier from there. Pressing and trying to do too much at the plate, I tried to make up for lost time. The last month of that season was almost a total disaster. I couldn't hit water if I fell out of a boat in the middle of the ocean. All that hard work leading up to the pulled hamstring seemed to be for nothing. The only thing that saved me from jumping off a building was a late surge in the last two weeks of the season.

Having missed 27 games, all due to injury, and still leading the club with 16 homeruns and 60 runs batted in, I was doing what I needed to do to be noticed but it was like all had their eyes closed or looked the other way when it came to me. I began to feel like an unappreciated housewife. She cooks, cleans, takes care of the kids, does all the shopping and laundry, keeps the house in order, and all she wants in return is to be loved and respected for what she brings to the table. Instead, her husband comes home, plants himself on the couch to watch television and totally ignores her. Before long she starts to wonder why she is even bothering. That is what was going through my mind after we played our last game of the season. I felt like the Cubs didn't even know I existed. And at this rate, just like that unhappy housewife who would no doubt eventually get frustrated and give up, it wouldn't be long before I gave up on my love, baseball. If 'things' didn't take a drastic turn for the better it would all be simply a matter of time.

Orlando Cubs 1994:

Games	At Bats	Runs	Hits	HR	RBI	Average	2B	3B
115	401	5	104	16	60	.259	17	5

Trip Down Memory Lane

Because I have traveled the country and have friends in every time zone, I am no stranger to calls in the middle of the night. When on the East Coast I've been known to get a call at three or four in the morning when someone I know out West gets home from an evening on the town after a little too much to drink, and feels they just have to call me. I've had some pretty funny conversations under such circumstances. When my apartment phone rang on one August night and I looked at the clock through sleepy eyes to see that it was 3:30 in the morning I thought I was in for one of those talks. I groggily answered the phone, but came to immediate attention when I heard the voice on the other end of the line; it was Lee!

My first thought was that something had happened to my son. Calmly Lee informed me that he was fine so I relaxed and sat up in the bed to find out what was behind the call. Much had changed in her life. She and Teddy had moved to Utah, following her parents. And there was another addition to her family; they were the parents of another baby girl. But that information did not seem to be the purpose of her call. When I asked how she got my number she told me she had called my mother in New Jersey. My parents kept an open line of communication with her, not pressuring her by calling but expressing that she was always free to give them a call if ever she had a need. They knew of our arrangement and they respected it.

Of course, I wanted to know more about Eddie. According to Lee he was growing and adjusting well. Though present, I kept him in the back of my mind so as to not miss him or wonder how he was doing so much. It hurt to think about him. After we discussed Eddie there wasn't much I had to say so the talk turned to idle chitchat. Still, I was curious to know why she had called me. Finally, I came right out and asked.

Her response nearly rolled me out of my bed and onto the floor. Lee wanted to know what had happened between the two of us. "Why didn't things work out?" According to my recollection, she should already know the answer to that question. Subtle in responding, I tried to steer clear of placing blame. I put it all off on the fact that we were young and in different places at the time. Now I was really confused.

What had brought this on? Why was I on her mind? The stroll down memory lane had been nice, but it was late and all of this had caught me off guard. I hadn't thought about her much because I was still upset myself. I definitely hadn't put any thought into what had gone wrong with our relationship, doing my best to put all of that behind me. When it came time to hang up, there was one question yet on my mind. I would not resist asking it. "Where was her husband while she had me on the phone at this late hour?" As soon as I raised the question I realized why I was getting this call. Teddy was in the living room with his brother playing video games. The luster on his shine was wearing off. The knight in shining armor was not living up to his full potential. I didn't get the full report on the state of affairs, but I did get the feeling that Lee was forming a different opinion. "Maybe Ed wasn't as bad as I made him out to be back then," I could imagine her thinking. I couldn't help but smile a little as I lay in bed once we finally hung up. It took me a while to finally get back to sleep. The conversation opened some old wounds and had me thinking about a lot of things I had buried far behind the walls in the back of my mind.

Locked Out (Round One)

Major League Baseball turned itself inside out as a nasty fight turned into an all-out war between owners and players. This was the year of the lockout. On August 12, 1994, the major league season came to an abrupt halt because the two sides could not come to terms on a new collective bargaining agreement which expired on that day. Both sides were childish and refused to budge on any of the major sticking points: salary cap, revenue split percentage and arbitration. It wasn't called a strike because the players' association was willing to continue working; the owners simply closed the doors and the season stopped until an agreement was reached.

On September 14, no agreement anywhere in sight, the baseball commissioner announced that the rest of the regular season as well as the playoffs and World Series would be cancelled. The Series had been played every year since 1905, surviving two world wars and the Great Depression. None of that mattered as the two sides punished the loyal fans. While salaries and ticket prices slammed through the roof, the game's integrity and quality diminished. Two sides, both crying poverty, actually tried to convince the public that is what they were dealing with. Imagine that: billionaire owners and millionaire players standing in soup lines if either conceded anything to the other!

As minor league ballplayers, we would eventually be caught in the middle. The collective bargaining agreement did not have a thing to do with most of us, so we went on, business as usual, until our season ended. Once complete, the owners and players started trying to butter us up, knowing we would play a part in the whole mess if it weren't resolved by the spring of next year. Both camps dug in, preparing for the long haul if a compromise couldn't be reached. Naturally, this all spilled into the following season.

I learned some interesting facts as the off-season began. The clock ticking on the deadline for the expiration of the existing collective bargaining agreement, positioning of both sides was in effect long before the lockout began. Teams purposely made very little player movement. If they promoted a player to the big leagues during that season he would become part of the Major League Baseball Players Association, another soldier for the other side once the fight began. Yes, everyone was going to sit right where they were. I didn't know it then, but I wasn't going anywhere no matter what I did that year. The business of baseball was now stealing the love of the game from me. I was tired of giving it all I had and getting nothing in return. The end was near and I could see it clearly now. I just waited for the last straw to break the camel's back.

In what would become my last baseball off-season, I got my first winter ball job in the Dominican Republic. After spending the first month of the fall season in New Jersey, I got a call from a scout for one of the teams looking for a big power-hitting infielder. Caesar Bernhardt, teammate and my best friend, had given my name to him. I first knew Caesar from the early days with the White Sox and we reacquainted as we spent a couple of months in the Cubs organization in Orlando, 1994. Caesar was nearing the end of his career and spent his off-season in Indiana rather than returning to his homeland to play during the winter. He, too, had been part of the 'Hreniak Experiment' and through the ringer with the Sox for years. They had finally gotten the best of him as well. He now resided, accompanied by wife and baby daughter, in South Bend, the city where he and I first played together way back in 1989.

All nine of Caesar's brothers were involved in baseball one way or another. One happened to be a scout for the team in San Pedro and I happened to be that for which he was looking. After a couple of days of price negotiating, we agreed on a figure, $4,000 per month, cash. I was scheduled to depart the end of October. I would give up valuable recuperating time, but the exposure and money would be well worth it. And, hopefully, by the time I got back the mess that baseball had worked itself into would be resolved. Teams had put a stop to signings of all types, including free agent minor leaguers, so when I left I was a man without a team.

My first trip out of the country was an eye opener. I was in a country where the majority of the population looked just like me, but that is where the similarities stopped. The second I opened my mouth I stuck out like a sore thumb. I had picked up a good deal of the Latin language befriending players from the Latin countries and we traded off in teaching the other our native tongue. The problem was: I spoke very well in slang and phrase but had a severely limited grasp on the language as a whole.

Only five American players were allowed on the roster of each winter ball team, so I was a true minority and a long way from home. I wasn't used to the prevalence of guns in the country either; everybody seemed to carry one and there was no law against it. It was nothing, while traveling to and from games, for almost every player on the team to pull a piece out of his pocket so it didn't accidentally go off while we played cards. And when we locked up our valuables to go out on the field to take batting practice, my watch, wallet and jewelry were packed up along with twenty or so guns! And it didn't stop there. Military, armed with machine guns, patrolled every game we played. To say that I never felt truly comfortable in the Dominican Republic is an understatement.

The baseball I played there, however, was the best with which I was ever associated considering I never made it to the big leagues. I played on a team replete with future Hall of Famers. Young Sammy Sosa was one. Together in the White Sox organization back in the late 80's and early 90's when he came over in a trade from the Texas Rangers, the first time I saw Sammy he was a young, stringy kid with a big bat. He was also well on his way to becoming the 'Slamming Sammy' that we all know now.

Winter ball was the proving ground for all talent on the verge of breaking into the big leagues as well as many players already there trying both to stay sharp through the winter and to make more money while doing it. Therefore, games were taken seriously. There was no tolerance for losing or not playing well. The Latin version of the big leagues, games were televised nightly and those who played well were heroes. Similarly, a couple of bad games meant one's head was being called for.

I got off to a banging start, playing every night at third base and spraying the ball all over the field and out of the park. The first month I was given a bonus (not unusual) for playing so well, and I couldn't go anywhere without being noticed by the locals. Though I never understood a word they said, their smiles informed me that they knew who I was. My four American teammates and I stayed in a hotel in Santo Domingo, the country's capital, traveling an hour each day for home games in San Pedro. And we rarely strayed far from one another. The reason behind that was the poor surroundings in our home city. Poverty was both evident and rampant in the country; if you weren't rich you were poor. Every day we passed shacks without running water or sewage. I couldn't believe people could live like that, but they did. It all made me appreciate how blessed I was to be living my life. An old saying repeatedly came to mind, "There but for the grace of God go I".

I sailed along as smooth as silk for the first month of the season through Thanksgiving and right into the middle of December, but a bad decision coupled with a stroke of bad luck was about to intervene and derail me once again. Returning to my hotel room with my teammates late after a December game, I looked forward to the morrow's rare day off. We talked about going out to hit the town for a bit as the clubs in the Dominican Republic stay open until the crack of dawn, but opted instead for a night of video games in one of our rooms. A couple of us were hungry and it was too late to go out for a bite to eat, so we called down to the front desk hoping we could talk someone into bringing up some room service for us.

Always eager to take care of us because we were big tippers, they obliged. My order was a cheeseburger and some fries with a couple of cokes. We lost track of time playing video games but realized almost an hour and a half had passed before we got a knock on our door. By then I was starving. I bit into my thick burger and immediately recoiled at what I saw; had it been cooked any less it might have still been mooing. Disappointed, I put the burger down and considered calling down to the front desk to have them bring up another but, because it had taken so long for the first one to arrive, I figured that was a waste of time. Stupidity and hunger got the best of me and I decided to eat around the cooked edges; that and the fries would have to hold me over until morning. That decision I soon lived to regret! The next day I felt a bit under the weather but the full effect of what I had done didn't hit until the third day.

The first sign that something was really wrong? Uncontrollable stomach cramps accompanied by frequent trips to the bathroom all through the day. Added to the intense pain similar to someone stabbing me in the gut with a pitchfork was a burning, sweat-producing fever. That night: the exact opposite – shivering, shaking and freezing accompanied by cold night sweats. It was impossible to concentrate on baseball, but I tried to for the first few days of my mystery illness.

The training staff, I'm sure they'd seen a variety of illnesses, were still stumped by what had gotten a hold of me. We all knew it was caused by the burger, but no one knew how to treat it other than simply letting it run its course. Problem: all the Pepto-Bismol and antacids prescribed did nothing for me. After playing through it the first few days, I had to shut down. I attended every game for ten days without performing. Instead, I sat on the bench wrapped in a jacket while everyone else sported short sleeves in the tropical weather. And I couldn't put anything in my stomach without it being rejected from one end or the other. The only thing held down was pineapple purchased twice daily from a vendor in front of our hotel. Other than that I put nothing in my mouth because it brought too much pain to my stomach.

After a week and a half I knew I needed true medical attention unobtainable in the Dominican Republic. Scared I had something deadly, I addressed my concerns to both the manager and team owner. They sent me to a local doctor who provided no explanation. That was it. I either had to find out what I had and cure it or I needed to go home where I could get it under control.

The next day I informed the team that I wanted to return to the States. Nothing, including baseball, was worth this. The team owner suggested I give them a few days to see if the provided medicine took care of the problem. He even threw monetary incentive at me. I gave him one night and then returned with the same request. The next day, bags packed, and plane ticket in hand, I headed home.

On December 24th, Christmas Eve, I landed at the Newark Airport and took a cab to Browns Mills. Mom and Pops were in New Orleans for the week watching Irv finish his second season with the Saints. I spent a quiet Christmas at the house and drove myself to the doctor the day after. Seventeen pounds lighter than when I reported to the Dominican Republic, I was in pretty bad shape. Diagnosed with a parasite contracted through the meat I had eaten, I had done well to return home as it wasn't departing on its own!

A couple of weeks after returning to the States I was recovering and putting my weight back on, but I was also beginning to think someone was trying to tell me something. It seemed every time I was on the right track I got knocked off course. Could it be that I was traveling the wrong road? I wasn't sure what to think, but my patience was running thin. If there was a message I was supposed to be getting, I wanted to hear it loud and clear, no more whispering in the dark.

All sought answers lay mere months ahead. Just as I was getting back on my feet in early January teams began calling Don out in California. They expressed interest in acquiring me for the upcoming season. The best and most interesting offer came from the Cleveland Indians who were adamant about how well I would fit into their organization. It seemed like the perfect fit and the right team with which to take this next shot at making it to the big leagues. Approaching my twenty-fifth birthday that summer, I felt I had lived two lifetimes already. The disappointments were mounting and I desperately needed something positive to happen.

Hoping this year with the Indians would turn it all around, my optimistic thoughts were quickly dashed. Shortly after my signing with the Indians, the motive was revealed behind the mad rush by all teams to sign as many veteran free agent minor leaguers as possible. The owners were playing dirty pool. The lockout still dragging on and the resolution everyone hoped for during baseball's winter meetings in December having fallen through, the two sides almost seemed further apart than when they first butted heads in September. Neither side was willing to give an inch and even though it was only January, Spring Training and an on-time start to the regular season were already jeopardized. The owners, looking to turn up the heat on the Players Association, devised a plan: to use replacement players (scabs if you will) to start the regular season. Days after signing my contract I answered calls from both sides, team management for the Indians and individual major league baseball players. Arguments ran as follows:

Management tried to sell the dream. This opportunity was *the* chance of a lifetime. Every player on the cusp of breaking into the big leagues as well as those who had fallen by the wayside would get the chance to be seen and evaluated by all of the big league managers and scouts; this would be their moment in the sun. Each organization was supposedly rounding up the best talent and the product they put on the field was going to be comparable to the superstars they replaced. That was a joke, but that was what was suggested. While in camp and once the regular season started, each player would be treated like a big leaguer; money, accommodations and all of the fringe benefits would be first rate.

Management also attempted to turn one side against the other. They pointed out some interesting questions and facts:

What was the Players Association doing for minor leaguers? We had no rights down there, no benefits, no one representing us, etcetera, etcetera.

How did anything the Union fought for have any effect or benefit for a player who never made it to the big leagues? Fact is: the percentage of players that ever make it is minimal at best. While I had just signed a minor league contract with the Indians for $5,000 a month, the Union was fighting for the league minimum to be bumped up to $175k. They wanted a 58% cut of the total revenues that baseball generated rather than the 50/50 split the owners had on the table. And, they didn't want a salary cap to put a roof on how ridiculous major league salaries had and could become.

The **Players** were trying to sell the 'United We Stand' theme. If we allowed the owners to divide us we would forever be at their mercy; we had to fight for our rights together. They were, after all, fighting for each and every one of us, not just their greedy selves. Right? They were taking this stand for every future *Major League Baseball Player*. What they failed to cover: What about the player who never makes it? The many who work in factories, furniture stores, or car dealerships during the off-season to support wives and families? The ones who get released and never get to live the dream of playing in the big leagues? Where are their pensions? What health benefits do they have? What portion of the revenue do they get to share? Big league meal money during a season is more than most minor league ball players make in salary during a season. But we were supposed to stand side by side with our *brothers* in the struggle! Something was wrong with this scenario. The players actually came off as the side blowing the biggest cloud of smoke and piling up the most bull****.

Question: When the lockout was over what would happen to players who crossed the line as scabs?

Answer: Don't worry! **Management** was going to take care of every player when this was all over. They realized the incredible sacrifice in crossing the line, but the tradeoff would be worth it. They promised to find places for many players in the organization. A certain number of players would undoubtedly prove themselves assets and there were jobs in triple and double-A that needed to be filled. Neither was it out of the question for a player to make the big league team. As far as retribution from returning players? Out of the question. There would be no hard feelings once the two sides came to an agreement and things returned to normal. No, payback would be tolerated. Each organization would see to that.

The **Players** offered contrasting opinion. Any player that crossed the line would be considered a traitor. Not only would such become an outcast amongst his peers, surely the owners, using those as leverage would discard them like yesterday's news once they had outgrown their usefulness. And if, by some freak of nature, a scab did happen to stick around after the lockout was resolved and the union returned to work, he would be treated as a leper.

As for those players demonstrating loyalty to the Union?

Their commitment to the cause would not go without reward. We were in this fight together, right? So how could fellow soldiers turn their backs on comrades who fought so hard away from the front-lines? They would not be abandoned!

Decision: I was initially flattered when my phone started ringing and the thought of playing a form of big league baseball was presented to me. I'd be lying if I said I didn't seriously consider the offer. The Players Association and Union had some nerve. What did bother me most initially was I knew I had gotten a raw deal at least a couple of times in my career, courtesy of Management, but this was my first real dealing with the Union. And they wanted to make it seem like everything they were doing was for me. I knew that was a lie and saw through the empty promises they made. I wasn't going to be entitled to anything once they got back to work unless I was fortunate enough to one day join their fraternity. And if I wasn't, then I was free to go on my merry way; they didn't owe me a thing and I was sure to get exactly what they had given me to that point. Nothing!

In the end, my integrity won out. As much as I wanted to live out my dream, I could not do it this way. I wrestled with the thought and during the decision-making process had several talks with Don as well as my parents. When I informed all three that I would honor my minor league contract and not cross the line, I knew I had made the right choice. I valued the opinions of both my family and Don and I know that each would have supported me whichever way I leaned, but they were proud of the decision I had made.

And the truth should be told. I WAS NOT DOING THIS OUT OF SUPPORT FOR THE PLAYERS UNION; I cared about them as much as they did about me, which was very little. I just didn't want to taint my lifelong dream of making it to the big leagues. If I crossed the line now, I would wear the tag of scab for the rest of my baseball life and I didn't want that. Still, I would not hold anything against my fellow players who decided to take the opportunity because I was not in their shoes. I didn't have their families to support, I didn't live their lives or know what roads they traveled, and most importantly, I DIDN'T HAVE THE RIGHT TO JUDGE THEM. It was just something that I couldn't do for myself.

After informing both sides that I was staying neutral and that I planned to report to minor league camp the first week of March, I took off for Florida to escape the cold of the Northeast and management's continued efforts to get me to reconsider. They did not give up easily.

1995 Buffalo Bisons/Canton Indians

The Indians Spring Training home in Winter Haven, Florida had been alive for about two weeks when I reported the first week of March. The owner's plan was in full swing and the game was going on without its locked-out stars. Right away I noticed a large number of familiar faces on the field. The Indians had gathered up players that I had spent much time playing with or against at one time or another. And management started utilizing their persuasive efforts on me from the day I pulled into the minor league team hotel. Now that I was in camp to see how well the new major leaguers were being treated I might want to change my mind. They were still not going to let me say no and just walk away, especially now that they had me in sight.

All the way through camp, starting on the first day, whenever I bumped into an old friend or someone I knew, the conversation revolved around me making the move to 'Big League Camp'. If I did, when I did, I would be taking batting practice in the big stadium rather than on one of the four complex fields next door. I'd be hitting brand new baseballs every day instead of the recycled ones. I'd be eating like a king and not like a pauper. I'd be staying in the nicest hotel in town and getting big league money during Spring Training. And I'd be getting the opportunity to show the big league staff what I could do on the field. My answer to all of it: "Thanks, but no thanks." It should have ended there, but it didn't.

What I never understood was why I was such a hot commodity all of a sudden. The Indians had more than enough players in camp and the team they were fielding was most likely sufficient for the existing level of talent. For whatever reason, I was on the wish list. On three separate occasions I was specifically called off the complex field on which I was taking batting practice or shagging balls to talk to the big league manager, Mike Hargrove. He had come all the way over to see nobody but me. Pulling up on his golf cart, he summoned me. Every single time he asked what my hesitation was and every single time I gave him the same answer, "I just don't feel comfortable with it." He then reminded me of the opportunity I was letting get away: performing in front of his staff and himself every day. In turn I told him I just hoped that the work I was doing in Triple-A was not going unnoticed because that is what I was here for in the first place. After his third visit, half way through camp, he apparently got the message and delivered no more surprise visits.

Once left to go about my business, I did it with the confidence and professionalism expected of a nine-year veteran. I blazed through Spring Training showing off the talent with which I was blessed from birth. Nothing held me back now. Three and a half years removed from the nightmare of the Chicago White Sox organization, I was at the top of my game and playing better than I had my entire life. It had taken a lot of time and hard work but I had finally put it all together. Physically, I was in great shape but equally as important, I was mentally strong.

That part of my game had caught up. All of the potential seen when I was young and green now bubbled to the surface. This should have been the breakout season that I had been waiting to experience.

Locked Out (Round Two)

According to the *Villanova Sports & Entertainment Law Journal*, on March 15, 1995, the National Labor Relations Board (NLRB) issued a complaint against owners for unfair labor practices stemming from their failure to return to the pre-existing system of salary arbitration and free agency when they revoked their implemented salary cap plan on February 3 of the same year. Two weeks later on March 27 the NLRB voted 3-2 to seek an injunction against the owners. On that same day the owners submitted a new proposal to the Major League Baseball Players Association (MLBPA) calling for a 50% tax on all team salaries over $44m.

On March 31 a U.S. District Court Judge ruled in favor of the NLRB. Under the National Labor Relations Act, if a court determines that the NLRB had reasonable cause to issue an unfair labor practices complaint and that equitable relief is just and proper under the circumstances, an injunction is granted. The judge ruled these conditions had been met. The decision was based on a finding that the salary arbitration and free agency were mandatory subjects of collective bargaining and that the unilateral changes made to the free agency system by the owners in the absence of an impasse amounted to a refusal to bargain in good faith.

As players had pledged to return to work if the injunction were granted, the decision meant the end of the strike. Fulfilling their promise, players offered to end the strike unconditionally. The owners accepted the players' offer, released the 'replacement players' that they had hired in February at the start of Spring Training and postponed the start of the season until April 26.

Just like that, replacement players were history. The owners tried to save face by shuttling a few of them down to minor league camp but none of them lasted more than a couple of weeks into the start of the minor league season. Without a shadow of doubt in my mind I'm sure that was one of the stipulations put on the table by the Major League Baseball Players Association. Scab players were put on the 'black list', never to be heard from again. Many of my good friends became casualties when the lockout ended; discarded athletes, the end came swiftly and without warning. In retrospect, they got off easy. I was left to suffer and endure the long, slow and painful season as it sucked the love of baseball out of me.

After an impressive spring I headed to Triple-A Buffalo, one step below the big leagues, to start the season. If I could just build on what I had started, anything was possible. At this level big-time opportunity is only a phone call away. I was taking the field with players that had years of big league experience already under their belts. They were trying to return while I was trying to arrive.

I thought I had experienced cold in my life living through a Midwest winter, but Buffalo was no joke. Whoever put our schedule together to start the season was out of his mind; the first ten games of the season were home games. In that first home stand we managed to make it on the field to play five times, the other five were cancelled due to being rained out, snowed out and frozen out, and a game was called just because Bison front office management thought nobody would be crazy enough to come out and watch it. Finally through the cold start and out onto the road in the American Association, I realized that Triple-A was the next best thing to playing in the big leagues. We traveled all across the country: Oklahoma, Iowa, Nebraska, and Tennessee to name a few destinations. All along everything was first class. The long bus rides were behind me and I was finally living life like a true professional. Though not my final goal, this was my best experience so far.

In the first two weeks of the season I was one of the toughest outs in the league, making a statement at the highest minor league level! I played four positions: third and first on the infield and left and right field. Carrying three gloves out to batting practice daily, I could be at any of those positions during a game. Demonstrating my versatility increased my value. I was hitting right in the middle of the batting order, with power and driving in runs, doing just what I always knew I was capable of. And yet, the walls came crashing down before the month of April was even gone, not even three weeks into the season.

Before beginning their delayed regular season opener in Cleveland, the Indians came into Buffalo for an exhibition contest against us. I watched that entire game from the bench, never called to play. After the game it was announced that the big league roster had to be trimmed so a few players from the Cleveland camp would remain with us in Buffalo. Adding players to a roster meant releasing players from a roster, so a few of my teammates were let go that night. What happened to me was a crime and the Cleveland organization would have been less cruel, had they just let me be one of those casualties.

For the next fourteen days I sat on the bench and watched one baseball game after the other; one time sitting through a double header on the road in Iowa. After the first five days I went to our manager and asked what the deal was. Bluntly he told me that the Indians had ordered him to play certain people and get them as many at bats as possible. I played four positions, five if one counts the designated hitter, and yet I could not find my way into a lineup? He assured me that was because they were in a rush to catch up due to lockout circumstances; this wasn't going to last. So, I took him at his word and raised nary a fuss.

Nine days later I admitted his conversation a joke. I was hitting .375 (9 for 24), yet hadn't touched the field during a game for two weeks. A couple of hitters in the lineup played every day at my various positions and still hadn't reached my numbers. While I had thought years ago that I had reached the ultimate level of frustration, nothing compared to what I was going through now.

When I walked into the clubhouse on Day Fifteen and saw that I was in the starting lineup, I thought it was a misprint. I was actually going to play after sitting down for two weeks? My teammates joked that the end of the world must be coming. They witnessed the ongoing injustice and wisely used humor to deflate the situation. True, I was near boiling over every time I walked by our manager and I know they expected me to come in and snap one day, but I kept my cool through the ordeal.

That night I got right back into the lineup and both hit a homerun and got a walk. I didn't want to shake our manager's hand when I returned to the dugout but I played a bigger man than I felt. That homerun practically forced him to play me the following night, which he did. After I got no hits that game he called me into the manager's office. That's when he dropped the bomb; the organization was sending me back to Double-A. He actually looked me in the eyes and told me it was a good thing, that the demotion would allow me to play every day. I told him the truth: "That was bull****! I could've done that in Buffalo. I was able to play four positions in the field or be the Designated Hitter if that is what they wanted me to do and he couldn't find a spot for me in his lineup?" Right then and there I almost told him to tell the organization I was not going to accept the assignment, but that was not in my character. I didn't want it to end like this. Before I left his office, he thanked me for handling the situation as I had and gave me the token, "I'm going to fight hard to get you back up here." My question to him should have been: "Why was he not fighting hard to keep me there?" Instead, I walked to my locker and packed my bags. The next and last stop on this part of the journey was Canton, Ohio. I would return to the bus leagues for the last round.

Take That:

During my brief tenure with the Bisons we faced all three of my former teams, the White Sox, Brewers and Cubs. In the middle of my exile to the bench I never made it on the field to play the Cubs, but I did take some revenge against the other two. In a televised afternoon game in Buffalo against the Brewers, my best friend (I had been the best man in his wedding back in 1993), Mike Farrell, stood on the mound. He left an off-speed pitch up in the zone and I took him deep over the left field wall for one of my homeruns. We went out after the game and he immediately wanted to discuss the 90mph wind blowing out to left field. The way I remember it, the wind was blowing straight into my face at about 95mph. We both maintain our different recollections to this day!

Later in the season against the White Sox, then making their Triple-A home in Nashville, Tennessee I took even more pleasure in hitting a high fastball about 450ft. The ball clanged off the top of the left center field scoreboard, and smacked a smile the size of the Grand Canyon on my face as I trotted all the way around the base path. "Take that," I thought as I ran!

Buffalo Bisons 1995:

Games	At Bats	Runs	Hits	HR	RBI	Average
13	31	4	10	3	9	.323

The first thing I did not appreciate about being sent back down to Canton was that the Indians wanted to cut my pay because I was returning to the lower level. When I called Don we agreed that was out of the question! I wasn't being sent down because I had performed poorly, so why should I be punished? We stood firmly on that; if they were demoting me for the reasons stated, I should not have to suffer any wage loss. If they disagreed they could just release me and let me move on. And if they did not want me making that kind of money in Double-A, they could find a spot and play me in Buffalo.

Reluctantly, they allowed me to keep my salary. If I was supposedly being sent down to get playing time and they intended to return me to Buffalo, why any concern over my salary? Easily answered! They never had any real intention of sending me back up, but were looking to save themselves some money while they buried me in Canton.

The three and a half hour drive from upper state New York to northeast Ohio might as well have been a million miles. My new team was on a long road trip in Connecticut, so I drove to Ohio and left my car at the old rickety stadium in Canton, stuffed with all of my belongings, and hopped on a flight to Bristol to meet them. I really tried to keep a positive outlook once I joined the Canton team but it was hard and I was tired. This was my first time in the Eastern League and I wished I'd never seen it. The majority of ballparks were old, the facilities and hotels were second rate, and the travel was brutal- the worst I had experienced in my nine year career. Canton was the only team in Ohio; everyone else was located near the eastern seaboard from

Bowie, Maryland all the way up to Portland, Maine. Our shortest trip was eight hours and the longest fourteen. Some of the most miserable hours of my life were spent traveling on a bus throughout that summer.

A good book and headphones allowed me to make it through our long road trips but I couldn't escape the cast of teammates surrounding me. There were some great guys on that team and I got along well with the majority of my co-workers. I just didn't have a thing in common with any of them away from the ballpark. The team held a lot of Indians' young talent and reminded me of my first year in South Bend. Partying and skirt chasing were the major discussion topics every day in the clubhouse, at home or on the road. Those weren't big parts of my life now. The only thing I really wanted was to get out of Canton and back to Buffalo. That just wasn't going to happen, though.

After a month in Canton I lost all hope. I totally gave up! I didn't have the energy to fight. For nine years I had ridden the minor league baseball roller coaster. It finally got the best of me. I had worked, made sacrifices and tried to respect the game, giving it all I had, but it seemed all for nothing. This time, rather than act out by drinking and running the streets, I turned into a recluse, spending all of my Canton free time holed up in my small, one bedroom apartment. I purposely got a place that none of my teammates knew of or lived at. That way I could maintain whatever level of peace and quiet I desired. After a game I would come home, cook and watch television until I fell asleep. Then I'd get up and repeat the cycle.

On the road, I did pretty much the same thing. It was tougher having a roommate to deal with in the hotel, but I kept to myself as much as was humanly possible. Nobody on this team could relate to what I had experienced in all of my years, so I kept it all bottled up.

On the field in Canton I started off well, but when I realized I was to be there for the duration of the summer, I lost focus. A four hit game might as well have been a no hit game as far as I was concerned; who cared what I did anyway? I had days when the only thing I thought about was packing my bags and calling it quits. At those points the ONLY thing that stopped me was that I knew I would disappoint my parents. They had taught me to never give up on anything, so I mainly stuck it out for them. As far as I was concerned though, this was it; I was finished with baseball at the end of this season. I had no idea what was next in my life, but it surely had to be better than this.

Then, on a rainy evening in late June 1995 I had an epiphany. The day had started out promising. When I got out of the bed it was already raining heavily and the forecast called for the wet stuff to fall from the sky all day long and into the late evening. I hated the thought of going to the ballpark, so I prayed for a rainout all the way to the point of heading for the stadium in Canton. I didn't even bother getting dressed in the clubhouse, just waited around all afternoon hoping the rain would keep coming. When the game was finally cancelled, I was the first one in the parking lot. From there I headed home for a nice meal and some television.

The pork chops I had left marinating in the refrigerator were outstanding and I was settling in for a quiet night on the couch, when my mind started to wander. I envisioned what my life might have been had I decided to go to college instead of turning professional right out of high school. At the very least I might have had an education on which to fall back. And what if I had decided to play football instead of baseball? I might be playing in the NFL with my brother now. Through the years, even at the worst of times, I tried my best never to think in this fashion, but I gave in on this night; I hated where I was and what

I was doing with my life!

Then, out of nowhere, a thought jumped into my mind, "What if I tried to play some football now?" I knew it sounded stupid, but did that mean it couldn't be done? I hadn't put on a football uniform since I was a senior in high school back in 1986 and I had never gone to college, but did that make it impossible? Nothing said it did! After wrestling with the possibility of getting back on a football field for at least a couple of hours, I called the one person who could legitimately either shoot the idea down or give me the slightest bit of hope: Irv. Enjoying his second off-season in New Orleans, he was about to get a call from his big brother.

Irv reported that he was organizing things around the new suburban New Orleans home he had recently purchased. Two seasons into his career, he played starting tight end for the Saints and was doing well for himself. The more he talked and the more I thought about what I was going to ask my brother, the crazier it sounded even to me. I almost chickened out and didn't address the subject of me playing football. However, the only way I was ever going to get to sleep that night was if I asked the question, so I presented the idea to Irv almost expecting him to laugh.

First though, I danced around the main topic of discussion, catching Irv up on the mountain of frustration with which I was dealing. I explained how I had given all I could to the game of baseball and that there was nothing left. The moment of truth descended moments later when I asked, "What do you think of the idea of me taking some time, getting in shape and taking a shot at playing some football?"

There was absolutely no hesitation in my brother's response, "If you put your mind to it there is nothing you can't do!" What shocked me most was Irv's amazing enthusiasm.

Though we both knew the odds were a million to one at best, by the time we hung up the phone we had even talked about the possibilities of playing in the National Football League on the same field one day! Irv's vote of confidence re-charged me. I told him that my plan was to finish my season in Canton, not quit. Once the season was over, I would begin the process of transforming my baseball body into one resembling a tight end in the NFL! Meanwhile, he would keep his eyes and ears open from the time he reported to training camp in two weeks and through the season to see how he might be able to help me. And, just like that, the plan was put into place.

The following day, before heading off to the ballpark, I called out West to talk to Don. When I told him about my new direction, he exhibited more excitement than I had. If anybody knew how much I had been through over the last few years, it was Don. He supported my plan and agreed to jump on board to help in any way he could. And we both agreed this would be our little secret until after the season; nobody needed to know what we had up our sleeves.

With two full months to go in the season, I had a chore ahead. I still loved the game of baseball, but my heart was nowhere near it now. The politics of the game really had sucked the life out of me. What I did not want to do was embarrass myself heading down the home stretch of my final days on the diamond. I wanted the last memories of my long career to be good ones. That feat would be tough, riding it out in the Eastern League, but I chose to make the most of it. Somehow, I had to find my lost love of the game. The business of baseball provided a bad taste which lingered. It was important for me to clean my palate, to find a way to walk away from the game on my own terms; happy with how I performed on the field and satisfied that I had tried to give the game the respect it deserved even if I had not received it in return.

Losing My Mind?

I didn't know what Mom and Pops would think about the decision I was making and what I was about to attempt. My plan was to tell them after baseball season. The odds I faced actually scared me and there were nights I considered myself absolutely crazy for thinking I could play football after all these years. I think I may have been keeping my secret partly because if I got cold feet at the end of the season I could just drop the plans and only have Irv and Don with whom to discuss my temporary insanity! The fewer people who knew, the fewer people there would be to try and talk me out of it or look at me like I was crazy.

A few weeks after my deciding night, my parents drove out for a visit. I saw a lot of them through that summer playing in the Eastern League. Because many of the cities were within a few hours drive from Browns Mills, they made frequent trips to catch games on weekends. On that particular visit to Ohio I was in the middle of a bad and frustrating streak at the plate. Any hopes of the Indians calling down to bring me back to Buffalo were long gone. If they had I might have reconsidered my plans, but that was something about which I never had to worry. I wanted nothing more than to put on a great show for my mom and dad during their stay. More than likely, this would be the last summer they would have to watch me on the baseball field. Even if I didn't make it trying to resurrect myself as a football player, I did not think I wanted to come back to this lifestyle again.

My parents were proud of me throughout my entire career no matter how I performed on the field. Right now I was pressing a little, trying to do too much. That, combined with the frustration of keeping my secret, resulted in my looking out of sorts. I didn't notice I was acting any differently but my mom and dad knew something was wrong. Having stayed for three days, they were leaving for New Jersey after an afternoon game on Sunday. I didn't perform well that day and was really upset with myself. My parents probably saw me cursing under my breath on the field after booting a ground ball, striking out and pitching a little fit to myself in the dugout or something of that nature. Out of character. I didn't realize I was acting out.

After the game Mom and Pops stood beside my car. We talked in the parking lot for a few minutes and then it was time for them to head out. I hugged my mother first and then my dad. When I pulled away he passed an envelope to me, telling me it was a letter from the two of them; they wanted me to read it when I got home. I started toward my car but curiosity got the best of me and I opened the letter right there.

The short of it? My mother and father thought I was *losing my mind*. In a two page letter they suggested that I start talking to someone, maybe even a professional, because they sensed I was not dealing with things well. They thought I was handling my frustration poorly and that I would explode if I continued to keep it all bottled up. Quickly turning back, I caught them exiting the lot. Then, I let them have the whole story. I wasn't crazy, I assured them; I was just holding something back.

My plans spilled out of my mouth like gushing water. There was absolutely nothing wrong with me; I just wasn't happy playing baseball any more. It was time, I explained, for me to get away from the game. I was a little afraid of what their reaction would be and that is why I had not yet told them. I had kept a lot inside only because I didn't think I had anybody to talk to about this besides Irv and Don. The second I got it all off my chest I knew I had been wrong for not including them in the circle from the beginning.

Their smiles and words were enough to convince me of that. Like Irv, they felt if I put my mind to something I could accomplish it, no matter how big the odds. They would be behind me in all of my endeavors. Their support lifted an incredible weight off all of our shoulders and when they pulled out of the parking lot smiles replaced the former looks of concern. I was smiling too. I felt no pressure from that evening on and that allowed me to play the remaining days of my professional baseball career with one thing on my mind, having fun! My last days on the baseball diamond would not be about the business.

On September 4, 1995 I played in my final game as a minor league baseball player. I packed my bags and said my good-byes to my teammates, still playing the role as I told them I'd see them in Spring Training or somewhere out there in the baseball world. I left Canton a couple of days later, heading for New Jersey, and my baseball career flashed before my eyes as I drove. I had a lifetime of memories in the nine years I had spent chasing this dream. I was now about to walk away from it all and head toward the unknown. I was scared but I thought back to an earlier time when I had trusted my heart years ago. It was time to let it be my guide again.

Canton Indians 1995:

Games	At Bats	Runs	Hits	HR	RBI	Average
103	365	41	88	11	52	.241

Farewell Tour:

So many amazing things have happened in my life that I absolutely believe in a higher power. Sometimes a true blessing is provided and either we don't recognize it or we don't understand what we have been given until after the fact. The trek through the Eastern League in what would be my last season of professional baseball took me through Trenton, New Jersey; the very city I was born in and where most of my family resided. Trenton was the home of the Double-A affiliate of the Boston Red Sox, only in their second year of existence. When I first realized I would be going back to play in front of the home crowd after all these years I felt humiliated. I saw myself as a failure for not living up to what everyone expected of me. After nine years in the game I wasn't returning to play at Veterans Stadium over in Philadelphia or the Meadowlands in north Jersey but coming back as a member of the Canton Indians. I felt I should have been, for them if not for myself, and so, felt somewhat distraught.

We traveled to Trenton that summer and played in a stadium only five miles from the hospital where I was born. My grandmothers, neither of whom had never seen me play a professional game in their lives, came to watch me on the field. Every member of my family, plus friends and teachers all the way from grade school through high school came out to see me play. Even the reporters who had written about me and followed my career, from freshman year at PTHS, gathered around me in the clubhouse to get the scoop on what was going on now. All of the attention was bittersweet because of the disappointing circumstances surrounding my return.

After an abysmal start in Canton, I had turned things around. Still, statistics were not of real concern for me now that I had planned 'The Great Escape'. In two separate trips to Trenton (a total of six games) I did not disappoint those who came to see EZ! I didn't lack focus when it came time to play the Trenton Thunder! In those six games, back in front of the hometown people, I hit three monster homeruns along with a barrage of other hits and received standing ovations even when I made an out.

I couldn't have scripted the last summer of baseball much

better than that. How many players enjoy the privilege of going home for a farewell tour?! I was able to show all of my supporters that I was still hanging in there no matter what they might read in the papers. And for anyone who doubted my abilities, this was a taste of what I had been capable of all along if life had just 'played out' a little differently.

I refuse to think my last stop being the Eastern League was mere coincidence. Rather, I was given a gift as a reward for all my hard work and sacrifice. It was time to move on now, but I had been provided the wonderful opportunity of leaving everybody with a small glimpse of what was a very long, memorable career. Perhaps many people would have said that I wasted my time- that I would have been better off going a different route. Who were they to judge if they hadn't walked a mile in my shoes? I followed my heart and chased my dreams. The days weren't always sunny, but I dealt with the rain as it came. At the end of this season it would be time to press forward and write the next chapter in a journey that was not ending, but heading in a new and promising direction.

Final Numbers:

Most interesting about my career statistics is the final average. A .250 hitter is considered average according to baseball's historical standards. I never considered myself merely average. I ask myself all the time, "What possibilities would have existed if not for the bad timing of being in the White Sox organization during the earliest and most important developmental years of my career?" The time spent with them was bad enough aside from the time it took to repair and correct the damage done there. That organization destroyed me as well as countless other hitters heard from never again- numerous forgotten soldiers. For only minimal gain, a great deal of power, consistency and production were sacrificed early- and all because of an experiment that went horribly wrong and could never be fully rectified.

Career Statistics:

Games	At Bats	Runs	Hits	HR	RBI	Average
997	3517	443	878	76	485	.250

*Ed, Michael Jordan and
Terry Francona
(Birmingham Manager)
1994 Orlando Cubs vs.
Birmingham Barons*

Homerun - 1994 Orlando Cubs

1995 Canton Indians

ED SMITH   3B

ED SMITH   3B

ED SMITH
Infield
Sarasota White Sox

Ed Smith   Sarasota White Sox

Ed Smith 1B
Stockton Ports

STOCKTON
PORTS

SMITH

EL PASO
DIABLOS

ED
SMITH
EL PASO DIABLOS • IF

Ed Smith
Orlando Cubs • IF

Smith's 2 homers, 5 RBIs lead Cubs

COMPILED FROM STAFF REPORTS

KNOXVILLE, Tenn. — Ed Smith hit two home runs and drove in five runs Saturday night to power Orlando past Knoxville, 9-6, in Southern League play.

Smith, who totaled four hits, had a two-run homer in the first, an RBI triple in the fifth and a two-run homer in the eighth. He leads the team in homers (14) and RBIs (51).

Pedro Valdez also was 4-for-5 in Orlando's 16-hit attack.

Marty Clary (2-3) pitched seven innings, allowed seven hits, one earned run and struck out three. Giovanni Carrara (13-6), the league leader in victories, was the loser.

The teams play a doubleheader today at 1 p.m. Amaury Telemaco (3-5) and David Hutchson, who was recently promoted from Daytona, will pitch for Orlando.

Smith's 7 RBIs power Cubs

TONIGHT'S GAME: *Carolina (Ramirez, 0-0) vs. Orlando (Hutcheson, 0-2), Tinker Field, 7.*

☐ Orlando downed Greenville, 8-3, behind Ed Smith's record-setting performance.

By Peter Thomson
SENTINEL CORRESPONDENT

With its Southern League Eastern Division title already wrapped up, Greenville bore the brunt of one of the season's most impressive individual performances by an Orlando Cubs player on Wednesday night.

Third baseman Ed Smith set a club record with seven RBIs, including two homers, as Orlando defeated Greenville, 8-3, in front of a crowd of 4,891 at Tinker Field.

Smith's offensive heroics were more than enough for fellow New Jersey native and starter, Jason Ryan (2-0), who went the first six innings and allowed four hits and struck out five.

"I was a lot more relaxed out there tonight," Ryan, 18, who won his first start last week against Birmingham. "I think I had a better game plan tonight. I kept the ball low, my changeup was working and I was able to spot the ball around."

Orlando manager Dave Trembley was equally impressed with his young pitcher, who graduated in June from Immaculata High School in Bound Brook, N.J.

"We got a great job from a young guy," Trembley said. "On top of that, he's an athlete."

The one performance that overshadowed Ryan's was Smith's. His three-run homer in the first hit the top of the scoreboard in left-center field.

"I was fortunate to get ahead on the count," Smith said. "That hit [first homer] was my pitch, not the pitcher's pitch. I found that sweet spot on the ball on that one."

In the third, Smith connected again, driving his team-leading 16th homer just inside the left-field foul pole, and tying the club record of six RBIs (set by Phil Dauphin in 1993).

Smith's double in the fifth drove in Doug Glanville to set the single-game record. It also gave Smith a team-high 59 RBIs for the season.

Wednesday's box
Cubs 8, Braves 3

GREENVILLE	ab	r	h	bi	ORLANDO	ab	r	h	bi
Warner cf	4	0	2	1	Brown 1b	3	1	1	0
Wollenberg 2b	4	0	0	0	Bernhardt 2b	4	2	1	0
Hughes lf	4	0	0	0	Glanville cf	4	1	1	0
Grijak 1b	3	0	1	0	Keschnick lf	4	1	1	0
Rios 3b	4	1	1	1	Smith 3b	4	2	3	7
Robinson rf	4	1	2	0	Larregui rf	4	1	1	0
Swail c	4	0	1	0	Petersen ss	4	0	1	1
Cerrabalo ss	4	0	0	1	Campos c	3	0	0	0
Koller p	2	0	0	0	Ryan p	2	0	1	0
Brock p	1	0	0	0	McDonnell ph	1	0	0	0
Gillis ph	1	1	1	0					
Totals	35	3	8	3	Totals	33	8	10	8

| Greenville | 000 | 100 | 002 | — | 3 |
| Orlando | 304 | 010 | 90x | — | 8 |

E—Petersen. LOB—Greenville 8, Orlando 2. 2B—Warner, Grijak, Glanville, Smith. HR—Rios, Smith 2. SB—Larregui.

Greenville	IP	H	R	ER	BB	SO
Koller L	5	10	8	8	1	2
Brock	1	0	0	0	0	2
Burgess	1	0	0	0	0	0
Thomas	1	0	0	0	2	2
Orlando						
Ryan W	6	4	1	1	3	5
Gavlick S	3	4	2	0	0	2

CHAPTER FIVE

Behind the Scenes & Inside the Game

Much goes on during a single season of minor league baseball and I was fortunate (or unfortunate depending on how you look at it) to play nine of them. I saw more in that stretch than the average person might witness in a lifetime. While much of what one hears about athletes is exaggerated, a goodly segment is not. I know I lived right in the middle of my fair share of mischief, crazy times, bizarre moments and unbelievable circumstances. I've "been there and done that" and if I haven't, I most likely know somebody who has. The good thing is that I always had some limits, including only associating with those who held similar boundaries. Drugs and anything physically dangerous was out of the question. But, just about anything else was fair game. We were a bunch of overgrown kids, men playing a child's game for a living. Lots of free time led to lots of fun times, trouble and some hilarious moments.

Practical Jokes & Game Etiquette

Boys will be boys when they have too much time on their hands and that includes grown men playing minor league baseball. The national pastime is loaded with practical jokers and pranksters. Within the ranks, one really learns to keep his eyes open! When I first started playing I was green but the veterans took mercy on me because I was quiet and kept to myself. The prime targets were loud mouth rookies who needed to be taught a lesson. In most cases the jokes are harmless, but I've seen scuffles break out when the victim of the joke takes it a little too seriously, the joke misses the mark, or crosses a line. Kinnis was the first of our group to go down.

Three Man Lift

This ultimate baseball joke I first saw in Instructional Ball. Setup and execution take time and need be choreographed for perfect effect. In our particular case, after a day on the field one of the vets was in the weight room. Someone called him out, making reference to him being a weakling, and a verbal back-and-forth broke out. A third party from somewhere across the room offered up a challenge. The 'Three Man Lift!' could settle the dispute. Tall and very lanky, the insulted player accepted the challenge and the big event was scheduled for a week from that day. Just like every other rookie, I had never heard of this 'Three Man Lift', so I got the scoop from someone who had seen it. Three men lay on the ground side-by-side, interlocking arms and legs. When all are in place, this resembles a large pretzel. The man in the middle is the key. The lifter's challenge is to lift all three men off the ground and hold them for a count of three.

Hype built through the week, with bets taken for both sides. I got into the action wagering ten dollars against the success of the lift. Meanwhile, our gangly contestant had everybody in hysterical tears through the week in the weight room as he worked out to Rocky music, grunting, growling, and throwing weights around the room.

Held at lunchtime, the lift was an event even our instructors wished to see. Chosen as a wingman, I would be right in the mix of the action myself. Kinnis was in the middle and a big, strong veteran served as anchorman on the other side. Three of the biggest men in camp meant a lot of beef to be hoisted off the ground. When it came time for our mid-day break hardly anyone went in for lunch. Our lifter disappeared along with a couple of others but almost every player and coach stayed put on the field for the 'Big Event".

When the lifter returned, he walked toward the lift spot trying to look buff and swollen; he had a headband on, socks tightly fastened around his biceps and a sweat already worked up from a supposed last minute workout in the weight room. A blaring boom box, carried by a member of his entourage, enhanced the atmosphere. Final Instructions: interlock our legs over Kinnis' and each wrap an arm underneath and around his neck. Because the lifter would grab Kinnis, it was important to lock him in solidly.

As the entire team gathered around the three of us on the ground in our uniforms, the lifter took his place and the crowd threw themselves into a frenzy. He stood over Kinnis, ready to attempt to lift all three of us off the ground. Grabbing Kinnis' pants by the front, he began to get his grip. Something was wrong, though. Kinnis' belt, in the way, cut into our lifter's hand. He quickly undid it and took it off of Kinnis, the three of us still tangled on the ground like a pretzel. It was now Showtime! Stretched to the capacity of its elasticity, Kinnis' pants were nearly ripped on the first attempt, but not one of us moved an inch off the ground.

Our lifter, buoyed by the crowd and determined all the more, shifted into Hulk Mode for the second try. Yielding a mighty scream, he grabbed Kinnis by the pants and pulled on them as hard as he possibly could. This exposed a mighty throughway down the shoot and to the middle of my good friend's legs. Then I spied, out of the corner of my eye, two players approaching from behind and they were carrying something very big: a Gatorade cooler. The contents were 'dispensed' right into Kinnis' pants, into his lap, and down his legs. And it was the most foul and disgusting concoction imaginable. Victims of small splatters, my fellow anchor and I survived unharmed. Kinnis, however, was a mess. Players and coaches laughed hysterically as poor Kinnis clambered to his feet. His midsection was covered in filth and the bulky contents of the bucket had collected at the bottom of his pants trapped by the elastic.

The 'Three Man Lift' was, indeed, all a sham; the bets were fake and the entire event was just a setup. The week leading up to the big event existed expressly to build the hype and prepare the cooler.

The cooler included:
- Discarded soup, fruit and sandwiches
- Spit
- Atomic Bomb rub from the training room
- Black shoe dye

AND

- Only God knows what else!

Added to daily, the 'soup' marinated for a week.

Later I learned I was nearly selected by the veterans as the candidate for the lift from the belief I seemed an easy target. And they were correct because they would have had me hook, line and sinker. Kinnis was ultimately chosen because the veterans wanted to quiet him down a bit. Humbled briefly, Kinnis acted as his old self not long after.

My eyes were eternally opened after that afternoon. Unless one wanted to be the butt of a joke he had to constantly stay at least one step ahead of the pranksters. I tried to maintain a two step advantage at all times.

Hot Foot
Anybody can be a victim of this prank. First, distract the target, usually with conversation in front of him. Meanwhile, place a fuse on the shoe of the unsuspecting prey. It is best to use toilet paper with some gum gently pressed onto the heel. Once everything is in place, the fuse is lit and the dance begins. When the hot foot lights up, jumping and kicking follow shortly. This version of Stomp is not going to win any awards for its step sequence.

Shaving Cream/Bubblegum Top
This may happen a dozen times in one night depending how long it takes for the joke to wear thin. The object? Put something on top of a player's hat or batting helmet without him knowing it. Then get him to walk around looking like a fool for as long as possible. The most commonly used props are a glob of shaving cream or a huge piece of gum blown into a bubble and placed on top. I have seen a player spend an entire inning out in the field or walking to the plate with something on top of his head. Most umpires will <u>eventually</u> say something, but I've also seen them let it slide, enjoying the laugh themselves.

Brawls
A baseball brawl can look like a total melee but in reality the average is about as physical as a good game of musical chairs. Baseball players don't want to hit anyone! There are instances when brawls occur resultant of outright hatred between particular players or teams, but the majority of these tussling matches consist of a lot of ass-grabbing and hand-holding in the middle of what looks like fisticuffs. There is a degree of etiquette involved in fighting and the rules are pretty simple:
No cheap shots, i.e. hitting a player when he is not looking

or from behind.

No use of weapons on the field, bats, helmets or balls.

Keep it as clean as possible as nobody really wants to get hurt.

There are also responsibilities involved in brawling. As first or third baseman, I protected our pitcher on the mound as the second line of defense. The catcher, first line, pops up and jumps in front of hitters to discourage them from charging when the thought crosses their minds. He has to be on his toes at all times. In a case where the bull gets out of the gate unexpectedly or too fast, the catcher's job is to catch him before he gets to the mound. If he is late, good corner men are to the rescue.

Several times in my career I had to fly like Superman to wipe somebody out before they reached their intended destination. By the time anyone else arrives to assist, the brunt of action is over. Everyone going at each other from then is mostly a lot of talk and little action. Nobody actually wants to be hit or have to throw a punch.

In over a thousand regular season games and eight Spring Trainings I never charged the mound, but I experienced my fair share of brawls due to the stupidity of others. I had to experience the bottom of the pile on several occasions but never suffered serious injury. I would only classify a couple as serious fights; in all the others we might as well been playing ring-around-the-rosy on an elementary school playground.

Early Shower

In my entire career I was never tossed out of a game. That's not because I never argued or disagreed with a call, but because I knew how to do so. Umpires do not like to be showed up in any way and sometimes run on short fuses. Just about every umpire I encountered knew me as a good guy. There were a few that I didn't particularly care for or whose calls I consistently disliked, but I gave what they wanted, respect. Only human, they will make mistakes, just give them a break when they do and don't embarrass them.

To discuss what you might think is a bad call at the plate, do NOT turn around and loud talk them. It's okay to turn around and ask a quick question, but don't start drawing lines in the dirt to show them how far inside a ball was or raise your hand to show them how high. My favorite technique was to keep my eyes looking out in the field toward the pitcher, and then state my opinion on a pitch, "I thought that one might have been a little low or outside." That way no one knew I was questioning him. Another was to ask the question, "Is that the bottom of the zone?" This method came across in a non-threatening manner.

You would be surprised how many times I heard an umpire admit that he might have missed that one – and that meant one very good thing, makeup call! Frequently, a bad strike call was made and on an ensuing strike, a ball right down the heart of the plate at knee high level, the call of 'ball' was signaled. While umpires don't compromise the game's integrity, they do return respect for respect.

One magic word in the English Language, beginning with "F", must not be said to an umpire, I don't care who you are or what type of relationship you enjoy. If you say that magic word, before you get to the "K" at the end, the ump's arm is up and you are done for the day. Even bringing family (Did your mother know she was raising a blind child?) into conversation doesn't guarantee an early exit. You might actually get a smile for being so creative, but that four-letter word will deliver an automatic 'Early Shower'!

Bullpen

When I wasn't in the lineup some of the best days of my career were spent down in the bullpen. At some point in each of those games I spent some time with the relief pitching crew. Those guys really have too much time on their hands. Always on call, up and down during the course of every game, warming up in a hurry and then sitting down in an instant, these are the stepchildren of any baseball roster. Taking a bat with me and going through the motions of staying loose in case I was needed for a pinch hit somewhere during the game, I masked my true intention of simply joining them and getting involved in whatever was going on! Some highlights included:

Every team seemed to boast a bug eater; some crazy, backup catcher would put anything in his mouth if the price were right. When someone came across a crawling creature that looked worth the money, the bet was offered up (I dare you to eat this for $20!). On a busy night bug eaters could make $100 easily.

If hungry the fastest way to get a meal was only a baseball away. Kids, running around the stadium, spent most of their time at the ballpark hanging around the bullpen asking for foul balls or bullpen balls with which the pitchers warmed up. All a player had to say was, "I'll give you a ball if you get me a hotdog or cheeseburger," and they were off and running, looking for their parents. An experienced vet could get a couple of kids to make separate runs. After all, one needs a drink to wash the meal down and if the fries at the stadium are good, what to do?

My mouth watered as I watched the process, Mom or Dad granting the request, someone standing in line to pick up the food and returning with order in hand! The exchange had to be done on the sly as did the tasty morsel consumption. I wasn't so inconspicuous more than once, causing an umpire to say something to me on my way back to the dugout; his advice usually something like, "You'd better wipe the mustard or catsup off your chin before your manager sees it."

The bullpen was usually a great place to do some crowd watching. Pretty ladies loved to drift and gravitate toward the bullpen area where the players were either out in the open and accessible to the public or hidden in a corner deep down one of the outfield lines. Either way, this was a nice spot to stand and scope out the cuties, especially on the road. Every now and then, someone got lucky and a prospect got close enough to actually make contact. Phone numbers might be exchanged or hotel and room number passed along. If the fortunate one was a 'team player' he sometimes informed the young lady of the bar or restaurant we might all frequent that night, stating that it would be nice if she came along with some of her friends.

Unless a signal was flashed from the dugout or the bullpen phone rang, nobody paid much attention to the game while down in the bullpen. On quiet nights we played the popular game: 'What would you do for _____ dollars?' The monetary amount was usually filled in according to the question. One could learn an awful lot about teammates on those nights. Depending how much money was offered, some were willing to do just about any and everything.

Superstitions

Years after my last day of baseball, I remain a superstitious person. I embrace faith that a higher power is guiding me through the days of my life, but why take chances? I say that facetiously, but there is a hint of truth behind my words. Baseball players are creatures of habit, so anything that throws the routine can be detrimental; anything that is considered bad luck is taboo. Show me a black cat and I'll show you my back as I head quickly in the other direction.

Superstitious behavior surfaces in many forms and degrees of sensitivity. For instance, if one afternoon I had chicken for lunch and a great day at the ballpark, I returned to the same restaurant and ordered the same exact thing the following day. And it didn't stop there; I would eat that meal as close to the exact time as I had the day before as well!

Another critical event was the order in which I put on my uniform. An outstanding day at the yard might encourage recollection of what order every article of clothing went onto my body that day. This was then repeated until the magic wore off. I remember getting dressed one day after a two-homerun evening the night before. I was nearly fully dressed when I realized I had started by putting the first sock on the wrong foot. I got undressed all the way down to bare nakedness and started all over.

The same goes for a special bat or glove. Hot bats came into contact with nothing else! I had a special place in my locker for any piece of lumber that showed me serious love. For anyone else to touch him was against the rules too, a <u>serious</u> no-no. And when that bat finally died, I hoped he went out as a soldier; meaning he got me a hit in his last official game time duty. If there was any way possible to salvage him and put him to use during batting practice (sometimes it took an entire roll of tape) I did whatever I had to do. On the flipside, if any equipment: bat, fielding glove, batting gloves, wrist bands or even jock strap gave off negative vibes, they might be totally banished from the rest of the contents of my locker.

I also had at least two or three driving routes to any home stadium in which I played. A particular route might yield more hits than another, so if one went ice cold it was time to put another to good use.

Last but not least, there are two proven, uncontestable

facts when it comes to the game of baseball: 'The fool-proof method to break out of any slump is the 'the all-nighter', and 'Never walk away from a woman who has hits in her or hang around one that doesn't!

The All-Nighter

Not something pulled off the shelf due to a couple of bad games such as back-to-back 0 for 4's, the all-nighter is for the times that a hitter is about to climb a clock tower after a consistent stretch of failure. A good 5 for 50 stretch can take one there and I had a couple of those in my day! When it feels like there is no other conceivable alternative, it is time for your fellow teammates to step in and bring you out of the darkness.

The all-nighter is usually very spontaneous, rarely planned. Required: that the struggling player go out with or show up where teammates that care are waiting to cure him and set him back on the right track. The premise of the night is to get that player as drunk as possible without taking it to a dangerous level, and he is not allowed to pull out his wallet or money clip all evening. Once goal is achieved, the player is safely returned home or to the hotel where the mother of all hangovers awaits him. Head pounding, he is left to go about hitting a baseball. The theory is that the hangover takes over your brain. You aren't thinking about the fact that you are not keeping your hands back, that your hips are flying out, or that you are pulling your head or stepping in the bucket at the plate. All you want to do is take your swings, put the bat on the ball, get back to the dugout, and be done with this game as soon as possible, so you can go home and sleep away the tiny, little man with the jackhammer pounding in your head! The success rate of this procedure is remarkably high and in my career I did test it out a few times. Some of my best days and slump turnarounds came because my teammates cared enough to take me to hell and back.

She's Got Knocks

It's a known fact amongst baseball players that some women have knocks (hits) in them and others don't. I'm not trying to sound barbaric but that is the level of thinking that goes on sometimes when you are dealing with a bunch of potentially and purposefully immature men. This 'hits' theory didn't pertain to married men because they had everything they would ever need in life waiting for them at home (Can you sense the sarcasm in that?) If an unattached player started seeing someone and suddenly went on a hitting tear, that woman was pretty much assured of getting calls from and seeing him consistently. Perhaps not the prettiest or cutest girl in town, if she had some hits in her she was like gold and one might want to treat her like that so no one else came along and scooped her up. Conversely, on rare occasions, it sometimes didn't matter how beautiful a woman was if she wasn't producing for you. Nobody threw away a perfect '10', but a young lady might not receive quality time depending on the superstition depth of the particular player.

Looking back, baseball players, myself included, have a bunch of screws loose. Too much time on our hands, nothing is off limits. My fondest memories revolve around the silliest of situations that only coincide with living this particular lifestyle. Logic sometimes thrown out the window, each has his own way of approaching the game or dealing with the daily grind, fighting off boredom, handling relationships, and so on. A silly smirk sometimes appears across my face for no apparent reason when I reminisce about the 'good ole days'. The memories are priceless!

Groupies

What about groupies? How do they come into 'play'? The first is probably the most asked question of all, especially from male friends trying to live vicariously through me. Baseball lifestyle is fast, the women sometimes faster, and it can be a wild ride. Remember, "I've seen just about anything you can imagine"! I'll leave the rest to your imagination! Groupies at the minor league level are just as pretty, just as conniving and just as cunning as those chasing millionaires in the big leagues, NBA or NFL. They fall into the same categories and it is usually very easy to pick them out of the crowd; they're definitely not your 'Quality Girls'!

1 – Take Me Away

This young lady looks for rescue. She may feel trapped in her small city, and may be living with her parents or in another unfavorable situation, and is possibly taking care of children she can't afford. Whatever the circumstances: BEWARE. Before you know it, she is practically living with you during the season and making fast plans for the off-season. She is usually more interested in home team players because they are more accessible and around town on a consistent basis, but she is not against traveling to visit you in another city either. After all, her goal is to get out of town. She's not trying to sell herself short, but if you're not the most attractive guy on the team she might be able to look past that, just as long as you take her with you at the end of the season!

2 – Girls Just Wanna Have Fun

These girls just like hanging out with ballplayers. They love to be around the action and can party hard. They can be spotted at the ballpark during the games and know where the players are going to be hanging out that night afterwards. They aren't looking to get serious; they just want to have fun. Whether you play for the home team or visitors, the entire league might know these girls. When there is nothing going on at the club, these fun-lovers have been known to make house calls, showing up with drinks in hand and smiles on their faces no matter what time of night.

3 – Home Team Girl

This girl loves the hometown team and will do anything to show her support. One week she is 'dating' the left fielder and the next she is 'spending time' with the first basemen. And it's not against her rules for the two players to be friends or even roommates. She is at almost every single game during the season and you can usually spot her waiting for someone outside the clubhouse at the end of the night. She likes to take care of her man, whoever he may be that week, cooking him dinner, baking him cookies and doing whatever she can to show how much she cares. She likes to think of herself as the 'summer girlfriend'. You can tell her there is someone back home and she might not care less; she's only interested in the 'here and now'. It only becomes complicated when she feels she might have a chance at becoming the 'number one girl'; issues can get really complex when it comes time to pack your bags and head home for the summer.

4 – Road Kill

This girl is not about to destroy her reputation by spreading herself around for the home team. Instead, she will only date the players that come in for three and four game series throughout the season. How much you see her depends on how many teams in the league she is affiliated with. Even then, she would rather take her out-of-town beau to dinner or back to her place, away from all the scrutiny of being singled out as one of 'those girls'. This helps to keep her business out of the street and her reputation as a good girl intact. If she does show up at a club, she is not likely to throw herself all over anyone; that would be too obvious. She will stay in the background, almost always surrounded by at least a couple of her friends for camouflage. Unless she snags a steady man, players around the league will start to spread her name on the circuit. If one is looking for a good time in that particular city he only need run into this young lady. An easy hit on the road, you can leave it all behind once you break out of town.

5 – Part Time Girl

This girl will start out by telling you that she seems to always end up dating an athlete, baseball players in particular, because only they approach her. In reality, they are all she is looking for. She is a part-timer because she does actually try to date seriously. She knows where to find the team, but isn't on the prowl. She puts the bait out there and lets the lion come to her. She can and will be selective because she is looking for more than just one night. Once she has her man, the two usually aren't seen at the clubs consistently; she likes to do the couple's thing, such as dinner and a movie. When or if things don't work out between the two of them, she is back out and looking. Low and behold, she is soon dating again and guess what, he's a baseball player!

6 – Baby Daddy

This girl is the most dangerous of all; she is looking for a 'baby daddy'. If she can land the right player, she might be set for the rest of her life or at least the next eighteen years. You don't ever want to trust this girl if you have the slightest idea about her real motives. If she says she is on the pill, bring your own condoms anyway, because you don't want to be using one with a hole she poked in it. This girl can disguise herself as one of any in the above categories, so she is a tough one to spot. Avoid her at all costs or you may be paying for the mistake a long time.

Through my travels, I have experienced or witnessed a multitude of women from each of the categories described above. Regardless of her particular objective, inside each woman I encountered, there was some 'good'. Just as I have, some went through a maturation stage and moved on to bigger and better things. Others found what they were searching for, whether it be landing that ballplayer or escaping the small city. And a small number may still be 'playing the game'. Groupies go along with professional sports just as apple pie does with America. God bless them all!

Where Were You When..........?
Part I

Moments in our history as a country and as individuals ultimately define the era in which we live. While some events can be of great sociological impact, others can be quite trivial. In most cases the events simply illustrate a point in time, frozen and embedded in our individual minds forever.

My mother and I frequently hold incredible meaningful and insightful conversations. A few years ago she stimulated thought as she recounted moments frozen in time in her memory. She recalled her location and the moment she heard that John F. Kennedy was assassinated in Dallas. She told me which song was playing on the radio when the newscaster broke in to announce that Martin Luther King had been shot and killed. She remembered the day man first walked on the moon as though it was last week.

Since that conversation I make concerted efforts to remember where I am and what I am doing when those moments come along in my life. Following is list of moments frozen in time in my mind. And the question should also be asked, 'Where were you when...?'

Space Shuttle Challenger Disaster: Tuesday, January 28, 1986

Tuesday morning started off no differently from any other in my junior year at Pemberton High School. I was waiting out the last few minutes of my history class and looking forward to lunch, which was coming right up. We had finished our lesson early, so I was in a conversation with a classmate seated directly behind me. Laughing about something, I did not pay attention to our principal's voice as he began to make a very sad announcement: the Shuttle Challenger had exploded just 73 seconds after liftoff at the Kennedy Space Center in Florida. The crew of seven was lost. Tragically, one of the members on board was the civilian teacher, Christa McAuliffe. Part of the NASA Teacher in Space Project, she was basically just along for the ride.

I remember sitting at my desk, recognizing a moment of silence and saying a silent prayer. Our tiny town was located minutes from a military and air force base (Fort Dix and McGuire) and that directly impacted how somber the mood around school was for a long time. I felt sorry for the families of all the astronauts, but especially the teacher. She was probably fulfilling a lifelong dream when all came to a sudden and tragic end.

Magic Johnson HIV Announcement: Thursday, November 7, 1991

The press conference that changed the American view on the AIDS epidemic took place on a Thursday afternoon. I had just returned to Sarasota, Florida from New Jersey to begin my off-season. This was the year of my mid-season trade to Milwaukee and Lee's wedding in September. I was drifting in no particular direction. My first full day back in town, I had no plans whatsoever so I went to a restaurant where I knew one of the waitresses. Sitting at the bar, I had a bite to eat while she ran back and forth stopping to chat with me when she could slow down. I could not hear the television as it was either muted or the sound drowned out in the crowd noise, but the special news conference set-up on ESPN caught my eye. As Magic Johnson and his wife, Cookie, came in and sat down, the noise around the bar decreased and the bartender turned up the sound. When Magic made his announcement you could hear a pin drop. Immediately I began to think of my own promiscuous activity. Though I was careful and almost always used a condom, there were those times when I got caught up in the moment. At that instant AIDS, no longer the 'homosexual disease', placed all at risk. If Magic could contract it, anybody could! It was a moment to think about one's mortality. I was not invincible, and at that moment I truly realized that fact.

O.J. Simpson Slow-Speed Bronco Chase: Friday, June 17, 1994

The brutal murders of Nicole Brown Simpson and Ron Goldman occurred June 12, 1994. Five days later, on a Friday night, my road roommate, Doug Glanville, and I were eating at our favorite restaurant, The Waffle House in Raleigh, North Carolina. In the Southern League playing for the Orlando Cubs, we had just finished a game. Leaving the team bus at our hotel, we crossed the street to eat before likely spending the night watching SportsCenter on ESPN and maybe Madden Football on the Sega Genesis. After my usual, a ham and cheese omelet, bowl of grits and a waffle, we made our way back across the street. We found every one of our teammates gathered around the lobby's big screen television. Some sitting on the floor, all were glued to the action on the tube; O.J., Al and the white Bronco were heading down the highway. The slow speed chase was captivating and reporters dribbled off all sorts of incriminating evidence that pointed to O.J. as the newly designated prime suspect. Early on, everyone picked sides. Most thought he had to be guilty. I, initially, tried to stay neutral. That was a tough stance to take, not very popular either, and I was in the minority because nothing O.J. did seemed the actions of an innocent man. 'Innocent until proven guilty' though, right?! Doug and I watched the rest of the bizarre night unfold on the television in our room. The trial and persecution of O.J. Simpson sparked racial debate that divided the country for quite a long time. And the topic remains a fiery one to this day.

O.J. Simpson Not Guilty Verdict: Tuesday, October 3, 1995

The "Trial of the Century" dragged on for what seemed like forever and I spent a lot of days in front of the television, like everyone else, trying to decide if O.J. had killed his ex-wife and her friend. Some days I thought there was no way he could have committed such a heinous act of violence; others I couldn't help but think he was guilty. The evidence built up over the course of the trial and by the time the closing arguments were to be delivered, sixteen months after the bloody murders, I still hadn't made up my mind.

Finishing my last season of baseball in Canton, I was in the baby stages of putting my football plan together. I was staying with Mom and Pops in New Jersey and after taking about a month off to gather strength for the long and uncertain road ahead, I determined it time to get into football shape. With my YMCA membership about 30 minutes from our house in Browns Mills, every Tuesday and Thursday I played lunchtime basketball. The group of men I played with was diverse, mostly middle-aged businessmen trying to stay in shape or keep the competitive edge.

That particular Tuesday, both sides had delivered closing arguments and the judge provided the jury final instructions. The great debate in full swing, everybody prepared for a long deliberation; nobody expected the jury to return as quickly as they did. I was on the basketball court running full speed when someone burst into the gym and loudly announced that the jury had a verdict and it was being televised now. The basketball court cleared as if someone had yelled 'fire', every one of us sprinting to find out what the jury had to say.

By the time we made it into the TV room, it was standing room only. Gathered were about 50 people representing every race, age group and cultural background imaginable. Sweating profusely, I stood flanked by a white businessman and a white female, front desk employee. The moment the judge asked the jury for their verdict, the chatter-filled room became silent.

When 'Not Guilty' was announced I felt more uncomfortable being a black man than I ever had before in my life. Every African American and minority in the room cheered and all white people cried out in disbelief. A woman standing near me actually started crying. She looked at me as if I had stabbed and murdered Nicole and Ron. I looked around and saw high fives exchanged in the quickly emptying room. Amazed, I stood hand over mouth, unable to mutter a word. To this day I can't say I believe wholeheartedly one way or the other whether O.J. committed the murders. The one thing I do know is that he will have to face his Maker one day and that is when true judgment will be delivered.

As I Walk Away
What I Miss The Most............

I miss the fans! Baseball at the minor league level is such a personal experience. The tiny towns looked at us as 'their boys' for the summer. They treated us like big league Stars and, in some cases, cared for us like we were part of their own families: housing, loaning cars and feeding us on a regular basis. They made it difficult to move on at the end of a season- they would be missed by us as much as we were missed by them. Thank you to all loyal fans on behalf of every minor league baseball player, Past, Present, and Future! Some of us wouldn't have made it without you.

I miss the wacky days! The San Diego Chicken, Philadelphia Fanatic, the late great "Clown Prince of Baseball", Max Patkin and Morgana, "The Kissing Bandit" are just a few of the characters who made life on the field fun and unpredictable.

Any time one of the personalities was scheduled to appear at a stadium one could guarantee a sellout crowd. Watching Morgana come out of the stands to plant a big, wet one on an unsuspecting player was a sight to see. I was amazed the several times I saw her that she didn't topple over from the weight of her two incredibly large front assets.

I miss the sights, sounds, and aromas of the ballpark! The smell of freshly cut grass on a mid-summer's eve night. The crack of the bat striking a pearly white baseball, followed by that long homerun trot as you gallantly rounded the bases, 'all eyes on you'. Peeling a dirty, dusty uniform off after a long night of stealing bases or scrambling to one's feet in the infield to throw runners out after a diving play.

I miss my teammates! While there were numerous personality conflicts due to the diversity and forced time together, some of my best friends today were teammates back when. We now belong to a strong fraternity and share a common, lifelong bond.

To all who made it out of the trenches and up to the top: Congratulations! To all who never made it to the show: We didn't fail; it just wasn't meant to be for one reason or another. God had a different plan for each of us. We all had a lot of fun along the way. Let's celebrate that reality!

What I Miss The Least............

– Fourteen-hour bus rides.
– Sleeping on an air mattress in the middle of a bus aisle
  during a bumpy ride through the wee hours of the night.
– Truck stop and convenience store dinners.
– Cheap motels.
– The vagabond existence.

LIVING
THE LIFE

———◦•◦———

CHAPTER SIX

Frankfurt Galaxy

At best I knew I would have one and only one shot at pulling off the improbable task of returning to the football field after nearly a decade away from the sport. My first thought after finishing the 1995 season on the baseball field was, "It's not too late to turn back". I was getting ready to walk away from nine years of my life, out of the comfort zone, and into a black cave of uncertainty. It was like walking a tightrope a mile above the ground without a safety net below; if I fell I was going to be in for a very hard crash landing. It would take every star to align and every stroke of good luck to move to my side just to get near the door so I could knock. The scariest part was knowing that even when I got 'there' I had not one guarantee that anyone would let me enter. For all I knew, I could be throwing my baseball career out the window and making the biggest mistake of my life.

I let the plan marinate in my mind for a few weeks in New Jersey before moving full steam ahead. I gave myself time so if I got cold feet or just realized I wasn't thinking straight I could just scrap the whole plan and go about business as usual. Still, I couldn't shake the thought of returning to the gridiron, so, in early October, I made up my mind once and for all- I was going to give it everything I had! There was absolutely no turning back now!

The plan was very simple in design. Its execution would

be the tough part. We'd have to deal with everything as it pre-sented itself to us; nothing was going to go according to a script. The first thing I had to do was get into football shape. Always big and intimidating on a baseball field, playing between 220 and 230lbs., I was getting ready to enter a world where I would be considered a lunch snack at that size. Irv came up with the first great propelling idea. The head baseball coach at Notre Dame, Pat Murphy, had, a year prior, traded the snowy Midwest for the scorching heat of the desert and now served as headman at Arizona State University (ASU). Now in his second or third year, he was comfortable and established. He and Irv had been close while attending Notre Dame and now were best friends. I knew Coach Murphy pretty well myself; young in heart and age, he had allowed me to work with his team during my off-season in South Bend back in 1989.

Initially, I was just looking for a warm-weather place to work out and use facilities, but, as luck would have it, I was going to get more than I anticipated. After a discussion with Irv, Coach Murphy devised an idea. He approached his assistant coach, Jeff Forne, former outfielder in the Cincinnati Reds minor league system. Recently retired after spending his entire career in the minors, he landed his first coaching job as Murph's right hand man. Only a few years older than I, it was no surprise that our paths had crossed numerous times prior. After hearing the story from Coach Murphy, Forne called me in New Jersey.

Though starting coaching at the college level, Jeff's ultimate goal was to work in the big leagues as a strength and conditioning coach. In retrospect, this was the first of a series of events that many would explain as coincidence. I don't buy that at all though. The Force working in my life was putting pieces on the board and moving and using them according to His Master Plan.

Jeff and I weren't on the phone for more than five

minutes before agreeing that we definitely had a reason to work together. He was exactly what I was looking for because I realized that it wasn't humanly possible to do all that I needed to on my own. I needed someone to take me places my mind and body had never ventured. Jeff stressed only that we either did this all the way or we didn't do it at all. He described an intense, months-long program. I had a tough job ahead of transforming my baseball body into something that remotely resembled an NFL tight end. If I were willing to commit, he was willing to get me into shape. And in the end, if it all worked out, I'd both have my body ready for some football and be a walking advertisement for Jeff and his unique workout methods and techniques. We chose November to begin. That would give Jeff time to clear things on his side and allow me to get settled in the desert. I had a long way to go, but every journey starts with the first step and this one offered up hope.

The circle of people in-the-know was still purposefully small. My family, Pat and Jeff out in Arizona and Don in California were the only ones aware of the fact that I had played my last baseball game. The strange thing is that, for whatever reason, according to the number of calls that Don received on my behalf, I was never more popular. A number of teams wanted to sign me to a minor league contract and one even said that a big league camp invite wasn't totally out of the question. A year before I would've snatched that offer up in a heartbeat. I was now in a different place with other things on my mind. Don and I agreed that his response to the teams would be that I was not signing right away because I wanted to explore all available options. That way, if I fell flat on my face trying to pursue football I might use that new safety net after all.

Another big part of the plan was to get my name into as many ears as possible. With baseball officially on the backburner

I had nothing holding me back. The most critical aspect fell into Irv and Don's hands. They would keep their eyes and ears open and put all feelers out; we had to find someone not only interested in what I was doing but willing to help. After all, what good would it do to get into shape if nobody cared about what I was doing or if we never connected with the right people?

Amongst the three of us we were convinced it would take the help of many to pull this off, but one had to be a *special* contact. We hoped that the theory of 'six degrees of separation' would be on our side; somebody had to know somebody who knew somebody else who could help! It was a while before we were successful in finding that special person, but fate would be on our side at the twelfth hour, just in the nick of time.

At the end of October I was back on the road, heading across the country once more. I probably traveled well over a million miles during the first part of my professional life on the ground alone. I spent so much time in the back of a team bus or crammed in a packed car that it was second nature for me to rattle off fourteen hours without blinking an eye. When I was at the wheel the front seat always had a stocked cooler in it, a steaming hot cup of coffee next to me, and music forever loud and bumping. The Camaro I bought just before graduating high school was gone, replaced by a burgundy Nissan Pathfinder in my second year in El Paso (1993). The added space was much appreciated but not totally necessary at this time; living life on the road meant accumulating as little as possible. My worldly possessions included my clothes, a stereo, a huge music collection of compact discs and my Sega Genesis.

When I returned to the desert I had a very nice place to call home. My old roommate's parents still owned their house, but nobody lived in it. Jennifer had lived there alone for a time but decided it was too much for her so had moved into an apartment. Her parents were now looking to sell the house but it would be a little while before they put it on the market because they wanted to do some home improvements. Timing couldn't have been better if I had planned it myself. Jennifer helped and before I left New Jersey I had a four-bedroom home waiting for me. The rent was minimal, the family was glad someone would be staying at the house so it wasn't vacant, and I promised to help with the home improvement projects. The best part was that I would reside fifteen minutes from ASU. Just the beginning of the project, I had a good feeling about the recent turn of events. The ball finally seemed to be bouncing my way.

Jeff and I hooked up right away once I got into town. There was no time to waste and the schedule we came up with was cut and dried: five days a week, early in the morning on a side training field directly across from the university. The athletic department's weight room would also be on our routine's hit list. I worked hard in Arizona that year, believe me! There were days when I thought Jeff must have dreamt that I was the one who killed his favorite childhood pet. I thought I worked hard preparing for a baseball, but this was pure hell compared to that. The first day Jeff met me on the field he promised me one thing, "I'm going to show you how much a ten pound weight can hurt you." And he did.

Most amazing was the methodology Jeff used to trans-form my body. I had an idea that my workouts would include a whole lot of heavy weights in the gym to bulk up and some run-ning up and down a field for endurance. That's not what I got. For the first week together we only made it across the street to the weight room once. I performed every imaginable agility drill while either pulling a weighted sled, wearing a weight jacket or carrying weights in my hand. For the three daily hours we met, the man tried to break me down. The small shed storing all needed equipment for the daily torture session included everything from large rubber bands for resistance to medicine balls for monster abdominal workouts.

It was very important to get football back into my system. I'd been away from the game for a long time and catching a football, something that I used to be able to do with my eyes closed, had to be reintroduced. I used Irv's expertise in this area by picking his brain over the phone for every bit of information he could pass on. I talked to him about everything from stance to techniques in getting off the line of scrimmage to routes to run and how to run them. This was always kept for the very end of the workout when I was dead tired. For the increased level of concentration, I would have to dig down to complete my training for the day. Another form of conditioning, Jeff also took great pleasure in running me until I was about to drop.

Everything we did was 100% natural! I had never used a steroid or muscle enhancer, didn't then and never will. I noticed a marked appearance difference about three weeks into our grueling work. Walking around the house shirtless after a workout one day, I passed a mirror and took a quick glance. I stopped dead in my tracks; I had to go back to take a second look. The reflection in the mirror was not the big, lean man I was used to seeing. Out of nowhere arms protruded biceps, chest heaved pectorals and a set of big, broad shoulders <u>commanded attention!</u> I was starting to look the part that I so desperately wanted to play.

While I had a goal in sight, life goes on, bills need to be paid and groceries have to be bought, so I called for a favor and reclaimed my bouncer job at the same nightclub from a couple of years back. Some of the same women frequented, playing the same game; my improved physique made me even more popular! Working late hours that took me early into the following morning, I sometimes lost focus and chased after skirts, but made sure the number one priority was always met. A day of training wasted was a day I might be taking away from myself in the NFL.

While I took care of my part in Arizona, Irv and Don demonstrated that this was a total team effort. Our first big contact, not the special one, came from an idea of Don's: Why not approach a big time football agent to garner interest in this unique story? Such an individual would have nothing to lose; we weren't asking for much other than helping us get my name out. It would also be great publicity for anybody assisting if, by some miracle, I actually pulled it off and made it to the NFL! Don made a few calls and got the attention of one of the biggest and best firms out there- a short list of whose clients included Troy Aikman, Drew Bledsoe and Steve Young- three of the highest paid league quarterbacks. Don made the initial contact, I talked to the agency on the phone, and a San Francisco meeting was set for the end of November to discuss further detail. All came about in the matter of a couple of days and I was as giddy as a little schoolgirl, thinking this was *the* huge break.

Right after Thanksgiving Don and I met in San Francisco. He had turned into a best friend and proved this with something he said before we met the representative. Baseball, he reminded me, was his specialty and he was not connected in the world of football. He felt that in order for me to be successful once we got things rolling he should necessarily defer to whoever needed to call the shots. His sole purpose was to help me and he sought nothing in return. That spoke volumes about the integrity of the man who took me on from the very beginning with no guarantee that he'd ever get anything for the time he committed to my baseball career.

Our meeting in downtown San Fran was like any job interview in corporate America. The representative sent on behalf of the agency was low in the chain of command, but his job was obviously to scout me out to see if there was any chance that I could do what Don and I suggested. My developing body was not an issue, but he had to find out what I had on the inside; if I didn't have the heart to go with the body, we were all wasting our time. Look like *Tarzan*, but hit like *Jane, why even bother?* After a little bit of back and forth dialogue I got the feeling that the rep was at least slightly sold on the possibilities; the idea wasn't totally ludicrous.

With the state of the NFL as it was at the tight end position, who knew what might be possible?

That position is difficult to fill, requiring a special athlete to pull it off because of its hybrid nature. Most football positions are a dime a dozen, but it takes a particular type to be able to play tight end because so much is demanded. One must hold one's own against men that outweigh at the line of scrimmage, tangle with linebackers as strong as a mule all over the field, and deal with pesky defenders from secondary while moving up field.

There was an extreme shortage of multi-purpose tight ends in the league at this time. Most were either excellent blockers with no speed to get up the field or lightweight/undersized versions that couldn't block. If I could prove able to do both well, my stock could actually be worth something. Teams always sought quality backup help. If they had a good tight end, he was usually the only one as performance dropped significantly from one to two and so on.

The meeting a huge success, a great idea surfaced in our discussion. While I was setting my immediate sights on the NFL, the firm suggested I would be better off getting my feet wet in the World League of American Football, a more realistic goal. The league was not then affiliated with the NFL, but in a couple of years that would change. It is known today as NFL Europe. No connection between the two at the time, the NFL did use the league to send some players for development and also did a great deal of scouting during its season. The World League played a ten game schedule, early April to the middle of June, the six teams scattered through Europe. Holding a mid-February draft, they filled the holes left by players departing for the NFL or just moving on.

If we could get my name onto the wire and somehow get drafted, we might be able to use that as our first step. While the agency promised me nothing, they did say that they would help in the process. And down the line if things worked out, they would definitely consider representing me. By the time Don and I parted ways after our meeting, we were both riding high. Neither of us had expected to be so far in such a short period of time. I was to keep in touch with the agency while I was in Arizona and Don was going to continue to look for opportunities. My contact representative would work on helping me to open the World League door. I was his new project. The idea that at first seemed ridiculous was taking form and we *might* just pull it off!

Back in Arizona, I got to work immediately. With seemingly more at stake, the goal seemed a bit more attainable also. I actually began to tell people what I planned on doing. All the way through Christmas and into the start of the New Year I had a one-track mind; I didn't know where, but I was going to play some football. More good luck, the Super Bowl just happened to be played at Sun Devil Stadium in Arizona that January. This was just another sign that I was where I was supposed to be, doing what I was supposed to be doing. In the week leading up to the big game on Super Bowl Sunday, every team would be represented; coaches and front office personnel would be everywhere. And that special contact might just be one of the people with whom I happened to rub elbows!

Over the two months leading to that busy week I kept in close contact with my representative at the agency, providing frequent progress reports on my field and weight room development. By the end of January I was in shape like even I never thought possible; in three months I had gone from a 225lb. baseball player to a 250lb. man dying to put on a football uniform and hit something. All I needed now was the chance to prove myself on the field.

Irv was already coming into town for the parties, festivities and socializing that go hand in hand with Super Bowl week. This was his third year in a row making it to the host city for the big game, and this year he appeared with an extra item on the agenda: helping to spread Ed's name to anybody who had something to do with football. With all the support Don was giving to the cause, it just wouldn't have been right to not have him by my side as I got ready for what I thought would be the biggest week in my professional life. He was more than excited to fly in for the week and accompany me everywhere I went. We three felt like it was only a matter of time before we ran into the one person we were looking for.

I had considerable expectations, mostly due to the positive feedback I received from my California agency representative. According to him there was a lot of interest in what I was trying to do. The plan was for me to attend as many big functions as possible, including a huge party thrown by the agency itself at the Phoenix Zoo the day before the Super Bowl. All big names were going to be there including the biggest clients, but that is not what I was most excited about. What I most anticipated was meeting the two agents who owned the firm and actually represented those millionaire clients. That would be my big chance to make that first impression and if I were lucky it would be a lasting one. The problem was: while I thought I had the right people backing me, it would all fall apart quickly. The relationship I thought was developing turned out to be nothing more than a lot of lip service.

The week turned out to be a big bust and major disappointment. I made it to a few of the biggest parties and met some very important people, but my agency rep had overstated the amount of work he was putting into my project. I realized that when I introduced myself to one of the lead agents at the big party at the zoo and he didn't even know who I was. That really shouldn't have shocked me, but it did because I had allowed myself to think that, for the first time in forever, everything seemed to be going exactly according to plan. I had gotten used to hearing good news over the last few months and it felt good to think I was finally on the right road. The party culminated a disheartening week. I discovered that I was not nearly as close to accomplishing my goal as I thought. The plan wasn't dead but we definitely experienced a setback.

As quickly as everyone had descended on the city, they disappeared, most before the opening kickoff of the game on Sunday. Again alone and only twenty minutes from the stadium but a million miles away from the playing field, I watched the Steelers and Cowboys play the game out on the field from my living room sofa. Before Irv and Don left town on Sunday they encouraged me to stay positive; we had come too far to just give up now. But it was very easy to feel like I had made a big mistake. In a few weeks baseball would be back, Spring Training right around the corner, and I apparently had wasted all this time chasing my tail in the dark, fantasizing about an impossible dream. To add insult to injury I soon realized I had false allies in my camp. I got the hint the following week as my California agency calls went unreturned. The harsh reality was: besides the obvious support of my family and Don, I was pretty much on my own.

The next devastating blow landed two weeks after Super Bowl Sunday. Included on the list of potential World League draftees, I was nothing more than a name on a sheet of paper. With no statistics, college credentials, game tape for teams to view and no one in particular that could or would vouch for the fact that I had ever played football, I'm sure I got as much consideration as the man on the moon. What was I thinking? What allowed me to believe I could pull this off?

If I felt badly a couple of weeks prior, I really wallowed in self-lament now. I felt like the stupidest person on the earth as I recalled telling some of my old baseball teammates about my plans to walk away from baseball. And, I had turned my back on several offers. Don, looking at the big picture from every angle, reminded me that it might not be too late to contact some baseball teams to see if they still had a place for me, but my pride wouldn't allow me to even consider it. When I walked away from the game I did it on my own terms. I was not about to return, tail tucked between my legs. I had made the decision as a man and I would stand by it. I knew I had been brought to this point in my life for a reason. Again, as ever, I had two choices: allow uncertainty and fear of the unknown to turn me back or stand firm and find another door to open. I had come too far to turn back now, so the choice was an easy one!

By the first week of March I was ready to give up. World League camp opened, baseball was underway, and I was in Arizona working out- for what? Jeff now had bigger responsibilities to tend to with Sun Devil baseball, so I was on my own. My day consisted of working out in the morning and sitting by the phone the rest of the day. I don't know whom I expected to call, but didn't want to miss them if they did. I considered everything done and over because, obviously, nothing was going to happen until we became proactive rather than passive. Still, I had no idea what to do next. I was about to pack my bags and call it a day when the phone finally did ring one morning. Irv posed an idea that just might be crazy enough to work. The only thing he needed to know from me was: Would I beat some doors down if I had to? The answer, without a second of hesitation? Yes!

Time was not on our side. If we were going to make anything happen it had to be right now. The last hour was upon us. Less than three hours after talking to Irv I was in flight from Phoenix, Arizona to Atlanta, Georgia: home to all six World League training camps. Irv wanted me in the city because he had just stumbled across the best and most promising piece of information to date. While I was in the air he would make calls to track down our "special person"!

In the spring of 1993 when Irv was preparing for the NFL Draft he had played in one of the College All-Star games, the Senior Bowl, to show the scouts how he stacked up against the rest of the top senior athletes. He was then invited to the NFL Combines, a week of drill and physical examination held in Indianapolis prior to the draft. There he met and befriended one of the Combines' top organizers, Les Miller. Les was now League President of the World League of American Football. If there was anybody who could help us it was him.

My only knowledge of Atlanta was gained through the window of a bus traveling from one city to the next in my two years in the Southern League. I didn't know one person in the entire city and didn't even have a place to stay. Irv had arranged for me to fly in and when I got there I was to rent a car, then stay with one of his best college friends, Amy Irvine. Then he would call me and inform me of my next move. If all else failed and Les could do nothing for us, I could at least appear at each of the training camps, walk up to individual coaches and offer my services to them. That was our last alternative, but if it came down to it, what did we have to lose?

By the middle of that evening I got a call from Irv at Amy's apartment. He had given Les the full story of what I was attempting. Not only impressed, Les offered full support. He told Irv to have me ready for anything the next morning because he would see what he could come up with by then. Having returned to my apprehensive state of mind and not wanting to get my hopes up too high, I was pretty much prepared to hear bad news the following morning if the telephone rang. It did and the call was for me. The first time I had ever talked to the man, Les addressed me as if he had known me my entire life. One team of the six had given him the green light to see me. I was to drive to Suwanee, Georgia immediately to meet the head coach of the Frankfurt Galaxy. The supposed half hour drive felt like two hours but probably happened in twenty minutes. Nervous the whole way up, I didn't know what I would say once there, but I knew it had better be good; this was more than likely the best and only shot I had at getting a look.

The six teams used facilities spread out through the Atlanta area. The Galaxy were staying at the Falcon Inn, training camp home of the Atlanta Falcons, and using their practice fields to prepare for the season. The team was between their first and second daily practices when I got out of my rented car and began my search for the head coach. I basically planned to beg for the opportunity to show him what I could do on a football field if he would just give me the chance. Finding the right room, I knocked and heard a very gruff voice. "Come in! The door is open." My heart pounded as I turned the knob. The only words to escape my lips were, "Hello, Coach. My name is Ed Smith and I was told to come and see you."

Cutting me off before I could go into my spiel and never looking up from the papers at which he stared, he told me that he knew who I was, the trainers were waiting on me and if I passed a physical I was expected to be ready for first practice the following morning.

"Thank you," I said, then turned and walked out the door. I stood immobilized, stupid smile on my face, for probably a minute. An hour later found me at a local hospital being poked and prodded, examined inside and out. I passed my physical with flying colors, was taken back to the hotel where I was fitted for my first football uniform in ten years and given a playbook that looked more like a phone book and told the first practice started at eight the next morning. And, if I wanted to get taped, I'd better be early because the lines got long. Everything transpired so quickly that I didn't know if I was dreaming or awake. None of it hit me until I was nearly back to Amy's apartment to pick up the week's worth of clothing I had brought just in case something actually happened and I needed to stay in town.

Free Look

I wouldn't learn the whole story about what Les had done or said to get me the opportunity of a lifetime until weeks after the fact. He called the head coaches of all six teams, one after the other, and offered me to them as an exemption on their roster. I wouldn't count against them and if they decided to keep me around past first cuts it was entirely their choice. If they gave me a look and felt it wasn't worth the time, they could let me go as soon as they wanted.

Frankfurt's Coach Ernie Stautner was the last team he contacted. The first five said they had all the tight ends they needed and with the first roster cuts two weeks away I wasn't going to get a look in their camp; I'd be wasting their time and mine. Coach Stautner had four tight ends, but figured it couldn't hurt to bring me in. He knew I hadn't played football in a decade but he wasn't giving anything up, so what was it costing him to take a look other than a cheap hotel room?

I remember that first day of putting my football uniform on like it was yesterday. As nervous as a little kid on his first-ever day of school, I felt every eye on the team was looking at me as we got dressed. Camp had been going for nearly a week and a half and now a strange face shows up. And the story about this baseball player trying all of a sudden to play football trickled from locker to locker. After getting situated in my hotel room, I had stayed up looking over the enormous playbook. It might as well have been in a different language. I saw x's and o's with strange terminology mixed in and had no clue as to what I was supposed to be reading. Talking to Irv I got every piece of advice on how I should attack my first few days on the field. The best thing he told me was, "When you finally get in there, even if you don't know what you are supposed to be doing, just go as hard as you can."

On the field I was starting totally from scratch. All the work with Jeff was great, getting in shape, but now I thought I was really in over my head; nothing made sense to me. My first thought was once again, "I had made a mistake thinking I could make this type of switch." I took part primarily in drills the first two days so as not to throw the offense out of rhythm while I tried to catch up with learning the offense. Nothing felt comfortable right off the bat. I felt like I was wearing a heavy suit of armor and I felt out of place amongst players who had been doing this for years.

Very tough on myself, much insecurity had to do with my self-conscious nature. Because I was still in camp three days after getting started, I knew I must have showed the coaching staff at least a little something. The offensive coordinator mentioned that the following day they would turn me loose in practice a bit. A scrimmage against the Amsterdam team was upcoming and if I was going to show the staff that I could play it would have to be soon; cuts were approaching and jobs were at stake.

Practices hard-hitting and intense, the pain I experienced on the field and at night lying in bed was something I was not used to after nine years of baseball. If this was something I was going to do for a while I knew I'd have to get past it all so I put it out of my mind; the mental toughness to work through anything was the first lesson I learned on my own in my new football world.

I was getting a small grip on the playbook mainly because I kept Irv on the phone for almost an hour at a time when I called him at night. He gave me every benefit of the knowledge he had gained from four years at Notre Dame and three seasons in New Orleans. I crammed that night and just prayed to God that I didn't fall flat on my face the following day.

In my first full go practice with the team I was all over the place. The technique I talked about on the phone with Irv, worked on in Arizona with Jeff and tested out against blocking sleds in the first three days went out the window; it was a man's world on the football field and nothing like high school days I remembered. The first snap I took at the line of scrimmage against one of my own potential teammates nearly got my neck snapped. The 280lb. defensive end lined up across from me threw my 250lb. body aside like he was throwing away a piece of trash. Aware of everybody watching, I quickly picked myself up and made my way back to the side as one of the other tight ends went in for the next play. While I waited to see if I would even get another chance to line up on the field I debated: get tough or get going. One thing I refused to do was to embarrass myself.

A few plays later the offensive coordinator sent me in. As I listened to the play call in the huddle I made up in my mind that I wasn't going out like a punk; I had to earn the respect of myself if not of any other person on that field. When I put my hand on the ground in my stance, across from the same beast that had rag-dolled me the last time, I was ready to come off the ball and hit something. My first step was direct, my hands fired out and locked onto their target and we fought until the whistle finally blew and the play was over. In that one play I surmised that I was up for the challenge- as did both other players and watching coaches.

Number five on the tight end depth chart, I had very little time to move up the ladder. I had some work ahead of me if I was going to depart with this team's April 1- destination: Frankfurt, Germany. Three of the tight ends with whom I was in competition with had spent some amount of time in NFL training camps or on actual regular season rosters. They were using the World League as an opportunity to get back into the NFL. The remaining tight end was a German national. Unique to the World League, each team necessarily had seven National Players on the roster. During games at least one of them had to be in the game on alternating offensive and defensive series. Another concern was the smaller number of 45 total players allowed on each roster in the World League as compared to 53 plus practice players in the NFL. The fact that one of our tight ends was a national, almost assuring him a spot on the roster, and that we might keep two others at the position didn't aid my comfort. The only thing I could do was take advantage of every chance I had. That was the only thing in my control.

I experienced new things every day in my new line of football business. Baseball is a very tranquil sport, things rarely get intense and bad blood between opponents is not normal. A typical day preparing for a baseball game is filled with jokes, laughter and joviality. There was none of that the morning leading to nor once we took the field for our afternoon scrimmage against the Amsterdam Admirals. Practice pace appeared in slow motion once the first whistle was blown and the two teams got it on. Standing on the sideline, I watched the violent hitting, trash talking and bone crushing collisions the first three quarters of the contest and thought I wasn't going to get in at all, but the offensive coordinator told me I would play in the fourth quarter. That is when the butterflies really started to flutter. I couldn't let them see fear in my eyes out there on the field though, no matter what I did, so it was time to put the mean face on.

From the first snap I was on the field I took Irv's advice: "Even if you don't know what you are doing, go hard."

And it paid off in the end. I felt like I was on a war battlefield. Signals called, I tried to remember what I was supposed to be doing each play while defenders moved and shifted on the other side of the line, grunting and snorting as we both prepared to come off the ball. Everything moved at lightning speed and though it took everything I had, I kept up with my teammates as well as with the opponents; I looked like I belonged and that was one of the most important pieces. If I stuck out like a sore thumb it would be very easy to get rid of me. I intended to stick around for a while.

I didn't do anything spectacular that first scrimmage but did find a moment to stand out and separate myself from the rest of the pack. On a simple running play to the right side of our formation I took on a linebacker. I held my ground long enough for our running back to squirt through the hole, breaking through the next level of defense and running for about a fifty yard gain. Exactly fifty yards down the field I threw one more block right in front of our running back who nearly made it into the end zone. That play was run forward and backward on the big projection screen in the film study meeting the next morning and my hustle was commended several times by our offensive coordinator. I was making my impression.

The first real thought that I was at least on the right track came a couple of days after that first scrimmage against Amsterdam; one of the tight ends was released and it wasn't me! I had been in camp a little over a week and there remained two weeks before the team left for Germany. I hoped there would be a reason to dust off my passport.

Ever a big fan of those who can do things that I can only dream about (like playing any musical instrument, performing delicate surgery or singing with a beautiful voice) I have always wondered if people viewed me in that same light due to my God-given ability as a true athlete. As I demonstrated the gift on the football field after being away from it for such a long time I quickly gained confidence and became more comfortable in my surroundings. Resultantly, my old abilities quickly began to resurface. Though away from the game for quite some time, I found the instincts still present. I just needed some time to polish the old skills up a bit. Given a chance, I might just be a pretty good tight end for someone.

Regardless the outcome, making the final cut or not, I was proud. There was no way I should have been competing for a job in the World League but here I was, getting a look and opening some eyes. During those two weeks leading to final cuts and eventual departure to Germany, I did everything I could to make that football team. I started getting more reps during practice and in the final scrimmage played an equal amount of snaps as the other tight ends. I had fun, learned something new every day and experienced an athletic rebirth that can only be described as exhilarating. Suppressed on the baseball field for so many years, I had almost forgotten what it felt like to be respected as an athlete.

The final cuts came three days before D day (departure for Germany) and there were still four tight ends on the roster. Each got equal playing time in the scrimmage against the London that afternoon, so it was time to sweat it out in the evening, waiting for the call that might send me home. One thing was certain; regardless of whether or not I made this team I had earned the respect of every one of my teammates, coaches and opposing players. Most importantly, I had not given up on myself. It was now time to let the chips fall where they may!

The pre-cut drill was simple: take the early part of the evening off and then be in your own room from 6p.m. to 7p.m., when the coaching staff would make those calls that nobody wanted to receive. If you didn't hear anything by 7 o'clock, you were free to go about the rest of your night. About a week into my stay at the Falcon Inn, I had taken a roommate, a place kicker named Oliver. We had become pretty good friends in a short period of time, our late arrivals resulting in us both feeling like odd men out. I had spent so much time in my room studying my playbook that I really didn't make much time to socialize with many of my teammates. Oliver and I grabbed fast food and returned to our room to eat.

When six o'clock came the two of us tried to take our minds off the phone sitting on the nightstand between our beds. If we were lucky, the next hour would be silent; there was no need for anybody to be calling us! For 55 minutes Ollie and I talked nervously about a whole lot of nothing and then it happened, the phone rang! Mere minutes before the deadline, someone was calling one or both of us. Closest to the phone, I reluctantly picked it up. The lump in my throat impeded my ability to get 'hello' out of my mouth. The voice on the other end was one of a staff coach.

Our short conversation went exactly like this:
"Is this Ed"?
"Yes."
"Could you put Oliver on the phone?"

I looked across to my roommate and handed him the phone. Ollie listened, got up, and quickly walked out of the room, leaving me alone with less than a couple of minutes before 7p.m.

When the clock in the room hit the magic time, I ran out of my room, heading for a pay phone. If they made a mistake and forgot to call me they would have to come find me because I wasn't staying in that room for one more second than necessary. I immediately called Mom and Pops to give them the incredible news. Irv was next, then Don out in California. Each shared in my triumph and gave thanks to God for making it possible. In just a few days I would be flying out of the country with my new professional team, playing my second professional sport, football!

The next day's schedule involved time to take care of personal business before leaving the country for two and a half months. I had a lot to do. Mom came to the rescue with a last minute trip down from New Jersey- I was short on everything from deodorant to toothpaste to clothing. The delivery was actually just an excuse as she really wanted to see me before I jumped across oceans to another country. I did my best to close all business in Arizona. Jennifer's family allowed me to store belongings at their house and I left my truck in Coach Murphy's garage. Numerous others also played a part in helping me out and I appreciated them all so much.

Before I knew it I was seated on the nine-hour plane ride

to Germany. Had I awakened to learn I had been dreaming, I wouldn't have been surprised, but that was not the case. I was really going to play professional football after being away from the game for nearly a decade!

Final Cut

We arrived in Germany a week before our first game with three tight ends on the roster. My first concern of just 'making the team' quickly changed to what type of role would I be playing. The offensive system I was learning and trying to fit into was one of wide-open, vertical attacking featuring wide receivers. Still, a good tight end could make a great deal of difference if used properly. Concentration upon the deep part of the field would yield much room inside the soft, vacated middle. I had to be on the field to take advantage of that though; sitting on the bench behind someone and doing a lot of watching would defeat the whole purpose of being in a uniform.

Landing in Frankfurt, we literally began work immediately. Departing Atlanta at 5:30 p.m., the sun just on its way down from the sky, we touched ground in Germany nine hours of flight time later, 8:30 a.m. the next morning. Shocking our body clocks into order, we deposited bags at the hotel and re-boarded the bus; no rest for the weary. At our practice facility we got right at it: a full-padded, hard-hitting, physical practice.

No players, myself included, knew we remained in competition. Though I split all reps with the other two tight ends during the practice, I was asked if I had ever played fullback. I told our offensive coordinator I had not but was willing to do anything he might have in mind. When I wasn't in as tight end, I took snaps lined up in the backfield and served as lead blocker for our halfback. I considered this a sign that I would not play much at tight end. In reality, it demonstrated my versatility and value.

Our sleep deprivation did not end after this initial practice. After quick showers and lunch at the facility, it was back to our hotel for just enough time to unpack our bags and change into clothes minus Nike swooshes and logos. Next stop was a big reception dinner thrown by the city of Frankfurt on our behalf. Incredibly tired, the only thing I could deeply think about was sleep, but free food was enough to keep me occupied until I eventually made it back to my room where I was out before I hit the bed.

The following morning I awoke and headed down for our first meeting of the day, special teams. I noticed somebody was missing, my competition at tight end. I asked around thinking he had overslept. Truth was: he had been released and placed on his way back home all before we got to that first morning meeting. We had flown all the way to Germany with one extra man on the roster because I was still being counted as an exemption! At some point the coaching staff decided I could handle the job and was the best and only athlete they wanted to keep as tight end. I don't know when they officially made the decision, but I would never want to know how close I was to being the one re-packing a bag just after unpacking it. That would have seemed the longest flight in history. The way it worked out our German national would back me up and play on the designated series when there had to be a national representative on the field. And that answered the question I had been asking myself on the way over: my role on this team? Starting tight end! For an ex-baseball player I wasn't doing too badly for myself.

As much as I had already done and been through in that short amount of time, it was all just the beginning. I was in for quite a wild ride through spring and into summer. Over the next ten weeks my mental and physical endurance would be tested to and beyond all limits- as would parts of my faith. I had good days ahead, but they would be mixed and matched with never-far trials and tribulations.

Football 101:

Before I get deep into the season's progression, allow me to fill you in on the incredible football education crash course in which I enrolled. No luxury of being spoon-fed, I had to eat it all at once. I wasn't playing for the Pemberton Hornets and this wasn't high school football. The easiest part of the whole learning curve, digesting the playbook, was similar to translating an unknown language. Life only toughened after that. What fans in the stands see going on down on the playing field- the pointing, communicating back and forth before each play, and shifting and moving right before the start of the play on both sides of the ball is all choreographed chaos. Nothing is as it seems on the field; each team is out there to confuse and disorient their opponent.

– Assignment

From an offensive standpoint, there exists no guarantee that what you prepared for all week is what you are going to see on game day from your opponent. Tendencies are studied with one objective: exploitation- but your opponent schemes all the while against the tricks your coaching staff might have up their sleeves. To be totally prepared you have to cover every single possible scenario, a single running play can be blocked four or five different ways and all go into the game knowing that. Depending on what looks the defense provides, there could be combination-blocking going on between the tackle and tight end, leaving the guard on his own. Another look might send the tackle down to help the guard, leaving the tight end alone on the island to block the man over him. In some instances every man is covered, calling for man-to-man blocking all the way down the line. Another example, one might get a late shift or overload so the play cannot be run against that front at all. That the case, it is the quarterback's responsibility to check the play at the line and run something else. If he is out of time or doesn't recognize the disadvantage, it can get pretty ugly and the play can be disastrous; those are the times when it looks like the offense has absolutely no clue what they are doing. Yet another scenario includes the play being called at the line of scrimmage. You could have a combination of two running plays for the quarterback to choose from depending on what he sees on the other side of the ball, or he might choose to go to the air if the secondary coverage looks exploitable. The side to which you run can be swapped as well, changing all assignments. It's all a big chess game going on out there and you must be on your toes and know your assignment or you become the weakest link. One player destroying a play with a blown assignment can turn out to be the difference between a six-yard gain and a sixty-yard run for six points.

– Audibles

As I just mentioned, the play taken to the line of scrimmage may not be the one run. The quarterback is the general on the field and when he sees something he doesn't like he can get out of it at any time. You are expected to know why he is making the change and carry out all new obligations. One should be thinking right along with the commander on the field. Players need the entire playbook logged into their brains along with action code words and colors to alert that there is a new plan of attack.

– Communication

Linemen and tight ends walking to the line of scrimmage or settling into their stances, pointing and talking to each other indicate sorting out of the big defensive presentation puzzle. The center, second in rank to the quarterback, identifies the defensive front, relays it down both sides of the offensive line and designates the plan of attack. After his initial call all may change as defensive shifting begins. Blocking assignments and combinations are alternately confirmed or denied. Up until the snap of the ball one may have no clue as to whom to block. The last thing wanted is confusion or being on the wrong page while a man goes screaming up field to make a play, but it happens all the time. The defenses' job is to disrupt and that is what they do.

– Coverage

Tight ends are the hybrid animals on the football field. Our duties include extreme hand-to-hand contact with the interior beats and up field running contests with the hard-hitting headhunters in the secondary. Even running a route is complex – nothing is as simple as it sounds. The route run could be solely based on secondary coverage read first while getting into stance at the line of scrimmage and then checking to confirm it at the snap of the ball. Coverages are masked and disguised to throw off both receivers and especially the quarterback. Assignments can vary in the following manner: When you approach the line of scrimmage and get into your stance you see "Cover 2"- two deep safeties responsible for two halves of the deep field. On this particular play, you run a deep post if the coverage remains the same. Here is where it gets tricky. As you come off the line, your first job is to get clean release from the linebacker trying to hold you up; if the safeties have rolled into a "Cover 3"- a cornerback has dropped back, joining the two deep safeties, the middle is closed because the three men split a third of the field. Now, instead of a deep post route your task is to maneuver up field through traffic and run across the field at twelve yards. What happens if you get straight man-to-man though? If a defender latches on at the line of scrimmage or picks you up right off the ball, your entire route might change. Sound confusing? Then too, little intricacies like finding windows and settling in the middle of zone coverage or running away or past man coverage make it all the more fun.

– Blitz/Hot

To complicate matters even more the defense throws in the blitz and all hell breaks loose. A well-timed blitz is disguised and can come out of nowhere; the purpose is to bring too many men for the line, backs and tight ends, to pick up or to block. The complicated schemes can also send defensive linemen into coverage while defenders from the secondary come screaming off the edges to destroy the opposing QB or RB. Tight ends or receivers going out on routes must ever mind that the need may arise to become an immediate outlet for the QB. A good offensive coordinator has built in 'hot routes' for each passing play in the game plan. Do not be the one continuing on a route up the field and missing that emergency situation unless you want to catch the ire of your QB.

– Halftime/Adjustments

Upon exiting the field after the opening series the offensive unit huddles to discuss what everyone saw. Sometimes it looks exactly like what you prepared for all week and at others it doesn't resemble it remotely. Still overhead pictures are sent from upstairs, players talk on phones and headsets to coordinator or coaches high in the booths and chalkboards are pulled out and scribbled with the diagrams of what to change or keep. If a team is doing something totally out of character and the whole plan of attack has to be changed right there, then so be it; forget all studied that week. The same goes for halftime, when activity really gets crazy. The coaches come down from the booth and there is much yelling, screaming, and communicating back and forth. Those are some of the fastest and most furious twenty minutes players ever see.

– Trash Talking

Nothing is off limits in the trenches; some opponents will talk horrendously about you and your family to get into your head. The first tactic is to try and punk you or test your heart. If an opponent feels he can make you his 'bitch' for the day, he will straight up call you out: "I'm going to have you washing my drawers and cooking my dinner by the end of the night, punk!" With a lot of 'trash talking' going on all over the field, it is best to simply walk away, but that can be tough to do. One may choose to let actions speak, but 'good' trash talkers won't let it go; they keep digging and digging until they strike the nerve. It takes a great deal of mental toughness and strong fortitude not to fall into the trash talk trap.

World League Teams

Frankfurt Galaxy (Germany)   **London Monarchs** (England)
Scottish Claymores (Scotland)   **Barcelona Dragons** (Spain)
Amsterdam Admirals (Amsterdam) **Rhein Fire** (Dusseldorf, Germany)

The six teams all played each other twice, once at home and once on the road. The team with the best record after five games was the first half champion and hosted the World Bowl on June 23, 1996. The team with the best overall record at the end of the ten game schedule was the opponent for that first half champion.

I wasn't totally transformed into a football player overnight; I had a lot to learn about the game of football on a live field. It was one thing to learn a playbook and practice against my own teammates in a controlled setting but it was different altogether when the lights and cameras were turned on. Only the strong survive.

An early obstacle to overcome, which I didn't realize at first, was getting rid of the baseball mentality I still carried around. In my old world, a day at the park was a peaceful one filled with laughing, joking and joviality. Holding conversations with opponents before, during and after games, nobody was an enemy. In my new world I was to be as nasty, punitive and vicious as the man across the line from me or I would get myself killed out on the field. There is no place for laughter on a football field and you have no friends out there when the clock is running. In the third game of the season I figured that out and the lesson that brought the point home was a painful one. Once I learned it though, I needed never be taught it again.

My first professional football game was against the Rhein Fire on 13 April 1996 in front of 33,000 fans. The only two teams in the league residing in the same country, this was a rivalry game with bragging rights for the two cities at stake. The intensity level in our locker room and on the field for pre-game warm-ups high, I sat back and watched some of my teammates get charged up while keeping my cool, which is my nature. Probably more fired up on the inside than anybody in that locker room as there couldn't have been a bigger day in my life, I am just not wired to demonstrate it outwardly. When we ran out of the tunnel and onto the field for the opening kickoff, I had butterflies in my stomach, my heart was pounding so hard I thought it might jump out of my chest and I felt like I could run through a brick wall.

The pace of the game was the biggest surprise of the day for me. How we flew around during practice was nothing compared to the assault that took place on the field that afternoon. The speed lightning fast, everything happened in a flash. Vicious collisions produced the violent crunches heard in the first few rows of the stands. And the chess game was on, both sides scheming against one another.

Not about to embarrass myself that first game, I not only looked like I belonged, but I performed well. While I took every snap at tight end, I found myself acting as decoy most of the game- running a lot of routes to clear out zones and avert the opposing secondary's attention. I caught a couple of short passes, but the wide receiver crew got all the glory. Doing my best work as a run blocker, I showed that I was capable of handling myself one-on-one against whomever I was matched. We walked off the field that day with a hard fought victory undecided until the last minute.

Final Score: Galaxy 27-Fire 21

The morning after game day I awoke to the introduction of a new life element. I felt like someone had been hitting me with a jackhammer all through my night's slept. Every muscle, joint, bone and ligament called out in pain; even my eyelashes hurt. To make matters worse, we had stayed over in Dusseldorf, our flight was in the mid-morning. The change in air pressure was nothing but an agitator. By the time I got back to my room that afternoon, it hurt just to blink my eyes. Difficult to get used to, this simply came with the game. No pain, no gain!

Week two of the season, our first home game against the London Monarchs, I started rolling. The jury was probably still out on me up until I showed them what I could do in actual combat that first week. Even I didn't know I was going to do as well as I did. Confirming that they had made the right decision in keeping me, the coaching staff made it clear that I would play an effective part in the offense through our next week's preparation. They were true to their word and I took full advantage of the moment and made the play of my life, the one that would mark my official arrival into the football world.

Sports Machine

In game number two I introduced myself to the world. By the beginning of the contest's fourth quarter we were in total control- all that was left was the exclamation point at the end. Personally, I was having a good game with some short passes over the middle and a good day of blocking. Knocking on the door again deep in Monarch territory, a play action pass play was called; a running play is simulated in order to deceive the defense. The main objective is to fool the linebackers, suck them in toward the line of scrimmage and allow receivers to sneak in behind them, occupying their voided territory. In our heavy formation, two tight ends and two running backs lined up in the backfield, I sold the run by blocking down hard on the man lined up inside of me. Then, after a quick delay, I released for the back corner of the end zone. Meanwhile the quarterback went through a heavy run fake to the deep running back and then rolled out to my side; I was option number one. The play executed to perfection, I found myself running free toward the back pylon in the right corner of the end zone. The defense eventually sniffed out the play and the linebackers duped by the fake turned and started searching out all eligible receivers. As our quarterback rolled, he saw me and lofted the ball toward the back corner of the end zone. He'd put a little too much air under it though and it sailed. Not to be denied my reward, from the moment the ball left the quarterback's hand, everything entered slow motion for me. I couldn't see or hear a thing as I knew the ball and I were the only entities in the entire universe. As the ball seemed to be drifting away from me, I let instinct take over and I left my feet; I was perpendicular to the ground, four feet up in the air, hands outstretched. The ball touched my fingers and I locked onto it and pulled in, preparing for my crash landing. And when I finally hit the ground I did it with a big thud, the ball tucked into my breadbasket causing every ounce of air to rush out of my body. Then, the roar of the crowd bought everything back into fast motion.

I should have been keeled over as I got up gasping for breath but the rush of the moment took over. The whole offensive unit rushed me and I was hit from every angle. I didn't know it at that moment, but I had made one of the best catches ever witnessed by a multitude of fans. Such opinions were substantiated at the end of the following week when I got a call from back home in the States. A national sports television show, "The George Michael Sports Machine", had selected my touchdown catch as the 'Sports Machine Play of the Week'! That single catch took me from the back of the line to the front; I was now a player to be watched. And in my mind I was doing what I had set out to do; changing the perception that I was a baseball player trying to play football to now being a football player who used to play baseball.

Final Score: Galaxy 37-Monarchs 3

My laid-back personality caught up with me in week three and I learned another valuable lesson in Barcelona, Spain the following week- a true wakeup call! Still a nice guy on the football field, I wasn't out there to hurt anybody; I just wanted to play some football. I learned truly that not everybody shared my frame of mind. Early in the first quarter I was going about my business, deep up the field on a post route. I took a look back to see what was happening behind me and saw my quarterback about to be sacked. When I returned my vision up field the only thing I saw was a green Barcelona Dragon helmet as it landed squarely under my chin. Knocked silly, my feet flew straight into the air over my head, which hit the ground first. The safety who took the cheap shot had launched himself from about five feet and his illegal hit was nothing more than malicious but went un-penalized. Sprawled out on the field in a daze undoubtedly accompanied by a mild concussion at the least, I refused to give anybody the satisfaction that they had knocked me out. I hoped that the signal for four wide receivers in the game was held up on the sideline, but that wasn't the case. I literally wobbled back to the huddle, not even sure of my own name. And when we broke huddle the only thing on my mind was not falling over in my stance; I was *literally* out on my feet.

Thankful that the play called was a running play and not to my side, I did my best to get in the way of the defender across from me as I tried to regain my faculties. After that play I was headed off to the sideline; we failed to convert on third down so it was time to punt. I spent the next few minutes trying to put my jaw back in place as I boiled on the sideline and vowed revenge; somebody wearing an opposite color jersey was going to pay for that hit and I didn't care who it was.

What goes around comes around. Late in the first half I had my chance for a legal hit retribution. I felt a bit of guilt because the man I took out wasn't the one who hit me, but that wasn't my problem. I ran a route up the field, this time keeping my head on a swivel and my eyes up-field, and when the ball was dumped off to a running back out in the flat he went wide trying to get the corner and make it down the right sideline. I turned and ran a half circle back toward the action. Then, right in front of our bench, I threw a block that wiped out one of the would-be tacklers; he never saw me coming or knew what hit him. My entire bench went crazy and I felt an inexplicable rush as I looked down into a face that resembled what mine must have looked like just a short time ago; a glassy eyed, dazed and confused expression was plastered on his face. That was the day I found that inner beast inside. I knew the mentality I had at the moment I went looking for that hit was the only one I could safely

run around with on a football field; hit or be hit, kill or be killed.
Final Score: Galaxy 33-Dragons 29

I was riding high heading into week four but it was time to come crashing down; lightning was about to strike yet again! I didn't get a whole lot of action in Barcelona as the ball just didn't come my way, but I did have a good game. The fact that I never complained and was only interested in doing whatever I could to help the team made me a favorite with the coaching staff and especially with my quarterback. When asked about my job at tight end, the staff remarked that I was doing an outstanding job and that the coming week's focus was to get me more involved in the offense because they didn't want to waste the talent they had. Once again, they said it and they did it. By the end of the first half I had five catches and a touchdown, my second of the season. We were destroying the Amsterdam Admirals in Frank-furt. Right before the end of the first half the game got ugly, frus-tration had set in on the Admirals' side of the field, and that set the tone for a second half street brawl.

I don't know what the Admirals talked about at halftime, but they came out with blood in their eyes. All game long I had been having my way with the two defensive ends lined up on either side of the field. What I was doing to them must have been seen from upstairs, so they had to have gotten their butts chewed off during the twenty-minute intermission. When they came back on the field they were both howling like the wind; talking more sh** than a little bit. I couldn't keep them out of my face. After every play one of them came looking for me and the action didn't stop just because the whistle blew. We lost our starting quarterback to injury in that second half and became unraveled, almost losing a 21 point lead. On the verge of totally giving it all up and losing our first game, we put one last drive together in the closing minutes of the fourth quarter, up by only five points.

On a first and goal play we ran an off-tackle play to my side. I was engaged with one of the boorish defensive ends when the running back got tackled before he made it through the hole. The entire pile landed on my left knee, which was firmly planted on the ground and trapped with nowhere to move but inward. I instantly felt and heard a loud pop and went down in an instant. The whistle blew and the pile rolled off me but I wasn't getting up; I was hurt and I knew it. For the first time in my life I was lying on a field and didn't think I could get up. I wasn't going to try until one of the menacing, defensive ends came looking for me and found me on the ground. I was flat on my back and he came and stood directly over me, straddling my body. Bending directly into my face, he uttered the words that would not allow me to stay where I was for one more second, "What's wrong, bitch? Do we need to call an ambulance?" In that instant he totally demoralized me. I would have felt less than a man if I didn't pick myself up. Fortunately, the Admirals had called a timeout to stop the clock and that allowed me just enough time to search deep enough to find the strength to go on. I have no idea where I found the will to get off the ground in that instant but I did. For three plays I hobbled around on one leg at the goal line before we got the ball across and put the game out of reach with less than two minutes left. The offensive unit never returned to the field as time ran out as the Admirals attempted to score, so I spent the last few minutes of the game conferring with my trainers about what I had felt in the knee. Encouraged that I was able to stay on the field actually walking normally, their first diagnosis was maybe a strained ligament or joint but no serious damage, a slight tear at worst. If all was well I might not even miss a day of practice. The doctors confirmed their belief as they examined me on the table after the game, twisting and rotating my knee in every direction for 30 minutes. Still, an MRI was scheduled for first thing the following morning.

Final Score: Galaxy 40-Admirals 28

I was hoping for some good news the following morning after the MRI, but no such luck. After my sitting in the waiting room at one of the local Frankfurt hospitals for nearly an hour, the doctor came out and called me into his office along with the two trainers who had kept me company as I hoped and prayed for the best. He led us into his office where the MRI results were already lit up on his wall screen. Ever so nonchalantly he told me that I had suffered a total rupture of my Medial Collateral Ligament (MCL); the picture showed the detached ligament curled up on opposite sides of my knee. The first thing that ran through my mind was that my football career was over as fast as it had begun; my head fell into my hands and I almost cried right there in that office. All I had worked so hard for was taken away in an instant!

The fact that the MCL was the damaged ligament was the best possible news I could hear. Damage to my ACL would have meant I could have missed an entire calendar year. The way the doctor explained it I would not even need surgery. Rather than reattaching a ruptured MCL, the new procedure was to rehabilitate the knee to function without it. The scar tissue formed during rehab would take the place of the ligament in holding the knee in place, keeping it from slipping out interiorly. The best scenario would be my missing four to six weeks if my knee took to rehab.

As far as I was concerned, my season was over; outlook meant at least four weeks on the shelf with only six games left on the schedule. While I was gone someone would be doing my job so the coaching staff might not even want me back by the time I finally recovered. I had come far in short time, but the ride seemed to end just as I prepared for take-off. While I didn't have a very positive outlook about returning to the field before the end of the season, my trainers were much more optimistic. Happy it was the MCL, according to them it was possible to make it back in time. My rehab would have to start immediately though, and it was going to have to be done back in the States as such facilities did not exist in Germany.

The next morning I was on the first flight heading back across the water to, of all places, Birmingham, Alabama! The World League had an affiliate with Health South and all players requiring surgery or any type of major rehabilitation were sent there. I had a lot to think about on that long flight back across the water. Life did not seem fair. I worked hard, tried to be a good person, treated people fairly, and, most importantly, had a strong belief in God. I knew He was guiding me through my life and always by my side. Why was this happening, then? I know all things happen for a reason, but what was the reason behind this? I had a million questions but no answers. The only thing I could do was rely on my faith; all things would be revealed according to God's time and not mine. I would later find out that the knee injury was a blessing in disguise; a last chance to do something very special.

Insult To Injury

What was even more depressing about the sudden derailment was the fact that my mother and father were actually flying into the country as I was leaving it; we might literally pass each other in the air. The following week was to be the first time my parents watched me play football live since I was in high school. I called my mother as soon as I got my bad news, but there was nothing they could do to change their plans due to ticket restrictions. They would fly over and use the trip as a vacation. I flew out as they flew in. They ended up having a great week in Germany as the Galaxy treated them as if I was still there. Though they took in all the sites and culture, I know they missed seeing me on the field as much as I missed being there. We all really had been looking forward to the visit. It would have to be another time and place though, if ever at all.

It was May 7th when I landed back in Birmingham. The sports rehab specialist who would be helping me get back on the field the following morning discussed with me the road to recovery. It included but was not limited to two sessions of rehab every day during the week, one early morning and the other in the late afternoon. On Saturdays I would have one in the morning only and Sunday would be a day of rest.

I approached my rehab with narrow-minded focus: Get back on the football field! Some of the many familiar faces from around the league in Birmingham worked a different agenda. Workmen's compensation kicked in and all still received portions of their $35k salaries while rehabilitating. A couple preferred to take that money and lounge around the pool in place of getting healthy enough to rejoin their teams. I associated with them little. Desiring to be in Birmingham not a day more than neces-sary, I was actually told early on to slow my pace. I was putting too much pressure on my damaged knee the first week; the workload was too heavy.

That first week of rehab didn't go well for me in Birm-ingham. The problem with my knee was more severe than I had anticipated. Lacking stability on the interior part of my knee and without the MCL to keep it in place, it popped out of the socket when I applied pressure in that inward direction. If I couldn't walk and make a right turn without stopping and turning my entire body, how was I going to play on a football field any time soon? I resigned myself to the fact that I was probably done play-ing football for now and I was convinced that although I had a great four game run in Europe, it wasn't enough to find work in the NFL. And, there was no way I was going to sit and wait another whole year to take another shot; I was turning 26 in less than a month and that was a late start for professional football as it was.

One of my biggest fears was that I would be forgotten about while away from the team. The day I flew out, another tight end flew in. I figured it would be one of the guys who had been in camp with us but I learned the Galaxy went out on the wire and found an ex-Philadelphia Eagle looking for work. He was an experienced veteran, someone who could handle coming into an offense and learning it in a short time. That was very important because the next week was a crucial one. Only two teams remained undefeated. The Scottish Claymores were also 4-0 and the winner of that game would win the first half and host the World Bowl. Unfortunately, the following weekend ended disappointingly in Germany. The Scottish Claymores stomped us on our home field by a score of twenty to zero.

I wallowed in my own self-pity for the first week and half of my stay in Birmingham. Feeling sorry for myself, I tried to figure out why I just couldn't catch a break. And in that time I lost the opportunity to receive the special gift that God had intended for me *all along*, the chance to see my grandfather alive one last time! I got a call in my hotel room on May 16th, 1996 from my mother in New Jersey. The man who had given me my first car as a teenager in high school had passed away from diabetes complications. I'd been in town for over two weeks and hadn't gone to see him because I got caught living and thinking in my own little world!

In 1994, when last I saw Granddad, his health was bad. He had managed to hold on for almost another two years before losing his battle. In January 1996 my mother made a visit from New Jersey to see my grandfather for what she felt would be the last time. Totally bedridden and in a coma-like state, Granddad seemingly did not know who Mom was while she stood by his bed. Very difficult, the visit was something that she needed in order to have peace of mind.

I didn't immediately go to visit my grandfather because I didn't want to see him like that. I hadn't spent a lot of time with him in the last few years, but he had been quite special in the early part of my life. His decision to return to the South was both his own and the reason he lost touch with most of the family, but I continued to love him as much as I had when I was a little boy. I didn't want to see him as my mother had described, so I kept putting off my visit. At first I was too busy with rehab, then I didn't have transportation or it just wasn't a good day; I'll go tomorrow or wait until the weekend. I put it off one day too many and lost the chance to say good-bye. Amtrak gave my grandfather his 'last ride' on May 19th, 1996. The company he had worked for for over 30 years transported him from Birmingham to New Jersey; he was laid to rest on the 22nd. I felt a great deal of guilt but my mother eased my pain a little. She reminded me how proud my grandfather was of me. He knew in his heart how much I loved him and that was what mattered the most.

Granddad's death put life back into perspective for me; we shouldn't put things off until tomorrow because that day is not promised. I was determined to get back on the field now. Pushing my knee to cooperate, I found progress slow. In Germany there was an urgency to get me back as soon as possible. Trainers called for progress reports several times a week at the coaching staff's request because things were unraveling there. The first loss to the Claymores was followed by two more, a (27-7) shellacking at the hands of the London Monarchs and (20-17) loss to the Claymores in Scotland. Apparently, I was a more important piece to the offense than anyone thought, myself included.

Exactly four weeks after my injury and one more loss in Germany (a 31-8 beat-down by the Rhein Fire) the moment of truth finally arrived; I would be allowed to take a required running test to determine if I was healthy enough to return to the field. If I passed I would be released to play immediately, but if I failed I would miss at least one more week. It was a Monday afternoon when I stepped onto the local community college football field around the corner from the Health South facility. My test included a rigorous workout which required I run forward, do angled cutting work and run routes. For part of the workout I was allowed to wear my knee brace, but there was a small portion of it wherein I had to remove it and demonstrate that I had at least a small degree of stability solo. I tried to maneuver my way through the workout, but the test was set up to expose any remaining weakness. I could run straight ahead, but not yet at full gallop. I was okay making cuts, but I had to cruise through them; there was no explosion into or out of them. And, I was still in a great deal of pain.

By rights I should not have been cleared, but I think all the hard work I had put in over the four weeks influenced our head rehabilitation specialist. He told me himself that he didn't think I was quite ready but with only two weeks remaining in the World League season he would let me go. If I thought I was healthy enough (I didn't but told him I was) and my team wanted me as desperately as they obviously did, he would let me return. On Tuesday afternoon, June 4th, I was on a plane heading across the ocean for the season's last two weeks and one more shot at fulfilling my new dream.

Arriving back in Frankfurt on my 26th birthday, June 5, and seeing my teammates were the best presents I could have given myself. Going through the same time mix-up as when we flew as a team, I left the States at night and arrived just in time to put my bags in my room and join my team for the first meeting of the day. They were as happy to see me as I was to see them; the tight end that had replaced me was gone, shipped back to the States, and I was going to be right back in the mix of things as if I had never left. The only problem was that I didn't know how much trauma my knee could actually sustain; one hit and I might be down again. It was Wednesday morning. We had three days to prepare for an important game against the Barcelona Dragons. I would find out soon enough.

Our situation in Frankfurt was plain and simple; win the last two games against the teams we had to leapfrog for the spot in the World Bowl or lose one or both and call it a season. Four consecutive losses during my absence had put us at 4-4 and a logjam was created; Scotland was the only team that kept winning all through the season.

The instructions sent from Health South to my trainers included keeping my left knee as braced as possible. The brace was re-enforced with enough tape (from the middle of my calf all the way to the top of my thigh) to make me look like I was wearing a cast. And I had to wear this thing every day. Testing my leg in practice, I gained a little confidence that I might be able to be somewhat effective in the game; the biggest worry I had was the unpredictability and violence of real live action. The controlled atmosphere of practice was one thing. The mayhem of game day was another.

On Saturday, June 8th, I stood in the tunnel ready to be introduced with the starting offensive unit when the same butterflies from game one paid a second visit. I needed to get that first contact out of the way so I could feel confident that I could make it through the game. What I really didn't want was to get out there on the field and not be able to do my job. That would just be too much of a disappointment after what it took me just to get back here. When it was my turn to come out of the tunnel and the public address announcer told the crowd of over 33,000 Galaxy fans that I was back, the stadium almost flipped upside down with applause. That huge roar gave me one of the greatest feelings I had ever had as an athlete: I had been missed and I was appreciated. It was good to be back. I only hoped I would not let my fans down.

Because we got the ball on the opening kickoff, it was right to work. As I walked out of the huddle I took a deep breath. The moment I looked down at the new pair of receiver's gloves sporting my grandfather's initials I dedicated the game to him. I wanted to make him proud. Our first play from scrimmage that day was a running play that ran right up behind me. I suffered a serious case of déjà vu because it was almost the exact play that had put me out of action in the first place. This time around the running back made it through the hole and I was still standing after the play. The one getting off the ground? The man I had just blocked. My next obstacle to overcome was running a route- taken care of on the very next play. Obviously a step slower, I could get up the field. After that second play of the game I put all worries out of mind. The knee was not 100% but I had enough in it to get the job done.

I couldn't have scripted my return any better. I don't know what was missing while I was gone but we came together to succeed. The team to which I had returned was that which I had left, not the one I had sadly watched and heard about while in Alabama. On that first possession we marched the ball all the way down near the Dragon's goal line. After two unsuccessful run attempts trying to get the ball across for the score, the boot- leg was called- my 'Sports Machine' play. The defense bit on the fake run again and this time I was alone in the back corner of the end zone with no need to dive for my third touchdown of the season. The crowd went crazy and I was mobbed by teammates; they too had missed me. The game wasn't decided until our defense made a big stop with little time left on the clock in the fourth quarter, but we defeated Barcelona and kept our World Bowl hopes alive. If we could win in Amsterdam the last week of the season, we'd play Scotland for the championship!

Final Score: Galaxy 24-Dragons 21

How ironic was it that the Admirals and their two trash-talking defensive ends were the last team standing in our way if we wanted to play one more game that season? In an uncomfortable amount of pain through the week as I got ready for what was undoubtedly going to be hell dealing with the two loud-mouths, I sucked it up and made it through. Those opposing ends began with me during pre-game warm-ups, so I knew it was going to be a long day. I kept my cool and didn't let them get into my head. My plan was to do the same thing I had in our first meeting- beat the two of them up and down the field all day long. If that didn't shut them up, nothing would. While I didn't catch a pass that day, my true value was in keeping the two defensive ends busy all game long. That was both my best blocking performance of the season and what I was primarily needed for that day. When the last whistle of the day went off and the game was over we headed victoriously to the World Bowl.

Final Score: Galaxy 28-Admirals 20

On June 23rd, 1996 I made my first appearance on National Television when Fox broadcast the World Bowl live from Scotland. By now word of my sports switch had gotten out to all of my old friends and acquaintances. Now they would see actual proof that I had pulled it off and they would get a chance to see me at my new profession for the first time, playing for a professional football championship!

The game in Scotland was my most exciting life event to date. The game went back and forth, both teams exchanging the lead all the way to the last minutes of the fourth quarter. I shone early, catching a few passes, and got a lot of praise from the broadcasters. In the second half I wasn't much of a factor, but I did manage to have a good game. In the end, the Claymores narrowly escaped with the victory, recovering a fumble on our last possession as we moved down the field for the possible winning score.

World Bowl 1996: Galaxy 27- Claymores 32

Standing on our sideline and watching the Claymores celebrate was a tough pill to swallow, but I didn't let that take away from what I was feeling. After losing four games in a row we could've just phoned the last two in and gone home. Instead we pulled it all together and fought to the end. I was proud to be a part of this team and what I had accomplished personally made me feel even better. I hoped this wasn't the end of the road for me, but if that turned out to be the case I had nothing of which to be ashamed. I had done what few thought possible; I was now a football player. Where the Good Lord took me from here remained to be seen, but for the time being I could take a quick second to bask in the glow. I'd done pretty well for myself over the last ten months. Three days after the game in Scotland I was heading back across the water to New Jersey from Frankfurt. I wasn't sure what, if anything, was waiting on me but I was feeling pretty good about my direction.

Edward Smith

Frankfurt Galaxy
1996

Frankfurt Galaxy
1996
Catch & Celebration

CHAPTER SEVEN

Washington Redskins & St. Louis Rams

My transition phase was a grueling one, September of 96 to June of 97. The only way I made it through was with the constant support that never left my side. Without my family and small, select circle of friends there is no possible way I would have been successful. Had I been alone the many obstacles and reasons to give up would have prevailed. If it wasn't my parents supporting me, it was Irv. And if it wasn't one of them, it was Don out in California encouraging me to complete the incredible mission I had started.

Had you asked me how the family was doing when I returned from my European tour I would have said, "Not bad, we're all making out pretty good." As a whole, the family was actually still recovering from the loss of my grandfather. Even while I was away and busy I could feel the pain of missing him. His sudden return to the South and the fact that he had been away from us over the last few years didn't diminish the role he played in my life. He would be missed incredibly and remembered always. Collectively, we were moving on with life after death.

Individually, we were all making our way as well. Irv was in New Orleans preparing for his fourth year with the Saints. Only a couple of weeks from training camp when I returned, he was enjoying the last few days of freedom prior. A major reason our family was doing as well as it was, Irv continued to live the way we were brought up – always looking out for others. The fact that he had an incredible amount of money did not change that. When I first signed my minor league contract I had his role on a much smaller scale. I remember getting calls from Irv when he first started college. Whether it was a bike to help him get around campus or help paying a couple of speeding tickets he preferred our parents not know about, all he had to do was call. Now he was the one who helped anyone in our family when they were in need.

My father was succeeding where he had long failed in staying clean and sober. It was now a lifestyle change and not something he wanted to get control of just for the time being. Now mentoring and sponsoring in our community, he also chaired, spoke at and organized meetings for addicts in need. His new motto was 'one day at a time'. If you asked for any more than that one, you were being greedy because none of them are guaranteed to us in the first place. All the years of bodily abuse had caught up with him by this time. He had already experienced six major back operations. Three were disk removals and three were scar tissue/mess clean-up procedures. His addictive personality was responsible for just about all of the damage in one-way or another. Whether it was a car accident while under the influence or stopping on the side of the road to load a tree stump into his trunk for the firewood, my father just didn't have any limits. And his back paid for it over the years. Sometimes he seemed in pain and he had frequent mobility issues, but his spirits were high. He was growing wiser as he aged, so there was hope for him yet.

All the while my mother was the rock that couldn't be moved. When most women would have thrown in the towel, she stood by my father. The reward came to her now; she had a good man on whom she could depend and would stay by her side.

Still working at the same community college, Mom had moved up the ladder all the way from the library to the accounting department. Whether a question I needed answered or something troubling me, it was 'Mom to the Rescue' with comforting words of wisdom.

During this time I had many questions. Numerous days I doubted what I was trying to do professionally. Toward the end of my baseball days, during the attempt to make the switch to football and through my first football injury Mom was a constant source of strength for me. No matter where I was or what I was doing, I could call her and she'd move me back into the right frame of mind; sometimes without even knowing I sought answers because I disguised my questions. While that was comforting, the most important thing my mother gave to me was a release for the internal struggle I experienced intermittently. Having developed a bad case of tunnel vision as I tried to turn myself into a football player, I suppressed a couple of things to keep from having to think about them, but they seemed to pop up when least expected. The biggest issue was the son that I felt I had abandoned. I thought about him almost every day and it hurt to think of him growing and learning without even knowing I existed. I blamed myself for letting things happen the way they did. I also looked at the fact that it wasn't me who walked out the door, but me who was asked not to return. I was truly conflicted. The only person I talked to about any of this was Mom. She never candy-coated anything when she talked to me; she gave it to me straight even when we discussed this. And I believed what she told me, "One day it will all come full circle and you will have a chance to be in his life."

In the beginning of my quest to make the jump from one sport to the next, nobody expected much of me. I know I surprised most by getting a look in the first place and then making the team was another amazing long shot. Even after I did those two things I can imagine that anybody involved with football expected me to be exposed; I couldn't be as good as I looked. After all, it was the World League of American Football, not the NFL. I was bound to eventually find myself in over my head. When that didn't happen initially, I'm sure I shocked at least a few doubters. And I may have turned a few into believers. Then, all seemed to come to a sudden halt. The injury was probably the expected end to the whole experiment as far as some were concerned. Nobody knew if I'd recover in time to even finish my season and more evaluation was yet needed to determine my skills.

Not only did I make it back from my injury, I picked back up as if I hadn't missed a beat! It was also pretty evident that my team missed me while I was gone and when all was said and done I didn't just look like I fit in on a football field; I stood out in a positive light. The question in front of me was: Did I do enough to show anybody back home that I might actually be able to play at the highest level? I didn't have a whole lot of experience backing me, but hopefully someone was curious enough to want to find out.

I didn't know what to expect after that stint in Germany. Don continued to do everything he could on my behalf, but he wasn't plugged in to the world of football. He also had to tend to his growing flock of baseball clients. We discussed options and contacts right when I got back, but it was going to take time to get in touch with the right people. And that was something we didn't have a lot of with the opening of NFL training camps only a couple of weeks away. If I didn't get in now while the iron was hot I might not make it. For the first couple of days back all was quiet. Then the phone started ringing. Somebody *had been* watching while I was over in Europe.

The calls originated from agents interested in representing me. The phone didn't ring off the hook, but there were three who felt they could help me take the next step. One stood out from the rest because of a personal connection. Amy, Irv's friend initially and mine now, worked for an agent who had been following my progress from Atlanta. More of that 'six degrees of separation' was in effect. The agent's name, Pat Dye Jr., rang an immediate bell. He was the son of Pat Dye Sr. who had coached the Auburn Tigers Football program for years and became a legend in the South. Pat Jr., heading up his own sports agency firm, Pro-Files Sports Management, followed my story from the start, obtaining updates from Amy along the way. Now interested in working with me, he stood out from the others because of his integrity. I had never met the man before, but I could tell he had the same type of values as Don- rare in the dirty business of sports agents. I could tell by talking to him that he was more interested in my talent and the possibility that I could play in the NFL than the publicity it might bring him just to be representing me. The latter was the feeling I got from the other two agents. I decided to work with Pat. He made no promises but was going to do everything he could to get me to the front door. If I got the opportunity, it was up to me to prove that I could play the game in the NFL. That was all I could ask for.

I had a lot of personal business to take care of after being busy with football for the last few months. My travels had taken me from out West to the South and across the water and back twice. And it had all happened at the drop of a hat so there were things that needed tending; my personal belongings and truck were sitting out in the desert. With no time frame for how fast anything might happen, I decided to go out to Arizona to get things in order and take a short vacation. My tired and beat-up body could use a few days. I hadn't had half a day to catch my breath out there when I got a call on my brand new, self-gifted cell phone.

On the job fast, Pat found interest surrounding me had already escalated. He was already receiving feedback from teams looking to fill their training camp roster spots with a quality tight end. And I was high on their lists! Time was of the essence. We didn't want to miss out on an opportunity this late and close to the opening of training camps, so we conversed back and forth via phone all day long. We narrowed the best situations to the Washington Redskins and St. Louis Rams and the final decision was made before the sun set on the West coast that evening. My first stop in the National Football League would be in St. Louis. By the end of the following morning, July 6, I had received and returned my faxed contract. It was official. In ten months I had gone from playing my last minor league baseball game to preparing for my first, hopefully not last, NFL training camp. If I was dreaming I didn't want anybody to pinch me because I did not want to wake up.

My reporting date was one week from the day I signed my contract, July 13. Once again I headed into uncharted territory with no clue what to expect other than what Irv told me. And although his detailed account of what was ahead painted a vivid picture, it still could not prepare me for all I was about to go through and all I would be expected to absorb. The first thing I had to do was forget about my experience in the World League. Though a great learning tool, I would start from scratch at the bottom of the totem pole again. Football at this level is like nothing imaginable until experienced firsthand. Hearing or reading about it is one thing, living it is another. I was about to find out what it meant to be pushed beyond my limits.

To compare football in the NFL to football in any other form is like putting a Rolls Royce next to a Pinto; the only similarity is that they are both cars. Nothing I had been through in my life could have prepared me for the experience that awaited me.

I flew into St. Louis and was transported to the team facility. All players who opted to travel with the team then boarded buses for the drive to Macomb, Illinois, home to Western Illinois University. During the summer hiatus a large dorm on campus would house us as we made our way through two-a-day practices. I got the sense that my new work environment would be nothing like any I had experienced. Minor league baseball life seemed a hundred years ago and a million miles from here.

– Bling-Bling

Pulling into the dorm parking lot at Western Illinois University, I saw what looked like a car show in progress. The big boys definitely liked their toys and paraded them decked out with chrome wheels and explosive sound systems. Competition. Who had the nicest ride? Loudest sound system? Newest model? My '93 Pathfinder was parked in a garage back in Arizona and I was proud of it but they would have laughed at me had I pulled into training camp with those factory wheels. Jewels, expensive clothing and electronic equipment comprised other extravagantly sported items.

– There Is No "We" In Team

I quickly learned that it was a dog-eat-dog world in the NFL. With millions of dollars possibly at stake there remained very little time to worry about the next man. Veterans separated themselves from the rookies and vice versa and there existed certain cliques, but mostly egos made it tough for a great deal of bonding to transpire. Even on field teamwork pitted two sides against each other, offense versus defense. It was hard to be too friendly at lunch with someone who had literally tried to rip your head off in morning practice.

– Size Does Matter

The size and strength of NFL players is unbelievable! To watch a 330lb. offensive lineman come out of his stance, pull around a corner, and throw a block downfield is amazing. Your eyes tell you that those big fellas are just not supposed to be able to move like that, but there they go. And to see a 290lb. gargantuan with arms the size of tree trunks in a three-point stance across from you at the line of scrimmage can be somewhat intimidating. Bigger, faster and stronger- that is how they breed them today. Years ago a tight end in the NFL was big at 220lbs. At 255lbs. I was considered average at the position and almost small on the field when you consider whom I lined up next to and across from.

– The Scheme Of Things

When I was handed my playbook in training camp I got dizzy just examining the first few pages. The width of two phonebooks, its terminology and diagrams looked like something that should be on the chalkboard of a physics class at Harvard University. All plays, formations, line calls and audibles learned in Frankfurt had to be thrown out the window because they were useless now. In baseball you can only do a bunt defense so many ways. On a football field there are no two similar ways to do or call anything according to each offensive coordinator; everything has a different code name. I was expected to learn this offense in camp, adding new plays and formations in both the morning and afternoon practices and without excuse for missed assignments. I spent hours lying in bed at night after bed check reviewing everything we worked on that day and trying to stuff new additions into my brain so I could be prepared the next morning. It was like cramming for an SAT test with one week's notice. Difference was: if you missed a question on the SAT you weren't going to have a coach ripping you a new one in front of everybody.

– No Pain No Gain

When I was in Europe I thought I knew pain. Practices intense and hard-hitting there, they compared to training camp in the NFL like playing tag in the Browns Mills backyard when I was a little boy. If the World League was like being in a car accident every day of the week, the NFL was like being in the same accident with a Mack Truck replacing the other car. The crash resulted in one being thrown from the vehicle and run over several times by oncoming traffic unaware of your bloody and bruised body lying on the road. For two and a half hours, twice a day, we did individual position work, one-on-one drills against the defense, plus full contact teamwork that could result in the loss of up to ten pounds of water weight in a single day. With the sweltering heat and high humidity I almost melted like a snowman in a sauna when in full uniform. After the first workout on the first training camp day, nobody at a physical position (that subtracts kickers) runs at 100%. From that point in time something on your body is going to hurt through the rest of the year up until about a month into your off-season. By then, maybe, your body will start to feel some relief. And you will be expected to play through anything not considered a major injury. Dislocated fingers are popped back in on the field and taped to other fingers to keep them as far from harm's way as possible. And no crying in football! If it hurts that bad, just bite your upper lip.

– Pick Up The Pace

As there is no recovery time on an NFL football field, one false step or misread means the play is over. Somebody running past you heading for your quarterback or running back produces an unpleasant end result. Because field action moves at lightning speed, you better keep up. Three hundred pound plus men run 4.7 forty-yard dashes and bounce around on light feet. Collisions are that much more violent because of the size and strength of the men involved. The crunches one sees and hears while sitting in a favorite living room chair actually feel and sound ten times worse. There is nothing remotely pleasant about getting blind-sided by even the smallest man in the defensive secondary on any field in the NFL. While you never get used to the pounding you take, every hit as bone-jarring and teeth-rattling as the one before, you learn to deal with and avoid the carnage. There is a true art form to avoiding direct hits; you don't want to take too many of those if you can help it. Just because taking on head-hunting linebackers and defensive ends that might outweigh you by 30lbs. is part of the job description doesn't mean you have to stand in front of them like a sitting duck. No need to go looking for extra contact.

Rich Brooks, head coach of the St. Louis Rams, ran an intense training camp. Coach Brooks wanted his team to have hard-hitting attitudes and believed the best way to get that across was to have us practice beating up on each other every morning and afternoon. Some type of pushing and shoving match broke out almost every day. By the end of the first week I was so tired of hitting that I found my own attitude developing. When you spend your entire day banging and brawling, a pleasant disposition is not so natural!

Training camp opened with 80 players on the roster. With first cuts roughly two weeks into camp and each additional week thereafter, the roster is shaved down to the magic number of 53 a week before the regular season starts. In addition, each team places five players on the practice squad. Fifth on a depth chart with six tight ends, I was followed by an un-drafted rookie free agent. Nobody knew what to make of me that first week of training camp due to the odd path I had taken to arrive there. The coaching staff treated me just like any other player with no excuses for missing assignments or penalties. If I couldn't handle the game at this level, I'd be on the first bird out of town, my baseball background irrelevant. The players, on the other hand, knew my story and initially treated me somewhat like an outsider because I didn't really fit into a particular group. Never having played in college, I had no alma mater, old teammates or former opponents to vouch for my abilities or myself. The veterans didn't consider me a rookie because of my age and the rookies didn't consider me a veteran because I had no years of experience of which to speak. I could demonstrate that I belonged only by my on-field performance.

Though the level of competition could intimidate most, I backed down from nothing. Regardless from where I had come or how I had gotten there, I was in camp just like everybody else. I made mistakes in the beginning but quickly caught up as I adapted to the pace on the field. When all else failed I fell back on Irv's old advice, even if I didn't know what I was doing I went hard at it. Before long I earned the respect of my teammates, young and old, and the questions about who I was and what was I doing there faded (or 'disappeared').

At first, the odds of me making my first NFL team in this camp were off the chart. The numbers simply didn't work in my favor. My goal all along to show that I could play at this level, even if I didn't make the team I had to show that it wasn't for lack of ability. Hampered a bit entering camp, I didn't let on. I downplayed my knee injury. The day I reported the training staff wanted to take a look at it. Of course, they knew the day I hurt my knee and had every report on file. They knew I finished my season in Europe wearing a knee brace that could have fit an elephant and had just over two weeks of recuperation time between the end of the World League season and beginning of training camp. Not wanting to alarm them in any way, I told them the knee was fine and insisted I didn't even need a knee brace. And that was the last time we talked about the knee. I couldn't afford to allow anything to appear to be wrong. Instead, after each practice I performed my own maintenance. I studied my plays sitting in bed with ice packs covering my aching knee.

After three weeks of taking our frustrations out on one another, it was time for our first preseason game and my first taste of live bullets in the National Football League. Our opponent the Pittsburgh Steelers, we played on West Virginia University's campus. I saw no action until the last portion of the game. By the time I ran onto the field for the first time there wasn't a veteran in sight as they had all shut it down for the day. Playing well, it was easy to see that I belonged on the field against that left-over competition but ultimately I wanted to be out there with the league's superstars. While my ambition was way ahead of my reality, I considered that the only way I could approach playing to be successful.

Over the four preseason games I weekly became more comfortable and improved on the field. In the second game, against Jacksonville, I caught the first pass of my career. A four-yard drag route across the middle of the field, it didn't officially count because it was only preseason. But it meant the world to me. That catch would turn out to be the only one I pulled in, but still I made it all the way to the final roster cuts, just one week before the start of the 1996 regular season. I was still around after seeing a lot of players pack their bags and leave camp released. The last cut, the one that would get the roster down to its official limit of 53, took place the day after our last preseason game. Having picked up on my story early in camp, the media had followed my progress all the way through. They made more of a big deal out of my staying power in training camp than did anyone else. The coaching staff was probably more pleasantly surprised than anything because they could see that I actually had talent. Raw and yet in need of development, I showed I could definitely handle myself on the field. Despite my positive performance, it wasn't quite enough to make the final last-day cut; I got a call to bring my playbook down to the coach's office.

By this time we had broken camp and were staying in a downtown St. Louis hotel. The elevator ride down to meet the head coach in a room designated as his office was a long one. The disappointment was eased when I entered his office and got at least a little bit of good news. I had made a good enough impression on the staff that they wanted to keep me around. Coach Brooks told me I had made it a tough decision, but they were only going to keep three tight ends on the roster. That, however, didn't mean there was not a place in the organization for me. Because I did not have more than one accredited season on an NFL roster I was eligible to be on the practice squad. I first had to be released and clear waivers, a period where my name was on the wire and other teams could sign me if they wanted to, but if I wasn't signed I would be welcomed back in four days when the team filled its practice squad spots. From there they wanted me to continue on the development path I had started. Meanwhile, if an injury occurred or staff decided to add me to the roster, they could immediately activate me. I left Coach Books' office feeling a lot better than when I had walked into it.

By the end of that morning my bags were packed and I was flying back to New Jersey for a few days, waiting to clear waivers. On the way to the airport I talked to Pat down in Atlanta. He expressed pleasure that the organization wanted to keep me around. We both would have preferred I be on the active roster, but this was a start. In the meantime neither of us expected to hear much, so the plan was simple: enjoy a couple of days off before returning to work.

I never got to enjoy those days of rest. By the time I touched down at Philadelphia International Airport that afternoon Pat was already trying to reach me. Two teams, the Washington Redskins and New Orleans Saints, had contacted him and wanted to fly me in for workouts to evaluate my talent. We set an itinerary. First, I would fly to D.C. to work out for the Skins and then I'd head down to New Orleans. We wanted at least to give the teams a chance to see me in person. Even if nothing happened now it might give them something to think about down the line when in need. I never made it down to the bayou or returned to St. Louis after that first workout with Washington.

Once there, I spent about an hour on the field running drills and catching balls and then a little more time being examined by the training staff. Though I was scheduled to go directly to the airport to fly down to New Orleans, the Skins were adamant in trying to keep me in town. They conversed with Pat while keeping me around the facility. Putting on a full court press, they told Pat how they liked my ability and maturity. Though their 53-man roster included three tight ends, they communicated how perfect they found me for both their practice squad and position fill-in. Result? Pat and I talked at length regarding my options of staying or returning to St. Louis. New Orleans was never really an option because that was Irv's place of business and I needed my own space to establish myself. Irv and I working together might have complicated things. Both Pat and I had the same opinion on that matter. Coming to the end of almost an entire day at the Redskin facility, we made a decision: I would join the Redskins on their practice squad. Appreciating the St. Louis opportunity, I necessarily recognized this was business from my player perspective as much as it was from their side. Pat informed the Rams I would not be returning and I had one day to fly to New Jersey to gather belongings at my parents' house. In a couple of days I'd be starting my new job in the NFL as a member of the Washington Redskin Practice Squad. I moved into a small one-bedroom apartment in Leesburg, Virginia, north of downtown Washington D.C., fifteen minutes from our practice facility in Sterling, Virginia. My goal? By the end of the season I hoped to live my dream of playing on an active roster in the NFL!

Rookie Haze

I was definitely happy that I need not go through the traditional rookie hazing of NFL training camp. Having heard stories from Irv after his rookie training camp, I got a firsthand look while in Macomb. Example? Rookies are expected to know and sing their alma mater fight songs upon command. This normally takes place in the middle of the cafeteria during a meal. Any vet in the mood for some dinner music had only pick out the rookie of his choice and order him to sing. That player then stood on a chair in the center of the room, introduced himself to the crowd, gave his name, what school he went to and the position he played. After that: time to sing!

Another tradition, slightly less painful, is the rookie talent show night. Rookies are expected to put together an act, collectively or solo, to entertain the organization. An entire evening is set aside late in training camp for this momentous occasion. Some sing, some put together little skits and others just get on stage and make complete fools of themselves in one stupid way or another. Nothing off limits, even the head coach is fair game during this fun night- he can be spoofed just like anybody else. (It's not wise to do it but it can be awfully fun.)

Last but not least is the final night of training camp. That evening rookies can expect doors kicked in and buckets of water thrown on them and all their belongings. Some rookies are literally picked up by a bunch of veterans and carried, kicking and screaming, outside and onto one of the fields where they are tied to a goal post buck-naked. That night promises trouble. One rookie will put up too much of a fight or truly take offense at something and it gets close to getting out of control. Usually internally squashed at a team meeting the next day, you can rest assured it'll happen again same time next year.

The higher draft picks tend to take the most rookie-status abuse because of their large signing bonuses; the vets like to bring them down a peg or two. Once again, men playing games for a living sometimes act like little boys with too much time on their hands.

Practice Squad Duties

As a member of the five-unit practice squad my duties included all grunt work to which players on the active roster turn up their noses. Part of the team, I did everything as if I were on the 53-man roster. I lifted weights three times a week just like everybody else, but had the worst, earliest reporting time, because I was on the practice squad. Responsible for being in all meetings- team, special and individual, I took part in everything the team did. The only things I didn't do were travel when the team went on the road or dress in uniform at home; I stood on the sidelines in civilian clothes for those games.

My on field duties spread far and wide. Most important of weekly duties, I gave the defense the proper reflection of the offense they would oppose in the coming week. Whether facing a tight end that ran all over the field, spread out wide or spent time lead blocking for the running back, that is whose identity I assumed. I ran card-diagramed plays against our first team defense with a goal of providing a realistic look. That was a fine line in itself. No starter wanted to look bad on film during the work week so I had to walk between giving a good look and not going too hard. I had to have a feel for what certain players wanted but also get my work in.

The defensive linemen wanted me to move fast and let them know how I was trying to block them, with minimal head-to-head collision. Running routes was a different story. The secondary wanted me to push to the limits full speed. The most exhausting part of my day, a post or corner route could take me all the way up the field where I turned around to make it all the way back for the next held-up play. There was no rest for the weary and nobody wanted to help me with my job because it was beneath them; that is why practice squad players exist. With the same responsibilities in every special-teams-aspect of the game, I also had to follow the game plan put together for the week. Thus I would be ready in case I got called to duty during the season. Additionally, the coaching staff constantly reminded me that I was there to get better and that they were watching; trying to keep both sides happy was sometimes a big juggling act.

The best part about my job was that my biggest, long, physical workdays were Wednesday and Thursday. The other days weren't nearly so tedious or painful. Leaving the facility by 2p.m. on Friday, I arrived home late morning Saturday. On Mondays I lifted weights and watched film of Sunday's game. Tuesday, my off day, I didn't go within ten miles of the facility if I could help it.

After all of the years of struggling I was about to open the door and cross to the other side, my ultimate goal of making it to the highest professional level now obtainable. The fact that this was not the original road I had begun to travel and that I had detoured mightily to beat some incredible odds made my story that much more personally satisfying. Time to settle in and get my feet wet, it was no time to get comfortable.

When I reached the halfway point of the season, things seemed to be moving right along. I was a member of the hottest football team in the National Football League, still on the practice squad but making my contribution and earning the respect of my teammates on the field. At 7-1 we were sitting on top of the Conference and already looking forward to the playoffs. Though a long way to go (the last eight games on the schedule much tougher than the first) we were riding high. I remember sitting in our individual tight-end meetings and listening to the three active guys talk about how many victories it would take to lock up home field advantage throughout the NFC Playoffs. I thought it was premature but they were confident and they had been getting the job done to this point so it seemed like the right attitude to have.

With things rolling the way they were I knew I was going to remain on the practice squad for the remainder of the season unless someone got hurt or another type of emergency arose. Still, I found it hard to complain. I was in the NFL, on a winning team, making good money ($76k) for practicing during the week. One day I'd be on a roster if I continued to work hard, paid my dues and most importantly, it was in God's plan for me! I felt like I had finally turned the corner in my life.

Wednesday and Thursday practices were my game days during the season. They were my hardest working days and I got to show all of the skills I had by working against the number one defense. I went head to head with our defensive linemen and linebackers in the run portion of the day and ran up, down and across the field against our secondary during the pass segment. I gave the coaching staff what they wanted to see and the players what they needed to feel to be ready for Sunday. I continued doing my job and doing it well, earning every penny of my salary.

A Strange Feeling

About the only thing consistent in my life, whether moving through good or bad times, was that I was moving through alone. My relationship with Lee far distant, I had made it a point not to let anyone past the outside gate and into the inside. I kept in contact with plenty of women on a regular basis and my travels afforded me the luxury of having them spread out all across the country. Having left behind the hateful mentality, I interacted respectfully. Even after I moved on I retained contact, sometimes even counseling women in their new affairs.

I loved women but promised myself I would never love 'just one' again. I just didn't think I had it in me after all I had seen and experienced. And the fact that I was like a rolling stone, always on the move, made it easy to justify never getting attached. I know there were women who cared a lot for me, might have even loved me along the way. I also know that I had stronger feelings for a couple but I could never let them know that. It wasn't the right time and I wasn't in the right place. I could have continued on this path for the rest of my life with little regret, but that was innocently interrupted. Things would never be the same after the day I met Randy.

Immediately attracted to the young lady who was the apartment manager of the small community I lived in, I found she wouldn't give me the time of day initially. And why not? One: she didn't date or socialize with residents. Two: I was a football player; the athlete stereotype is a tough one for many to overcome.

At this point in my life I was really settling into being a good man. I had been in every club, had enough to drink, been involved with my fair share of women and seen everything there was to see out in the streets. It didn't interest me any more. One good thing about living the lifestyle I had was that I got a lot of things out of my system. Curiosity satisfied, I now enjoyed the quieter life moments. Perhaps nobody would imagine that my favorite thing to do after a long day of work was to cook a good meal while listening to music and watch a movie afterward to complete my evening.

Therefore, I didn't take it personally when Randy turned down my initial request to take her out to dinner. Still, it didn't stop me from asking her again a few days later! She must have seen the good in me because she said yes. That night I took her out to Applebee's, right next to the apartment complex, and after that we started spending a good deal of time together. Really starting to like this woman, I actually looked forward to getting off work to spend time with her! For a month and a half we got to know each other and then she dropped some news that took the air out of my sails. Her company had asked her to take a transfer to Charlotte, N.C. where she would take over another property. An advancement for her, she saw it as an opportunity she could not turn down. In less than a week she was packed and ready to get on the road; she left on Halloween night. The way I felt I knew I had to see her again, but I got a nonchalant feeling in return, even on the very night she was to leave. I almost held back letting her know I'd miss her, still feeling I had to keep the facade erected to protect my hard exterior. I did tell her, shortly before she pulled out of the parking lot, but I don't think she truly believed me. Even when I mentioned I would keep in touch she gave me a look as if I were merely blowing smoke. I guessed we'd just have to see if things worked out down the road. The odds were not on our side though; absence doesn't always make the heart grow fonder.

Everything seemed to fall apart after Halloween. The first couple of losses after our 7-1 start were nothing to be alarmed about as we were still on top of our division but when losing continued through November and into December there wasn't just concern around our complex, but initial panic signs. In the second half of the season we couldn't win a single game. Meeting room talk moved from home field advantage and the coveted best conference record to, with a bit of luck, winning our division. A couple of losses later it went from that to getting into the playoffs as a Wild Card. Finally, in the last week of the season we sorely needed help such as a win of our own accompanied by at least two other teams losing. All said and done, the 7-1 start turned into an 8-8 season; the team reversing its fortune by winning at least one of the final eight games.

I never made it off the practice squad that year and was almost glad I didn't. While I would have loved to have had an opportunity to help the team when it counted on Sundays, I was relieved not to deal with the mass finger pointing going on as the losses piled up. Monday meetings when we reviewed game film turned outright ugly toward the end. The coaches blamed the players for not executing and the players fired back under their breath, of course, about the game plan itself. Funny thing was: it all worked and everybody had been happy not that long prior. There had not been enough backs to pat then. Sitting back, I saw a team with a soft schedule overachieving at the start of the year. When difficulty increased people started in-fighting rather than pulling together. My observation may have not counted but it seemed accurate.

Road Trip

Off the field I was a lonely man that second half of the season. That was unusual for me because in my world I could always find ways to entertain myself. I didn't need anyone as far as I was concerned formerly. Just that fast though, I had gotten used to having someone in my life on a consistent basis and didn't mind her being there. Now she was gone. That should have, I thought, returned me to my old state, but it didn't. I realized how lonely I was during that period. It was not fun any more.

To combat the sudden loss I went out and bought my first computer, a used desktop. Even America Online wasn't enough to take my mind off North Carolina. I talked to Randy on the phone every night but that wasn't enough. Just a week after her departure I suggested I make a road trip down to N.C. After our Saturday morning walkthrough, the team flying out on the road that afternoon, I jumped in my truck and drove six hours just to spend a day and a half with Randy. I knew then that there was something more to this than I originally thought. I admitted to myself that I cared for Randy and that was the beginning of a hot and cold, on and off relationship that would take us through the next several years. Sometimes good, sometimes bad, always interesting!

Out of Gas

To review, my football season hadn't started in summer training camp, but a whole year ago that November when I began the rigorous task of body transformation. I had gone from playing baseball to my first training camp with the World League in March. The European season was split in half by the knee injury, and two and a half weeks after my return to the States in late June I was starting my first NFL training camp. After seven weeks of training camp including four preseason games with St. Louis, I landed in Washington on the practice squad. And now the Redskins were riding me like a camel through the desert, trying to get everything they could out of me. My body gave me everything it had, but by late November it ran out of fuel; there was nothing left in my tank.

I felt a small tweak in my groin after a Wednesday practice. I thought a little ice at home on the couch would be all I needed but I woke up the next day in more pain than the night before, not a good sign. Barely making it to the end of my day Thursday, I saw no way to hide this from the trainers. After our Friday practice I went in to see our team physician for some treatment. He laid me on the table, examined me and said he thought I had a hernia. By the time I left the complex I was almost unable to drive my five-speed truck. Every time I moved my leg to work the clutch I felt like someone had shot me. I spent that night with a big bag of ice sitting in my lap taking anti-inflammatory and pain medication.

Saturday only a walkthrough and the team on the road that weekend, I had the luxury of spending my entire weekend on the couch. After watching another loss I reported for work on Monday. Because the pain and discomfort wasn't subsiding, I began to worry as did my trainers. We really didn't know with what we were dealing. During another examination that after-noon the team doctor suggested a radical approach: start shooting it up with cortisone. I'd been through this before and knew the drug only masked the pain but what was I going to do? I had to be on the field! So, as the good soldier always does, I agreed to the shot, dropped my pants and allowed them to plunge a needle filled with cortisone into my pelvis.

As the weeks slipped by I got worse, not better. The only way I made it from week to week was with that weekly Monday cortisone injection. I'd take my shot, use the off day on Tuesday to let it settle in, and by the end of the week be right back where I started at the beginning of it- barely able to walk a flight of stairs. Once, after making it home from practice late in a week, I sat in my truck for almost ten minutes just to allow time for the pain to ease so I could make it to my second floor apartment. Another time, toward the end, I took two shots in a week because the first just wasn't doing the job.

It didn't take a rocket scientist to figure out where I sat on the food chain within the organization. The coaching staff knew the type of pain I was in, but pushed me even harder down the stretch.

Losing has a bad way of changing the work atmosphere so our practices became more physical and intense as defeats piled up. Injuries had a lot to do with our second half plunge and we were really thin at the defensive line position. To add insult to injury, the coaching staff started using me to fill voids outside of my normal work description; I was playing on both sides of the ball during practice to give relief to other players. My regular duties on offense and special teams were already killing me and now I had to line up at a defensive lineman position against our first team offense. No longer fooling myself, I knew what I was really there for, but this moved beyond inhumane. I had trouble walking back up the hill to our facility after practice and they saw this. I guess as long as they were getting everything they could out of me they didn't care. Finally, with one week to go in the season, it was decided that I had enough. I was to take the last week off. Now they were trying to cover themselves; if it were about me they would have sat me down long ago. I watched the last week of practice from the sideline and behind huddles.

Through this whole ordeal I was never again examined or diagnosed. Rather, they stuck with the hernia guess. I'd have to go out on my own after season's end to find out what had been wrong.

Slide complete and last game lost, we found we had made a bit of history; no NFL team had ever started off 7-1 and finished 1-7. The last meeting of the season, Monday following the loss, was quiet and somber. Coach Norv Turner was at a loss for words. Nobody had an answer for what had happened in the second half of the season. The only certainty was that a long and tough off-season awaited us. My sixth sense told me that my off-season would not lead me back to Washington. First priority now was finding out about my injury and healing. Then I would more than likely be looking for work again.

My apartment cleaned out and truck packed before going in for that Monday meeting, I got on the road and drove the two and a half hours up to New Jersey immediately following. A week later Pat had a conversation with the Redskins regarding my future with the team. They informed him that they were not ruling out re-signing me but that it would be in my best interest to explore all available options. In other words, they had gotten what they wanted for the season.

Regardless, I considered my first season in the NFL a success. The mission wasn't complete and I had to get healthy in a hurry if I was going take advantage of the momentum created. This was no time to slow down or let anything stand in my way or discourage me. Having sampled a small taste of what the good life felt like, I wanted to live it for real.

Diagnosis

What the Redskins tried to pass off as a hernia turned out to be much more than that. In New Jersey I sought a second opinion. Several consultations and an MRI revealed the pain's origination: the lowest abdominal muscle had detached from the pelvic bone. Two solutions existed: I could either undergo surgery that would require months of rehabilitation or hope that scar tissue would develop and partially reconnect the muscle. I opted for the latter. It might have taken a miracle for me to be healthy in time for the opening of free agency signings in the middle of February, but I didn't have much of a choice. Again I had to deal with the choppy water, relying on my faith to get me through it all one more time.

REDSKIN REVIEW
Volume VII Issue 6 / Week Two 1996

For Background Only

Smith Shows It's Never Too Late To Dream

By Rick Snider
Associate Editor

Darrell Green is an inspiration to 30-something fans who know they can no longer play pro sports, but still have contemporaries that can. Thus, they're not really old as long as Green can run down opponents.

But what about the 20-something crowd. They're only a decade or less removed from playing high school ball, but the struggles of establishing a career and starting a family mean they'll never realize their dream of playing pro sports.

Meet Ed Smith. At 27, he should be way too old to start over. After all, he hadn't played football since 1987 when named tri-state athlete of the year in New Jersey, Pennsylvania and Delaware.

Now Smith wasn't some computer programmer or professor who would need the kind of miracle that movies are based upon. He was a third baseman batting .323 last year for a Cleveland Indians Triple-A affiliate. But after nine teams, eight seasons and three organizations, Smith grew weary of playing baseball and retired.

"I was frustrated with baseball and ready to move on," he said. "When you're not one of the so-called 'prospects,' you start to take a second seat to them. I started playing behind prospects no matter how good my numbers were."

Offered a football and baseball scholarship to the University of North Carolina, Smith instead signed with the Chicago White Sox in 1987 after being drafted in the seventh round. He spent four seasons in South Bend, Ind., Sarasota, Fla. and Birmingham before traded to the Milwaukee Brewers in 1991.

After never hitting more than .246 during his first four seasons, Smith never finished below .259 afterwards. He combined for a career-best 72 RBI in 1992 at Stockton, Calif. and El Paso, and batted .294 in 1993 at El Paso. Smith signed with the Chicago Cubs in 1994 and hit .259 with 18 home runs and 60 RBI. He signed with the Indians last year, but played only 13 games at Triple-A Buffalo before leaving.

Figuring he would never make the major leagues, Smith (6-foot-4, 257 pounds) considered playing football. He called brother Irv Smith, a 1993 first-round pick by the New Orleans Saints for advice.

"I asked if it was a crazy thought, and he said I had the ability," Smith said. "I didn't think I would get too far. It was a long shot to begin with."

Smith played for the Frankfurt Galaxy during the spring, catching six passes for 36 yards and three touchdowns. Frankfurt was 6-0 with Smith, but 0-4 without him while Smith recovered from a minor knee injury at midseason.

"Once I put the pads back on, everything came back pretty well," he said. "I had to get used to pounding again."

Afterwards, Smith spent training camp with the St. Louis Rams before he was released. Smith said the Rams wanted to re-sign him to their practice squad, but he signed with the Redskins practice squad instead.

"The Redskins just wanted me to come to develop," Smith said. "You never know. I might be activated in a couple of weeks or spend the whole season on the practice squad."

The Redskins are already well stocked at tight end, but the NFL means "Not For Long." It's possible Smith could get promoted next year or even this season given an injury to the active roster.

Maybe then Redskins fans will have another contemporary to make them remember it's never too late to try something new.

Rick Snider covers the Redskins for the Washington Times.

His e-mail address is: rmsnider@erols.com or visit his internet-based bookstore at http://choicemall.com/dc/dc177-01.

CHAPTER EIGHT

Atlanta Falcons "The Dirty Birds"

Recovering from the detached abdominal muscle took a little bit of time as I'd beaten myself up pretty badly during the season. The free agent signing period began in the middle of February, providing a bit of a break, but I also had to stay in shape. I couldn't just sit on my butt for the next six weeks. I started the off-season in New Jersey with the family. Once it was time to start auditioning for teams I wasn't sure where my travels might take me and after the last year and a half it was time for a break in the action. Soon enough it would be time to get back out on the road.

So contradictory to his personality away from the business, Pat was an aggressive agent. He put in a great deal of time on my behalf calling teams and trying to spark some interest. With a training camp under my belt and four preseason games on film, I was now easier to market. A full season on the Redskin practice squad was more proof that I had some talent. I hadn't made it this far for no reason at all. As I had hoped and he had expressed confidence regarding, Pat started getting return calls from teams interested in seeing what I had to offer on the field. Toward the middle part of February three teams contacted and scheduled me to fly in for workouts. My itinerary would take me out to Kansas City and the Chiefs, down to Atlanta and the Falcons then slightly further south to New Orleans; the Saints were still interested in seeing if my talent matched my brother's.

When it came time to go out on my auditions I wasn't yet fully recovered. I was still very sore and it hurt to do normal, everyday things like walking up stairs. In fact, my leg would be a recurring issue for the rest of my career. Even when you heal you don't just leave these types of injuries behind. Like bad dreams, they return to haunt you when least expected.

By rights I should not have let the Skins off the hook as easy as I had. They were partially responsible my current condition. I take at least half the blame because I could have always said no to the shot or asked for a more thorough evaluation. As badly as they had treated me toward the end though, I didn't want anything to do with their organization. My injury work-related, I could have easily gone after them, had them pay for a surgery and even gotten compensation until I was healthy. That's not what I wanted. My desire was to play football for someone in the NFL. If I went through that whole process I'd first be taking myself out of the game for a long time because of the surgery and I'd be informing every team in the league that I was hurt. Rather than go that route I decided to totally self-reha-bilitate. I did that by resting for a couple of weeks and then a lot of heavy weight-lifting to try and force scar tissue build-up. I had learned that from the situation with my knee. While I had no idea if my plan would work or was the right thing, I didn't feel like I had much of an alternative. The gamble paid off and although I was nowhere near 100% when I flew out to Kansas City, I had enough mobility to get by. That, combined with my seriously high threshold for pain, gave me some hope that I could pull the wool over enough eyes to just get on the roster. I'd worry about what came after that when I got to it.

I flew into Kansas City and spent a night in a hotel directly across the street from Arrowhead Stadium, home of the Chiefs. The next morning I was picked up and taken to the practice facility where I met the training staff. They had quite the surprise waiting for me. Anything I thought I was going to keep secret was on a sheet of paper in the hands of the head trainer. My medical records were like a rap sheet and he counted every item off one by one. He asked me to verify the injuries and as I did he checked them off. They went all the way back to my broken hand in South Bend, 1989. It wasn't long before I was stripped down and lying on a table as they checked me out, one limb at a time. The last request was for an X-ray and they had a machine on site so we got right to it. By the time they were done taking pictures of me from the inside I should have been glowing from all the exposure. And they didn't miss a thing on the list:

– Right hand broken by a fastball in 1989 in South Bend.

– Right shoulder- operated on in 1992.

– Left knee ruptured MCL buried beneath a mountain of scar tissue from the spring of 1996.

– Left groin- never diagnosed but documented by the Redskins as a possible hernia.

Surprisingly, I detected no concern on their faces as they looked at the x-ray results. I just knew they had to be thinking somewhere along the lines of taking me out back and shooting me to put me out of my misery. I didn't realize then that the average football player that has been through four years of college and put any amount of time in the NFL was probably worse off than I was. I could actually be considered par for the course. Next on the list was my workout on the field so I headed for the locker room and got dressed.

I wasn't alone on the field; there were also a big name quarterback and wide receiver being considered by the Chiefs. Before the three of us got together I had my own separate agility workout to run through. Included were the normal cone drills, running in every direction, touching lines and backpedaling. I didn't have a full burst of speed, never have for that matter, but my leg held up enough that I didn't look like a lame horse on the track. And when I ran routes for the quarterback I did so without looking hurt and I caught everything that came my way. Finally done somewhere in the early part of the afternoon, I had a plane to catch for Atlanta. I hit the showers, shook hands and was on my way. The coaching staff liked what I had done on the field and gave me positive feedback. They also explained their situation to me. They had two very good tight ends on the roster and they were looking for a solid third to back them up. I fit the bill for what they sought and they'd be in contact with Pat to discuss the matter further. One down and two to go.

I was met at the Atlanta airport by one of the Falcon team equipment managers and we enjoyed good conversation on the 30-minute ride to the hotel. The team had just been taken over by a new head coach, Dan Reeves, and the roster was in a total shambles. For the last few years they had been under the direction of June Jones who ran the Run and Shoot offense, all pass and no run, and they didn't even have a tight end on the team. Coach Reeves was a big fan of using tight ends; he'd proved that while coaching the Broncos and New York Giants. The most encouraging news was that I was the first tight end coming in for a visit. That was even more reason to really put on a good show the next morning.

This was only my second time flying into Atlanta, the first being almost one year prior. Much had happened in that span of time but the feeling of déjà vu began to creep over me as we pulled into the Falcon Inn, my hotel for the evening. How ironic to be pulling into this parking lot as an invited guest of the Falcons when just last year I was there getting out of my rental car, looking for my first football opportunity with the Frankfurt Galaxy.

Settled in my room, I checked messages. While not surprised to hear Pat's voice, I was floored by what he said. The Kansas City Chiefs had offered me a contract! That was good news, one workout down and a contract already on the table. I quickly returned his call, again appreciating that he made himself quickly accessible all through the day. Because training camp was months away and this was the first few days of free agent signing, we were afforded time to mull things over. There was no rush to do anything immediately. The Chiefs knew I had other teams to visit and the deal should be there when I was done. There was no guarantee but it was encouraging to know that I could make a good enough impression to warrant an offer. If this was the case as we continued, it gave us the ability to look for the best-fitting job and not just the first available. In comfortable position, I fell asleep easily that night.

My interview with the Falcons stood in total contrast to that in Kansas City. Taking over a disheveled roster, Coach Dan Reeves had an array of holes to fill, tight end being one of the focal points. My physical examination was thorough but quick. The Falcons were more interested in what I could do on the field and not how many dings my body had. The workout was also different, a more intimate affair. The only player on the field, I was accompanied by the tight end coach and an assistant. I ran through agility drills, scrambled off the ground running to and around cones and then caught passes off of a ball machine. This was a very condensed version compared to the previous day's work. When done, I was off to hit the shower as I had the day before. I had another flight to catch.

After that shower I hung around in the locker room awaiting instruction on my next move. I figured everything would move similar to the day before. The Falcons would call Pat as the Chiefs had and talk to him while I made my way to

New Orleans. Hopefully, they liked what they had seen. A contract offer might be in order. The small bit of interaction with training staff and coaches in the halls and around the facility was all good. It would be nice to be a part of this organization; everybody seemed friendly and it was a wide-open opportunity. Since the coaching staff had just taken over and they were totally starting from scratch I'd be in on the ground floor.

Though I found it a bit strange that I was still sitting and waiting, I didn't put too much into the fact. Soon the tight ends coach, James Daniel, came down and took me back up to his office. He told me to sit at his desk, pick up the phone and punch the button for line 2; Pat was on the phone and he wanted to have a talk with me. Coach Daniel left the office and I picked up the line. My agent was waiting with good news: the Falcons were ready to sign me right now! I would be the first tight end on the roster, not the last. They recognized that I would be a nice fit within their scheme of things. Discussing the matter quickly, Pat and I viewed this as a no-brainer.

We couldn't have asked for a better situation. All I needed to know was where they wanted me to sign the contract. I hung up with Pat, knowing he was making the call to the Falcon front office while I found Coach Daniel in an office down the hall. A handshake sealed the deal between my new tight end coach and me. He welcomed me aboard and directed me to one of the administrative offices where contract business would be conducted. A few short hours later I was part of the Atlanta Falcon family and my dream of playing football in the NFL was back in high gear. I signed that contract February 20, 1997, one of those "happy days" that you never forget.

Now I had a little time on my hands. Pat had prepared me for the worst-case scenario, one that a lot of players face; I might not find a job until the last minute when camps were about to open in July. Having found a job in the first week, I had over a month before the voluntary off-season program even started near the end of March. There was no rush to do anything right now and I felt like I was sitting on top of the world.

With no immediate plans once I flew back to New Jersey, I probably could have just spent the few weeks up north and leisurely made my way down to Atlanta, but there was someone in North Carolina who I wanted to see.

Randy was doing well for herself and in her new position. She was about as surprised as I was that we had even kept in contact; both of us thought we'd just move on since we had only known each other for a short period of time before she left D.C. We hadn't seen each other but had stayed on each other's minds. Since I had a bit of time before reporting to Atlanta, and since North Carolina was on the way, I drove down early and spent some time with my 'quality girl'. This was trouble for anyone else I was talking to at the time because I started to realize what I was feeling for this woman; she was particularly special. After spending a couple of weeks with Randy it was time to go but tough to leave. It wouldn't be long before I saw her again though; I started commuting between Atlanta and Charlotte whenever I could, which was all the time. The four and a half hour drive between the two cities became a weekly ritual through the spring and into the summer leading up to training camp.

I was very frugal with my money at this time. All of the years of minor league baseball had forced me to be so. When you didn't have it you couldn't spend it and that was the case all the way through my career. I had gotten so used to scrimping and scraping to get from one off-season to the next that I didn't know how to live with money in my pocket. It was something I could get used to though.

For the time being I had everything I needed. The off-season program was totally voluntary with a hint of mandatory participation implied. There were incentives if you made a specific amount of the workouts but the most important thing was being there to show the coaching staff that you were willing to put in the time. My home for the next few months was to be the Falcon Inn and when I arrived at the end of March my old friends and teammates were in the home stretch of World League training camp. That is when I realized how far I had come in a year! One year ago I had pulled into the parking lot of that hotel hoping, praying and almost begging for a job. I now returned as one of the only members of last year's Galaxy team who had a job in the NFL. The baseball player who tried to play football was now the football player who used to play baseball. It was incredibly cool to see my old coaches and teammates and get their congratulations. And it was special because there was no way I would be where I was if I hadn't been given the opportunity by the Galaxy staff and been accepted by the players. My experience with the Frankfurt Galaxy turned everything around and started me on the new path when it seemed like I had made a big mistake.

A Little Satisfaction

I ran into a familiar face a few days after my arrival at the Falcon Inn. While my Frankfurt teammates were nearing the end of their training camp and preparing to go across the water, so were the Amsterdam Admirals who stayed in a neighboring hotel across the street. This year they shared the facility with the Galaxy, alternating practice times. Early one evening I left my room to grab a bite to eat at one of the restaurants on the strip. Pulling out of our parking lot, I headed for the main street and saw someone on foot. Not a Falcon teammate, I guessed he was one of the Galaxy or Admiral players so I pulled up next to him, put the passenger side window down, and asked him if he needed a ride rather than walking on the busy street. When he turned toward me I saw that it was one of the Amsterdam defensive ends that I had fought tooth and nail with last year. In fact, he was the one who stood over me and asked me if I needed an ambulance when my ruptured MCL had me flat on my back. He looked at and recognized me just as I realized who he was. Accepting the ride, he jumped in. Neither one of us acknowledged last year or the ugliness on the field. We drove about a mile together before he pointed out his destination. During the conversation he asked why I hadn't been on the field with the Galaxy and I pointed out that I was not there with them but with the Falcons. Deriving some satisfaction from letting him know that, I avoided gloating. God doesn't like ugly! I offered to pick him up on the way back as I was going to grab my food and head to my room to eat in peace, but he declined; he was going to sit and have his meal there. At least that is what he told me. I never saw him again after that day, but I'll always remember him because he is the one who 'made' me get up off the ground. And for that I thank him.

During the off-season I was getting paid (only a few hundred dollars a month but it was still money) to work out and get ready for training camp. The collective bargaining agreement in the NFL only allows a certain amount of organized work where the coaches are involved during the year and limits the number of days players work as well. Four days a week is the limit for player participation. Our strength and conditioning coach encouraged us to take Wednesday off to give our bodies a mid-week break but if we wanted to go four straight that was up to us. We had a specific program in order; certain days were weight room days and others were heavy conditioning days on the field.

The goal was to make at least 90% of workouts during off-season so as to obtain a small bonus and exemption from the training camp conditioning test that could turn grown men into little girls.

Our roster was taking shape, Coach Reeves filling necessary holes as the days went along. I was one of three tight ends by the time the NFL Draft rolled around in the middle of April. One more was added to our group in the third round and that would be what we went to camp with in July. Running last on the depth chart because of my obvious lack of experience, something in my gut still told me I was in the right spot. The collection of tight ends that had been brought together would eventually be close, almost like brothers, as we bonded and got to know one another. A fourteen-year veteran led the way. Next was a journeyman who had followed Coach Reeves down from the Giants, then our drafted rookie was touted as the next great talent, and there was me. It was the beginning of something special.

My routine changed a bit from time to time during the off-season but was pretty consistent. It allowed me to get my work in every week and spend just about every weekend up in North Carolina. If I took Wednesday off I'd leave after a Friday workout and get to Charlotte right about when Randy finished her day. Sometimes I'd work four days straight and leave on Thursday to make it a long weekend. Every now and then I'd stay in North Carolina an extra day, heading back to Atlanta Monday night. And then I'd finish my week Tuesday through Friday. However I did it I was dedicated to two things: the off-season program and what was becoming something of a relationship.

All the work on the field, in the weight room and traveling back and forth on Interstate 85 caused the time to fly by and before I knew it camp was just around the corner in early July.

The advantage of being in the organization from the start of the off-season was the advanced look I had at the playbook and the new system. Coach Reeves featured tight ends who had to know more than one position. We played a huge part in the running game on the line of scrimmage as well as off in motion and lined up in the backfield. It was almost like playing multiple positions. We had three mini-camps that spring/summer and I had a grasp on the system by the time our summer break was over. The degree of difficulty increases once training camp starts because of the physical and mental demand that becomes prevalent. 'Hell on earth' is the only way to explain every NFL training camp in which I was 'fortunate' enough to be involved.

The heat and humidity of a Georgia summer are enough to make anybody want to leave the state and never come back. Draped in full gear and topped off with helmets to make sure body heat has nowhere to escape, we pushed through one of the toughest stretches known to man. Coach Reeves knew how to reward his players for hard work, we alternated two a day practices, but there was no cutting back on the work when we were on the field. As I said earlier, our tight end unit was one of the closest knit on the team. All in competition with each other, the pecking order was established early and we all accepted our roles. Ed West was our fourteen-year vet and the starting job was his. The biggest concern with him was whether or not his injury-ravaged body could make it through the season. Fourteen years is a long time to be beat on for a living. Our drafted rookie, O.J. Santiago, was the tight end of the future. When he was ready for the game at this level he would take over the reins. How well Ed held up was going to determine if that came sooner or later. Brian Kozlowski was the journeyman most familiar with Dan's offense and his role was as the H-back tight end, playing off the ball and in the backfield most of the time. Then there was me.

My role was to learn to do everything from the line of scrimmage, off the ball and in the backfield. I'd need to know all blocking assignments, blitz pickups and routes. All of that would help me stick around if we kept four tight ends. It was a strong possibility but no guarantee.

The schedule got a little lighter once the preseason games began and the Dan Reeves era got underway in Atlanta. In the four games we played we showed signs of being a good team but it was going to take some time for us to gel. Our final record was 1-3 in the exhibition season, one of those games being at home against my former employer, the Washington Redskins. I caught two of my three passes during the off-season against the Skins and took great satisfaction in that fact alone. If they thought I was done and they had gotten the best out of me, I was going to prove them wrong.

I played in the fourth quarter of all four games after the starters and next in line got in their work. I tried to show the coaching staff the same thing that I had in St. Louis and Washington. Forget the fact that I had spent nine years playing baseball and didn't have years of experience on the football field; I could play in the NFL.

Again, I made it to the last weekend of training camp. And again the scenario worked itself out as it had last year in St. Louis. This time, instead of getting a call in my room to take my playbook down to the head coach's office, there was a knock on the door. Coach Reeves had an administrative assistant who made the rounds on foot, in charge of doing the dirty work of informing players he needed to see them. When I opened the door he gave me the news but made a comment that it wasn't as bad as I thought and that there was some good mixed with the bad. At first, I didn't understand his words but when I got to the office, playbook in hand, Coach Reeves released me but said he wanted to keep me around as a member of the practice squad where I had one more year of eligibility. It had come down to numbers again, keeping three tight ends instead of four, but I knew I was much closer than I had been last year to breaching the barrier and playing in the NFL. It was just a matter of time now.

The process was the same, a two-day separation of service from the Falcons, and once I cleared waivers I would rejoin my new team. This time around everything went as planned. There were no workouts to seek a better situation out there because there wasn't. I don't know what it was but I felt like I had found a home. I took a two-day break from football, went up to see Randy, and returned to sign my practice squad contract and get to work.

Down In The Bayou

Now, as a member of the Falcon organization, I was in the NFC West Division along with my brother and the New Orleans Saints. Our two teams were scheduled to play against each other twice during the season. In the fifth and final year of his original contract with New Orleans, Irv and his happy football marriage had hit a bumpy road. Irv missed nine games during the last regular season (1996) due to knee injury. Up until then he'd played in all sixteen games three years consecutively (93-95). He pulled in 45 catches in 1995 alone. The NFL, however, is a "What have you done for me lately?" society and the Saints displayed no loyalty for all he had given them. Pressure on for a big season in '97, the dreaded contract year, the posturing began early. The Saints wanted to resign Irv early and cheaply. His goal was to wait it out and stick them after a good season. If it didn't work out he might have to test the free-agent waters. For now, my team would face his twice. This would be a great subplot to my story if I were to play on the same field as my little brother. That was one dream we had discussed when this whole thing started. That would be something if it all played out to fruition, wouldn't it?

Though I had the same job title and description in Atlanta, this stint on the practice squad was nothing like that in Washington. A respected member of the team here, I was appreciated and recognized for the work I was investing. And although it was my duty to take the majority of reps on the scout team, my fellow tight ends never shied away when it appeared I needed a helping hand in carrying my heavy workload. Even Ed West, a fourteen-year vet, jumped in from time to time taking a scout team snap when he saw I was overloaded. I also worked with the first team offense on a regular basis, getting in on the weekly game plan. Right in the mix of things, I felt more a part of this team than at any time in Washington.

Coach Reeves is one of the best players' coaches in the game. A demanding man, he is also very personable and fair. Even though I was on the practice squad he knew and spoke to me every day as if I were on the 53-man roster. And I felt no different than any one of the other players. Strangely enough, which happens rarely in the NFL, there existed a big family atmosphere around our camp. While we had a couple of egos on the team, it was overall a very low-key, humble locker room. Almost everybody seemed to get along. And there was little division internally (the type of separation that mostly occurs between the offensive and defensive sides of the ball). That was important considering the season's start.

We were winless in the four football weeks of September and that trend spilled over to the first one in October, off to a 0-5 start. We were actually not as bad as our record but something seemed to fall apart each of those weeks. One week we'd score a bunch but give up more and another we'd shut the other team down but couldn't put enough on the board to claim victory. Morale was low in that first month; it was very disappointing.

I did what I thought was my part each week, giving the look and following along in case I was called into action. During at-home weeks I watched the games from the sidelines at the Georgia Dome and when the team went on the road I took my own trip up to North Carolina to spend a nice relaxing weekend with Randy while watching my team on television.

Our bye week came in week six (couldn't have come at a better time after the fifth loss) and the following week we were headed to New Orleans for our first meeting with my brother and the Saints. The game was on the 12th of October, the day before Irv's 26th birthday, so I asked Coach Reeves if I could fly down with the team and watch the game on the sideline. He thought it was fine and also allowed me to spend my time in town with Irv. I would return with him the following morning for the game and watch it from on the field.

Irv picked me up from our team hotel in downtown New Orleans and we spent the remainder of that Saturday hanging out like two high school teenagers – laughing and having a good time. The next morning we pulled into the New Orleans Super Dome and he went one way and I went the other, toward our separate locker rooms. Half the dream was realized that Sunday afternoon in New Orleans. I wasn't playing in the game, but my heart was still pumping and pounding hard as I stood on the sideline directly across from Irv during the National Anthem. I couldn't believe I was on the same field as my brother. And when Irv was out there during a break in the action he'd look over and give me a nod or thumbs up to let me know he knew I was there. While I was rooting for a Falcon team victory it was hard not to cheer for my little brother during his day of work!

The most important thing was that he come out of the contest healthy, but it wouldn't hurt if he grabbed a bunch of balls and maybe even a touchdown along the way.

Because both struggling teams could use the victory the game was a good one. The Saints came in 2 wins and 4 losses. When the smoke cleared and the dust settled Dan had his first win (23-17) as the Falcons' head coach. I hugged and congratulated Irv on the field after the game and we joined the group prayer at the 50-yard line, giving thanks for that day. Wishing him a happy birthday, I then joined my team in the victory. Irv and I would see each other in a few weeks when they came to Atlanta for the second match-up. And I'd be on the sidelines for that one as well. Our locker room was jubilant, it was good to get that monkey off our back, and I felt good to be a part of that first win even if I hadn't stepped on the field. I knew if I continued to work hard my time would come.

In the NFL there isn't much time to savor victory. The next two weeks brought us back down to earth. Midway in the season we sat at the bottom of our division with a 1-7 record. In our Monday morning meeting, after that seventh loss, Dan brought us together and challenged us. As he put it, the time had come to stop making excuses. So what if it was a new system and everybody was trying to learn it as we went along? So what if a lot of players were trying to learn to work together for the first time? And forget about the first half. Our character would be defined by how we responded from this point on. Do we lie down and continue to take beatings or get up and fight?

After that speech the team came out fighting the rest of the way through the season. In the second half the Falcons actually became one of the hottest teams in the NFL. And I got my chance to be a part of the action on the field sooner than later. The dream was about to be realized and I was going to play football in the National Football League.

We split the first two games of the second half, both at home, and then it was time to go out on the road to St. Louis to play the Rams. In this eleventh game of the year, I really hoped I would get my shot, but it didn't look like I would. I might spend the entire season on the practice squad again. I didn't travel to North Carolina that weekend as I was probably fighting with Randy about some nothing; we did that from time to time. Rather, I was sitting on the couch in my apartment watching the game when O.J., then the starting tight end, went down on the field late in the second half. It didn't look serious, but he never returned to the game after that. Ed, next on the depth chart, had begun to wear down a couple of weeks ago and it was getting harder for him to compete; fourteen years of wear and tear had caught up with him but he plugged on. He and Koz shared the tight end duties to finish the game, which we won 27-21.

After the final whistle blew I settled into lounge mode for the rest of my relaxing Sunday around the house. I enjoyed those times of peace and quiet and took full advantage of them. When I went in for work early Monday, the first thing on my agenda was some weight lifting before film study. When I walked into the weight room our strength and conditioning coach called me over to his desk and whispered that I'd better be ready because my time might be coming. I didn't know what he was getting at but he quickly filled me in. O.J. had broken a bone in his leg in yesterday's game and might be out for the remainder of the season!

I left the facility on Monday not wishing O.J. to be hurt, but finding it hard to contain my excitement about the possibility of standing on the sideline in uniform the upcoming Sunday. I didn't want to jinx myself so I didn't say a word to anybody, which was especially tough all the way through our day off on

Tuesday. On Wednesday, first thing in the morning, it was confirmed. O.J. would go on the injured reserve list and I would be activated on Thursday November 20. I'd become a member of my first 53-man roster! I'd take reps with the first team during practice week and preparation for our next opponent, the **New Orleans Saints!** That first time, a few weeks prior, when I had stood on the sideline in street clothes had been merely a practice run for the real thing! This time around, in my first regular season game ever in the NFL, I'd be wearing my uniform while looking across at my brother in his.

No way would an event like this transpire without my parents, so I flew them in that Friday. It seemed like a dream to me. I had imagined what it would be like preparing for my first week in the NFL, but nothing compared to the actual reality. The fact that my brother was going to be there playing for the other team was incredible. This was just too good to be true; stuff like this happened in the movies but not in real life!

Friday night, after dinner with my parents, I finished the night off with a study session in bed. Saturday morning my brother and the Saints came marching into town. I went to pick Irv up at his hotel after my morning walk-through practice. Next, we had dinner as a family and hung out at my apartment before returning Irv in time for bed check. It was hard to believe it, but Mom and Pops would sit in the Georgia Dome the following afternoon watching their two sons- one on each side of the field.

From June 2, 1987 my career had gone all the way from the Chicago White Sox farm system to my first game in the NFL on November 23, 1997. While I was third tight end on the depth chart, I was still expected to get some snaps during the game. Ed was on his last leg and Koz would need some help so I had to be ready. As the game started I stood nervously on the sideline waiting for my number to be called. Meanwhile, Irv would be on and off the field doing his regular good job. On our first posses-sion I was told to go into the game for a two tight end formation. My knees were knocking by the time I got into the huddle.

I remember the play like it was yesterday. I started on the right side of the formation off the ball and went in motion to the left. The play was a running play to the strong side of the for-mation, which I had just vacated. My job was to cut off on the backside, creating a lane if our running back decided to cut back. The play happened fast with a lot of hitting, spitting and grunt-ing going on and I was right in the middle of it. Trotting off the field after that play, giving way to a wide receiver coming back in, I smiled on the inside like it was Christmas morning and I had just awakened to a room full of toys.

As the game unfolded I participated in about fifteen snaps. Blocking and running a couple of routes, I felt like I truly belonged. On a couple of occasions I was in the huddle during a television timeout while my brother called me from his sideline. I felt like I was back in high school. I could see how proud he was to be my brother that afternoon; I had accomplished an unbe-lievable task and he liked telling the story! Maybe more than I did. All of his teammates knew who I was, some remembering me from when I visited him in New Orleans as a baseball player. To see me on the field playing for the Falcons was almost beyond comprehension. It didn't matter who won that day on the field because the Smith family would celebrate this day for the rest of our lives!

The Falcons did come out on top though. After giving thanks in prayer after the game Irv and I trotted to the stands behind our home bench where our parents were seated. We stood side by side in our uniforms for some pictures, then headed in opposite directions to our locker rooms. After a shower, my parents along with Pat and Amy from Pro-Files Sports, waited outside my locker room to give congratulations. From there, the group went around to see Irv and his teammates off as they boarded buses with their destination the airport. Later, I took my parents out for a victory dinner at one of my favorite restaurants, The Cheesecake Factory. That concluded one of the best days in our family history! They were headed back to New Jersey the following morning and I had a busy week ahead of me preparing for my first road game and another monumental day on this incredible journey.

Final Score: Falcons 20-Saints 3

As I check things off on the 'to do list' I replaced them. I try never to rest satisfied because there is always something else worthwhile to be done. Once I cracked the 53-man roster and played in my first game, I had to move on to another item: I wanted to make the box score. That meant doing something significant. Already living the dream with each day that passed that I could say I was in the NFL, there was no telling when the ride might end. I was here now and I was going to play and enjoy the game like there was no tomorrow!

In the very next game I checked off two very significant milestones. Ed West was having a terrible time with the knee that had bothered him all year. The night before our game in Seattle against the Seahawks, he made it clear that unless it was absolutely necessary or an emergency situation he would rather not put himself through the pain of playing. That meant Koz and I would share all the duties at tight end. The next afternoon, our first offensive possession of the contest, we took the field in a double tight end formation and I was credited with my first NFL start. Later in the game, I caught my first pass. The reception showed up in the paper the next day as a four-yard gain. To me I might as well have caught a touchdown in the Super Bowl. Along with my first NFL reception we outplayed Seattle that

Sunday and the second half push continued as we won our fourth game in the last five weeks.

Final Score: Falcons 24-Seahawks 17

The game against the Seahawks turned out to be the last time Ed West would dress in his career. His knee forced him to discontinue playing. He voluntarily moved to the injured reserve list before the next week's game in San Diego. A third tight end was brought in to back up Koz and me. I was now the number two tight end on the depth chart. We picked up another victory on the second part of our West Coast swing against the Chargers and I was getting extensive playing time. It really was true! I was a tight end in the National Football League!

Every time I took the field or looked around and saw where I was or what I was doing, I had to pinch myself. My new world was far to the extreme opposite of my old one in minor league baseball. We traveled first class, stayed at the finest hotels in town, ate at the classiest restaurants, and were mobbed by fans everywhere we went. Game days a frenzy of activity, it would have been easy to get caught up in all the hype, but I remained grounded. My early humble existence was forever embedded in my memory – along with the bad taste of truck stop burgers and beef jerky in the back of my throat. I hadn't come so far that I couldn't remember the difficult times which almost forced me to give it all up. It was all by the grace of God that I was there and I knew it could all be removed in the blink of an eye. So, I'd better enjoy it, but most importantly appreciate it while I had it. This was truly living the life.

As a team we almost made history with the second half of our season. The year prior with the Skins we turned a 7-1 start into an 8-8 finish. This season with the Falcons we came up a game short of doing the same thing in reverse. No team had ever started 1-7 and finished with an 8-8 record. We came home from the West Coast to beat the Eagles in the Georgia Dome before going out to Arizona for the last regular season game of the year. At 6-1 in the second half, we had worked ourselves into a position for an outside shot at the playoffs. We still needed a couple of teams to lose, but nonetheless, we had aspirations going into the game. Ahead late in the contest with victory in our grasp, we were that close to the record books, but the Cardinals drove the ball almost the length of the field to score a touchdown with four seconds left on the clock in the fourth quarter. The playoffs had actually slipped out of sight just as our game got underway when the Lions won and locked up that last playoff spot that we eyeballed so hopefully.

Still, the mood in our locker room after the game was good; we'd made Dan proud. In the second half we showed the character that Coach Reeves looked for by not giving up on our season when everybody thought we were a wounded dog. Our strong finish was something to build momentum on in the off-season.

I was also especially proud of what I had done individually. Five NFL games under my belt, I now felt greedy- I wanted more. I'd have to wait and see what the beginning of the off- season might bring. I didn't want to have to pack my things again. I was comfortable. I liked it here! But, you never know what life in the NFL is going to toss you next. If anybody could vouch for that I could.

Final Scores:
Falcons 14-Chargers 3
Falcons 20-Eagles 17
Falcons 26-Cardinals 29

New Addition

Our last game of the season was on December 21st, leaving me little time to get up to New Jersey for Christmas. That would not deter me. In all of my travel across the country and world through the years I still made myself a regular around the Christmas tree. Irv was also rarely missing in action from Mom and Pops at that time. Christmas has always been a special holiday season for our family, but this one would hold a little extra added flavor.

A couple of days after Christmas Irv and I readied to head back to New Orleans and Atlanta, flying out on the same day. I sat in the living room watching some television before gathering my remaining belongings. Irv and my mother stood around the corner in the kitchen having a conversation. Suddenly, I heard Irv call out, "Ed, you are going to be an uncle!"

The first question to my mind was which one of my cousins was pregnant or going to be a father. For a second I tried to figure it out in my head. Then, the little light bulb went off! In order for me to be an uncle, my brother had to be the child's father! I looked up to find Irv peaking around the kitchen corner, a huge grin on his face.

A young lady he had been seeing for the past four years in New Orleans would bring the next little Smith into the family. The look on his face told how excited he was at the prospect of being a papa and I was immediately happy for him. As I gave my brother a big congratulatory hug and held him, thoughts of my own son crashed into my mind. I hadn't heard anything from Lee in a very long time. I didn't know how my son was or what he was doing. His ninth birthday just a couple of days away; I was nowhere in his life, not even in thought. That hurt and I missed him so I pushed the thoughts to the corner of my mind and concentrated on being happy for my brother. I hoped he could be the father for his son that I had not been for mine.

New Lease On Life

Returning to my Atlanta apartment right before the New Year, I found myself with time on my hands. This was unusual because I normally packed up and moved on when a season closed. In no hurry right now, there were a few things I had really wanted to do in Atlanta if I landed the opportunity. The good news I received right after returning to the South now allowed me to do just that.

The news? Pat had already been in contact with the Falcons and, very satisfied with my performance filling in at the end of the season, they wanted me to remain with the team and offered a one-year contract to do so! Due to the collective bargaining agreement the deal was worth a little more than the league minimum, $250k. I nearly fell off my chair when Pat gave me the details. No reason to even think about the offer, I chose to stay. The very next morning I did something I hadn't done in ten years of living my life on the road as a professional athlete: I RENEWED MY LEASE! Then, feeling incredibly comfortable, I even bought furniture, appliances and dishware for the first time. And, I rid my place of all I had been renting up to that day!

Higher Education

Because Atlanta felt more like home than any other place I had ever lived, I had hoped to find myself staying there. I had great friends on my team, loved the area, and definitely didn't want to have to start all over again after a great year. When I got my wish, I put another plan in action. I had been talking to our Director of Player Development, Billy "White Shoes" Johnson, about eventually getting an education. Billy, huge in the community, pulled some strings to help me enroll into Georgia State

University (GSU) for the winter quarter. I was going to school.

GSU is located in the heart of downtown Atlanta and my commute was about 30 minutes without traffic. I took a medium-sized class load of evening classes, general and business courses. That way, once the off-season program started in late March, neither would interfere with the other. I felt like an old man at 28, taking first year courses with a bunch of youngsters, but that was beside the point. My parents were proud of me and I was proud of myself. Making the Dean's List at the end of that quarter was one of my greatest accomplishments.

By the time I finished first quarter at GSU our off-season program was just underway, the theme for the upcoming season-"Keep it going". Our strong finish of '97 was supposed to be our fast start of '98. My personal job through the spring and summer all revolved around getting into the best physical shape possible for the upcoming season. The body that used to run around on the baseball field, streamline and quick enough to play the hot corner, was now thick and muscular and there was no going back to what it used to be. I resembled the prototypical tight end in the league and I found it hard to imagine looking any differently even though it had not been that long that I scrambled off the ground to throw a baseball across the diamond.

I noticed that a hazard of my new profession was the fast aging process which accompanies the regularly occurring punishment and beating I now put my body through. The off-season is a great thing because it is a time to recuperate. And if you are able to do that early you may spend most of it in only a limited amount of pain. I was fortunate not to have anything major from which to heal at the start of my break. My status:

– Left knee probably looked like shredded lettuce on the inside due to ruptured MCL and the ton of scar tissue holding it all together.

– Dislocated left ring finger snapped back in place by myself on the field during the Seattle game so I could stay on for the next play.

– Right shoulder no doubt in need of another surgery after tearing it up time and time again.

– Countless other pulls, strains, slight tears, bumps, bruises and contusions that went hand in hand with life in the NFL.

I was getting off lightly compared to some of the carnage seen every day in this line of work. If you've never heard it explained this way, it might bring some light to what actually goes on during a season in the NFL: One week in the NFL is the equivalent of being in a head-on collision car accident. Imagine having one of those every week from early July to the end of December! Sound like that might hurt a bit?

On the same off-season schedule as last year, this season I wasn't staying in the Falcon Inn. There was another significant change in my situation. Randy had taken another job transfer to revive yet another property; this was now becoming her specialty in the property management field. She was good at what she did and her climb up the ladder came with choices. Having accepted the new position, she had moved to Columbus, Ohio. That eliminated my weekly off-season commute back and forth to North Carolina and put an even bigger strain on a relationship that was all long distance. While we tried to continue to make things work, it was tough. The distance seemed too much to overcome. This became one of our off times.

Many of us work hard so we can play hard. Money in my pocket and time on my hands to do whatever I wanted with any day I chose, it didn't take me long to adapt to my new lifestyle. The hours I put in during my four working days each week were followed by a routine of hanging out around my apartment and bowling with my two best friends on the Falcons- Nate Miller and Calvin Collins. Both buddies were offensive linemen, Nate having been with the team for the past couple of years and Calvin just drafted in the fifth round before the '97 season. The three of us bonded through the year, becoming inseparable. We tried to work out at the same time each morning during the off-season and then head to our apartments. Nate and I lived right across the street from each other, in different apartment communities, and Calvin was only a few miles away. Next, we'd rendezvous at a local bowling alley and spend a couple of hours each day competing on the lanes. Sometimes at the alley before they opened, we waited for someone to come and let us in. If any of us had an itch to get into something anytime during the day or evening each could count on a call to see if the others wanted to tag along.

Coincidentally, my relationship with Nate and Calvin was not unique on this Falcon team. Very little separatism on this unit made it unique in the NFL. I could walk into our facility at any time and hold conversation with any coach, trainer, administrator, or member of the team. Even the owner's son was seen in the weight room every now and then getting a sweat on and talking it up. I enjoyed a certain feel not experienced at my two previous stops – caring versus strictly work. While we worked our butts off in the weight room and on the field, we didn't mind coming in for the punishment as much because we were amongst friends. This good chemistry aided in our improvement efforts.

Bayou To The Bay

After five years in New Orleans Irv decided to leave the organization, testing the free agent waters and signing with the San Francisco 49ers early in the off-season. The Saints had offered a contract, but Irv felt he needed a change of scenery. Playing for an organization accustomed to winning appealed to him. During his tenure in New Orleans the team had never made the playoffs, their best finish an 8-8 record in his rookie year. Each of the four after that was a losing year, one of them a miserable 3-13. That had gotten to him. The move to San Fran kept him in the same division so that was a good thing because if I were able to remain in Atlanta by making the team we'd play each other twice during the regular season!

Many workouts and two mini-camps later we approached training camp mid-June. Thanks to the collective bargaining agreement, wherein teams have to shut down and give the players a break, there is a mandatory two-week period before camps open. My last bit of freedom until the end of the season, I elected to head to New Jersey to spend some time with family.

During that break we experienced the loss of my Aunt Barbara to a condition she'd fought for several years. The youngest of my father's two sisters, her alcohol abuse early in life caught up with her and she experienced kidney failure. She carried a personal dialysis machine while waiting for a transplant. As she waited, her heart weakened and her doctors advised that she actually needed a double transplant for any chance of survival. Both operations would have to be done at the same time as the risk of doing them separately was too great. She carried a pager which, when sounded, would signal that the hospital had found matches and needed her in for surgery immediately.

Irv had also come home from New Orleans for a few days before we both went off to camp. Just before we were both scheduled to fly out, Aunt Barb's pager went off; they had found matches and she was going to get her new heart and kidney.

Aunt Barb was one of my favorite aunties; she seemed to have the funniest stories from our childhood and told them to anybody who would listen. I really loved her. She had even made a road trip with my Aunt Betty, the oldest of the two sisters, back in 1994 to visit me in Orlando when I played for the Cubs. One of her biggest thrills was getting an autograph from Michael Jordan while waiting for me after a game against the Barons.

She was quickly rushed to the same hospital in Philadelphia where I had my 1992 shoulder surgery. By the time we arrived doctors were already working on her. When they exited the operating room and addressed our large family group, they provided a cautious thumbs up. Aunt Barb had come through the surgery well and her signs were good.

For two days everything seemed well. Then her body started rejecting the heart and she slipped into a deep coma. The family had to decide whether to take her off support or leave her hooked to machines. The difficult choice made, we individually entered her intensive care room to say one last good-bye. Aunt Barb, body still open from her extensive surgery, showed no resemblance of the woman who made me laugh a thousand times in my life. The roughest part of the entire ordeal, you never want that vision to be the lasting impression of a person who meant so much to you. After the last members of the family paid their final respects, the machines were turned off and Aunt Barb was allowed to peacefully pass over to enter the Heavenly Kingdom.

A day later another decision had to be made by both my brother and myself as our family prepared to lay Aunt Barb to rest. Training camp started for both of us in three days and funeral services weren't scheduled to take place that soon. There was no question in my mind that I was not going anywhere; the Falcons would just have to wait until I got there! Irv felt likewise about the Niners. My parents disagreed. They felt that Aunt Barb knew how much we loved her and would want us to honor our commitments by joining our teams on time. This was a very important year for both of us as Irv was joining a new organization and fighting to be the starter on the team and I would be fighting for my spot on the roster. Other members of the family, including my grandmother, all urged us to proceed with our original plans. They would honor our aunt's memory on our behalf. Getting on that plane and leaving New Jersey was tough. It was one of those sacrifices that goes unnoticed by a public who sometimes judges athletes by what they see without knowing what we endure in our daily lives. My family takes priority over everything else in my life and there is no way I would have made the choice I did without their support. To this day, though, I still regret that I wasn't present when they celebrated Aunt Barb's life and laid her to rest. I reluctantly returned to Atlanta and prepared for training camp with a heavy heart.

The Dirty Birds Take Flight

No one could have imagined the magical ride the 1998 Atlanta Falcons were about to embark upon. Our impressive late season play of 1997 hadn't made a lasting impression on anyone analyzing prospects for the following year. Predicted to finish near the bottom of our division, we were expected to be mediocre at best. Training camp opened and we got to work, focused on proving the seers wrong.

During that off-season there wasn't much movement at the tight end position. We were actually minus one. Ed West had called it quits at the conclusion of the previous year, accepting a coaching position with the team. O.J. had made a full recovery from his injury, Koz was still with us, and then there was the battle for the third spot on the depth chart between the late season replacement from last year and myself. While confident that I was a better athlete than he, I took nothing for granted, continuing to work as hard as ever I had. Keeping a positive attitude through the off-season, I headed into training camp feeling I could beat him out and make this team.

We got right to it from the first day in camp as Dan put us through his version of the cruel and inhumane punishment that we get paid to endure. An extremely hot and humid summer in the South, it was a good thing that Dan had a heart because somebody could have died out there otherwise. Over the first few days we were subjected to two practices a day, but he let up on that and we went to an every-other-day schedule; two sessions, then one, and so on.

With a full season under our belts, everything was much crisper the second time around. Familiarity and cohesiveness are great assets for any football team. Knowing the man next to you makes working together on a football field much easier. It's one thing to know your responsibilities, but another to be on the same page with those you work side by side with. Much improvisation goes on when you are in the trenches with little time to think when the bullets are flying. To know that someone's watching your back is a very comforting thing. Because of all the work put in during the off-season, we enjoyed that early and experienced it all way through the year.

Locked Up

For those with any doubts about training camp being hell on earth, I recount a little story about how I lost 15lbs. in ONE DAY! Toward the end of our two-a-day schedule, right before our first preseason game, dawned a day just like any other. My playing weight for the season set at 260lbs. by our strength and conditioning coach, I had beefed up a little with all my off-season training and entered camp at 265lbs. One never exits camp how he enters, part of which is the ease of shedding a few pounds. Mandated to weigh in before and after every practice, weight is entered on a little chart right next to the scale by the shower. This is done to monitor players as losing too much weight is just as bad as not losing enough. I got on the scale in the morning before practice and it read 264lbs. Then, I went out for practice

I'm a sweater. I know I get that from my father because I've watched him eat a bowl of my mom's chili with a towel on his shoulder, sitting next to an open patio door to catch a breeze, while wiping his face down as the sweat poured off. On a football field in Georgia, dressed in full gear, in the heat and humidity of a July day, you can't imagine how much water I lose through my pores.

By the time I came in, just two and a half hours later, I was down to 256lbs. I went up to the team cafeteria for lunch and took my food and drinks back to the room.

The small nap-time window before heading back down for taping is valuable sleep time if fit in. It feels more important than eating.

That day I did try to get something into my system, mostly fluids, then was quickly out like a light in my bed. The alarm sounded just before two and it was time to go back down to get taped for round two. When I got on the scale it read 258lbs.

By the tail end of the second practice I began feeling the effects of the extreme workday. I was having trouble concentrating and felt disoriented. My trainers were keeping an eye on me, obviously checking the weight chart before we hit the field, and whenever I came off to the side or had a split second, they had me guzzling water from one of the portable water coolers or squeezing it into my mouth from a bottle. The faster they put it in the faster it poured out of my system. When we finished that second practice and conditioning session, my circuits were fried. I felt like I was going to puke and could barely see straight, but I made it inside and got undressed in front of my locker. A sign that I was heading for trouble was my toes cramping and curling up while I tried to remove my socks. And I wasn't done for the day; I still had to lift weights. Out of my uniform, I put on some shorts and a tee shirt and went over to weigh out; I didn't want to be fined for missing that. The scale read 249lbs., minus 15 for the day.

I entered the weight room knowing I was going to have to fake my way through my workout because I didn't have it in me. Addressing my ab work, I moved to the floor to do my crunches. That was the worst thing I could have done. I started to go into a full body cramp. The first thing to lock up was my stomach, so I jumped off the floor and started running for the training room, out the door and down the hall.

I made it halfway there when my legs started cramping. One of my teammates grabbed me as I started to go down. The trainer alarm sent out, they came running for me. Having literally carried me the rest of the way, they threw me on the table. That is when my entire body turned into a big knot of water-deprived muscle going into shock. I screamed in agony as the medical staff, on hand during the dog days of training camp for just such an emergency, went to work trying to get IV's into me. I've obviously never experienced it, but I felt like I was giving birth to a baby. The pain would ease up providing a quick minute as my muscles relaxed and then I could feel the cramps coming back on like contractions; my body was trying to lock up. On the table flat on my back, a nurse searched for a good vein on my arm, a trainer holding me down and two others at the end of the table trying to straighten my feet as the cramps intensified. My toes felt like they were trying to turn themselves inside out.

Funny thing is, I was just one of many to fall victim that day; each of seven tables occupied by a player with an IV running into his arm. And yet another player was on his way. He had gotten all the way up to the cafeteria, then fell out in the middle of the room. When he arrived in the training room, trainers had to work on him on the floor because there wasn't a table available. Because it takes a while for the IV's to take effect, I went through a lot of pain for a long time on that table. A line running to each arm, my body received two bags at the same time. That stuff freezes from the inside out so I was wrapped in a sheet to keep warm. Like a mummy on the table, I lay bundled and still shivering. When the staff checked my chart and saw how much weight I was down, they insisted on inserting a third bag's contents so I remained on the table for a total of about an hour and a half.

The process complete, I sat up slowly with my feet off the table for a while before I hit the shower. Sadly enough, I had missed dinner and our night meetings had already started, special teams being the first, so I had to go grab a plate of food and plenty of drinks to go sit in my meeting while I ate. My last meeting didn't conclude until ten that evening and it wasn't until then that I could finally get in the bed to try to shake off the day's trauma. My reward? I had to get up the next morning and do it all over again!

Junior

On August 8th, 1998 Irv got a call from New Orleans. His girlfriend was going into labor and the baby wouldn't be too long coming. He flew out from Stockton, California, training camp site of the 49ers, and made it back in time to witness the birth of his son, Irvin Martin Smith Jr., early the following morning. Little Irv was a healthy baby and my brother, a proud father.

When he left a message on my cell phone that day I could tell how much witnessing the birth of his son meant to him. Both mother and son would join him in the Bay area once camp was over and the season underway.

Liftoff

Our 2-2 record during the preseason didn't do much to change the minds of the critics who considered our maximum potential that of being an average team. Dan, however, continued to impress upon us that we could be better than anybody thought if we played within the system and ourselves. He persuaded us that we were not as mediocre as the outsiders might believe. Two goals he set at the end of camp were: 1) To win our division, placing us in the playoffs and 2) To secure a home field game in those playoffs. He told us that if we got to postseason play anything was possible.

While as a team we played hot and cold during the preseason, I personally contributed and made my claim for the third tight end position and won it. I caught one pass for 14-yards in our third game against the Steelers and my role on the special teams units was increased as well. When the last cuts came at the end of training camp no one knocked at my door. I would enter the season wearing my number 86 jersey from the opening kick-off of the year!

The season opened with two victories- a road win against the Carolina Panthers was followed by one against the Philadelphia Eagles at the Georgia Dome. Dominating neither of those games, we did just enough to pull them out. An early break followed our 2-0 start as our bye week occurred in week three. Despite a lot of locker room confidence (maybe too much) a true test loomed when we returned; week four was on the road out West against the defending division champion, San Francisco 49ers and my brother Irv. Family bragging rights were at stake early.

Final Scores:
Falcons 19-Carolina Panthers 14
Falcons 17-Philadephia Eagles 12

Family Affair Part I – September 27, 1998

My brother and I could not be on a field without my parents being there, so they flew out to San Fran a couple of days before the Sunday afternoon game. When we arrived as a team early Saturday my brother picked me up from my hotel and took me to see Mom and Pop as well as my new nephew. He was the tiniest little thing and it brought tears to my eyes to hold him for the first time. It also brought back memories of the first time I held my son. After a family dinner it was time for me to get back to my hotel.

The next time I saw Irv was on the field for pre-game warm-ups at Candlestick Park. We Falcons were riding our two game winning streak and feeling good about ourselves. Planning to enter the game and dethrone the seemingly arrogant 49ers, we were in for a rude awakening. The Niners probably crossed the fine line between confident and cocky, but they had the right. An experienced team with future Hall of Famers like Jerry Rice and Steve Young leading the way, when they came out of their tunnel it was almost as if they had already beaten the opponent, the game just a formality. They looked at us as if to say, "What are you even doing here?" And when the opening bell rang they showed us what the old saying 'to be the man you've got to beat the man' means. They smacked us around the field that day as if we had refused to give them our lunch money and they wanted to teach us a lesson. The final score was no indication of how badly they actually put it on us that day as we did score a couple of times late, after it was already a decided game. I only made it on the field for about ten snaps; the tight ends took a backseat as we fell behind early and played catch-up the entire day. All done, Irv and I met in the middle of the field where he was all smiles. Round one had gone to him and his 49ers. They had to come see us later so we had a chance at redemption but there seemed a long time before that day. Our return plane ride was not a happy one and Dan was set to make some changes when we got together the next day.

Final Score:
Falcons 20-San Francisco 49ers 31

Coach Reeves tore into us in our Monday meetings. We had allowed ourselves to think we were better than we were. The 49ers showed us how good we were be by beating us up and down the field in every aspect of the game. One of our players actually lost his job after the game; one of our defensive backs was shown the door early Monday morning. He got his point across, singling out players on film and calling them out in front of the whole room. This was the most animated and upset I had ever seen Coach Reeves. I knew he had it in him but he had never showed it. This time he held nothing back. We had a lot to think about as we left the facility that day and when we reported back for work after our off day we got back at it with an intensified focus.

Using the San Fran debacle as motivation, we took that frustration out on our next three opponents, starting out by beating the Panthers for the second time in the early season at home. The following week was a road trip up to Jersey and the Meadowlands to play the Giants and that was like a homecoming for me. Family made up the biggest part of my fan club but there were current friends and even teachers who went all the way back to when I was a little boy. These were all the people that never lost faith in me when it seemed like I was going to die a slow death in the minor leagues. I felt like a superstar as the big group congregated near my team buses after the game. It was almost like being back in Pemberton playing for the hometown Hornets.

The last of the three victories came with a price as our starting quarterback, Chris Chandler, went down with an injury late in the home contest against the Saints. We held on late, walking away victorious against my brother's old team, but the price tag was hefty. Chris was going to miss at least a week of action. Next? A return engagement to the Meadowlands to play the other New York team; the J-E-T-S, Jets, Jets, Jets!

Final Scores:
Falcons 51-Carolina Panthers 23
Falcons 34-New York Giants 20
Falcons 31-New Orleans Saints 23

We marched into the Meadowlands for the second time in three weeks with a 5-1 record but we were a wounded duck without our starting quarterback, so we waddled into a straight ambush. Our backup quarterback, 44-year-old Steve Deberg, was more than experienced enough to back up Chris but the Jets' defense treated him like a piñata. They blitzed him from every angle, throwing everything but the kitchen sink at our offensive line. Never in the game, we didn't come close to scoring a touchdown, only managing a single field goal for the day. Humbled for the second time of the season, it would be the last time we walked off a field as the losing team for a long stretch.

Final Score:
Falcons 3-New York Jets 28

Chris resumed the helm the following week at home

against the Rams and we got back on course, finishing the first half of our season with a 6-2 record. We still didn't garner much respect throughout the league because we were considered a pretender. Supposedly, the biggest reason we were winning games was because of our so-called soft schedule. The 49ers and Jets had exposed us and nobody was to believe we were as good as our record. The second half of our season when we headed to New England was believed to be the beginning of the end for us. Then, when we went into Foxboro and put a beat down on the Patriots, a 1998 AFC playoff team, a few eyes opened around the league and people started taking notice of that new phenomenon, the "Dirty Birds". We were sitting at 7-2 and it all set up nicely for the showdown to see who would take sole possession of first place in the NFC West Division. The San Francisco 49ers (7-2) were coming into town for round two.

Final Scores:
Falcons 37-St. Louis Rams 15
Falcons 41-New England Patriots 10

Taken Away

Merely a spoke in one of the wheels of a big rig gaining momentum as it rolled down the hill, I averaged fifteen to twenty snaps a week at tight end, started on a couple of special teams units, and backed up everywhere else. Not shabby for an old baseball player, I continued to work hard in practice. That was still my proving ground. A young practice squad player on our roster, picked up right after camp on waivers from the Jacksonville Jaguars, assumed the job I had done not long ago.

Having played the entire season to this point without a catch, a majority of my action coming in short yardage and goal line situations, I found myself standing in the front of the end zone against the New England Patriots with a football in my hand. Touchdown! The game was already in hand late in the fourth quarter; we had been knocking on the door one last time. In our jumbo set, three tight ends, I was to the left, on the weak side of the formation. Six yards out from the goal line we ran some crossing routes and as I found myself in Chris Chandler's sight, he put the ball right on me. I caught it and just stopped in my tracks in disbelief, cradling the football like it was a newborn baby. But, excitement and euphoria was quickly removed when I saw a yellow flag hit the ground and a referee run toward the umpire to notify him that there was a penalty on the play. The call was illegal procedure on us and my touchdown was *taken away*. Sick to my stomach, for a split second I wanted to go get the man who threw that flag so I could shove it down his throat. The jumbo package was called off the field, but we did score two plays later after yet another penalty pushed us even further back. I was that close to the ultimate item being checked off of my list- it just wasn't meant to be this time around.

Family Affair Part II – November 15, 1998

Game two of the Falcons/49ers-Smith Brothers' Battle for Supremacy was considered a "Clash of the Titans". Even the fickle Atlanta sports fans started to take notice. Years of futility on the football field had left them skeptical, but they decided to come out and see what the hype was all about; it was the first football sellout crowd at the Georgia Dome in quite a long while. Mom and Pop sat front row and center after what was becoming a nice football weekend ritual: a family dinner Saturday night before watching their two boys play on the field Sunday afternoon.

That same look of invincibility in their eyes when they came out to face us, the 49ers probably didn't notice until somewhere in the first quarter that they were not playing the same team they had slapped around early in the year. We took it right to San Fran and when they punched back we didn't flinch. I was right in the middle of a lot of the action because our running attack was a big part of the game strategy. The outcome came down to our last drive, up by five and trying to hold onto the ball to keep it out of the potent hands of the Niner offense. Instead of sitting on it, though, Dan called for a long pass play that caught the defense sleeping, the result of which was a long touchdown up our sideline. That sealed the fate of our opponent. This shocking event, a big monkey to get off our backs, proved that we could do more than just play with the big boys. We could beat them as well.

At 8-2, a one game lead in our division, we began to see the light at the end of the tunnel. The goals set so long ago in training camp seemed in sight if we could stay the course. On this Sunday when we met at the middle of the field after the game Irv was smiling as usual but mine was obviously bigger than last time! Round two had gone to the "Dirty Birds" and big brother Ed. While this was our last meeting of the regular season, it was possible to meet in the afterlife of the post season if all the stars aligned properly.

Final Score:
Falcons 31-San Francisco 49ers 19

The little engine that could kept moving along on the tracks toward goal number one: a division title. Three more wins followed the defeat of San Francisco but the 49ers kept winning each week right along with us so we ended up accomplishing our objectives out of order. A win down in New Orleans on December 13 would help us wrap up a playoff spot but not guarantee a division title. The noisy Super Dome was packed to the brim and even though the Saints were struggling under Coach Mike Ditka, they were not going to lie down and let us walk into the playoffs. As the two teams do not particularly care for each other, it is considered a rivalry almost like a "battle of the South".

The contest back and forth, we finally took control late in the fourth and as we realized the magnitude of the situation a great celebration began on the sideline. Like Dan said, "Once you get in, anything can happen." We were in now and ready for anything! Incredibly, that win took us to 12-2 for the year. Never mind about our opponents or supposed soft schedule – what we were doing was simply winning football games! Riding high in our locker room after the game who could predict we would come crashing down just a day later when faced with some very frightening news.

Final Scores:
Falcons 20-Chicago Bears 13
Falcons 21-St. Louis Rams 10
Falcons 28-Indianapolis Colts 21
Falcons 27-New Orleans Saints 17

Heartbeat Of The Team

After a game on the road, our buses escorted by the police, take us from the stadium directly onto the runway where our chartered plane waits to fly us back home. There are normally about four buses filled with coaches, players, team doctors, administrators, media and whoever else gets clearance to make the trip. On this trip in the long line of people loading the plane I stood behind one of my favorite trainers, Harold. He held something strange in his hands which I recognized from the many times I had seen it on television. Harold held a defibrillator, one of those machines used to shock a heart back to life. When I asked him why he had it, he told me it was for one of the elderly administrators who had complained of chest pains. I didn't think another thing about it but found out the next morning that Harold had lied to me.

When I went in to do my weight workout before watching the game film, I saw a swarm of reporters hovering around the entrance to our facility. When they saw me getting out of my truck they came running. They wanted to know what my feelings were or if I had any information about Dan. The defibrillator hadn't been for the elderly administrator but for our head coach. While sideline coaching during the New Orleans game, Coach Reeves had experienced chest pains and shortness of breath. He said nothing to our trainers until after the game, so the machine was brought on the plane in case of emergency. Coach Reeves' wife, who made him go to the hospital when he got home, more than likely saved his life. He was immediately admitted for emergency quadruple bypass surgery. Suddenly, football became very unimportant.

Coach Reeves came through his round of surgery well but it was a tough week to concentrate on football. Assistant and offensive line coach, Art Shell, took over for Dan while he recuperated in the hospital for the first few days. There was no time-frame on his return and there was concern that he might not get back on the sideline for the rest of the year. Practice and preparation did not run smoothly. We were going to Detroit to face the Lions. A victory would allow us to accomplish goal number one and two on the list and a little something *extra*. A win meant the NFC West Division Title, at least one home game during the playoffs, and the *bonus*, a first round bye. The last was something we hadn't even considered at the beginning of the year.

Having completed our Saturday walkthrough, we were in the last meeting before breaking to shower and get to the airport when we got all the inspiration we would need for the weekend. In walked Coach Reeves, fresh out of surgery five days prior, to speak to his team before we departed. The room became dead silent as he was helped to the center, obviously weak and unsure of foot. Standing before us, he told us how we had come too far to turn back or falter. The fact that he was not going to be there was of no consequence; we were in good hands. There was no excuse for expecting and accepting anything less than success. A whole room of grown, testosterone-filled men was almost in tears by the time he was done. And as we filed by him one at a time on the way out the door, he shook every one of our hands. That emotional moment defined the spirit of 1998 Atlanta Falcons. We were a family.

Fighting like champions Sunday, we pulled out a late victory against the Lions. It was all about Dan that day. During our celebration in the locker room we got a phone call from him in Atlanta where he had watched the action from the comfort of his living room. He was proud of us. I don't know about the rest of my teammates, but I felt like I had reverted to early days of childhood hearing his voice over the speaker in the middle of that room. It was like I had done a job well and my father was letting me know that I had found favor in his eyes.

Final Score:
Falcons 24-Detroit Lions 17

Our final weekend of the season at home against Dan Marino and his Miami Dolphins posed a chance to do something never done in all the franchise's years. A win would complete the first undefeated home season (8-0) in Falcon history. "Dirty Bird" mania gripped the city. In the previous year and through this remarkable run, the city's skepticism prevailed – thousands of seats empty in a dome that held 72,0000 spectators. I recall two games from the 1997 season (when the Tampa Bay Buccaneers and Oakland Raiders came to town) in which the stands were filled with more of their fans than ours. Those were like playing road games at home. This game only our second sellout of the year, San Francisco being the other, electricity filled the air. Inspired by the return of Coach Dan Reeves, who sat in a booth upstairs only two weeks after his quadruple bypass, we marched past the playoff-bound Dolphins and achieved our perfect season at home!

Our theme song, a very unusual one to be played in an NFL stadium right before kickoff, was "I Believe I Can Fly" by R. Kelly. In so many words, the song said everything there was to say about our team- everything the "Dirty Birds" believed. Our 1-7 start from the previous season proved beneficial to forming our humble nature. I couldn't believe what I had become a part of, but here I was, a member of the NFC West Division Champions. With a 14-2 overall record we were winners of our last nine games of the season. And like Dan had said, "Once you are in, anything can happen!"

Final Score:
Falcons 38-Miami Dolphins 16

The Minnesota Vikings were an equally big story in the NFL that season. Top team in the league with a 15-1 record, their only loss came in Week Nine to the Tampa Bay Buccaneers, 24-27. Randy Moss, in his rookie year, along with Chris Carter and Randal Cunningham had set a new standard for scoring; their season total of 556 points was a new NFL record. We joined them as the other NFC team lucky enough to have the bye week but they had the advantage of home field throughout the playoffs. Bye week was crucial as it allowed for a week of rest after a long grueling season and meant one less game on the road to the Super Bowl. Because Dan gave us plenty of well-deserved time off that week, I sat on my couch the following weekend rooting for my brother and his 49er teammates as they took on the Packers. A Niner win would set up a third meeting between us. In Irv's six years in the league this was his first post-season and it would be something else if we met up for the season rubber match to see who would go to the NFC Championship game.

(12-4) San Francisco 49ers defeat (11-5) Green Bay Packers 30-27

(9-7) Arizona Cardinals defeat (10-6) Dallas Cowboys 20-7

A Little Extra Incentive

The ultimate goal in the NFL is to win the Super Bowl but the extra incentive is certainly the money. Each round in the playoffs represents unplanned bonus money. The reward for our bye week was a $12,500 check. For a time, during my minor league baseball days, that was more than I made in an entire year on the field. The following week of playoff football was worth $15k, and the Conference Championship game $17,500. The Super Bowl purse jumped all the way up to $34k to the loser and a mind-blowing $50k to the winner. If that wasn't enough to get you motivated, nothing was.

Family Affair Part III – January 9, 1999

The San Francisco win meant round three. At stake was a chance to take one step closer to the single most-watched event each year, the Super Bowl. After a nail biter against the Packers on the West Coast the 49ers had to jump all the way across the country to face a rested Falcon squad. This weekend was a magical moment in our family history. My parents were on a cloud as this was the third time they would watch their two sons' teams play in one year. It was a little agonizing for them because they did not want to pick sides, knowing this game meant a lot to both my brother and me. Mom, admittedly, had rooted for my side in the second match-up of the year because Irv had won so decisively the first time out but this time she was perplexed.

The game was an instant classic. The old guard fought to keep their title while the new kids on the block looked to knock them off. As the game played itself out, my stomach was in knots on the sideline and on the field. I'm sure my parents were just as bad off as my brother and I were. When the last whistle blew only two points separated the winner from the loser: Falcon's magical season continued while the 49ers season came to an end that afternoon. The Dirty Birds were moving on to face the high-powered Vikings up in Minnesota to decide who represented the NFC in the Super Bowl. Irv hugged me on the field after the game and promised to be in the stands supporting me next week. Next stop: Minnesota!

Final Score:
Falcons 20-San Francisco 49ers 18

NFC Championship Game – January 17, 1999

We went into the title game on the road as an eleven-point underdog. With fifteen victories under our belt that little amount of respect still remained the only type which we seemed worthy. About the *only* people who believed we had a chance were those on our field in Atlanta.

The Metrodome in Minneapolis is one of the noisiest and most intimidating stadiums in all of professional sports. The fans seem like they are almost on top of you and the noise has nowhere to go as the domed top reverberates it right back to the center of the field. To combat those factors, we worked on a silent snap count. All week we prepared by running our offense between two large speakers. Cranked to full capacity whenever we huddled and through the plays we ran, blaring out of them was something that simulated a frenzied horde of rowdy fans, the equivalent of standing next to an airplane engine as it roared.

The plan was simple. When Chris walked to the line he and the line would communicate blocking assignments and blitz pickups by yelling and pointing. The offensive line would be responsible for passing the information down the line until it got to the last man. Once all necessary information was translated, the center would put his head down (seeming to look back between his legs) and lift it back up. The ball would then be snapped a count later if the call were on one. In an attempt to keep the defense honest there was also a two-count version. Our center would simply repeat the head down and up a second time before snapping the ball. The key for the offensive line was to watch his head and try to go off the center's cadence. The tricky part for the tight ends was the fact that we were the farthest from the ball and it was tough to peek all the way down to see what was going on with a man across the line. Even more difficult was the position I would be in a great deal that day, off the ball in a wing position or on the move across the formation. Without a visual of what was going on, I was at least a second behind all those capable of observing our center's movements, including the defense.

Coach Reeves, who had gotten full clearance to be back on the sideline before the San Francisco game, put all this in place. Fumbling with it during the early part of the practice week, we had it down when it came time to fly to Minnesota. Though we were in for the fight of our lives, Dan had us believing in ourselves even if no one else did.

My role and participation in our offense had increased due to the loss of our fullback, Bob Christian, a few weeks prior. Koz had stepped into his role as the lead blocker for Jamal Anderson, which meant I was the second tight end. Our practice squad tight end had also been activated in case of extreme emergency.

Irv sat in the stands when we took the field that Sunday afternoon but, of course, the sea of purple-clad fans there to see their Vikings destroy us on the field swallowed him up. The section of supporters from Atlanta was so small they could not readily be seen.

Can You Hear Me Now?

If not for the brilliant plan, the silent count that Dan came up with, it would have been on the other side of impossible for us to get off a single snap in the Metrodome. The crowd noise was beyond deafening. At the opening kickoff I yelled at the top of my lungs on the sideline just to see if I could hear myself. I could not. Before I went on to the field for the first time I tried a little trick; I put tape over the ear holes of my helmet to see if I could stop the noise from penetrating. That only made it worse! The noise blasted into my helmet and, with nowhere to go, rattled inside. I quickly removed it. No, there was no escaping the ferocious clamor of the screaming fans and loud Viking horns blown throughout the domed stadium.

Unintimidated by the Viking team, we stayed even with them through the first period of play with a 7-7 score. Then, the wheels seemed to fall off our wagon as the Vikings capitalized on our mistakes and jumped out to a 20-7 lead late in the second quarter. They were going for our throat, deep in our territory, when our defense forced a fumble to give us one last chance to close the gap before the intermission. A long drive culminated in a momentum-shifting touchdown to breathe life back into our team. At the end of the first half the score was 20-14, advantage Vikings.

With one half of a football game separating us from a trip to the Super Bowl, we rallied the troops in the locker room in the most intense twenty minutes I've ever experienced in sports. We had put doubt into the hearts of the Vikings. They had expected to run over us and had almost done that in the second quarter.

When we pulled closer to them at the close of the period there was a different look in their eyes. You could tell they knew they were in for a fight to the end. There would be no easy win on this day.

Back on the field to start the second half, a sense of frustration was setting in on their sideline and on the field. Neither team crossed the opposing goal line in the third quarter and only we managed to put points on the board, a field goal pulling us within three points and pushing the score 17-20. Halfway through the fourth, the Vikings scored a touchdown and we followed that up with another field goal to make the deficit seven points; the score was 20-27. With the ball in their hands and the clock their friend, the Vikings started to wear our defense down with a steady dose of running the ball right up our gut. Minnesota, deep in our territory with just over a couple of minutes left on the clock, looked to seal our fate. Having come so close we were apparently going to come up just a little short of pulling off the miracle.

The Vikings drive stalled on our 21-yard line and out came their veteran kicker, Gary Anderson, to put us out of our misery. A successful kick with that little amount of time left would put the game out of reach. Considered automatic, he hadn't missed a field goal in two years and was a perfect 39 for 39 during this regular season. As the Vikings lined up, I walked in the direction opposite of where the ball that was going to end our season was headed. Helmet in hand, I started to feel the weight of the moment. We'd had a great season, but it was about to come to an end. We didn't have anything to be ashamed of after all we had put together. We weren't even supposed to be here in the first place, according to the experts.

Everything moved into slow motion mode as the ball was snapped and Gary made his approach. From my standing angle the ball looked like it was dead center, but then began to hook a little to the left. As I leaned with the ball, it seemed to float in the direction I tilted. As it passed the uprights wide left, a mighty roar was heard on our sideline while the rest of the stadium of 65,000 fans let out a huge moan of disbelief. Gary Anderson had missed the kick! We were still alive! We had one chance to move the ball 71 yards for a touchdown that would send the game into overtime.

Our season had come down to this *one* drive with 2:07 left in regulation. In dramatic fashion, Chris led our offense down to the Viking sixteen-yard line with seconds left on the clock. On the eighth play of the drive he connected with Terance Mathis, one of our wide receivers, right at the goal line for a touchdown. The extra point was added and the Vikings and their fans were stunned! After the ensuing kickoff they knelt on the ball and accepted overtime as the period in which this game and championship would be decided.

Winning the coin toss, the Viking offense would get first crack at winning the game in sudden death. Overtime became a seesaw affair as the Vikings failed to score on two offensive possessions and we failed on our first. The game took a turn in our favor when O.J. made a spectacular catch and run up our sideline and into Viking territory. A few plays later we sat in the same exact spot, going in the same direction as the Vikings had when Gary Anderson missed the field goal that would have effectively ended the game in the fourth quarter. Our field goal unit called into action, I ran out on the field as the left wing to see if we could complete the upset. As we lined up, the Vikings called a timeout, attempting to rattle our kicker, one of the most prolific, Morten Anderson. We were one play away from the "Promised Land".

In that huddle, every one of us was nervous. Before the

end of the timeout we got our last instructions: NO PENALTIES. No one wished to move early or hold a defender and warrant a flag from one of the referees. My job as left wing was one of the tougher. I first had to step down to protect the inside gap between myself and the end then step back outside with a solid left hand to impede the man screaming around the corner diving to block the kick. As I settled in my stance the ready call was given and I could feel my heart beat through my shoulder pads. With 3:22 left in the first overtime, the ball was snapped. Unlike watching their field goal unit from the sideline earlier, this play transpired in warp speed, not slow motion. I stepped down firmly to secure the inside gap, made it back out to get a good piece of the missile racing around the corner, and finally peeled back deep in case the kick was blocked. The ball cleared the line of scrimmage and from the second it did I had the perfect view. It soared right down the middle of the field and cleared the goal post. THE FALCONS WERE GOING TO THE SUPER BOWL FOR THE FIRST TIME IN THE 33-YEAR HISTORY OF THE FRANCHISE!

Final Score:
Falcons 30-Minnesota Vikings 27

I felt like I jumped ten feet off the ground with my hands high above my head as the ball soared through the air and came to rest in the net behind the goal posts. The crowd formerly screaming at the top of its collective lungs went dead silent as I turned and started running in the direction in which Morten had taken off in his excitement. The first person I ran into was Koz. Leaping into the air simultaneously, we caught each other mid-flight in a hug, and landed on the hard Metrodome turf with a thud. Complete pandemonium broke out on the field as I bounced from teammate to teammate, yelling and hugging in a frantic state. When our jubilance finally subsided hats were quickly handed out, scribed with the words 'Atlanta Falcons, NFC Champions'! The reality of what we had just done finally hit me as I stood with my best friend, Calvin. We both started crying in each other's arms.

The dazed Minnesota fans remained in the stands, disbelieving the truth of what they had just witnessed. A stage quickly erected in the middle of the field indicated it was time for presentation of the championship trophy. It was also time for Coach Reeves to honor a bet that he had made with the team. If we won the game he was to perform the "Dirty Bird" dance onstage. Surrounded by players, he put his best foot forward, began to dance, and the party was on!

When we finally hit the locker room, more hugs and congratulations were handed out. I have never in my life seen so many grown men crying at once, but it was totally acceptable considering the circumstances. Then, Dan finally got our attention to say something that will stick with me for the rest of my life. He said he wanted us to savor this moment but to also realize one thing, "As good as you feel at this very moment, enjoy it and remember it. It is the highest of the highs. But, if we don't finish what we set out to do in two weeks you will experience the lowest of the lows." He was speaking from experience after having lost three Super Bowls as head coach of the Denver Broncos (Super Bowl XXI, XXII and XXIV). Coincidentally, we would face his old team in Super Bowl XXXIII. (They had defeated the New York Jets in the AFC Championship game later in the day, after our victory, 23-10.)

By the time I was showered and dressed I had cried enough to last me a long time. Waiting for me outside was Irv, standing near our buses. As I first approached him, he flashed one of his huge smiles. Then, the tears streamed down his cheeks. We hugged in that parking a long time but I couldn't muster another tear; I was all dried out. Irv stayed with me until it was finally time for us to load up and get the airport so we could return to Atlanta. The plan was already in place. I would fly my parents in and Irv would spend the whole week with us in Miami for the Super Bowl festivities. I called Mom and Pops as we pulled out of the Metrodome and felt I had conquered the world by the time we ended our conversation. Life just kept getting better and better.

Shining Moments

I had not been a mere spectator during this remarkable game, but had both made my way on and off the field all day and made my way into the statistics with my second catch of the year. I caught a pass from Chris late in the third quarter down near the Viking goal line. We ran a bootleg to our right and Chris used me as an outlet with a man in his face. I was hit immediately after catching the ball and almost managed to get away from the defensive back that had gotten a hold of me around my legs. Just as I was about to break free I took shots from two linebackers closing hard and fast. A small contribution, it served as proof that I was out there battling with my teammates.

And later in the game I had to convert from an offensive to defensive frame of mind in an instant. In a dual tight end formation, O.J. and I were both up field en route. After catching a pass O.J. fumbled the ball, a Viking defender scooped the pigskin up in-stride and started toward our end of the field. I peeled back and once again made my presence felt with a solo tackle on our sideline. Again, not bad for an ex-minor league baseball player!

Our return to Atlanta was not what we were used to during the regular season. On any other given Sunday that we returned from the road, I could walk through the terminal unnoticed by a single soul. When our plane pulled to the gate this time we could already see the huge number of fans waiting to shower us with love. Crowding around waiting there may have been a thousand fans along with reporters from every radio and television station in the Atlanta area. In this madhouse even a lowly worker bee like myself was bombarded. I had cameras and microphones in my face while fans reached out to shake a hand or offer a congratulatory pat on the back. It was quite a while before I made it through the crowd and to my truck.

By the time I walked into my apartment late that evening I was exhausted. It had been a very long day packed with excitement but if I thought it was all over and that peace and quiet awaited me the remainder of the night, I was mistaken. My home phone voice mail was full (twenty messages) and the phone rang off the hook well into the early morning. It was funny how many people had come out of the woodwork. The first thing a lot of my callers wanted to do was congratulate me but the next was to pose the Super Bowl ticket request. I was only to have a few and I'd have to pay for those myself so some dreams were shattered. It was to be hectic leading up to our departure for Miami in two weeks.

With a bye week between the NFC title game and Super Bowl the excitement around the city was incredible. As players we wanted to get right to the game; the extreme hype and wait were excruciating. Coach Reeves and his staff worked on the game plan during that week and we practiced lightly. Once in Miami the week before the game we'd go back to work full speed. Coach had warned us about not getting too distracted with all the in-town attention and demands. It was tough! Calvin and I spent a lot of our free time preparing for our departure by shopping for all the essentials; cameras and camcorders to capture the experience and clothes to make sure we looked clean when we got there. We could go very few places in that city of over four million without someone noticing us and making a fuss.

On Saturday, the night before we flew to Miami, I got a surprise knock on my door- several friends from my apartment complex. They had all come over to see me off in style, drinks and food in hand. They stayed as long as we could justify playing loud music in my second story apartment, then left me to pack and get ready for the biggest week of my sporting life.

The next day the team met at the facility to get on buses which were to transport us to the airport. A parade was scheduled for us, win or lose, when we got back into town so Coach didn't want any of us driving to the airport individually. Also planned: a detour through downtown Atlanta and Centennial Park en route to the airport to give the thousands of fans who wanted to wish us good luck a chance to do so. As we made our way south on Interstate 85 fans that couldn't wait to see us stood on overpasses and outside parked cars waving flags and honking horns in support of their "Dirty Birds". I videotaped the whole amazing ride from my window on the bus. The park itself was so packed with fans that our police escort was the only possible way through the crowd. Faces were painted, banners were displayed and everyone wore Falcon red and black. This was fan support at its finest.

The Royal Treatment

When we got to Miami the red carpet was pulled out. Everything was first class, nothing spared. Every player got his own suite; no roommates on this trip! And, we all drove our own rental cars for the week. Besides our individual rooms, we also each had another room for guests. Mine was used by my parents.

Additionally, two more rooms were available at neighboring hotels if needed. Separate entrance and service elevator available solely to players meant we did not have to walk through the lobby and all the fans during our stay. And, when we traveled as a team to and from practice, we had a police escort that stopped anything moving so as to provide a straight shot to our practice facility at the University of Miami. To top it off, twice during the week after knocks on my suite door, bags were set inside. One was from Reebok and the other compliments of Nike. They were filled to the top with shoes, sweat suits, tee shirts, jackets and hats. The first time it happened I stopped the delivery man before he closed the door and told him he was making a mistake as I already had all of my personal baggage. He asked me my name and when I told him he said, "The bag is a gift for you." That was all I needed to hear- I accepted!

Media Day

After an off day on Monday, Tuesday was our last chance to take a breath before getting down to business. The first part of that day was Media Day and the rest we would have to ourselves. A bus picked us up in the morning and drove us to Pro Player Stadium where we dressed in our game pants and jerseys to prep for media coming from almost every nation on the globe. It was a huge free-for-all in which I walked around the field and sat in the stands with my camcorder filming the crews filming us. I also did interviews and gave sound bites to radio and television stations from around the world, including one for my old home city, Frankfurt, Germany. I joked with Stuart Scott from ESPN and rubbed elbows with people from Comedy Central to the FOX network.

The week was almost too much to handle as more media demands came from everywhere. Once we started practicing on

Wednesday we still had media obligations at the hotel in the morning and at the end of each day of practice. Plus, during allotted times we had to make ourselves present for the media in the big hotel ballroom. Each player had his name on a table where he had to sit and wait just in case someone wanted to talk to him. I was late the second day, thinking my presence wasn't even needed, but when I got there reporters came directly over to me and started interviewing me. They all wanted an in-depth look down the road I had traveled to make it as a member of the Falcons. My baseball past was catching up to me in a good way. One reporter, Bob Ryan, could be seen almost every week on a Sunday morning ESPN show, "The Sports Reporters". He had done his homework on me and really wanted to know my story. That is when I felt like I had arrived. I didn't expect anybody to know my name, let alone want to talk to me, and here I was giving my story to one of the most respected sports reporters in the business. By the time we were done, I could see the impression I had made on him. It was later reflected in a published article he put together.

After Friday's practice, the only thing left was our walk-through on Saturday at Pro Player Stadium. I could no longer wait to finally get to the game. All of the attention and hype was way past too much. It was tough any more to concentrate on why we were here in the first place. The serenity of being on the actual field on which we were to play the next day was the only thing that brought it back into perspective. I'd seen my share of fields to this point, but this surpassed spectacular. Not a blade of grass was out of place, the field paint and end zones were immaculately done and everywhere you looked there was something proclaiming the fact that you were at the "Home of Super Bowl XXXIII". Looking around I got goose bumps and found it almost possible to hear the crowd even though the stadium was empty. Tomorrow we would play before the whole world for the National Football League Title.

A Moment Of Indiscretion

Irv had been in town since Tuesday and my mother and father flew in on Wednesday, so my Super Bowl experience was entirely with family by my side. Calvin and I had taken one of our cars down to South Beach Sunday and Monday evenings to see the glitz and glamour of the city, but once that was done we had nothing but football on our minds. After that, all concentration went into being prepared for Sunday. I'd go to dinner with my family, then turn the keys to my rental over to them so they could enjoy all the sights and sounds they wanted.

Saturday morning arrived and I started to feel under the weather. This was no time to come down with anything, but the body has its limits. By the end of that day I knew I was flu-bound, so I went to get medicine from one of our trainers to try and hold it off until after Sunday. At dinner with my family that evening, I experienced butterflies in my stomach even though we were almost 24 hours away from kickoff. When I returned to my room that night, I got into bed, ordered a pay-per-view movie, and called it an early night so I could get the rest I needed. I drifted off to thoughts of doing something special the next day to help lead my team to victory.

About 7:30 the next morning my telephone rang. It was Calvin on the other end. If it wasn't for the fact that he was my best friend I might have cursed him for calling me that early. After all, I was really hurting and then I was suddenly startled and abruptly pulled from my sleep. What he was calling for though was enough to shake me and wake me instantly. He first asked me if I'd heard the news. I told him I didn't know anything about anything; I spent my night and this morning isolated from the world. He told me to turn on ESPN and call him back after I got caught up with the shocking news that was unfolding as we spoke. I grabbed my remote and sat up in the bed. This had to be something big – I could hear it in his voice.

The very first thing I was hit with when I found the channel was a picture of one of my teammates, Eugene Robinson. What followed was devastating to our cause. Eugene was many things to us, he provided veteran leadership, was our starting free safety and most importantly provided a spiritual presence that helped to bond this large group of men. He had been out the night before accepting an award for his humanitarian achievements but made an ill-advised stop on the way back to the hotel where his wife and children were waiting. In what I can only imagine as a moment of indiscretion, he decided to make a detour on the way home. He propositioned an undercover police officer for sexual favors and was arrested around nine o'clock. The news hit the wire like a ton of bricks. His rental car was impounded, he spent the night in jail and Coach Reeves had to be called to bail him out. Nobody would have ever thought something like this would happen, especially the night before the Super Bowl, but bang, there it was!

I called Calvin back and grilled him for information, but he knew about as much as I did. The only thing to do was get up and go down for breakfast to see what we could find out. There was nothing but whispering going on downstairs; nobody wanted to say a thing. And it was that way all the way through the day until we got to our team meeting a couple of hours before the buses were scheduled to take us to Pro Player Stadium. When Coach Reeves walked into the room, all chatter ceased. He quickly got to the heart of the matter, addressing it ever so briefly. We were, he stated, surely all aware of what had happened the night prior but there was nothing we could do about it. We couldn't allow it to be a distraction and take our focus away from the job we had before us. Eugene would join the team later. And that was the end of it. If anybody asked, we were to have no comment. I'm not sure that was the best way to handle the matter, but it was the way he chose that afternoon. As team members, we were left to wonder where Eugene's priorities were the night before the biggest game of our lives, but he had more important issues in front of him, mainly his family. Dan moved right past the incident and began trying to re-center our focus and energies.

By the time we arrived at the stadium I was sick as a dog and getting worse by the minute. I took every possible medication that day but nothing helped. Eugene did not show up to get dressed until we were almost ready to go out for our pre-game warm-ups and not a word was said by him nor was a question asked. No excuses can be made for how we played on the field that day, but the distraction was obvious both as an entire unit and individually for Eugene.

Super Bowl XXXIII – Sunday January 31, 1999

Unmatched by any other sporting event in the world is the pageantry surrounding a Super Bowl Sunday. It is the single, most widely watched yearly event. From the moment I walked onto the field to the moment the game was over I tried to burn emotion, feeling, and images into my brain. I did not want to ever forget one single moment.

And yet, it was obvious that something was missing as we made our way through the tunnel that night. We didn't have the same fire or look in our eyes as with Minnesota. Meanwhile, the Broncos, led by one of my football heroes, John Elway, were attempting to win their second Super Bowl in a row. They had been here before and done it all just last year and we could almost sense their calm as we passed them going on and off the field. Our minds weren't where they should have been while their focus led them to look like they were going for a walk in the park.

The moment of truth arrived. It was finally time for us to run out of our tunnel, over 80,000 fans in the seats and millions across the world watching. As sick as I felt, that moment was still absolutely the most breathtaking, exhilarating and awesome thing I had ever done as a professional athlete. I felt my heart would jump out of my chest. The roar of the crowd, the flashing camera bulbs and the thought that so many eyes were on me made me feel like the strongest man in the world; I could do anything. And if that weren't enough, when we finally lined up and down our sideline for the National Anthem I stood right in front of Cher as she sang. I tried to hold back the emotional tears pushing the corners of my eyes, but it was a useless fight. I got so lost in her spirited rendition that when the fighter planes came roaring over the stadium, disappearing in an instant, I nearly lost it. The coin toss immediately following meant I only had a little time to compose myself. It was time to get mean again and go to work. Super Bowl XXXIII was about to start!

From the opening kickoff of the game I was never without a cough drop in my mouth on or off the field. Our offense got the ball first and on that drive we moved the ball 48 yards and deep into Bronco territory before settling for a field goal. Being on the board first lifted our team, but it was a short-lived high. On the ensuing drive Denver marched down the field and eventually scored on a one-yard touchdown run. Late in the first Denver once again held the ball, but an interception by our defense set us up on their 35 yard line. We failed to capitalize on the momentum shift and turned the ball over on downs when we were stopped on a fourth and one play. Denver took the ball down the field after that and cashed in with a field goal to bring the score to 10-3.

On our next drive we responded by taking the ball all the way to the Denver eight-yard line before stalling again. When Morten's 26-yard field goal sailed wide right, you could almost feel the air escape us. On the next play, disaster struck. Eugene, mentally not in the game, was exposed and exploited for an 80-yard touchdown pass by Elway. Our missed field goal combined with that play turned a possible 10-6 game into a 17-3 Broncos' lead. And they never looked back. We managed a field goal near the end of the half and went in at the intermission down 17-6, but there was already a sense of desperation in our locker room.

I only stepped on the field a few times in the last 30 minutes of the game as we played catch-up the rest of the way. It was agonizing to helplessly watch everything unfold. We had our chances to get back into the game but two consecutive possessions resulted in interceptions inside the Broncos' twenty, stopping us and resulting in two Denver touchdowns. Their lead expanded to 31-6. We made the game respectable with two late scores, the last one being a long kickoff return for a touchdown with 2:04 left in the contest. But, it was way too little too late.

We shot ourselves in the foot all night. Priding ourselves on protecting the football and forcing our opponent to make mistakes, we were out of character and sync from the first whistle. We drove inside the Broncos' 30-yard line seven times, but came away with one touchdown and two field goals, throwing two interceptions, missing a field goal and turning the ball over on downs once. The Broncos were the better team that day and John Elway was going out of the game on top, winning MVP honors in his final game.

With a couple of minutes left in the game I stood on the sideline, along with many of my teammates, and discovered what Dan truly meant in the Minnesota locker room two weeks prior: the highest of the highs and lowest of the lows. I didn't look around much to see but I know I wasn't the only man on that sideline with tears in his eyes. Looking across to the other side of the field, I noted the celebration was on. That should have been us over there. I walked to the far end of our sideline and just stood by myself, reflecting on our season. It didn't help to think about what we had done. I could only feel the pain of what had slipped through our fingers. As the final seconds ticked off the clock I couldn't stay on the field one second to watch the Broncos in their victory. There were no hands to shake or congratulations to give out. I only wanted to be in front of my locker and away from the sight, so I trotted toward our tunnel and never looked back.

Final Score:
Falcons 19-Denver Broncos 34

Not much could be said after that game. Dan gave the best speech he could muster, but I don't remember much of it. I could still hear the commotion from outside on the field. Until we were on our bus heading back to the hotel where the huge tent party awaited us, I don't think I said a word to anyone. I'd almost forgotten how sick I felt but that came back as my body reminded me it was trying to shut down. Once in the parking lot and off the bus, we had to navigate through a stream of family and friends. One of the first familiar faces I saw was my mother, trying to be strong. When she saw the pain in my eyes, she started crying. Stopping to give her a hug, I told her I'd meet all of them under the tent after a quick run upstairs.

I did take a little time to compose myself before joining my company downstairs. Besides my family, Pat, Amy and members of the Pro-Files family were to be my guests. We enjoyed the evening as best we could, but eventually parted ways. I was flying out first thing in the morning with everybody else doing likewise shortly thereafter. Up in my room again, I succumbed to the flu battling to take over my body.

By the next morning I could barely get up for the wakeup call. I barely made it to the bus but eventually found myself on the plane returning us to Atlanta and a scheduled parade through the city. One of my trainers repeatedly checked on me during our flight. As we approached landing, he recommended that I not attend the parade. Neither he nor I felt I had the strength to do so. Moreover, the weather was going to be something that would only make my condition worse; it was 40 degrees and raining.

Missing a parade with all my teammates riding on fire engines through downtown Atlanta was the last thing I wanted, but the decision to go home and get rest was best for me. From the airport I got on the lone bus headed for our complex in Suwannee, put my bags in the truck and went home to my bed. It took every bit of strength to make it up the stairs to my front door, and I dumped all my stuff right at the threshold. I turned the television on to see the parade, but that upset me because I wasn't there. I turned it off and fell asleep instantly. The next time I woke up I was lying in a puddle of sweat. I moved just enough to get to the other side of the bed. I didn't hear a peep until the next morning when my telephone rang and woke me up at 7a.m. It was one of my trainers calling to check and see where I was as I was scheduled to take my mandatory year-end physical. I told him I could not get out of the bed; it felt like I was near death. He told me I had to do everything I could and called me twice in the next hour to get me up and into my truck. I went in, got my physical, turned in all my equipment and playbooks and had one last meeting with my tight end coach and Dan. From all indications, the organization was pleased with my work for the season and I would return. The only thing I was truly concerned with at that time, though, was getting back to my bed so I could crash. I finally got back to the apartment, turned the ringers off on every phone, got under the covers, and didn't move for seven agonizing days.

The Walk Of Shame

One of the first to board the plane from Miami to Atlanta, I had my own row and sat in the seat next to the window so I had something against which to lean my head. I casually watched the plane fill, but took no real notice until a couple got on the plane – Eugene Robinson and his wife. She must have been mortified as they walked to their seats in the extreme rear of the aircraft. The kids had boarded a second plane, also chartered by the Falcons, so they were spared the humiliating walk of shame. I wouldn't have wanted to be in Eugene's shoes for all the money in the world from the look on his wife's face.

Eugene's tenure with the Falcons ended early in the off-season after they released him from his contract. His decision that fateful night in Miami was a 'bonehead' move, one he undoubtedly wishes he could take back. He let his teammates down, but more importantly, he betrayed the trust of his family. Eventually reconciling with his wife, my hope is that the Robin-son's were able to leave the nasty chapter behind and move on with their lives.

Slow to recover from the flu, I lost valuable time being sick. Participating in the Super Bowl had taken us all the way to the last day of January and after being in bed for a week, the short month of February was about to fly by. The second week I got good news from Pat- another one-year contract from Atlanta was on the table. All I had to do was go in and sign on the dotted line. It seemed things would continue to roll in a positive direction; the light seemed to be shining brightly on me. With time on my hands and a lot of money in the bank, I settled in for a few weeks of rest and relaxation. It wouldn't be long until the end of March, off-season workout program underway and in full swing yet again.

A couple of weeks after the end of the season I got word from Columbus, Ohio. Randy. We hadn't talked much over the last half year since her latest job transfer. The distance and our schedules made it impossible for us to see each other and we had ended our relationship in training camp during the previous summer. All we seemed to do on the phone was argue, mainly because we missed each other, but there was nothing we could do about that. She called to let me know that she had been offered another relocation- this time, Atlanta.

Of course, we had done some drifting apart during this time. I didn't know what she was doing up in Ohio and I had overall returned to life as a single man. I wasn't looking for anything (nobody could get as close as she had to my heart) but at one point I thought she had moved on, so to keep what little sanity I had when things got complicated between us, so did I. The news that she would be coming down to Georgia as early as March was good to hear, but we would have to get to know each other all over again. And that was probably going to be as friends initially. I was excited that she was going to be close, but didn't know what to expect. And, I knew for a fact she had no idea what to make of me at this time. I scarcely knew what to make of myself.

Expansion

Irv was in the process of relocating to Phoenix, Arizona, after selling his home in New Orleans. He was no longer playing there and was no longer a fan of the city. Even though he had never officially lived in the Southwest, he had ties to the area. One such was that he and his college roommate, Nick Smith, had started a Smoothie King business in Scottsdale.

Irv was going through a bit of a mess with San Francisco. Even though he had a good season for the 49ers, they wanted to restructure the next portion of his two-year contract. He wanted no part of that, so had taken a firm stance. The 49ers had limited options on how to deal with the situation. If they couldn't convince him to take a pay cut, they either had to release him and get nothing in return or find another team that wanted to make a deal for him.

This was the year the Expansion Cleveland Browns were to return to the league. The city had been without a team since Art Modell had moved the franchise to Baltimore after the 1995 season. Starting from scratch, a proven tight end was high on their wish list. A deal was worked out and Irv's tenure in San Francisco was over after just one season of work.

For me, life couldn't seem to get any better. I had problems just like anybody else, but they seemed less pressing when all of sudden I seemed to have everything needed in the palm of my hand. Money has a way of masking everything. It made it easier to push things to the back of my mind and to come up with something else to keep myself occupied rather than facing certain problems that might exist, like missing out on watching my child grow up.

For about a month after the Super Bowl run, my biggest concern was what I was going to have for dinner at the end of the day. I also spent a lot of time at the bowling alley with my two best friends, Nate and Calvin, and doing whatever else whimsically crossed my mind. Randy had come back into town in the middle of March and we saw each other a few times to again get to know each other on a friendly basis. The relationship strained in the beginning, the attraction was still definitely there, so it was only a matter of time before we started seeing each other on a romantic basis once again.

We were a couple of weeks into the off-season program, upcoming season goals already in place, when the NFL Draft came upon us. I was doing things around the apartment, not really paying attention as the teams made their selections since the Falcons weren't on the board for a long time. Because we had gone to the Super Bowl we had the second to last pick in the first round at number 30. When they chose a defensive end out of Virginia with the first pick I didn't raise an eyebrow, but when they selected a tight end twelve picks later at pick number 42 I stopped in my tracks.

It didn't take a rocket scientist to determine that we were going to be log-jammed at the position. Even O.J., the starting tight end, questioned that pick. It seemed the most unlikely selection the team could make. There had to be bigger holes on the team to plug than that one! With that instant addition we had five tight ends on the roster. And I was number four on the chart without a doubt. We normally kept three and one on the practice squad, so what did that mean for me?

The rest of the day Saturday was a blur and by Sunday I had to talk to someone. I called Pat. He was equally concerned so the first thing on his agenda for Monday was a call to the Falcon front office. I got word back from him the next afternoon. The Falcons simply explained the move as picking the best available player on the board. It didn't make much sense, but it was what it was. My security within the organization vanished. The last thing I wanted to do was work all the way through the off-season and into training camp where I would become a victim of the numbers game. I didn't think I had too much of a choice, but Pat had an idea. The Cleveland Browns were still forming their roster and needed athletes at every position. They had Irv penciled in as their starter, but nothing really behind him. They might be interested in acquiring me if I became available. The way to do that was to opt out of my contract with the Falcons if they would allow me to do so.

The idea instantly lifted my spirits. The thought of playing with my brother on the same team! It was going to take a few phone calls, but Pat was on the job immediately. By the next morning he had talked to the Browns. They would indeed pick me up, having first rights. Pat called the Falcons and they agreed to release me from my contract if that was what I wanted to do. In the blink of an eye my days with the Atlanta Falcons were over. That's just the way it happens in the world of professional sports.

By the end of that afternoon I had been to the Falcon complex and packed all locker belongings. After all I'd been through in the last two years that was a tough thing to do. I felt like I was walking away from a part of my family. Twelve years in the business will result in thick skin, though. It was time to move on. The business said so and it was what I had to do. No time to look back.

Ed and Irv ▲
Falcons vs. 49ers

Irv and Ed ▶
49ers vs. Falcons

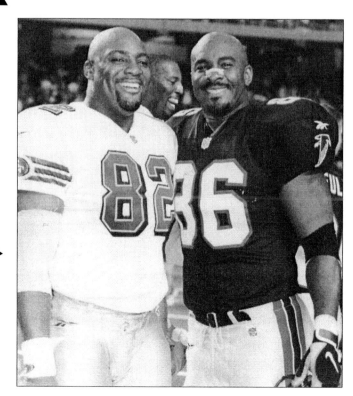

Nate Miller amd Ed
Falcons and Chargers, 1997

Calvin Collins and Ed
Super Bowl Week, Miami

Super Bowl
Media Day

ASSOCIATED PRESS

Atlanta tight end Ed Smith takes a break during a final walk-through session in Pro Player Stadium before today's Super Bowl.

JAN. 27, 1999   TO SUBSCRIBE: 404-522-4141

SUPER BOWL COVERAGE

Falcons media day
is a full-court press

SPORTS, F1, F6-12

50 CENTS

Super
Bowl
Send
Off

Ed Smith's success stuns Reeves

By Reuben Frank
BCT sports writer

When Falcons tight ends coach James Daniel first recommended to head coach Dan Reeves that the team take a look at an unknown rookie named Eddie Smith, Reeves didn't take him seriously.

Smith had 10 years of pro experience — eight years playing minor-league baseball and one year each in the World League and on the Redskins' practice squad.

So the fact that the 28-year-old Smith could not only make an NFL roster but contribute to a team with playoff aspirations ranks as one of the most surprising stories of his 36-year coaching career.

"He's amazing," Reeves said. "It doesn't happen very often for a guy to be out of football that long and come back and play on this level."

Smith, a graduate of Pemberton High School, signed a letter of intent to play football and baseball for North Carolina but instead signed with the Chicago White Sox, who had made him a seventh-round draft pick. He spent the 1987

through 1994 seasons playing baseball before turning to football.

Younger brother Irv Smith was a first-round pick of the New Orleans Saints in 1993 and Reeves said the Falcons took the bloodlines seriously.

"That definitely helped," Reeves said. "We knew (Irv) was a good athlete and we knew Eddie was a good athlete, too."

Smith spent some time on the Falcons' practice squad this year but when two tight ends — promising rookie O.J. Santiago and former Eagle Ed West — suffered season-ending injuries, Smith was promoted to the active roster.

Last week, in a win at Seattle two weeks ago, Smith caught his first NFL pass — two-yarder from Chris Chandler. It's a start.

"Eddie's really surprised me," Reeves said. "He's a hard worker, a good blocker, a good receiver and very athletic. He's got talent. We thought he had a future and he's played well over the last two weeks.

"It's unusual, but it's a great

story. Sometimes, all somebody needs is an opportunity. And when O.J. and Ed West got hurt, Eddie got his."

●

Tiki Barber never ran for 100 yards before he saw the Eagles. Same with Jay Graham.

Cory Dillon and James Stewart had one 100-yard game apiece before they faced the Philadelphia defense. And Emmitt Smith? Against everybody else this year, he was a shadow of his former self. Against the Eagles, it was 1994 all over again.

There was a time when the Eagles just didn't allow 100-yard backs. In the five-year period from 1990 through 1994, only nine opposing backs ran for 100 yards or more.

In just 49 games since Ray Rhodes was named head coach and Emmitt Thomas took over the defense, 13 backs have surpassed 100 yards, including six this year. That matches the most against the Eagles in any season since 1983, when Eric Dickerson, Walter Payton, John Riggins and Ottis Anderson (twice) were among eight

backs over 100 yards against the Birds.

But Tiki Barber? Jay Graham? James Stewart? They're not even starters. Yet all tore through the Eagles' defense like they were Dickerson, Payton or Riggins.

Going into today's game against the Falcons at the Georgia Dome, the Eagles are teetering on the brink of playoff elimination, and one of the main reasons is their soft underbelly. The strength of this team most of the year has been pass defense, so teams simply ram it up the gut against them. The result has been 1,720 rushing yards in 14 games, which places the once-proud Eagles 25th in the NFL against the run.

It also puts them on pace to allow 1,966 yards this year, which would be the second-most they've allowed since 1986.

"It's very uncharacteristic of the way we play," safety Mike Zordich said. "But it's not the physical, it's the mental aspect that's been the problem. We're a gap-control defense, and when one guy takes a wrong step and gets out of his gap, bad things happen."

FALCONS REPORT
LEN PASQUARELLI
■

Smith changes paths

He came to Suwanee as the longest of longshots, a 28-year-old football novice expected by most of the Atlanta Falcons coaches to provide little more than training camp fodder for a few weeks.

Just 11 days before the 1997 schedule kicks off, however, tight end **Ed Smith** is still around and no one is laughing about his chances for making the regular-season roster. "For a guy with a pretty unique background, he's done enough things well to give himself a chance," tight ends coach **James Daniel** said.

Smith could become only the second player in franchise history to make the team without having attended college, joining former center **Jim Weatherley** (1976) in that distinction.

Before one assumes a touch of **Walter Mitty** in Smith, however, it should be noted that the older brother of New Orleans Saints fifth-year veteran tight end **Irv Smith** was himself a standout football player at Pemberton (N.J.) High School in the late '80s. Selected in the seventh round by baseball's Chicago White Sox, though, Smith turned down a football scholarship at North Carolina and opted for third base over third downs.

That began a seven-year tour of the minor leagues — "I probably know every one of those little cities," Smith said earlier this week — in stints with the White Sox, Brewers, Cubs and Indians.

"I had a pretty solid career," said Smith, who was playing for the Indians' AAA affiliate in Buffalo when he decided to give up on baseball. "But the team was starting to make some moves and there were no guarantees concerning my future. I was talking on the phone to Irv about maybe going back and trying football again, and he didn't think it was so far-fetched. When he didn't react like I was crazy, it seemed like it might be worth a shot."

Smith signed on with the World League's Frankfurt Galaxy in the spring of '96 and then joined the St. Louis Rams in camp. Cut near the conclusion of camp, he moved to the Washington Redskins practice squad for most of the season.

Smith has three catches for only 13 yards in preseason but has demonstrated raw athletic skills and few regrets about his path to the NFL. "Sometimes I think about what would happen if I was five years younger, but there's nothing I can do about that now," he said. "Every day is a lesson for me here. We'll just see if I pass the test."

Coach **Dan Reeves** retained five tight ends/H-backs last year in New York and Smith is one of only four (**Ed West**, third-rounder **O.J. Santiago** and **Brian Kozlowski** are the others) in Suwanee.

Tight Ends All in the Family When 49ers, Falcons Meet

By Gary Swan
CHRONICLE STAFF WRITER

It's a family story, really, not a sports story.

Older brother is a three-sport star. He puts aside football to chase a professional baseball career, but almost a decade years later is still riding the bus in the minor leagues. Younger brother quietly makes his way to the NFL, becomes an accomplished tight end, winds up playing for the 49ers.

The younger one talks to the big brother. "Come back to football," he says. "It's not too late. You could still make the big time here."

It's with that kind of pride that 49ers tight end Irv Smith will greet his brother, backup Falcons tight end Ed Smith, before tomorrow's game.

"It's a great feeling to have your big brother out there. Especially with the things he's been through in his careers," Irv Smith said. "It's a

TOMORROW'S GAME

■ **WHO:** 49ers (2-0) vs. Falcons (2-0)

■ **WHERE:** 3Com Park

■ **WHEN:** 1:15 p.m.

■ **TV:** Channels 2-35-40

■ **RADIO:** KGO (810 AM)

special feeling for me to see it being done."

It started back in Pemberton High near Trenton, N.J. where Ed Smith was the Tri-State (New Jersey, Pennsylvania, Delaware) athlete of the year for his football and baseball prowess in 1987.

Irv watched his brother turn down college football scholarships to Penn State and Florida to take off after a pro baseball dream with the

▶ **49ERS:** *Page B7 Col. 3*

▶ **49ERS**
From Page B1

White Sox.

"He choose the baseball route, and people in high school were kind of mad at him because he was so good in football. It was like, 'You're the guy who put us on the map.' And when he didn't follow football, they pushed me so hard," Smith said. "It was like, 'Your brother was supposed to do it and now we have you left to get it done for us.' I was expected to be the next Ed Smith. But I couldn't play basketball like him and I sure couldn't play baseball like him."

Ed Smith worked his way through baseball's bush leagues, leading a league in fielding at third base one season, leading another league with home runs (16) in another. He was a teammate of Michael Jordan's on the Double-A Birmingham Barons. "He and Jordan are real close," Irv Smith said. His brother made it to Triple-A Buffalo and spent two years there, but the door to the majors had shut.

"He never made it to The Show. Never one day," Smith said. "It was the curveball that did him in."

Irv, meanwhile, had followed in Ed's footsteps only so far. He took that football scholarship to Notre Dame, where he didn't start until his senior year but became an All America. He played baseball, too, and was drafted by the Houston Astros. But he turned them down.

"I had reached my peak, and I knew that if my brother was still

struggling playing baseball that I was really going to have a tough time," Irv Smith said. "So I just gave it up. I realized my bread and butter was going to be football."

With encouragement from his younger brother, Ed Smith quit baseball, too, and signed with the Redskins as a free agent in July, 1996. He was a 27-year-old rookie who had not blocked an opponent or caught a football for nine seasons.

Last season, Ed made the Falcons' practice squad and, as fate would have it, was promoted to the varsity for a game against the Saints and his brother, Irv. Atlanta won, but Irv Smith caught two passes for 30 yards in a game he said he will never forget.

Tomorrow, Irv will start his third

game as 49er tight end. Ed, a third-string tight end, has played only on special teams.

But Irv Smith said having a brother like Ed made him the player he is today.

"It made me have to work hard every day. He had so much more natural ability that if I didn't work hard, I was going to fall short of accomplishing the things that he did, and that would have been a letdown because people expected so much of me," he said.

With all due respect, Irv Smith says he's the better player now. "I've got an edge because I've been playing so long, but he does a lot of things well," Irv said. "He's going to continue to get better."

Smith Family Reunion at Tight End

Ed Smith toiled to get to Super Bowl

By Sam Carchidi
INQUIRER STAFF WRITER

A little more than three years ago, Ed Smith was a down-and-out minor-league baseball player. Down from spending nine seasons in the minors without coming close to the big leagues. Out because he figured it was time to find a new line of work.

Pro football seemed unlikely. He hadn't played for a decade, since he was a star at Pemberton High. But today, Smith is a member of the Atlanta Falcons, a 6-foot-4, 253-pound tight end preparing to play in the Super Bowl.

Smith was on the field as a blocker for one of the most dramatic kicks in NFL history: Morten Andersen's 38-yard field goal, which gave visiting Atlanta a stunning 30-27 overtime win over the 11-point-favorite Minnesota Vikings.

After the win, "it was almost like I reverted to a 5-year-old kid, because it was impossible to contain your emotions," Smith said.

How he went from baseball's bush leagues to the Super Bowl is an unlikely and inspiring story that even a 5-year-old couldn't dream up.

Ed Smith, a graduate of Pemberton High, struggled for years playing pro baseball.

■

As a senior at Pemberton, Smith was named The Inquirer's South Jersey athlete of the year because of his dominance in three sports: baseball, football and basketball.

"He could have played any of them in college," Pemberton football coach Bill McDowell said recently. "I didn't care what sport he played, but I just wanted him to go to college. I thought he'd have more options after he got out of college."

Smith had been recruited to play football by almost every major college, but he decided to play baseball at North Carolina. He was selected in the seventh round of the 1987 draft by the Chicago White Sox, opted for the $60,000 signing bonus, and took off for the deep minors to play third base.

But in 4½ seasons with the White Sox organization, Smith hit only .230 before shuttling to the Milwaukee Brewers' farm system and then on to the Cleveland Indians organization. For a time, he seemed big-league bound, climbing to the triple-A level in 1995 with the Indians' farm team in Buffalo.

That was the same year major-

See **SMITH** on C2

After years of toil, Falcons' Smith soars to the top

SMITH from C1

league players ended a strike that had started in 1994. The March 31 settlement pushed back the start of the 1995 season about four weeks. The developments caused some late additions to triple-A rosters, and Smith lost out. Despite finally finding his hitting groove, he was demoted to double-A. He was devastated.

"It got to the point where, instead of going up the ladder, I was going across the ladder," Smith, 29, said from his home in suburban Georgia last week. "There was no reason for me to be back in double-A. I was second on the team in homers and RBIs, and I was hitting in the .320s after the first part of the season. And the next thing I know I'm on the bench. The guys who got sent down to triple-A from the majors bumped me out of a job."

Dutifully, he finished the season at double-A Canton/Akron, but a plan was brewing with the help of his younger brother, Irv, who had gotten to the NFL by a more conventional route. He starred in football at Notre Dame, became a first-round draft pick and starting tight end with the New Orleans Saints, and now plays with the San Francisco 49ers.

The brothers had always been close, speaking dozens of times a week. At one point, they were living in South Bend, Ind., where Irv played for the Fighting Irish and Ed labored for the White Sox' single-A farm club. Often, Ed, three years older, offered advice.

In July 1995, it was Irv's turn. Ed recalled the conversation:

"I went you to tell me if this is a crazy idea," Ed said to his brother.

"Go ahead," was the reply.

"If I get in shape and somehow get someone to look at me, do you think I can play pro football? Am I crazy?"

Irv told him: "If anybody can do it, it's you. If you put your mind to it, you can do it, I'd say go for it."

It was just the encouragement Ed needed. "But I never quit on anything in life," he said, "so I stuck out the last few months of the baseball season."

After baseball was over, Smith, who was living in Arizona, began working out at Arizona State. When the NFL season ended, he was joined by Irv, who left his home in New Orleans. After all, he said, his older brother was 'my hero.'

"Ed had four months of intensive workouts with a personal trainer, and my job was to work on the mental aspects with him," Irv Smith said. Irv took his big brother to a sandlot field in Mesa, Ariz., and, under the hot desert sun, gave him a refresher course, Tight End 101.

"It was the first time he had played football since high school. He hadn't even touched a football since 1986," Irv said. "So my job was to get him acclimated to the routes and the alignments and keeping the right leverage. The personal trainer got him stronger, and I worked on the mental part of playing football again.

"I had just finished my third year in the league, and I was showing him things that I had learned — and showing him things that he taught me originally," he said. "My sophomore year [at Pemberton], I had to play wide receiver because he was

Super Bowl XXXIII

Atlanta vs. Denver

Next Sunday, in Miami, 6:18 p.m., Channel 29.

---

the tight end, and he would show me what to do."

As the saying goes, what goes around comes around.

In the spring of 1996, Ed Smith went to an NFL-sponsored World League tryout camp in Atlanta. He won a starting tight-end spot with Frankfurt and was soon playing in Germany.

Smith made an immediate impression, grabbing three touchdown passes in his first four games. But in his fourth game, he ruptured his medial collateral ligament in his left knee, "and I'm basically thinking my career is over," he said.

It wasn't. He went through four weeks of rehabilitation and returned in time to play in the championship game in Scotland. When he got home to Arizona after the season, his agent was fielding calls from numerous NFL teams.

Smith signed with the St. Louis Rams and made it to the last cut.

The Washington Redskins signed him to their practice squad for most of the 1996 season. And when Dan Reeves was named the Falcons' head coach before the 1997 season, Smith took the free-agency route to Atlanta.

"They were getting rid of the run-and-shoot, and they had no tight ends on their roster," Smith said, "so it seemed like the best place for me."

He began the 1997 season on the practice squad, then was activated for his first NFL game on Nov. 23 against New Orleans. He got to face his brother in his first NFL game.

"I've been truly blessed to have the opportunities I've had," Smith said. "The ability I have isn't because of me, but because the Man Upstairs was gracious enough to give it to me."

Smith paused. He thought back to his nine scuffling seasons of minor-league baseball and to a knee injury that nearly ended his attempt to play pro football.

"For the longest time, I never seemed to be at the right place at the right time," he said. "And then just the opposite happened. Who knows what would have happened if there wasn't a strike [settlement] and some players weren't sent down to triple-A? Maybe I would have stuck baseball out one more year and then maybe I would have been too old to switch to football."

Smith is not an NFL star. He is a reserve tight end and a special-teams performer. He was activated for every Falcons game this season. Call him the Falcons' good-luck charm. The Dirty Birds have a pristine 20-3 record since he was activated on Nov. 23, 1997, including the 20-18 win over his brother's 49ers in this season's NFC semifinals.

"I know what my role is here, and I'm fine with it," Smith said. "We have so many weapons, and I'm just happy" to contribute.

In the playoff upset of Minnesota, Smith caught his first pass of the season. But his most memorable contribution, he said, was blocking a cornerback as Andersen nailed his game-winning field goal to put Atlanta in the Super Bowl for the first time in its history.

"All I kept telling myself was,

> "I've been truly blessed to have the opportunities I've had," said Smith, who was helped by his brother, Irv.

'Don't hold anybody, and don't let anybody get past," he said. "I think the first person to know it was good was Morten Andersen, and the second to know were the people on the field. We had a good angle, and all I could do was jump, because I knew it was through. It was like nothing I've ever experienced. Everything else was small scale compared to this."

As Andersen's kick sailed through the uprights, Irv Smith was sitting in the back row in the end zone. He couldn't contain himself, he said. Tears of joy swelled as he watched the Falcons celebrate.

"I'm in the Bob Uecker seats, in the last row in the stadium, and I couldn't believe what I was seeing," Irv said. "I'm saying to myself, 'That's my brother jumping up and down and going to the Super Bowl!' To see your blood and my closest friend in the world — I was in heaven."

So was Ed Smith.

"When Irv was at Notre Dame and then in New Orleans, I'd drive hours to be at his games," Smith said, "but this was the first time he was ever able to watch me play football from the stands on any level, and it meant so much that he was there. Irv was just as happy for me as if he won it, and I would have been the same. I have nothing but love for him."

The Smiths' parents, Ed and Patricia, who still live in Browns Mills, Burlington County, were also at the Metrodome in Minneapolis. And like Irv, they will be in Miami to watch Ed play in Super Bowl XXXIII against the favored Denver Broncos.

"Who knows if I'll ever be back here again?' Smith said. "This is the greatest achievement I've ever been a part of — unless it happens again on Sunday."

CHAPTER NINE

Cleveland Browns, Detroit Lions & Philadelphia Eagles

As 1999 progressed I felt like I was playing a game of musical chairs and just couldn't seem to find a seat. The day after I parted ways with the Atlanta Falcons I got a phone call from an administrator with the Cleveland Browns. There was a team meeting that night and the second mini-camp of the off-season started the very next morning. I hadn't even gotten confirmation from Pat that the deal was done, but they were calling to set up my arrival into Ohio. I took an afternoon flight, heading up to join my brother and new teammates.

I got to the team practice facility early in the evening, signed my contract, and made it just in time for my first meeting with the newly-formed Cleveland Browns. My brother had saved me a seat. The first thing I noticed was the large amount of players gathered for this information session. Because the Browns were coming in as an expansion team, the roster limitations were set extremely high; there were 114 players sitting in that room. As the off-season wore on they had to shave it down to the required number of 80 before the start of training camp. It was a mix of young and old; I was one of the latter.

Dave Palmer, new leader of the franchise, addressed the unit in a threatening tone, as if he were a dictator. It would be an understatement to say that I did not like him from the first time I heard his voice. Trying to use the scare tactic, putting fear into the hearts of the younger players, he was unprofessional in calling out certain veterans in an attempt to intimidate them as well. This was a drastic change from Coach Reeves' milder approach. This was Palmer's first head coaching job, moving from the offensive coordinator position in Jacksonville, so I understood what he was trying to do, but I disagreed with his technique. He wanted everyone to know he was the man in charge but there were better ways to go about it. This was definitely going to take some getting used to.

Things did not change once we got on the field the next morning and afternoon for the two scheduled practices. We were all learning a new offense, but he was cracking the whip as though we had been under his command for years and should know everything. The fact that over 100 players were all coming together for the first time, newly drafted rookies just coming out of college as well, should have been reason to exhibit at least a little patience.

But even Palmer's negative presence could not take away from the experience of being on the same field with my brother. We had six tight ends on the roster, Irv playing the role as the starter, three youngsters, one more veteran and myself. It was plain to see that I had more athletic ability than anyone else backing my brother. All I had to do was catch up in learning the offense and I could make this team. Irv and I went through a cram session the night before and he tutored me as we stood on the field; he was the teacher and I was the student. We even shared a locker because of the overcrowded nature of the huge roster. If not for little Napoleon leading us this would have been a dream situation. It was almost like being back in high school.

At the conclusion of the three-day mini-camp session I had a major decision to make. It was going to be very important to be in Cleveland for the off-season program and that meant spending the entire spring and part of the summer leading to training camp in Ohio. I returned to Atlanta and after taking a few days to settle all of my business I flew back into Cleveland leaving everything behind, including Randy. Ironically, she had finally landed near me just to watch me leave town.

Conclusion: Cleveland was a miserable experience! Through a connection of Randy's I got a two-bedroom apartment on the outskirts of town, supposedly for Irv and myself to share while we participated in the off-season program. But due to the problems my brother was going through in his relationship with the mother of my little nephew, I ended up spending the majority of my Browns' experience by myself, knowing no one in the city. Irv in town sporadically left the Browns and Palmer upset and me alone in a city in which I preferred not to be.

Just as I had been in Atlanta, I was a regular for my workouts. Every day I went in, but it seemed I was invisible. Unless he was asking me where my brother was, Palmer said not a word to me. The two of them did not hit it off at all and he viewed my brother's lack of participation as insubordination. In fact, though, off-season workouts are not mandatory but voluntary, and players do have lives to live outside of the world of football. My brother had issues to deal with regarding his son. That should have been enough to satisfy anybody questioning him. On the other side of that, I should not have been punished for any dispute not involving me directly.

After spending a month and a half in the city, going through another mini-camp and working out diligently for the organization, I was called into Palmer's office. I had just walked into the facility, headed for the locker room to get dressed for my workout when one of his lackeys stopped me and directed me to the headman's room. As a reward for all the work I had put in, the Browns let me go on June 3, just two days before my 30th birthday.

Palmer could have saved his explanation. As I sat in a chair facing him on the other side of his desk, the only thing I thought about was slapping this man across his face. I didn't need to hear his sorry excuse. Because they were an expansion team they wanted to start young, knowing they were likely to be initially unsuccessful. Irv was going to be the veteran starter and they were going to surround him with younger players so they could develop them. He wanted to let me go early so I could find another job. It didn't matter that I was superior to any of the other players he had at the position; he even mentioned that himself. It was all a bunch of bull but I took it like a man, shook his hand, turned and walked out of the office without saying a word. I packed the things I had in the locker I still shared with Irv, and got in my truck unemployed and uncertain of my next move.

Tough to find a job this late into the off-season, it was time to play the waiting game. I went back to Atlanta, but it was distressing to sit and watch the days go by with nothing happening. I became very depressed and disheartened. What a difference a year makes. Riding high getting ready to go into camp and the experience of my life just one summer ago, I'd worked hard and hadn't done anything wrong except being too old, if that's what 30 is. Rather than just sit around, I went up to New Jersey for a while, the comfort of being around my family exactly what I needed.

In limbo from that first week of June all the way through the last day of July, I had to come to grips with the fact that I would probably not be playing at the start of the year. Training camps had all opened up by the middle of the month and things didn't look good, as teams would be reducing rosters, not adding on. With no training camp I wouldn't be on anybody's mind when they needed someone in a hurry due to injury or any other reason. That could lead to me not being on the field at all for an entire season. And at this late juncture in a career that hadn't gotten started until age 27, it might be the kiss of death. I had to face the possibility that the end of the road had come. I thought this way to prepare myself in case that was how it all worked out. Pat was doing his part, continuously marketing me, but the business can be a real eye-opener.

Back in Atlanta after a nice stay in New Jersey I accepted the circumstances and prepared to move on. I didn't know what I was going to do with myself, but I had time to figure it out. I had a good deal of money in the bank because I had not thrown it all away as I earned it. Taking advantage of my free time, I started spending a bit of it with Randy. She had been getting situated in the city working at her new property and the two of us began a rekindling. I was actually at her house on the night of July 31, a Saturday, when my cell phone rang. It was the tight ends coach from the Detroit Lions.

Two of their veteran tight ends had gone down due to same-day injury. All they had backing up their starter, David Sloan, were two undrafted, free-agent rookies. They needed a veteran in right away to compete for the backup role and my name was high on their list having seen me on the field three times in the last two years with the Falcons: two consecutive in the preseason and once during the regular season at the end of last year. All the coach wanted to know was: Was I healthy? And could I step right in? They hadn't even called Pat yet, having obtained my number directly by calling Cleveland, the last team with which I had been affiliated. Having continued to work out while away from the game, I told him I was more than ready. That was all he needed to hear. I was to stay by my phone and receive contact again as soon as they got in touch with Pat. Two hours later I had an itinerary for a morning flight that would take me to Saginaw, Michigan and the Detroit Lions. It was once again time to say good-bye to Randy in a flash, but I'd be coming back for a quick visit real soon.

I stepped directly into the Number Two spot on the depth chart with the Lions. I was learning the offense straight on the fly, all of the new formations, audibles, the blocking schemes: everything! While I worked, the two injured vets watched from the sideline and I had a chance to demonstrate my talent on the field. Good fortune had shone on me and I was taking full advantage of it.

Barry Sanders

At the time, before Emmitt Smith passed him, Barry Sanders was the second leading rusher in NFL history (behind the late great Walter Payton) after ten years with the Lions. The big distraction surrounding training camp in Saginaw was the fact that he was walking away from the game with no real reason other than what seemed like a dispute over off-season workout participation. I was just walking into the situation but the word I heard around camp was that Barry wasn't happy with how things were handled within the organization. He also didn't see eye to eye with Coach Bobby Ross. Whatever Barry's personal reasons were, he could have become the all-time NFL leading rusher, setting the record so far out that Emmitt would have never caught him. He walked away from the game for his own peace of mind instead. It would have been nice to have had the opportunity to play with him, though.

I caught up and fell right into the mix with the Lions. As fate would have it, our first preseason game of the year was in Atlanta against my old friends and teammates. It was strange walking out of the visiting locker room getting ready to bump heads against the same players I had gone to battle with just a few months before. I had no hard feelings about how things transpired, but it was a chance to show the Falcons that they might not have tapped into all that I had to offer.

This was a different preseason game. In all those past, I waited until the second half to get on the field. Now I was on the field from the first whistle at tight end and on all of the special teams' units. By the middle of third quarter I was standing on the sideline with my helmet in my hand, done for the day and watching others finish out the game for a change. I grabbed three catches against my former team and left the Georgia Dome with a real sense of accomplishment. The game didn't mean anything statistically, being an exhibition game, but it meant the world to me.

For the next two weeks I put in the quality of work that should have solidified my position on the depth chart. I caught at least one pass in each of the following preseason games and was on almost every special teams' unit. My tight end coach, Danny Smith, used me as ammunition for the two veterans taking their time to get back on the field. "You are losing your jobs," is what he'd tell them. "Take your time coming back- we don't really need you now." Miraculously, in the last week of training camp both returned to health and I was bumped down on the chart, not by Danny, but by Coach Ross who didn't believe they should lose their jobs due to injury. In the last preseason game of the year I took a back seat to the two of them against another of my former teams, the St. Louis Rams. My limited playing time in the finale had me worrying about the impending final cuts the next day. When I got a call at my hotel the next morning, along with orders to bring my playbook in to meet with Coach Ross, I was very disappointed. On the ride over to the Silverdome I felt like I had been pimped. I came in and did all the work and when everybody was healthy I was just let go.

The first person I bumped into on my way upstairs to sit

with Coach Ross was Danny Smith. He wanted to make sure I stopped to see him before I left. Bobby Ross is one of the nicest men I've met in the game of football. As much as I hated what he was going to do to me when I sat in the chair across from him, it was hard to actually be mad at the man. He was sincere in his words and told the truth. He wanted to give the two tight ends a chance to win their jobs back and didn't feel comfortable releasing either of them because they had been hurt. They might have taken their time in the healing process, (we all knew that) but he was loyal. If something happened to either of them or there were performance problems he assured me I would come back to join the team. I left his office feeling dejected but with a hint of tucked-away optimism.

From Coach Ross' office I went in to see Danny Smith and he damn near shed a tear as we sat in his office, door closed. At the very least he believed that we should have kept all four tight ends. If one had to go it shouldn't be me. It wasn't his decision, all he had was input, but he vowed to do everything in his power to get me back there as soon as possible. With him on my side I had a feeling I hadn't seen the last of Detroit.

The Golden Ring

In the middle of training camp a special delivery was brought in and presented to me by one of the team administrators. It was my NFC Championship Ring. Down in Atlanta there was a big ring ceremony. Mine was dropped off while I sat in front of my locker after a practice still wrapped in my towel, fresh out of the shower. I opened the box up and every teammate in the vicinity came over to take a look or try it on. It was and still is the most beautiful piece of jewelry I have ever seen. It represents every struggle I have ever been through and all the adversity I have faced and stood up against along the incredible roads I have traveled.

Bumps and Bruises

My 30-year old body had been through the ringer twice. Going into my twelfth year of professional sports I had suffered just about every injury imaginable. I still considered myself lucky, not having to deal with anything catastrophic, but I was racking up an impressive list of bumps and bruises. In this camp I was to add one more to the list.

There were two practices scheduled for the day two days before our first preseason game of the year in Atlanta. In the first of the day we were doing a passing drill against our defense when I ran a deep out-pattern. The ball had either been thrown early or I was late coming out of my break. Either way it was on top of me when I turned my head and threw my right hand up in an attempt to make the catch. The ball directly impacted my index finger, dislocating it at the middle knuckle. Underneath my receivers' gloves I could see the bulge indicating a problem. Unlike the time I did something similar to my left ring finger in Seattle back in 1997, I couldn't snap this one back into place. Lodged on top of the back part of the knuckle, my trainers couldn't work it down either. They pulled as hard as I would allow them to (I was in a great deal of pain) but they couldn't get it back in place. After a few minutes they decided they had to take me to a hospital. Taking me inside they assisted me in getting out of my equipment, then whisked me to one of the team doctor's offices.

After first examination and a few good pulls, the doctor realized it was going to take a mighty yank to get my digit back into place. He would first shoot me up in three separate spots surrounding the joint with something I had become very familiar with during my career, good old cortisone. Then he would take one last shot at correcting the problem. If that failed, he warned me, I would require a quick surgery. He'd have to open up my finger to manually adjust it. That is the last thing I wanted.

I sat on the table with my hand under a towel so I didn't have to look at it for about twenty minutes while the cortisone took effect. When the doctor finally came back, he took the hand and I closed my eyes as he counted down to the mighty tug. One, two, three... PULL! The room was filled with a loud pop followed by a small scream. The good doctor had inflicted pain, but saved me from surgery.

When I was all put back together again, it was back to training camp where it was lunchtime. I bumped into Danny Smith and he asked if I thought I might be able to go during the second practice of the day. He probably expected me to say no and wouldn't have been mad if I had, but I wasn't gong to let him down. A little extra tape for stability was all I needed, pain and all, to get out on the field to finish the day. No pain, no gain. I made it through that practice without incident, but learned a valuable lesson the next day as we did our final walkthrough before flying down to Atlanta. It was a non-contact practice and I didn't think I needed tape on the finger, so I went without. I put my hands up to simulate a block during our last assignment session and didn't tuck my fingers inward. The finger popped right out again as I poked the man across from me right in the chest. It hurt like you can't imagine! This time my trainers were able to pull it back out on the field so I didn't have to make a return trip to the doctor's office. You can best believe I did not make that mistake again.

Back in Atlanta it was time to play the waiting game again. I watched the first week of the regular season from my living room, aching to get back out on the field. It didn't take long for the phone to ring when the Eagles called from Philadelphia. They had lost their first game of the season to the Arizona

Cardinals and weren't totally happy with the group they had at the tight end position, so they wanted to fly me in for a workout. That was a very exciting prospect as Philadelphia was almost right in my backyard, just across the bridge from New Jersey. Again, I was on a flight just hours after receiving a phone call. When I called my mother at work, already on my way to the airport in Atlanta, she could hardly contain her excitement.

In Philly I was taken to a hotel just 40 minutes from where I grew up. If this were to work out, it would be like playing at home. The next morning, after a quick physical, I was on the field with three other tight ends who looked like they had just graduated from high school, all young first-year players with no experience in the league. I outclassed them all as we went through a series of running drills, route running and ball catching. It was so obvious that when we all hit the showers I knew I had a new job if the Eagles were serious about bringing in a new tight end. The three young tight ends actually congratulated me in the locker room, saying they knew I had the job, and that is no lie.

When the tight end coach came out and told one of the rookies he had the job, my jaw fell to the floor. He directed him to an elevator so he could go upstairs to sign his new contract and then asked me to follow him to his office. Behind closed doors again, he first told me how I was recommended to him through my good friend Danny Smith out in Detroit. The two of them were good friends and talked all the time. Danny had passed the word to him that I was a quality tight end if he was ever in the market and with their current situation they were in dire need. Their veteran starter had gone down in the last preseason game and they had a young rookie and converted wide receiver manning the position for the time being. He explained to me that my workout had done nothing but prove what Danny had told him; I was a quality tight end. Money and age issues were the factors that led to first-year Head Coach Andy Reid's decision. I was scheduled to make much more than any of the first year players they had brought in. For anybody who doesn't think sports is a business, this is just more proof of that fact.

That was a tough pill to swallow. I knew I should be the one upstairs right now signing my new contract, but, instead I was gathering my things and heading back to the airport to return to Atlanta. I called Pat, then my mother, to give them the disappointing news before boarding my plane.

By the end of the day I was back in my apartment in Atlanta trying to figure out why I was putting myself through this. Was it just time to let it go? I had already accomplished more than anybody thought possible. The rejection was starting to get to me. In one year I had been essentially replaced by one team, the Falcons, and told by three others that I was good, but not quite what they were looking for. If this was the way it was going to be, I didn't know how much more of it I wanted to put up with.

For the next couple of weeks the phone was silent. Sundays were the toughest days to deal with. The only reason I had to even pay attention was to support my brother. I went to a local sports bar to watch him and his Browns play, and the green grass on the television called my name. I particularly watched the teams with which I had been affiliated. One score caught my attention at the end of the early games: Bills 26-Eagles 0 on the road up in Buffalo. I thought to myself, 'good for them.' They were 0-3 and I couldn't be more pleased.

On my way back to my apartment, my cell phone rang. The area code wasn't local and I didn't recognize it, but the voice sounded vaguely familiar. It was the Eagles' tight end coach. They hadn't even gotten on their team plane in Buffalo, heading back to Philadelphia, and he was already calling me to tell me they wanted to sign me. The young rookie experiment wasn't working out and they needed a veteran presence to help out at the position. He didn't want to wait until the next day to call me because of how fast things happen in the league. I might be on someone else's list and they didn't want me to be scooped up. He told me he was going to call Pat in the morning and set everything up. And just like that, I was back in the league!

1999 Philadelphia Eagles

If playing in the NFL was the cake, playing right across the Ben Franklin Bridge in Philly was the icing on it. Our practice facility was right next to Veterans Stadium, about a 35-minute commute from Browns Mills, so I stayed at the house with my family. The journey had come full circle and I was sleeping in my old room, on my old bed, with Mom and Pops right across the hall. I saw them every morning before I left for work and we had dinner together almost every night. A lot of times I'd just call them on my way back in and we'd meet somewhere for dinner or I'd stop and pick something up and bring it home. And they were front and center for every home game and the one trip we made up to the Meadowlands to play the Giants.

There was no magical ride for this team, because we weren't very good. Donavan McNabb, quarterback of the future, was just getting his NFL career started and Coach Reid was trying to turn the whole organization around, taking over a team that had finished 3-13 the year before. Right away, I was tight end unit leader because of my experience. Doesn't that sound strange? My three previous years in the league and trip to the Super Bowl made me the big man on campus.

Picking up the West Coast Offense quickly, I never got a chance to be involved in it to the degree that I wished. Each of the three of us had a specific role and mine was as the big, bruising, blocking tight end. Jed, the rookie, was the starter, but he spent most of the time confused as he was taking on a big load at an early stage. Then there was Luther-more of a big, wide receiver as he was kind of light in the pants. His favorite thing to do was catch balls and he wasn't shy about letting that be known. Getting dirty in the trenches was *not* his favorite thing and he was very happy letting Jed and me handle that part. It got to the point that I was the tight end that always went to point of attack on running plays even when there were two of us in the game. The three of us flip-flopped in and out, back and forth, all the way through. The one thing that confused me was that they never took advantage of my hands. I showed them in my workout that I could catch a ball. I accepted my place in the scheme, though, and just did whatever they asked of me. I could only give them what they wanted.

Kamikaze

I got my first *real* taste of kickoff coverage in Philadelphia. On this particular special teams unit I was a backup through my first three seasons. Soon, I would discover the distinction between doing it in practice and during live action on an NFL Sunday. As a constant member of the kickoff return team I watched a lot of film. A whole room could break out in hysteria when someone made the perfect hit and laid an opponent out. If you didn't want to be that guy sprawled out on the field in somebody else's meeting, you'd better have your head on a swivel as you came screaming down the field in search of the return man.

The blocking schemes are complex and well thought-out as the mind of a special teams coach is both creative and demented. He spends his day trying to invent ways to inflict pain and suffering on unsuspecting individuals. Double teams and wedges are just two simple ways to do so. The key is to set a cover man up so he has no idea where the hit is coming while he's at top speed. Well-trained return blockers will eyeball you as you come flying down the field, inviting your attention. The whole time you aren't even their responsibility, they are just trying to keep you focused on them and not paying attention to the man coming to knock your block off. The hits where you see a man leveled, his feet in the air above his head, are called 'de-cleaters'.

I remember my first time on the kickoff coverage team in Philadelphia. My heart was pumping four times its normal rate. The ten-yard run to get to top speed and the kick of the ball begins a rush like no other. Everything goes deaf and all you can see is mayhem. Opposing colored jerseys streak across your face as you run down with the 'head on a swivel'. Your first objective: Find the ball and zero in, making sure to stay in your designated lane. Then, recognize the scheme. If you've gotten deep across midfield, escaping the frontline assault and still have made no contact with the other side, you can rest assured there is a double team or wedge awaiting you at the second level. When you finally see where it's coming from, you have to attack it, bust through the double team or destroy the wedge as a human battering ram. And that's if you haven't been setup for the blind-side-shoe-removal hit. Your reward at the end of this five to ten seconds of chaos is a ball carrier with a full head of steam heading right for you, trying to crack a seam and take one to the house. Two objects, human bodies, come crashing together going at fast rates of speed from opposite directions. The impact is fierce and can cause great bodily harm. The rush you get from that one play is the equivalent of bungee jumping or skydiving- neither of which I would do. I did cover kickoffs and make tackles in the NFL, though!

The biggest asset in the kicking game and the thing "cover men" love most is a kicker that can consistently kick the ball deep into the end zone for a touchback. All ten cover men will run over to him on the sideline after he's done that just to pat him on the back or give him a hug. Touchbacks, equal no run-backs, and that means no punishment to endure.

My run in Philadelphia lasted for seven weeks, but came to an abrupt end out of left field. The Eagles eventually finished the season with five wins and eleven losses, myself present for three of the victories. I did exactly what they asked of me every single day. If they wanted more all they had to do was give me the opportunity. We had just beaten the Redskins on November 14 and preparing for the Indianapolis Colts to come into town the following week. We watched the Redskin game film on Monday and I enjoyed a day trip to Atlantic City on my off day, Tuesday. Back at work Wednesday, the day was long and hard-hitting. The two tights and I watched and critiqued our practice tape along with our tight end coach in his office. We were joking and laughing about something as we always seemed to be doing, when someone knocked on the closed door. An administrator apologized for the interruption, but said Coach Reid wanted to see me. Everybody in our tiny room looked at one another with the same puzzled look that I sported. What was this all about? I got up and walked around to the big office, knocked on the door and sat in a familiar spot.

Earlier in the day, the St. Louis Rams released a tight end and Coach Reid wanted to bring him to Philadelphia. In order to do that, he needed to clear a roster spot. And who do you think was heading out the door? I couldn't have been hit any harder from the blind side. First, a release in the middle of the week is almost unheard of in the NFL unless it is a kicker. I had just beat the hell out of myself on the field for what? Secondly, I knew there had to be someone on this roster less deserving than me of holding onto a job.

I returned to our tight end coach's office, which doubled as our meeting room, to give the news and say good-bye. They appeared as shocked as I was, but I didn't stick around long to figure out what had just happened. After signing the necessary paperwork in the main office, I went to my locker and grabbed my things, taking them out of the stadium in a green trash bag. I left that place so fast a cloud of smoke followed me. It was an interminably long ride across the bridge and back to the house in New Jersey.

My parents took the news as hard as I had. They had become accustomed to me being back around the house and they enjoyed watching me play. Pops was so angry he wanted to confront Andy Reid personally but I reminded him that it was all a business.

Though this all happened just eight days before Thanksgiving, I didn't have it in me to stick around. I was too close to the scene of the crime. A couple days later I was on a plane headed back to Atlanta. The roller coaster of 1999 was taking me up and down, round and around. And I was starting to get sick and tired of the ride.

A Little Justice

One good thing about my release is that it didn't happen until Wednesday. Because of that, the Eagles still had to pay me for the following game even though I was back in Atlanta. I was more than likely sitting in my favorite chair while they were on the field. My surprise check (the least they could have done for me after all I had tried to do for them) came in the mail in the middle of the following week just before Thanksgiving and I was thankful for it. To this day I hold bitterness toward the Eagles and find it hard to root for them even though the team included one of the nicer group of guys I have ever had the pleasure of working with.

The City Of Brotherly Love?

Philadelphia stained itself on October 10, 1999, showing why the city is sometimes considered to be home to some of the worst fans in all of professional sports. In my second game with the organization, the Dallas Cowboys came to town. The game was very competitive and clean on the field, but nasty in the stands. When future Hall of Fame wide receiver Michael Irvin went down on the field due to a neck injury and failed to get up the Eagles fans went into cheer mode. While he lay motionless on the field they celebrated broadly. At that moment I was embarrassed to wear the uniform. Down for quite some time, Michael had to be transported off the field on a stretcher. It turned out to be the last game of his stellar professional career. After twelve seasons he retired due to the injury sustained on the field *that* afternoon.

Top 10

The close of the century fast-approaching, everybody wanted to put some type of list together, celebrating the best of something in the past 100 years. Burlington County, the largest in New Jersey and the one in which I grew up, also got into the action and put one of their own together. They called it "The Top Ten Sports Legends Of Burlington County".

For ten weeks, starting October 31 and leading up to January 2, 2000, they would count down to one as they featured a male and female athlete. I came in respectfully at number ten on the list of male athletes and the company I was keeping was quite impressive. Some of the more famous names included on the list were:

Franco Harris

Thirteen-year National Football League Veteran

Nine-time Pro Bowl Running Back

Four-time Super Bowl Champion

Irvin Fryar

Seventeen-year National Football League Veteran

Five-time Pro Bowl Wide Receiver

Carl Lewis

Considered one of the greatest and most famous athletes of last century

Twenty-two gold medals (nine in the Olympic Games, eight at the World championships, two in the Pan American Games, two at the Goodwill games, and one at World Cup).

A prisoner of my chosen profession, I felt like a yo-yo-one minute I was up, the next down. I spent a quiet Thanksgiving alone in Atlanta, a couple of Cornish hens and a few sides to celebrate the start of the holiday season. With each week that passed I was more convinced that my season was over. I had at least made my presence felt in the league this season so there was always the possibility of someone being interested in bringing me into camp next year. Then, a week later, I got a surprise call from Danny Smith in Detroit. He'd seen my name on the wire and got the story from Philadelphia regarding the bad hand I had been dealt up there. He was calling to keep my spirits up and remind me to stay in shape in case something came about. That was encouraging, but it didn't look good for a return to the Lions; they were having a good season, 6-4 at the time, and things were running smoothly. Unless something drastic happened, there probably wasn't a need for change.

Three weeks later, Week Thirteen in the NFL, I was readapting to civilian life. An old friend from high school, Brian Jones, was in town. He was checking out the city because of a possible job transfer. We decided to meet at my Sunday hangout, the local sports bar. The two of us were digging into a big pile of wings when my cell phone rang. By now Danny Smith was programmed into my phone, so I recognized his name as it popped up on the screen. Over the crowd noise I listened to him tell me that one of the tight ends had gone down in their game against the Redskins. The severity of his knee injury wouldn't be known until the following day but if it was serious I would head back to Detroit. Halfway through Monday I got the call that I had anxiously waited for through a long, sleepless night. By afternoon I was shutting the apartment down one more time.

I walked right into the middle of another playoff run with the Lions. The 8-4 record that they had put together tied them for the NFC Central Division lead. The next game on schedule was a head-to-head battle in Tampa against the Bucs, the other 8-4 team. When I got back to Detroit it felt like I had never left and I fell right back into the mix of things. Number three on the depth chart, I was all over the field on special teams, stepping right into the shoes of the injured tight end. It was a good thing I made a good effort in staying prepared during my down time.

I felt like a bad luck charm during my second run in Detroit. All of the winning they had done in the first twelve games vanished once I got there. The first defeat came in a heartbreaking loss in Tampa. The game came down to the last seconds on the clock but we came up just short of victory. That was followed by a loss on the road in frigid Chicago and another in a Christmas Day home game against the Broncos. In the final weekend of the season we needed a win in Minnesota to secure a playoff spot, but fell short of that as well. Luckily, we got some help, a loss by another playoff hopeful, and backed into the post season at 8-8. That four weeks was very similar to the last half of the 1996 season I was in Washington with the Skins. Whatever could go wrong did. Fortunately, we managed to sneak our way into the playoffs this time though.

Like Coach Reeves said back in Atlanta, "Once you are in, anything can happen." It didn't matter how we got there, if we did something with the opportunity. And it definitely would have been a nice bit of personal satisfaction to have a part in bouncing my old team, the Washington Redskins, out of the playoffs in the first round. Sadly, we walked into an ambush in the Nation's capital and they sent us home to start our off-season.

Final Scores:
Lions 16-Tampa Bay Buccaneers 23
Lions 10-Chicago Bears 28
Lions 7-Denver Broncos 17
Lions 17-Minnesota Vikings 24
Playoffs: Lions 13-Washington Redskins 27

In less than ten months I had been a part of four organizations: Atlanta, Cleveland, Detroit and Philadelphia. I was tired and road-weary by the time I got back to Atlanta, finally home to stay for a while. After everything I'd been through, I figured if I could make it through this year there wasn't much I couldn't handle. Little word came out of Detroit as far as my future with the team, but that was the last thing on my mind right now. I had earned a nice long rest and it was time to get to it. I'd let everything work out according to God's plan. He was in charge!

TOP TEN
SPORTS LEGENDS
OF BURLINGTON COUNTY

Smith has traveled an impressive road

■ **EDITOR'S NOTE**: This is the first in a series naming the Top Ten male and female athletes in Burlington County history. The countdown will continue every Sunday with the top male and female athletes appearing Jan. 2.

By Jeff Offord
BCT sports writer

He played for 11 teams, wore 22 different uniforms, lived in two dozen apartments, slept in approximately 200 hotel rooms, played with more than 600 different teammates and traveled close to 60,000 miles.

All by bus.

And that's just his baseball career.

Wait until you hear about Ed Smith's life as a football player.

Smith, one of the finest, multi-talented male athletes in Burlington County history, has experienced more in his short lifetime than most of us could imagine.

As a child growing up with his mother, Pat, father, Ed Jr. and his little brother, Irv, in their two-story home in Browns Mills, Smith dreamed of being a baseball player. So when the opportunity arose to do just that shortly after his graduation from Pemberton High School in

Ed Smith

1987, Smith jumped at the chance, playing in minor-league ballparks from the Carolinas to California and a lot of places between.

Yet, when that dream ended after 10 years, he simply decided to live another. Why not try football, he thought? His high school football resume included Delaware Valley Athlete of the Year and Burlington County Player of the Year. How hard could it be to

MILLENNIUM

MEMORIES

See **SMITH** C7

Smith has traveled impressive road

SMITH From C1

strap on a helmet and pads one more time?

And with that, Smith embarked on yet another journey, one that began in Europe, continued through America's heartland, made a quick stop at the Super Bowl and now has left him right back home as a member of the Eagles.

Without a doubt, Smith has often traveled a sometimes bumpy road over the years.

But the trip sure has been exciting.

"How could I ever complain?" said Smith, who turned 30 last June. "There are so many people out there that go through life wondering what would have happened if they had done this or if they had done that. I've had the best of both worlds. I had some of the best days of my life playing baseball and I got a chance to play in a Super Bowl. How can you beat that? Sure, I've had days that haven't been very good. But who hasn't? I have no regrets."

Although he never made it to the major leagues, he is considered by many to be the best baseball player this county has ever produced. A pitcher with a wicked fastball, an infielder with a vacuum for a glove and a cannon for an arm, and a hitter who could slam a ball as far as the eye could see, Smith certainly had all the tools.

"We always tried to pitch around him," Rancocas Valley baseball coach Tony Lotierzo said. "Unfortunately, he'd still find a way to beat us. He had a great arm, a big bat and had lots of speed. No matter what we did he always got a couple of hits off us. And they were all bullets."

At 6-foot-3, 230-pounds, Smith's abilities on the football field nearly equaled his play on the baseball diamond back then. Smith could block as well as catch. And as a defensive end, few opponents ever escaped him. He also punted and played quarterback.

"Our coaching staff often talk about making sure that we know at all times where a particular player is on field. Well, Ed was definitely one of those players," said longtime Shawnee coach Tim Gushue, who often had the rather unenviable task of finding a way to stop Smith during the 1980s.

Thinking back, he was a man among boys when he played. But what a great person he was, too. I mean, there have been a lot of great players over the years. But he was the kind of player that you wished all athletes could be. He was such a gentleman. He would beat the devil

out of you but you still had so much respect for him."

Smith, according to his mother, was always a great athlete, even as a toddler. Said Pat Smith, little Eddie could dribble a ball when he was 12 months old and shoot it right through a hoop. As he grew older, Smith later fell in love with baseball but had a love affair with another sport.

Soccer.

"Eddie was always *The Man*," said Pat Smith. "I don't want to sound biased, but he was phenomenal. He was a natural at everything he tried. But he never really liked football. He was more interested in soccer.

"Soccer was the first true sport he played. He loved kicking the ball around the house. I grew up in a poor house when I was young, and my family never had the money for sports. So I vowed that when I had kids, I would make sure they had the opportunity to play anything they wanted. I bought baseballs, footballs, soccer balls. Ed just took to soccer."

His soccer days came to an abrupt halt when he got to high school. Already a young, up-and-coming baseball star, Smith started playing football as a freshman. Although still a novice, Smith made an immediate impression.

"The thing about Ed was that he was just so much bigger than all the other kids," Pemberton football coach Bill McDowell said. "But not only was he big, he had so much skill. I mean, when he was here he did everything for us. He was the tight end, he was a defensive end, he punted, he threw the ball. You name it."

By the end of his senior season, Smith had proven to be one of the county's all-time greatest athletes. About the only question remaining late that year was what sport Smith would pursue. And would his upcoming days be spent in college or as a pro?

Those decisions wouldn't come easy to Smith. He had a full baseball scholarship to the University of North Carolina waiting for him. He had most major NCAA Division 1 football powerhouses in the country hoping to sign him. Instead, Smith took another route. He decided to sign a contract with the Chicago White Sox, which had taken him in the seventh round of the 1987 baseball draft.

Smith received an estimated $70,000 signing bonus with the White Sox and was immediately assigned to their rookie club in Sarasota, Fla. From there, he played on nine minor-league teams from 1987 to 1995 without getting a call-up to the big leagues.

"I went with my heart," Smith said. "I went with what I thought would make me the happiest. I took advantage of what was in front of me. It didn't work out, but I wouldn't trade those days in for anything. I loved baseball. I still do. Even now, I still love going to the batting cages and swinging the bat.

"I love the game, but I had to be a realist. I was really getting frustrated. I mean, the travel wasn't that bad. But I had run my course in baseball. I always told myself that when the game was no longer exciting I'd move on. I could have continued to play, sure. I played with guys that are still in the minors. But for me, it was just time

to look toward something else."

Of course, that meant football.

With help from his brother, Irv, Ed began to make some inquiries. Irv Smith had enjoyed a spectacular high school career himself and later went on to star at Notre Dame. He was drafted in the first round of the NFL Draft in 1993 and is now the starting tight end for the Cleveland Browns.

After playing 997 games of minor-league baseball without a major-league call up, Ed Smith began his football career with the Frankfort Galaxy of the World League in 1996.

From there, he got a shot in camp with the Rams, then spent the season with the Redskins' practice squad. He spent the last two seasons with the Falcons.

Although he caught only seven passes in 20 games with the Falcons, he did see extensive action on special teams. Last year, he caught a pass in the NFC Championship game and got a chance to take on the Broncos in the Super Bowl in Miami.

"I remember the day he decided he was quitting baseball," said Irv. "He said he was done with it and that he wanted to get involved in something else. I really didn't know where he was going with it. Then he told me he wanted to play football. I didn't say anything for about five seconds. Finally, I said to him, "If anybody in the world can do it, it's you.

"Ed has always been such a gifted athlete. There really wasn't a rivalry between us because he's always been so much better than me. In high school, I was always chasing records or trying to win awards that he'd already won. He set the standard for me. He still does."

Ed Smith left Atlanta at the end of last season and moved on to Cleveland, where he teamed for a short time with Irv. After the Browns released him, Smith made it to Detroit's camp before being cut. He signed with the Eagles last month.

"At this stage of my life, I'm still extremely healthy," said Ed. "I didn't even play college football and I'm only 30. I know I can contribute. I enjoy playing special teams. Guys have made careers of playing special teams. But I know I can do some things as a tight end, too.

"If my body breaks down or my mind says I just can't do it anymore, then I'll quit. But I don't have a timetable. I can see myself playing until I'm 60."

Knowing Smith, he'll then quit football and begin a career as the oldest professional basketball player.

Hey, why not?

ED SMITH GLANCE

NAME: Ed Smith
SPORTS: Baseball, football
HOMETOWN: Browns Mills
HIGH SCHOOL: Pemberton
COLLEGE: None
ACCOMPLISHMENTS: All-County First Team football selection in 1985 and 1986. Made First Team both on offense and defense in 1986. ... At County First Team baseball pick in 1986 and 1987. ... All-County basketball selection in 1987. ... Selected as the Delaware Valley Athlete of the Year as a senior in 1987. ... Played minor league baseball for 10 seasons (1987-1995). ...Drafted in the seventh round of the major league baseball draft in 1987 by the Chicago White Sox. Reportedly received a signing bonus of $70,000 ... Hit .323 at Triple A Buffalo in 1995. ...Made the switch to football in 1996, first playing for the Frankfort Galaxy of the World League. ... First

NFL training camp in Los Angeles in 1996. ... After a short stint on the Washington Redskins practice squad the year prior, played in five games for the Atlanta Falcons in 1997, making five catches at tight end. ...Played tight end and on special teams for Falcons in 1998. Caught pass in NFC Championship game against Minnesota Vikings and played in Super Bowl XXXIII. ... Released from both the Cleveland Browns and Detroit Lions before signing a contract with the Eagles last month.
MISCELLANEOUS: Born June 5, 1969 ... Currently listed in the Eagles' media guide as 6-foot-4, 268 pounds. ... Brother of Irv Smith, who was drafted in the first round out of Notre Dame University. Irv Smith played for the San Francisco 49ers before moving on to his current squad, the Cleveland Browns.

CHAPTER TEN

'XFL' Birmingham Thunderbolts

There was one common denominator developing in my life. No matter what was going on and where I was coming back from, I always seemed to have Atlanta on my mind. And it is there that I landed; I seemed to have found a true home after all these years on the road. So, why not make it official? For a while I had been dreaming of owning a home. I had lived in every part of the country in one apartment after the other. To finally be in the position to put some roots in the ground was part of the dream.

I did some shopping shortly after returning from Detroit and it wasn't long before I found my dream home. Looking back it was more than I needed but as we all know, money can sometimes change how we think. I had lived so simply my entire adult life. After all I'd done and what I'd done to get there, didn't I deserve this? For a long time I could pack everything I owned in my tiny Camaro. And I still didn't own much. But I wanted to live like everybody else in the locker room. My vision was clouded and all I saw was this big, beautiful, four-bedroom house in the northeast suburbs of Atlanta. I had the money in the bank and that was all that mattered. I wanted a bigger slice of the American Pie. In a matter of weeks after my return, on January 31, 2000, I was sitting in an office, signing the papers to close on my first home. It was exactly one year from the day I played in Super Bowl XXXIII. The feelings I got as I walked through the door of my empty house in Lilburn matched how I felt running out of the tunnel that night. What a rush! No more apartment living for me, it was the high life from here.

Irv

My brother had reached the peak of frustration after his seventh year in the league. I could tell in his voice that he was becoming disenchanted toward the end of his dismal year in Cleveland and it spilled into the start of the off-season. Playing professional sports is not the happy-go-lucky life that everyone believes it to be. Along with the incredible pressures to perform and deal with the politics and business of the game plus constant sacrifices you have to make, you still have to live life and navigate all the curves it may throw you.

The rocky relationship between Irv and Palmer that started in the off-season festered through their 2-14 season. Throughout Irv tried to repair a relationship built on the fact of two people having a baby together, rather than on love. My brother had continued to learn lessons from me well after we left the comforts of Browns Mills and jumped into manhood. He knew the pain I had endured when it came to decisions I had made regarding my son. He didn't want what I had. Conversely, I wanted what he was trying to have but was unsure of how to obtain it. His relationship with Little Irv's mother was sinking and he was trying to keep it afloat, but it was tough when combined with NFL restrictions and demands. In the NFL no sick or vacation days exist in which to stay home and work out problems.

The season over, Irv became a free man. The Browns had picked up only the second year of his two-year contract with the 49ers and there was no talk of an extension or new deal. He couldn't leave Cleveland fast enough after that last game of their long season as he wanted to get to Arizona and his son who'd been back and forth during the year. As I watched his drama unfold over the months, a whole flock of emotions stirred inside of me. It was my turn to take another valuable lesson from him. Maybe it was finally time I did something about my situation.

I got lost in the frenzy of new home ownership. The simple things excited me. I didn't realize how many things I needed and shopping became a daily ritual as I bought everything from my first set of appliances to bathroom fixtures and window treatments. When my activity finally started slowing near the beginning of March, I should have been carefree, without a worry in the world. But there was something on my mind stemming from Utah. There was too big a piece of my life missing for me to be totally happy and content and if I didn't do something about it now I might find that it may one day be too late. It was time to find out if there was a place in my son's life for his father.

Nothing was happening on the work front. It was getting near the time when teams would be cranking it up and starting the off-season workout programs but Pat was coming up empty in the job department. My age and salary were weighing heavily against me. I would have gladly played for the league minimum but the collective bargaining agreement tied my hands. Someone would have to fork over $350k because of my three credited seasons in the league. That is a lot of money to pay a soon to be 31-year old backup when there are rookies and first year players out there for the basement bargain price of about $225k. It is all economics. Hopefully someone would look past the two strikes I had against me and give me a chance.

Nothing from nothing leaves nothing, so I decided to just call out to Utah one evening. At the very least I could see how Eddie was doing, catch up with Lee and see if they needed anything. It had been another long stretch since we'd had any type of contact so I had no idea how things were going. Not too much to my surprise it wasn't a slice of heaven. Lee was now a single mother, her husband having run out on her and their four children. My son, now ten years old, had three younger sisters ranging in age from seven to three. Our extensive conversation was full of surprises. Lee had been through a whole lot of headaches with her husband, culminating in him leaving her for another woman. Still some back and forth between them, it sounded like things were pretty much done. That left things wide open for my line of questioning.

I wanted to know what Eddie knew about me and if I had any place in his life? I wasn't sure if he only knew Teddy as his father or if they had ever told him differently; that is how far removed from the situation I'd been. Lee explained they had told him the truth recently when he started asking pertinent questions. His last name was different from his little sisters' and he wanted to know why.

That news came as a huge relief to me because I don't think I would have had the heart to turn his world upside down by destroying something he might have believed his whole life: that Teddy was his father. That opened the door as well; maybe it was time to introduce myself to him so we could start trying to build a relationship. It didn't have to be father and son from the start but I at least wanted him to know who I was. I asked Lee if I could come out for a visit and she agreed that it was probably long overdue. I had the green light to make plans for a visit with my son! I'd be laying eyes on him for the first time since I took him to the McDonald's Playland six years ago.

Reunited

A little over a week later Lee's father picked me up from the airport in Utah. I didn't know what her parents thought about me because I wasn't there to know what Lee might have been saying through the years. They only knew one side of the story and I know it couldn't have matched my version. It was all irrelevant for this visit though. The two of us talked casually as he drove me to the restaurant Lee managed. I had little butterflies as we pulled into the parking lot and when I saw her I was flushed with memories from the good old days. Motherhood and a bad marriage hadn't robbed her of anything as far as I could see from the outside; she looked very good. And once we started talking I sensed a level of maturity that comes with age and life experience. Neither of us was the same person we were all those years back. It felt like a lifetime ago that I'd even known her. This wasn't the woman I remembered and I'm sure she was thinking the same thing. The last time she laid eyes on me I was a struggling minor league baseball player. At the very least my new physical appearance had to be a shocker.

We exchanged nervous pleasantries as her father and I took a booth so we could have some lunch while she finished up a few things before leaving work for the day. After eating, her father took off and I sat by myself in the bar area of the restaurant for a short time before we headed out. The closer we got to her house the more nervous I became. I didn't feel this jittery getting ready to come out of the tunnel during the Super Bowl. When we pulled into her apartment complex I saw a young man running and playing with his friends. I knew instantly that he was my son. I held back tears. As we parked directly in front of Lee's apartment, the whole group of boys came running, Eddie leading the way. Stepping out I found myself facing my son with no clue what to say. He might have the knowledge that I was his father, but that didn't mean I had instant acceptance as 'Daddy'.

Lee walked around the car and introduced me by saying, "This is Ed." My first instinct was to grab Eddie, give him a big bear hug and not let him go, but I chickened out. I didn't want to make it too intense a moment so I gave him a quick embrace.

Then, I stepped back and reached into the car. Lee had given me a list of video games he had been asking for and I had picked one up, along with little trinkets for his sisters. His eyes lit up when I pulled it out and the first thing he wanted to know was if he could play it right then. Mom said yes and he and his friends ran for the front door, leaving Lee and me outside. I stood in disbelief. Surely there was no way the little boy who just stood before me was the baby I had once held. Sadly enough, it was though. I had missed all of the years in between and they could never be retrieved.

I had received what seemed like first approval from Eddie and his friends. We would necessarily have to feel each other out over the next few days, but I hadn't expected to bridge the whole gap right away; I knew it would take time for him to get to know me. And that would have to be done without piling a lot on him. He didn't need to understand everything at such an early age, just that I wanted to be a part of his life slowly but surely, if he would allow me.

The next big test waited on the other side of the apartment door, Lee's mother. She occasionally baby-sat for Lee and this was one of those days. I was prepared for a very icy reception. She and I had never had bitter words, but there was always that bit of tension when I used to call way back in the day when Lee and I were going through our times of separation during my early days of minor league baseball. No matter what happened I would be respectful but I was prepared for the worst all the way up to the moment I walked though the front door. Fortunately for me, Teddy had helped take the heat off me and built my image back up over the last few years by really treating their daughter badly. I wasn't such a bad guy now.

My original plan was to get a hotel room but Lee thought it would be easier if I stayed around their house, sleeping on the sofa downstairs. That was strange the first night but I quickly got over it. And it did make it easier to spend time with Eddie as well as to get to know his three baby sisters. I spent four great days with my son. I saw why Irv was fighting so hard to work things out in his situation and became angry that I hadn't done the same years ago. It wasn't an instant father/son bond but I was making a new friend fast and that was the first step. I took him and his little friends to a field and we played football, basketball and baseball in consecutive days over the weekend. And he and I spent a good deal of time alone, trying to get to know each other. We played video games in his room and traded off asking questions. I wanted to know all the little things about him, his favorite color, food, teacher, animal, everything. And he wanted to know all about my life as a professional athlete, especially the Super Bowl. We were getting along just fine.

I was trying my best not to rush things – not to overload his circuits. A grown man, it was hard for me to absorb everything and deal with all the swirling emotions, so I wanted to take special care in how I handled his feelings. It was a juggling act not to push myself as Daddy but to let him know that it surely would be nice if he someday wanted to think of me in that manner. At least that was my plan.

On the last night of my visit Eddie became a little despondent. I took Lee and him out for a quiet dinner while the girls went to stay with their grandparents. I was a little disappointed that he didn't have much to say. It was almost like he had stopped having a good time. I was flying out to Arizona the next afternoon and it would put a damper on the trip overall if this was how it ended. His demeanor didn't change through dinner. Lee told me he got that from me and that I shouldn't take it too much to heart. I've been known to slip into a quiet 'Gemini Mood' but he didn't share the astrological sign of the twin with me. The more I thought about it I figured the long weekend had just tired him out so I enjoyed the rest of the night enough for both of us.

Eddie was still withdrawn the next morning and trip time was running. As Lee loaded the car with kids I took him aside and told him how much this had all meant to me and how I was looking forward to us continuing to get to know one another. Maybe one day soon he could even come out to see me in Atlanta. He was very quiet in accepting my invitation and pretty much silent all the way to the airport. It was starting to feel awkward now. I didn't know what was wrong and definitely didn't know how to fix it. When we pulled up to the terminal I tried my best to reach out to Eddie one last time, but didn't quite get it right. I was new at this. The last thing I said to him was that I'd see him again soon. I got a half hug, not much enthusiasm, and took that as a sign of indifference. He just didn't know what to make of all this. It was a lot to soak in over a weekend. I said good-bye to everyone after collecting my bags and turned for the terminal. Even the way things had ended I still considered this a great first step. And I was going to make sure it didn't all end here.

I stood inside, preparing to check my bags, and reflected on the last four days. Lost in thought, I suddenly heard a familiar voice behind me; Lee was trying to get my attention from the front door. When I walked over she asked if I'd go out and talk to Eddie. Since last night he'd been holding something inside. That was why he was so quiet. And now he was crying in the car. While she stayed with my bags I went out to the curb. Eddie was in the back seat and his sisters were trying to console him. I opened the back door, got him out, and sat him on the trunk. When I asked him what was wrong he looked at me through a stream of tears and said that he was sad because he thought he would never see me again.

I'd misjudged the impact of our visit. Giving him a huge hug, I wiped his tears away. I should have been crying myself, but I couldn't stop smiling. He had just made me a very happy man. It took me a few minutes to eliminate his tears, but we both felt better after a little talk. I knew I would see him again soon and I let him know that. We would do everything we'd done this past weekend and then some. I put him back in the car and said good-bye to all again. As I walked back into the terminal I finally shed a tear. It was tough to board that plane to Arizona. I started to feel like Eddie; I didn't want this to end. This had been a great first step in the start of what I hoped was a relationship for life.

My Little Secret

Returning to Atlanta after our reunion presented a new problem altogether. Over the years I had developed a defense mechanism to push away the embarrassment of living my life as an absentee father. I knew my situation was different from most, but I still felt a sting of shame when the subject of children came up. I was scared to tell people that I had a son and I didn't even know where he was or what he was doing. What would they think? The last thing I wanted to be known as was a deadbeat dad. The only people who knew about my little secret were friends and teammates that had been in my life since baseball days and before. They knew what I had been through and the decisions that I'd made. The people that meant the most to me today had no idea about what I was holding back because I never let them in. I had never confided in Nate or Calvin and even Randy was still in the dark. You weren't supposed to keep secrets from the woman you might want to spend the rest of your life with (our relationship was back on) but it was tough to open up and let anybody in after living like a lone wolf for so many years.

After all the off and on time between us I had never let Randy into my protected circle. And now that we were in the same city and spending time together I didn't know what to do. How was I supposed to drop this bombshell on her after all this time? She didn't even know where I was going when I went out to Utah because I only told her half the truth, a bad habit of mine. She was under the impression that I was going to Arizona to visit my brother – which was true. What I failed to tell her was that the first leg of the trip was to Salt Lake City. Back home I was both excited and confused. I had a son who now knew who I was and I wanted to be a part of his life. The best thing I could have done was tell the truth but I stalled for time and continued to keep my secret to myself. I didn't realize that the longer I lived the lie, the more I complicated life.

When late May arrived and I was still unsigned, I began to worry about my football future. There was very little interest in a backup tight end who would turn 31 in June. The sad part is, it had nothing to do with having talent to play the game. If you were shopping for a lamp and had two to choose from, one being newer and cheaper, which would you buy? That is what NFL teams do, essentially. They seek younger, less expensive models. Pat was getting very little response, the word being, "We'll get back to you." The end of the road seemed to be right ahead as far as a future in the NFL.

While I sought work Irv was practically turning it down. He had yet to sign, but it wasn't because he wasn't receiving any interest; he was just unsure if he wanted to continue playing after seven long, grueling seasons. His first priority was taking care of problems in the ever-explosive relationship with little Irv's mother. He had come to the conclusion that although he did not want to continue with her, he did not want to lose his son.

She was making it pretty hard on him out in Arizona and threatening to make his life further hell because she held the biggest card in the deck, his son. With his attention divided it was hard to even put football into the equation, but the pressure to keep going was also intense. When the Redskins contacted him in early June and he eventually signed, I could hear in his voice that he wasn't too excited about obtaining the job. But it was what he was supposed to do according to just about everybody else. The fire that should burn inside every athlete only flickered in him. While I would have given my left arm for the job he had, I could tell he would have gladly given it to me if he could.

When training camps began to open up in July, I was still unemployed. I spent my days in my big house waiting for the phone to ring, but it might as well have been out of service because I didn't get the call. I worked out feverishly, trying to keep hope alive in my mind. A hard reality to face, it was possible the end of the road was not just in sight, but quite probably right in front of me.

Fear of losing the only identity known can be a scary thing. The only thing I had ever done was play sports. Consequently, all self worth was locked into how I thought everybody perceived me. If I wasn't playing sports, what or who was I going to be? Deep down I knew I was worth more than anything I had ever done on a baseball or football field, but the mind can play tricks on you when you let it.

I wasn't quite ready to give it all up yet even though it looked like the time had come. Some athletes hold on too long and I didn't want to be one of those, but something just wasn't right about the way everything seemed to be ending so abruptly. The dream couldn't end like this. I had accomplished a great deal, but I didn't feel like it was fair to conclude this way. There wasn't a lot I had left to do on the field, but I felt I deserved to leave on better terms. One last trip around the track, a victory lap, and then I could walk off into the sunset with peace of mind. I think that is what drives a lot of athletes to hold on past their prime. All you want is to feel good about how you walk away from something for which you've sacrificed so much of your life. That isn't a lot to ask. The nasty truth is: the game doesn't owe you a thing. If you are not prepared for the end, it can gnaw at you.

Late in the summer I became obsessed with staying in shape and being ready for 'the call'. Allowing myself to become consumed with getting that one last chance, I let it spill into other areas of my life. Sadly, two relationships suffered because of it. I kept pushing Randy away, never letting her in, mostly out of fear. And I was rarely 100% honest about anything. Even when I told her about Eddie, I made up bits and pieces to hide true facts. Even in truth I couldn't keep from lying a little. She had no idea who I was, because I didn't allow her to. I always hid behind something and this was another way to do it, focusing on finding work.

I really disappointed myself in regards to my son as well. I talked to him on the phone a great deal, but didn't follow through on seeing him as much as I should have with some of the time I had on my hands. The strange thing is, after spending all those years wanting to be in his life, I was scared to actually do it. I didn't really know how to get close to him, especially in phone conversation. It wasn't like stepping into a toddler's life; he was well past the early stages and had been through a lot. I was coming in from nowhere, all of a sudden, trying to be a father when he still considered Teddy to be that to him. Even though Teddy had run out on him, he still held that title. And that was tough to accept. To complicate matters, when I talked to Lee about Eddie and me spending time together in Atlanta, she wanted to make it a package deal. She didn't think he could handle the trip by himself, so she wanted to come along. That frustrated me. When things got tough, I re-erected my defense system and put the blinders back on. Things never seemed easy or I always made them tougher than they actually were. Either way, I wasn't handling anything the way I should have. This isn't how things were supposed to be going.

Hanging Up The Shoes

I was sitting in my home office, a converted bedroom upstairs, when my phone did finally ring in early August. The call from an NFL training camp came right in the middle of the day. But it wasn't an administrator calling my house, it was Irv! He was in the middle of two-a-day practices and I could feel his pain through the phone. As much as I wanted to be in camp, that was the part I just could not miss. The glory of playing football on a Sunday in the NFL is just barely enough to make it worth the while of punishment and abuse one goes through during the dog days of training camp. I would have a hard time wishing that on my worst enemy.

I had just talked to Irv the night before, so I thought this mid-day call was strange, but I know how good it is to hear a friendly voice when going through hell. He wasn't just up for idle chitchat though. He didn't waste a lot of time before he changed conversational direction and got to why he was calling; he needed some advice. Irv had come to the crossroad in his professional football career, he didn't want to do it any more. In camp going through the motions, his heart was not in the game. Having made the commitment, he felt obligated to fulfill it, but he was not happy. His question of me was what I thought he should do. It was very easy to answer him. I explained to him how I felt the night I called him and asked about the possibilities of playing football back in the summer of 1995. In choosing a different direction, I had to walk away from something I had loved since I was a little boy, baseball. I struggled with that back then just as he struggled today. Your heart is what leads you, and if it isn't where it should be you are not being true to yourself. And the last place you ever want to be in this world is on an NFL football field with your head and heart in the wrong place. It didn't matter what he thought everyone expected of him or what they thought he should be doing. He owed it to himself to be happy. No one else was making the sacrifices or taking the hits. And if he didn't want to do it any more he didn't have to.

I could sense the weight being lifted off my brother's shoulders. Before he hung up he promised to call me back in a bit; he had something to take care of. He first notified Pat Dye Jr. at Pro-Files Sports Management, now also his agent, and then the Redskins that he was not interested in playing football any more. Both tried to talk him out of it, but his mind was made up. They warned that this action would make it incredibly tough to find a job in the NFL if he changed his mind, but he was done with football. And he couldn't have been happier. When I talked to Irv right after he signed the papers in the Redskins' administration office, there was peace in his voice. When I asked him what his plans were, he didn't have any, so I invited him down to Atlanta and we sat together in my living room later that evening. Like two young boys at a sleepover, we talked all night long. The laughter we shared was good for both of us and exactly what we each needed. That is one of the things I love most of all about the relationship I have with my family. In times of need we are there for one another. Five summers prior I had called Irv, down and out about baseball, asking him for advice about breaking into football. This day he had called me asking for advice, wanting to get out of the game. Regardless of what it is, we always know where to turn.

Football out of the picture provided Irv opportunity to focus on issues of highest concern. He spent nearly a week with me in Atlanta and eventually flew back to Arizona to tend to his business. His unexpected retirement from football meant that for the first time in fourteen years neither of us was playing professional sports. I still wanted in, but it just didn't seem to be in the cards. Meanwhile, Irv was happy to be out. Every night before I went to bed there were many things I prayed for, forgiveness for my sins being top priority, but I also asked God for the chance to put closure to my career. That would mean a great deal and allow me to truly move on with life.

When you ask for something with a sincere heart, God not only hears, but He will bring you blessings. They don't necessarily come exactly when you want them, as it is according to His time, but He hears you. I was about to receive a gift in a strange form from a very unlikely carrier, Vince McMahon. Way back in February of 2000 the leader of the WWF (World Wrestling Federation) came up with an idea. He wanted to put together his own football league, the XFL. The "X" was for X-treme and that is what he wanted to give the fans, football with an attitude. He didn't want to compete with the NFL, but to fill the void created after the Super Bowl.

I hadn't heard much about what he was trying to do, but my first thought was that I didn't want any part of it. As much as I wanted to play the game, I wasn't going to make a fool of myself in some circus act. When my phone first started ringing in the beginning of September, coaches from the newly-created franchises called to see if I had any interest in playing. I was skeptical and critical. How were they going to combine football with wrestling? Were players going to be out on the field body-slamming and head-butting one another like they did in the pretend world of pro wrestling?

As I learned more about what the XFL was to include it didn't sound like such an absurd idea. McMahon is a marketing genius; one doesn't become head of a 100 million dollar industry by mistake. And when NBC stepped into the picture, putting up half the money to start the league along with a television deal, my attention perked up a bit. This was something of which I might want to take a better look.

Every time someone called I drilled for information. I was assured that the only thing players would be required to do in this league was play football. The game would be real and there would be no acting or crazy stunts involved, just football with an edge. That confirmed, I agreed to drive down to Birmingham, Alabama with my best friend, Nate, who was also out of work in the NFL since the finish of the 1998 season. Birmingham was one of the eight inaugural cities selected to host a team in the XFL and a group workout was to be held in late September. Each team would get a workout report and a draft would happen in late October. Both Nate and I felt that this could be a stepping-stone back into the NFL. For me, that would be nice, but if it never came about I might get a chance for the one thing I really wanted: that victory lap!

Nate and I drove down to the workout together and the hot topic between us was the possibility of playing together one more time. Nate had gotten hurt at the beginning of the Super Bowl season in Atlanta during training camp. He was on injured reserve all the way up to week eleven and the Falcons released him when he was eligible to come off and play. He found work in New York with the Giants after Atlanta let him go and finished that season there but missed all of 1999 when he couldn't land a contract. He and I did our best work together, him playing offensive tackle and me lining up next to him all the time when I was still on the practice squad in Atlanta. He was my best friend on and off the field and we looked forward to getting back out there as a pair if it worked out.

The first two things I noticed when we got to Birmingham were the number of players in for the workout and the quality on the field. There was much negativity floating around about the XFL before it ever got started. Most of the flack came from the media, who despised McMahon. I only met him a couple of times, but you could tell he lived by his own rules. Any publicity was good publicity, as far as he was concerned. The way he marketed the new league was as a raunchy, in-your-face type of game. Stepping across lines was nothing new to him. What was unfair was the criticism about the type of players to be involved in the league. NO draft had yet transpired. The team would consist of athletes in circumstances similar to my own. Not with my background, but facing the same situation as I was. For a thousand different reasons there were a lot of football players who could not find work in the NFL. If this new league were a possibility, why not take advantage of it? It is ludicrous to think the level of play would match the National Football League, but that isn't what anybody was saying. At the same time, the XFL wasn't going to consist of a bunch of bums either.

When Nate and I pulled into Birmingham for our workout, we ran into old teammates from Atlanta as well as an old Philadelphia buddy of mine. A modest number of the assembled talent had spent some time in the NFL at one point or another. This was encouraging because it would add to the credibility of the league and help to put a good product on the field. Also out there was a lot of unproven and young talent, fresh from the college ranks. From what I saw that afternoon if the other camps being held in the different regions had similar levels of talent, it would not be a far stretch to say they could put eight quality teams together. The more I thought about it, the better I felt about getting involved from the start.

Nate and I completed our workout and returned to Atlanta. During the month before the XFL draft my phone was very busy! All league teams wanted to make as certain that key players were onboard for the cause. I made it clear that if an NFL opportunity came about IT would take precedence, but that didn't seem likely. Nobody was knocking down my door. On October 28th the XFL held its first draft. In yet another twist of fate, Nate and I went back-to-back in the selection process. Of all the available players, we fell right next to each other. Our vision of playing as teammates went out the door, as he became the 97th overall pick, going to the Los Angeles Xtreme and I went 98th to the Birmingham Thunderbolts. What are the odds of that? I would stay close to home and Nate would jump across the country. I was going back to a very familiar city with family ties to keep me company. Funny how I always seemed to be landing in the same spots no matter what I was doing. It had to be more than just coincidence; there had to be a force working in my life.

Before the end of the calendar year I had made the two and a half hour drive from Atlanta to Birmingham three times for mini-camps with my new team. With much to accomplish and little time, the season starting in the first week of February, it was both exciting and crazy being on the ground floor of something like this! As mentioned, there was much negativity surrounding what McMahon was trying to do. As players, we were caught in the middle. All I wanted to do was play football, but there was so much focus on the wrong things. McMahon didn't help the cause by the way he promoted his new venture, but he was signing the checks so we had to ride the wave he created.

Old-Timer

At 31 years of age I was the third oldest member on my XFL team and affectionately referred to as 'Pops'. The other two in the 'geriatric group' were Casey Weldon, 31 but a few months older, and Reggie Johnson, a full year my senior. Reggie and Casey were teammates at Florida State University and amongst the three of us, with my four years of service in the league, we had twenty years of NFL experience under our belts. As we all got to know one another as a group and became comfortable, it was common to hear our third tight end, Scott Thompson, ride Reggie and me like horses. His favorite thing to do was ask us where our walkers were as we made our way out onto the field. All in good fun, we gave it right back to him. I reminded all that with age came great wisdom. We developed great relationships quickly, without all of the egos created by the money in the NFL, and a great work environment was established.

Early on I knew I would enjoy my XFL experience because it was just what the doctor ordered at the end of my long, lightly-celebrated career. It had been quite some time since I commanded the type of respect I now did on the field of play. I was like one of Gladys Knight's "Pips", a backup, in the NFL. In the XFL I was going to get one last chance to shine as one of the better tight ends in the league. I'd show them what an old man could do.

Once the holiday season of 2000 rolled around it was all downhill to the start of XFL training camp in Orlando, Florida. As I struggled with other issues in my life this was a great diversion- a chance to get away from it all. I shut the house down, preparing to be away the entire month of January, and boarded a plane New Year's Day.

XFL Teams

Eastern Division	**Western Division**
Birmingham Thunderbolts	Las Vegas Outlaws
Chicago Enforcers	Los Angeles Xtreme
New York/New Jersey Hitmen	Memphis Maniaxs
Orlando Rage	San Francisco Demons

Rules Of Engagement

Over the top! That is what Vince McMahon promised, then attempted to deliver. The league was promoted as if it was the WWF. That was probably the first mistake, turning off many people from the very beginning. What the cheerleaders wore, how they performed on the field, and who they were dating should not have been issues. Those topics gave the XFL a raunchy appeal, the stain hard to clean off once it was branded. A quality product on the field should have been the main focus. Then some of the ideas to make the game more interesting could have worked. Some rule changes, for example, were innovative. A work in progress, adjustments were even made after the season started. There was never a dull day in the XFL. Some changes included:

– No coin toss to determine which team gets the ball. Instead, action begins before the game even kicks off. A player from each team lines up on the 35-yard line. The referee blows the whistle and each player dashes to the 50-yard line in an attempt to recover the ball placed there. Recovering team chooses: kick or receive.

– Returning teams must run kickoffs back out of the end zone, unless the kick goes through the end zone: no touchbacks.

– Extra point after touchdown: pass or run, ball spotted on the 2-yard line. No extra-point attempt by the kicker.

– Receivers need only one foot inbounds for a pass

reception.

– Teams have 35 seconds to get a play off after previous play is ruled dead and 25 seconds following any clock stoppage.

– Quarterbacks who slide can be downed by mere contact and can't be hit.

– No in-the-grasp rule, the play stops when forward progress is halted.

– College football overtime system will be used. In overtime, each team will have at least one possession, a maximum of four downs from the opposition's 20-yard line, unless a defensive touchdown is scored on the first possession. However, if the first team scores a touchdown in fewer than four downs, the second team only gets that many plays to respond.

– Offensive backs and receivers are allowed in motion toward the line of scrimmage before the ball is snapped.

– No fair catches are permitted during the kicking game, but the returning player is granted a 5-yard protected halo wherein a member of the kicking team may not encroach until the ball is touched. The kicking team may not cross the line of scrimmage until the ball is punted. At the same time, any punt traveling more than 25 yards past the line of scrimmage is a live ball and can be recovered by either team.

In addition to the rules on the field:

– Cameras will to be located everywhere; locker rooms, sidelines, helmets and on the field in the huddles. Anyone can be miked.

– The base salary for each player in the league will be $45k. The winning team each week will be rewarded a bonus and the losing team will get nothing. The League Championship game is worth one million dollars, shared by the winning team.

– Players are allowed to put nicknames on the backs of their jerseys. In Birmingham we voted as a team to simply use our last names. "He Hate Me" was one of the more creative names on one player's back in Las Vegas. He explained the meaning behind his name in the first televised XFL game on NBC. Players on the opposing team hated him for what he was doing to them on the field. He looked across to the other sideline and pointed them out one by one: "He Hate Me, He Hate Me, He Hate Me!"

Birmingham Bolts 2001

The four Eastern teams held camp in and around Orlando while Western teams did so in the Las Vegas area. Our practice facility was a very familiar place for me and brought back some great memories. The field we practiced on was right outside the Citrus Bowl, which stood directly beside Tinker Field, my old home with the Orlando Cubs. My baseball life would never let me stray too far away without popping up to remind me of the good old days. Back in 1994, I played against Michael Jordan on that field. In 2001, I was walking past it to get to football practice. Life can be very unpredictable at times.

Training camp presented time to test the league's gadgets and ideas. With three preseason games slated for the month we were in town, all the props were brought out for a trial run in our first one. As we played the Orlando Rage in the Citrus Bowl it became obvious that this whole setup was going to take some getting used to. Distractions abounded! Some were:

– A cameraman on the field of play. In and out of our huddles and behind the play when it started, he was dressed in what looked like crash gear in case he got caught in the middle of the action. As any play came to an end he hunted a face in which to jam his camera. Very intrusive, this was part of what McMahon wanted: In Your Face!

– Reporters roamed the sidelines followed by their own

cameraman. At liberty to interview anybody they wanted to right in the middle of the game, they then broadcast the goods over the stadium's big screen. If this was how it was going to be during the regular season, I remember thinking they'd better be prepared to do an awful lot of bleeping.

– Casey Weldon, our quarterback, and one of our linebackers wore cameras mounted on top of their helmets. Everything that could be picked up on that camera and microphone was broadcast for fans to consume. The funniest thing about the oversized head-cam was how the one wearing it looked like "The Great Gazoo", the tiny green space man, from *The Flintstones*. Their heads looked huge with the extra, top-mounted part.

XFL training camp wasn't nearly as tough as one in the NFL, but we worked hard for the month we were in Florida. Cuts were made throughout and it looked like we were forming a pretty good team. The level of play and competition in this league was going to be just about what I thought all along, much better than anything I had seen in the World League but nowhere near what the NFL had to offer. In my opinion that still made it well worth the price of admission.

At the end of January we had one more preseason game against the team from Chicago. The day after that we would break camp and head to our individual cities. The starting tight end from Day One, I was going to fare well in the offensive scheme. It actually reminded me a lot of the one I played in Europe. Being wide open, and aggressive up the field, could mean a lot of balls coming my way and I was prepared to have a lot of fun with this. All nearly came to an end that last day in Florida.

Because I wasn't supposed to play more than two series in that last warm-up against Chicago the plan was to get a little work in and then shut it down for the day. On our third play of the game we ran a bootleg that came back out to my side. The run fake was executed for setup purposes and I blocked the defender lined up inside me to sell the play. Then, I peeled back out to make myself available for Casey as the outlet if he couldn't find a man deeper down the field. I was out in the flat when Casey decided to drop the ball out to me. With a man in his face, he had to float the ball over outstretched arms. The ball hung in the air a little. I made the catch and got ready to turn up field when I saw a black blur fly in around my ankles; it was a Chicago defender. Rather than try to tackle me up high the small defensive back decided to take me down by cutting my legs out from underneath me. He launched himself from about five yards away and landed directly on my ankle instead of through my legs. Everything buckled and it felt like my ankle broke at the moment of impact. Getting up, I put pressure on the leg, but it was hard to even stand. I hobbled back to the huddle, trying to walk it off, but could barely get in my stance the next play and came off the field immediately after the whistle. I was done for the day, spending the entire game sitting on a cart with my ankle wrapped in ice. I sat there wondering if my XFL experience might be already over.

I didn't want an MRI on my mangled ankle so I refused a hospital visit. Finding a break or any other serious damage would more than likely result in my trainers or the doctors trying to talk me into sitting down for a substantial amount of time. That was not going to happen. This was a one shot deal for me, the last hurrah. I was hoping it was just a high ankle sprain and for the time being I could just deal with the pain. It's not like I hadn't done that before. For the time being I would just bite the bullet and suck it up. All my trainers and coaches had to know was that I'd be ready for the first week of the season. When I got a chance to make it back to Atlanta I would dip into my DMSO stash to help speed up the healing process.

Don't Believe The Hype

When we rolled into Birmingham to kick off the first ever XFL season our reception was not good. McMahon's promotional blitz had us ill-perceived. While other cities in the league were more liberal we were in the Bible Belt of the South. Vince had everybody thinking our cheerleaders would be in front of the crowd swinging on poles and accepting dollar bill tips. A lot of people were offended and had made up their minds about what the league was going to be before we had even gotten into town. Sports writers beat us up in the papers and we got slammed on the radio religiously. You would have thought we were a bunch of known criminals instead of a professional football team in town to simply play some football. The general population welcomed us with mixed emotions, half embracing and half standoffish, but love us or hate us we were their hometown team for at least the next ten weeks.

Lights, Camera, Action, Kickoff!

We played our first game ever in the XFL on Sunday, February 4, 2001. Legion Field, located in the heart of downtown Birmingham was moderately packed with 35,321 fans. I had a large number of my Birmingham family in attendance and we treated them to a very good game of football against the Memphis team. I almost made it through the entire game but my ankle gave way after my second catch of the day late in the third quarter. The week's rehab brought me to about 30% mobility and I couldn't talk my trainers into a cortisone shot as they flat-out refused; they thought it was too dangerous to inject me in that area. All the tape in the world couldn't muffle the lightning bolts of pain shooting up and down my left ankle every time I moved, but with glory comes sacrifice. My day came to an abrupt end as I broke a tackle and ran into several hostile defenders. Three piled on top of me, one landing on the already-throbbing ankle, and that was it for the day. I watched the rest of the contest helplessly from the sideline. The game was exciting, coming down to the end, and the fans seemed pleased even though we lost. It was definitely a different experience with cheerleaders jumping and gyrating and cameras all over the field and in the player's faces, but when all was said and done it was just football. All the hype had blown things out of proportion. Now that the real product was on the field, it was up to the fans to decide what they thought.

Final Score: Bolts 20-Memphis Maniaxs 22

I had to sit out the one game on the entire schedule that I most wanted to play. In Week Two the team went up to New Jersey to play the Hitmen while I stayed behind. My ankle was still messed up, even after watching practice from the sideline all week. I was determined to play, but couldn't even make it through the walkthrough the day before the game so was deactivated for the week. While my team played in the Meadowlands on Sunday, I sat in my living room at the house in Atlanta with the lower half of my left leg submerged in a big bucket of ice, post DMSO application. In my absence and in freezing cold the team played well and won the first game in franchise history.

Final Score: Bolts 19-NY/NJ Hitmen 12

The most obvious thing about Week Three was the drop in fan support. Out of the 35,000 fans who came out for opening night, only half came back. My theory is that all the beginning hype was overkill. Fans initially came out because they were curious about all the controversy supposedly surrounding the league. Other teams in the league didn't experience the same drop we did; we finished second to last in total attendance for the season. They weren't playing in the conservative South, though.

I made it back onto the field Sunday afternoon, February 18, and caught three passes in a victory over the Chicago Enforcers. For the rest of the season I struggled with the ankle, always hurting, but didn't miss another game. Not one time during the year did I play free of pain and at best I probably ran at about 70% once or twice. The constant ache, day and night, was a lot to deal with but I wasn't going to let it rain on my parade. I knew this was more than likely my last go around so I was going to enjoy it for all it was worth. Some weeks I was able to put a full week of practice in and others I let my backups take most of the prep work. My job was to start on game days and that is what I did. And I put together a pretty good season along the way. I didn't care what the media said or how they tried to portray us. What they reported had more to do with their loathing for Vince McMahon than it did regarding us as players.

Final Score: Bolts 14-Chicago Enforcers 3

That second victory of the season turned out to be our last. There would be no bonus money in our checks after that. We ran into a couple of buzz saws the two weeks following the Chicago game, but the bottom dropped out of our season in the sixth game when we lost our starting quarterback, Casey Weldon, to a season and career-ending shoulder injury. It was all over. We were like a pistol minus all bullets. The seven consecutive losses were most frustrating but not enough to make me wonder whether I made the right choice in playing for this league. The friends I made on that team, players, coaches, trainers and administrators all included were some of the best from all my professional days. And I couldn't have asked for a better group to be surrounded by as I played out what would be the last days of my career. On Sunday, April 8, 2001, I played my last game as a professional athlete. I didn't know it at the time because the league was supposed to stay in existence and I was definitely going to return, but that all fell through. I walked off Legion Field that evening proud of what I had accomplished – not just in this particular season, but over a fifteen year career that took me through two professional sports. I had no reason to be ashamed. In fact, I had done a pretty good job! And if this was the end, I could now walk away on my own terms. I had nothing else to prove to anyone, myself included.

Season Highlights
– I put together my best game of the season against my best friend, Nate, and the L.A. Xtreme. I caught five passes, scored a touchdown against them, and added a point after touchdown as well. Nate said players were talking during the game about how to stop me. (Tommy Maddux, the league MVP, led the Xtreme to victory with a late touchdown and they were the eventual winners of the XFL Championship Game.)

– Minus the one game due to injury, I still led all tight ends in the league with 25 receptions on the season. My ankle slowed me down all through the year and took away most of my ability to work deep up field, but my veteran experience came in handy.

– My mom, dad and brother got to see me on the field one last time. I flew my parents out to Las Vegas when we played the Outlaws in March and Irv hopped a plane from Arizona. That was the best road trip of the year! I filled it with quality time with the family, a little football and some casino. Hard to beat that.

– In the middle of the season I discovered I had an XFL football card floating around. I started receiving fan mail with the Topps trading card on the inside. People from as far away as Hawaii wrote and requested my autograph on their cards. Only a limited number of players in the league were selected to appear on the cards and put into circulation. I was one of the chosen few.

XFL Folds

One month after the end of the first season, the XFL was still in existence. I had been in communication with the Bolts and down to Birmingham several times visiting the Health South Facility for consultation and rehab on my injured ankle and everything appeared full speed ahead for Year Number Two. The coaches were in New York May 2001 for meetings, preparing for the upcoming season. Rumor has it that they had actually convened and received phone calls after they returned home that McMahon had pulled the plug on the XFL. The most common guess about cancellation was the poor television ratings. Although they were low, that wasn't it. NBC had already made it clear that they would not be back for Year Two, but McMahon had already contacted cable networks willing to talk. TNN and UPN were still onboard too. McMahon had no problem turning this into an all-cable affair. From what I understand though, the other networks wanted to make changes to the format and promotion of the league. That's where they crossed the line with Vince. If it wasn't going to be done his way, it wasn't going to be done at all. Somebody didn't take that to heart and he folded the XFL in an instant. Doing chores around my house on May 10, 2001 with SportsCenter on the television, I heard the news that the XFL was done. Stunned, I couldn't believe my ears.

Nate and I went in search of answers for weeks after that,

but nobody had any. All offices were shut down in the matter of a month. Several players from the league made it into NFL training camps that summer, but only a few won jobs. As for me, I knew the page had turned on that chapter in my life. It was time to move on into the next phase of life. And now I could do that with peace of mind. Time to walk off into the sunset!

Ed , Coach, Reggie Johnson (#83) and Scott Thompson (#87)

CHAPTER ELEVEN

Behind the Scenes & Inside the Game

People always ask which of the two sports was my favorite – which I enjoyed the most. Baseball was my first love and always will be. But the six years I spent playing football, culminated by the dream of playing in a Super Bowl, is hard to top. The difference in the two sports was also like night and day. Baseball is laid-back while football is a straight shot of adrenaline. Baseball is a very individualistic sport while football is a total team effort. The difference between a 6-yard run and a 60-yard run for a touchdown is one person missing an assignment.

While my minor league career was a very happy-go-lucky existence, the world of the NFL was big business. There wasn't a lot of horseplay or practical joking surrounding the game. All business, especially when it came time to be on the field, there was very little time for anybody to be laughing about anything. The only time there was ever anything comical going on was in training camp, toward the end, when it was time to razz the rookies. Not a lot of superstition involved in football, it involves more blood, sweat and tears.

All broke and poor when I played minor league baseball, we grew close easily. Money changes everything. In the NFL, the large salaries create huge egos and jealousy even amongst teammates. If one player gets a new contract or extension, you can bet that, somewhere in the locker room, somebody feels salty or bitter because they should have gotten more or weren't offered anything at all. Therefore, football teams are not normally close-knit.

I was fortunate to be associated with a couple that broke the mold in Atlanta and Birmingham. Here is a closer look behind the scenes.

Groupies

All groupie categories exist and run similar games in the high profile world of NFL football as in minor league baseball. And let's be honest, big money can sometimes attract a certain type of woman. With that being said, the most obvious difference is the willingness to take things to the next level because of higher stakes - many disposed to do just about anything, anywhere, and at any time to land The Big Fish. These ladies dress nicer than their minor league counterparts, tend to travel in elite company, and aren't shy about letting any man know exactly what it takes to make them happy: M-O-N-E-Y! If minor league baseball taught me nothing else, it conveyed the message to avoid groupies like the plague. I worked too hard for my money!

Drugs

A series called "Playmakers" recently broadcast on ESPN has stirred up some controversy because of its totally negative representation of life in professional football. In one episode, the star running back sends a teammate to score some cocaine from his dealer during halftime outside the team locker room. The amount of surrounding security makes that ridiculously insane, and I find it insulting. Are there players in the league abusing illegal substances, including steroids? Yes. Does the NFL test and discipline the situation with severe punishment? Of course. Would that "Playmakers" scenario be conceivably possible? I don't think so!

The NFL has a severely strict drug policy: No Tolerance. Mandatory testing occurs in the off-season, through training camp, and during the season; one can be tested at any time. A random computer system selects players each week for every team in the league. If your name is on the list, any given day, you must provide a testing sample immediately upon arrival at the facility. One cannot leave that day before peeing in the cup. If any substance defined by the league as illegal is found in your system, you face an immediate four-game suspension without pay. A pretty hefty fine if you are making millions of dollars. You must also attend drug abuse counseling and once you return to the team you are subject to mandatory testing every week. The next failed test results in stiffer fines and penalties, leading up to banishment from the league for repeat offenders. Should that happen, you have to later petition for reinstatement.

Any test missed is considered a failed test. And if you have vacation plans during the off-season it is imperative to notify the league when you will be out of town. Randomly selected, even out-of-season, if the NFL cannot locate you that is a failed test. Lastly, when it is time to go, the person administering the test does not wait outside of the restroom. In front of the urinal, you drop em as he watches the sample hit the cup, filling it to the specified line. Amazingly, with everything to lose, I've had team-mates foolish enough to get popped for steroids, marijuana, and other illegal substances. Like Forrest Gump's mama said, "Stupid is as Stupid does!"

Fines

The NFL will take money away from you any way possi-ble. Between league and team fines it is very easy to give away a lot of loot if one is not careful. Late for a meeting, one second after the door closes, and you might as well consider yourself about $400 lighter in the pocket.

It's hard to punish millionaires by taking little amounts of money from them, but the league and individual teams definitely try to do their best in it. Following, more ways to lose hard earned money:

Weight – Every week you must make your required weight. Each Friday morning the strength and conditioning coach waits by the scale with his clipboard to register where you check in. If you are at or below, all is good. If you are over by one pound, you have a choice to make: lose the excess weight before the start of the first meeting or pay up. Each pound costs $375 for the first offense. After that, it doubles every time you come in overweight. Through my career I never had to pay, but I remember having to lose some weight in the mornings a few times. I always went in early just in case I had to get in the sauna to sweat off something I had eaten the night before.

Offensive and defensive linemen had it the roughest. Some of them were ten pounds plus overweight and they just gave up, paying fines each week that went up into the thousands of dollars. That money comes directly out of your check, you never see it, and it is donated directly to charity.

Training Camp – Every meal is mandatory during training camp. Personally, I would rather have used those precious moments in between practice and meetings to sleep. Trainers have a different opinion in this matter. Their main concern is getting fuel and liquids back into the tank. Even if you don't eat, you have to sign in to show you made it to the cafeteria. In my second training camp with the Falcons in 1998 I once ate in the dining hall and even had conversation with a couple of my coaches, but I forgot to sign in. An hour later Coach Reeves came in to our tight end meeting room and informed me that I had forgotten to do so. Even though he knew I was there and I could verify it through my tight end coach, rules were rules, and I was fined $375. He joked about that being one expensive meal I just had. I didn't find it funny though.

Curfews and Bed Checks – You don't want to get caught outside your room or miss a bed check after curfews on the road. That can get really expensive. The coaches designated for curfew detail give a courtesy knock before opening the door with a hotel master key. Once they cross the threshold you'd better be inside, not down the hall in another room, at the snack machine, or getting off the elevator heading in that direction. NO EXCUSES! And another thing, if you are daring enough to try and sneak a woman in, she better be well-hidden and quiet as a mouse. The most common place to conceal her is in the shower, tucked away, instructed to not make one single sound. But you didn't hear that from me.

Uniform violations – The NFL has "Uniform Police" that roam the field and sideline during pre-game warm-ups and during the game. If a towel hanging from your belt is too long, socks aren't pulled all the way up, a shirt is untucked or anything else defied on the long list of possible violations, you get one warning to correct the issue. If you do not, the cost is a hefty *five thousand dollars* per infraction. That's one reason many will argue that NFL stands for the "No Fun League".

Out Of The Closet

In October of 2002 on HBO's "Real Sports", Esera Tuaolo told the world he was a gay man. In most instances that would not be a big story, but when you are 6'3", weigh 300 pounds, and recently retired from the National Football League, you are going to grab some headlines. Esera played defensive tackle for five teams in nine years, leaving the game in 1999 and is only the third NFL player to publicly state he is gay. None of the three did so while still playing because of the stigma and retribution that might have followed.

A teammate of mine during the 1998 Super Bowl Season with the Atlanta Falcons, Esera's locker was directly across from mine on the last row. We roomed together on the road the entire season and I never knew he was gay. And I could have cared less. He was not just a teammate, but was one of the coolest guys I know. What saddened me was seeing his piece on "Real Sports" and then again on "Oprah" in November 2003, and realizing how much pain he was in because of the deep dark secret he hid. In his story he told how he pretended to lead the life of a woman-izing bachelor just to avoid the possibility of rumors. He endured hurtful jokes in the locker rooms without speaking up. He even contemplated suicide, simply driving his car off the road to end the pain.

I last talked to Esera in 1999 when we were both on dif-ferent teams. Playing for the Eagles, I faced him in Carolina while he was with the Panthers. Later, current and retired players were asked to comment on what would have happened to him had he come out while still playing in the league. I was shocked to hear the amount of negativity. Some players said that had he come out on a Monday during the season he would have never made it to Sunday for the game. Secure in my manhood, the sexual preference of another would never make me feel uncomfortable.

Obviously, that is not how the vocal majority feels. Shortly after hearing his news, I reached out to Esera, making a few calls and tracking down the number of a salon he and his life partner own in Minneapolis. I left a message for him just letting him know that regardless of anything he was still my friend and was a great teammate. He returned my call a few days later and we talked and laughed like we had in the past while sitting across from one another in the locker room or on the road in our hotel.

Esera has since gone on to do public speaking, hoping to help or save someone in the position he once was, living his life as a lie. We have spoken a few times. Most recently, I called him after he popped up on "Oprah". He is apparently happy in his new life out of the closet. I applaud him for his courage and efforts to reach out to others and wish him nothing but the best.

His story taught me another lesson. You never know what someone is going through in his or her life. Esera was always laughing and smiling, a jokester in the locker room. I never would have guessed in a million years that he was gay or dealing with the types of demons haunting him. It makes you want to be more sensitive and realize your words and actions could be hurting someone without you even knowing.

Where Were You When..........?
Part II

Diana: Death of a Princess: Sunday, August 31, 1997

I had just finished my first training camp with the Atlanta Falcons. Our last preseason game was on Friday night and I was released Saturday morning. Because I had to clear waivers before returning to re-sign as a member of the practice squad on Tuesday, I had a couple of days off so I drove up to North Carolina to spend time with Randy. Late Sunday night she and I were sitting on the sofa when a special news bulletin interrupted our regularly-scheduled programming. Unconfirmed reports out of London stated that Princess Diana had been killed in a tragic accident. Though not a big fan of the Royal Family, I was certainly rooting for Princess Diana. Her great humanitarian efforts gave her global appeal and her loss affected the world.

JFK Jr.: Death of a Prince: Saturday, July 17, 1999

Still two weeks away from signing with the Detroit Lions, unemployed during the roller coaster year of 1999, I was up in New Jersey spending time with my family in Browns Mills trying to keep my mind off of football. Meanwhile, JFK Jr. boarded his plane Friday, July 16. His family reported him missing to the coast guard at 2:15 Saturday morning. When I woke Saturday my mother was already watching coverage about his disappearance, the coast guard still calling it a 'search and rescue', but it soon became a 'search and recovery'. On Wednesday, July 21, plane wreckage with all three bodies still strapped in their seats, was recovered. My heart and prayers went out to both families. Tragedy and misfortune have no discriminatory factors. Neither money nor prestige guarantee you one more day on this earth.

Y2K: Friday, December 31, 1999

The world was supposed to come to an end when the clock struck midnight to ring in the year 2000. I was playing for the Detroit Lions and our last game of the season was in Minnesota against the Vikings on January 2, 2000. The NFL didn't want teams flying on Saturday, our normal travel day, because they bought in to the widespread national panic. In case of any problems, they didn't want us in the air that day. The Lions threw a makeshift New Year's Eve Party in one of the ballrooms of our hotel, but I decided not to attend because most all of my teammates were going to clubs and the majority of people at the party would be coaches and administrators. Since we were in the Central Time Zone at eleven, midnight Eastern Standard Time, I called my mother and father in New Jersey. All was well back home, the two of them spending a quiet night together. Midnight came in Minnesota with Dick Clark on television and me standing at the large window of my 30th-floor hotel room. Way down below and across the city I could see and hear fireworks; the world hadn't blown up. Everything seemed to be okay. Not long after, I turned off the television and fell asleep. That wasn't exactly the way I had envisioned ringing in the new millennium.

9/11 Terror Attack: Tuesday, September 11, 2001

Sitting at the computer in my home-office that fateful Tuesday morning, I witnessed the terrorist attacks in total shock. The first one could've been an accident, but the second sent the message; we were under attack. The images were horrible, people jumping from the sky to escape the agony and horror of a burning building. Then, when they came crashing down, it was like something out of a movie. What I was witnessing could not be real. I'll never forget that day as long as I live. It is burned into my memory as a day that will live on forever in infamy.

As I Walk Away

What I Miss The Most.........

I miss the roar of the crowd! There's nothing like standing on the middle of a field surrounded by tens of thousands of fans. You can use their energy whether they are cheering for you are against you. And when it is your moment to shine, making the spectacular catch, scoring the touchdown or making the big hit, all eyes are on you and you can feel the hair on the back of your neck stand up.

I miss the incredible rush of adrenaline! There is nothing like the moment before you come running out of the tunnel. Your heart is pounding, your blood is pumping and you can hardly stay in your skin. I used to feel like I could run through a brick wall as we came stampeding out and onto the field. And each hit during the game was like a sudden shot of adrenaline. My laid-back personality was replaced for a few hours each game day by a fierce and angry individual, an alter ego that knew it better be ready to inflict a little pain or accept the fact that it might be the one taking it.

I miss the high life! The best year of my professional sports career was the Super Bowl Season in Atlanta. During a stretch I felt like I was mayor of the city. Everywhere I went there was some sort of preferential treatment. When I parked somewhere and used valet service, my truck was parked right at the front door. If there was a long wait at a restaurant, all I had to do was ask for a manager and I could be seated in five minutes. We never paid cover to get into clubs or bars and someone was always buying me a drink. It was amazing. I made it a point to never go out of my way to ask for anything because I did not want to abuse the privilege, and most times I felt guilty for being singled out, but it was a great way to live for a while!

I miss that celebrity feeling! I still get singled out today, people asking if I play sports. It is a little different when you are still actually playing, though. When you are active, you know someone will make an extra effort to spot you on television or tell their friends they met you. I've been in airports, on planes and in restaurants and have seen people go out of their way to make it over to see who I was. I once had a gentleman on a flight come all the way to the back of the plane because he remembered me from my high school days, fourteen years prior, and had been following my career all the way to and through the Super Bowl. It makes you feel good when you see people pointing and whispering and you know they are talking about you. The best feeling of all is the look in the eye of a child when he finds out you are/were an athlete. That sort of makes you feel like Superman.

Just recently I learned that my #86 Atlanta Falcon jersey is hanging in a Ruby Tuesday restaurant in Florida. My good friend, Brian Jones, was passing through the small town on his way back to Atlanta when he and his wife, Tamika, spotted the jersey. He called me to tell me but I didn't believe him until he emailed a picture to prove it. A black home jersey, on the back was my number and name, 86, E. Smith. I will one day make a road trip to that restaurant so I can take a picture standing in front of it!

What I Miss The Least.........

I don't miss anything about training camp, it being one of the closest things to hell on earth as far as I'm concerned. Worth the price for the glory of an NFL football Sunday, it is no fun while in the midst of it.

I don't miss anything about astro-turf! Technology has advanced in recent years, but the recollections I have are nightmarish. Underneath that thin layer of carpet, an inch of foam separates one from a giant slab of concrete. Try landing on that with a few hundred pounds of manly flesh on top of you. The morning after a long day on that deceptive surface is one of the most excruciating known to man. Every joint and muscle in your body screams out for relief as you slowly attempt to climb out of bed. I purposely set my alarm 15-minutes early on Mondays to give myself the extra time needed to eventually put my feet on the floor. Then there's rug-burn, which scars players for life. Blood-soaked uniforms are what you see on television. In reality, fiberglass embedded in the skin is as common as sweat running down your face. And the post-game shower is anything but soothing. You might as well just slap some rubbing alcohol on an open wound and call it a day.

With money comes the incredibly large ego. Some people just cannot be humble. My background always kept me grounded, both my upbringing and years of struggle in the minor leagues. Just because I was now making a good deal of money didn't mean I was supposed to be ignorant and rude. The world did not revolve around me. Some thought it did though.

I don't miss sacrificing my life for the sport! As I wrote before, there are no sick or vacation days in the NFL. If you are on your deathbed trainers will still find a way to get you on the field; that is their job and the wishes of the coaching staff. Personal problems and business all take a backseat to football when you are on their time. It does not matter what you might have going on. That extends to off-season mini-camps and work-outs as well. Your *life* is football and everything revolves around that. All else is sacrificed.

WHEN THE LIGHTS GO OUT

———⟶⊙⟵———

CHAPTER TWELVE

Life After the Game

I had spent my entire adult life in front of the crowd and under the lights. Now, both were gone. That can be a very scary feeling if you are not prepared for an existence without them, but that is what the XFL did for me. I am still so grateful for that last opportunity to take pleasure in playing the game and not getting caught up in the business of it. Now that it was time to move on, I could do so with no remorse. There was no need to look back now; I hadn't left anything behind or undone on the field.

I had not, however, put much thought into what I would do when I stopped playing professional sports. Most athletes don't like to think about that. Even the smartest athlete can think that it is going to last forever when in the limelight. If you are not prepared for a good thing coming to an end, you could be in for a hard dose of sudden reality. I was ready to write the next chapter and get started with life after the game. I just didn't know where to start.

Things usually happen when you are not looking. Around the end of April I was working out at a local gym not far from home. Without an off-season program, I was now in charge of my own physical fitness and I didn't want to turn into one of those ex-jocks with the huge potbelly hanging over my belt buckle. There'd be plenty of time for that when I was old and gray, sitting on the front porch with a grandchild on my knee. I noticed a gentleman on a treadmill who kept looking in my direction. I got that all the time, my size and physical presence leading people to assume I was an athlete. The questions were who was I and how famous? Most admitted they'd never heard of me when they asked and I told them, but every now and then someone faked it, pretending they were one of my biggest fans. I always got a chuckle out of that.

When he was done on the treadmill, the gentleman got off and found me in the back of the gym lifting weights. The first thing he asked me was whether I played ball or not. If I had a nickel for every time someone asked me that question in the past fifteen years, I would be a millionaire. I had several ways to answer those questions. I could answer one way and lead to a long detailed conversation or in another vague way and leave the person wondering if I was even telling the truth. Thirdly, there was total denial that I'd ever played any professional sports (if I wanted a quick getaway). The last didn't work all of the time; people can be very insistent if they've made up their minds that you are someone famous.

Kevin, somewhere in his forties and very educated, introduced himself. We shook hands and I gave him the semi-detailed version of my sporting background, including my recent retirement. As I spoke, he listened and when I was done he went into a little bit about himself. Having just relocated to the Atlanta area from Boston, he was taking over a financial planning firm. A little red flag went up immediately. Once I told someone that I was an athlete, though now ex, it was very common to get a sales pitch. Everybody had something in which I should be investing or buying a piece of, or they should be handling my money for me. I almost cut him off, but he said something different than others had. He wasn't trying to get in my pocket, but wanted to talk to me about learning his business.

As I was looking for a new professional direction, he had

approached me at the right time and immediately caught my attention. Had I thought I might still be able to get back on the field or wasn't ready to give it up, I might have turned him away quickly. When he saw that I was interested, Kevin suggested we sit down and have an actual business meeting; the gym wasn't the place to conduct this. We agreed to have lunch in a few days.

Three days later I sat in my first business meeting in the corporate world. Shortly after we finished our meal Kevin got to the heart of why we were sitting down together. He had come down to take over a MetLife office in one of the black communities on the west side of town. The company was trying to do a few things including changing from strictly providing life insurance to more financial advising. Most importantly, Kevin wanted the office to impact the black community. He explained that, as a culture, we didn't look into the future enough, living mostly for today and not worrying about what tomorrow might bring. I listened to him for a while, captured by what he was saying. When it came time for my questions and comments I had plenty of both.

Explaining my entire situation, I pointed out the most obvious first. I'd been an athlete for the last fifteen years, had no college degree and only a few credits under my belt, had never been in the corporate world or held a job that didn't mostly involve how much I could lift or carry. And I had no experience in financial planning whatsoever. With all of that what could I do and how would I fit into his company or anything he was planning? If I wanted a job I knew this was not the way to go about getting it, but I didn't want to waste the man's time. With my lack of credentials I figured I'd just broken the deal. Instead I was something that Kevin was actually looking for. In short, he could tell that I was intelligent. I didn't have to have a degree to prove that. My sports background and the road I'd conquered to be where I was demonstrated the drive and determination that he wanted in the people he employed. If I were willing to put that type of dedication into learning his business and benefitting from his 24 years of experience as he mentored me, he would help me build a new career. It wasn't going to be easy, but he felt I was up to the challenge. I agreed. A handshake sealed the deal and my new course seemed to be charted. It would be a while before the company officially employed me as I had a lot of knowledge to acquire before that, but I was going to attack the business world as I had the world of sports. Walking to my truck after the meeting, I marveled at the power of God. He had brought something to me when I least expected it. He had led me to the next opportunity in my life and had given me a new direction.

Long Road Ahead

Before I could even think about being hired by Kevin and MetLife, I had those few things to address. Just to be considered for the opportunity, I had a list of required licenses and credentials to gather. I was going to have to jump into a new arena and start at the very bottom, learning and studying things totally unfamiliar. This wasn't going to be like figuring out a playbook; there weren't any X's and O's or blitz pickups involved. I was jumping into the world of finance without one stitch of knowledge. All of my football money was being taken care of for me by a hired advisor so I didn't even have my own experience as background. The first step in the process involved obtaining a life and health insurance license. The hard stuff would be next. Kevin advised me that I would go after my securities license, a Series 6, allowing me to work with mutual funds. If I were successful in accomplishing those, my Series 63 for state licensing would follow. Those three would land me employment with the company. To finish it all off he also recommended I be licensed to sell annuities; no hurry to get that, but it was on the list. This was intimidating, but I knew I could do it if I put my mind to it. So, I dove in headfirst, just like I had with most everything else in my life.

Eric Eugene Dixon

I thought I had all the friends I needed in my life. Over the years I had collected a great many good quality people that I knew had my back no matter what. After my initial meeting with Kevin he invited me to the home office, far on the west side of town. He wanted to introduce me to my future colleagues and give me a feel for the work environment.

My suburb in the north corridor meant long commutes once I started working for the company and Atlanta traffic is some of the worst in the country. On the day of my meeting I was right in the middle of rush hour traffic on the way back in. Since there was no hurry to get home, I stopped at an Applebee's down the street from the office, figuring I would have a quick meal and a drink, wait the traffic out, and then make my way home. I took a seat at the bar, not in the mood to sit alone at a table, and picked a spot next to Eric Dixon. We struck up a conversation and I knew from the second we started talking that I liked this 'fella'. He was *good people.*

Thirty-seven and the youngest of six children, Eric had been born and raised right there on the west side of town. That, in itself, is unusual, because 'everybody' who lives in Atlanta seems to be from somewhere else. Eric told me he stopped in the restaurant for a bite to eat before heading over to see his mother and father, something he did every single day of his life. I also learned he had worked for the Georgia Department of Revenue for almost twenty years right out of high school.

We laughed like we had known each other for years and I ended up sitting at the bar with him long after the traffic had dissipated. When it was finally time to depart, we exchanged numbers. You can never have enough good people in your life and from that first sit-down I knew there was a possibility we would become lifelong friends. I didn't know it that day, but Eric was brought into my life for a purpose.

My family was about to be rocked at the very foundation. I got a call from Mom in late May, her voice shaky. My father, always a strong man with a healthy appetite, had stopped eating and was not feeling well. In a matter of days he had lost all control of his body and could not get out of the bed. My mother was actually taking care of him like she would a child. They had tried to keep it from my brother and me, not wanting to worry us over nothing, but he wasn't getting any better and Mom was scared. Hearing the concern in her voice, I began to panic internally as well. Two days later, both my brother and I headed to New Jersey to see what was wrong with the strongest man we had ever known.

The doctors had no idea what was wrong with him. And they didn't seem to be putting much effort into finding out. At the time, Pops was actually working for the hospital we took him to. He had retired from working the 50-story boilers, not wanting that type of responsibility any more, and now worked on a smaller scale, still significant in keeping the hospital running smoothly. The first time we took him to the emergency room, they ran a series of tests and came up with nothing. According to the staff, there was nothing wrong with my father. We got him home and he remained in the bed, too weak to take care of himself. We couldn't just sit and watch him suffer so we took him back to the same hospital a day later. When they tried to tell us that they couldn't do anything for him, my brother went ballistic and demanded action. The second time they tried to turn us away it got ugly; my brother and I had choice words for the attending physician. Frustrated, we went for a second opinion at the hospital in Trenton where I was born. More tests were run and a few agonizing days later we got some horrifying news; my father had a small tumor on his spine. Surgery was needed. It was scheduled for June 5th, my 31st birthday.

There was no way I would be absent, so I returned to Atlanta to gather some things and get back to New Jersey. As Irv went back to Arizona to deal with some issues he had, the plan was to work in shifts. I would stay in New Jersey with him relieving me when it became necessary. On June 4 Pops entered the hospital, prepared to go under the knife the following morning for his seventh back operation. This time he wasn't dealing with a ruptured disk, scar tissue or a damaged nerve, though. More serious than anything we had encountered, we were all scared to death.

The morning of my father's surgery I was amazed to see how well Mom was holding up. I was putting up a front, not wanting her to know how scared I was, but she was a rock. We went down early to spend time with my father. It is a good thing we did since the doctors had decided to move my father's surgery up without informing us! When we got to his room they were preparing to take him away. He said later he had never been happier to see us than when we walked through that door. I saw the fear in his eyes as he hugged my mother and me. We all held on, not wanting to let go. Soon after, as he was wheeled to the elevator, I walked on one side holding his hand with Mom on the other side doing the same. When we finally got to a door and couldn't go any further, we had to let go. The look in Pop's eyes nearly brought me to tears, but I had to stay strong for both him and Mom. As the door closed behind him unthinkable thoughts ran through my mind. What if something happened during his surgery? Was this the last time I'd see my father alive? I couldn't imagine losing him. And what were they going to find when they looked inside? I pushed those questions to the back of my mind.

The surgery would take hours. Mom was a nervous wreck and I didn't want her sitting and worrying so I told her to go visit my grandmother who lived only ten minutes away. I'd keep watch. I had plenty to keep me busy, studying for my first exam, so I turned the hospital waiting room into a makeshift office. My laptop in front of me, I studied and took practice exams for my Life and Health license. Not knowing what was going on in the operating room made it tough to concentrate, but studying was the only thing that could keep me from thinking the worst.

Mom returned a couple of hours later, still showing her poker face, and we went downstairs to talk in the parking lot to put our minds in a better place. Once there we realized what day it was. Thirty-one years ago she had given birth to me in this very hospital. We started reminiscing about all the good days in our family history, going through the memories of our life. The good and bad times had made us the strong family unit that we were. We both mustered nervous laughter as we recounted some of our best times.

We had been back up in the waiting room about 30-minutes when my father's doctor came in to tell us surgery was complete. The procedure having taken nearly four hours; I don't know how much more I could've endured. The wait was tearing me up inside. The physician who operated on my father was the same who had performed Pop's previous six back surgeries, so he was a familiar face to Mom. I had never met the man before, but had heard good things about him. When he walked into the room, occupied by only my mother and me, he looked like he had good news on his face. The words that came out of his mouth turned my stomach in a thousand knots. I'm sure he was used to giving bad news and that is why he seemed so cold, but I wasn't prepared for what he said. He told us my father made it through the surgery fine, but the growth on his spine was cancer! The news hit me like a bucket of ice-cold water and I couldn't form a word to come out of my mouth. My mother, who had been holding it all in, started to cry and went limp in my arms.

When our initial hysteria wore off the doctor went into detail. The tumor they found was a result of a form of bone cancer and had something to do with my father's blood. They had removed the majority of it but not the whole thing because they felt it was too close to his spine. They felt that radiation and chemotherapy treatments would be the way to eradicate the rest. When I asked him what the prognosis would be as far as my father's future, he said only time would tell. He couldn't or didn't want to speculate now. Telling us someone would inform us when it was okay to see my father in recovery, the doctor left us alone to deal with the devastating news.

Through all the tough times in our lives Mom and Pops have never wavered in their love for one another. In that waiting room I got to see firsthand how deeply connected they are. Mom cried uncontrollably in my arms. She muttered words I'll never forget, "Your father is the only man I have ever loved in my life. I don't know what I would do without him!"

I kicked into gear; it was my time to become the 'rock' of the family. Comforting my mother, I held her up while she probably wanted to fall down. "Somehow, we're going to get through this," I assured her.

Finally, after what seemed like an eternity, a nurse came in and told us we could see Pops in recovery. He was still unaware of any prognosis and Mom and I felt it was not the time to tell him. When he was stronger the next day we would deliver the news together, just not now. He looked so helpless lying on that bed- tubes attached to his arms and a breathing instrument in his nose. When we entered he opened his eyes and smiled at me- probably like he did when he saw me for the first time 31 years ago that day. Groggy and still under anesthesia, my father grabbed my hand after Mom stepped away. He confessed the same thoughts I had had when they wheeled him away even though I had never uttered a word of what was on my mind. He had wondered if that was the last time he would see us. It was never so good to see and hear him.

Pops had numerous questions about his surgery, but we told him everything was a success. I planned to come down first thing in the morning to be with him before the doctors came in and broke the news to him. For now, all he needed to know was that he had made it through and that everything looked good.

I drove Mom home later that night, doing everything in my power to keep up her spirits. I refused any thoughts of her life with my father being cut short. The next morning Mom went to her office to take care of business requiring her attention. I had the alarm set and planned on getting down to the hospital right when visiting hours began so I could be there for my father. The last thing I wanted was for him to hear news of this matter without the support of his family. The plan failed. Instead, the house phone woke me. Mom sounded ruffled. The doctors had gone in and notified my father early in the morning and he had called her, obviously shaken. In a matter of minutes I was out the door, cussing the doctors and speeding to be by Pop's side. That was a nerve-racking 30-minute drive to the hospital.

I didn't know what state of mind my father would be in as I approached his room, so I braced myself before I walked through the door; I had to be strong. I put a big smile on my face, trying to hide my concerns, and entered. Pops was surely happy to see me. Amazingly, he was at peace and not in a panic as I had anticipated. That made it easy for us to talk.

As we shared, I realized where he was getting his strength, from his belief in God. My father had become a very spiritual man through all of his life experience. When he was younger he ran with the devil but fought hard enough to return his soul to its rightful owner when he thought he might lose everything. For that he was my hero. I let him know it that day as I had for the past ten years. He wanted to again apologize for all we had gone through when we were younger, but I wouldn't even listen to him. He had no reason to ask for my forgiveness, because that had been given a long time ago. We had talks about everything a son and his father could all throughout the morning. When he was tired I let him sleep, never leaving his side as I sat by his bed, reading and studying.

Later that afternoon Mom arrived and my father's eyes lit up like candles. I witnessed one of the most touching scenes in our family history when she approached his bed, already beginning to tear up. Asking her why she was crying, Pops requested she come to his side. He mustered up enough strength to almost sit up and embrace her and the two of them got lost in the moment, holding each other and feeling the love. I backed off and started crying myself. THIS WAS WHAT LOVE IS ALL ABOUT! I excused myself to go get my father some more of his favorite, apple juice, and gave them some time alone.

My father was in the hospital for the next week and Mom had to be in the office, so I kept him company during the day. I took our favorite chess set down and we managed a game every now and then, between his resting periods. When the doctors felt he was healthy enough, they released him and we took Pops home. An MRI was scheduled a couple of weeks out to determine the next moves in my father's treatment and recovery. That was all we had to go on for the time being. Mom and I decided it was now okay for me to head to Atlanta to take my exam. Once I did that, I would return to New Jersey.

Having held strong in my first opportunity to act as man of the house while my father was off his feet, I didn't realize how much I was keeping inside. It all hit me the moment I walked through my garage door in Atlanta where I broke down the second I put my bags on the floor. All we knew was that the doctors had found the tumor and removed most of it. If he had what they said, there was a possibility I might lose him. I broke down and cried right there at the island in the kitchen, releasing all my pain. Later that night as I was watched television, in some sort of twisted coincidence, there was a story on Dateline about Geraldine Ferrara, the one-time vice presidential candidate. Dealing with bone cancer, she was going through a health crisis of her own. Treatment options and chances of survival were highlighted. After the program was over I visited a website mentioned as a resource for more information about the disease. Reading only depressing statistics there, I could hardly sleep or even think about taking an exam over the next few days. Still, I forced my way through it, successfully passing the first test on my way to a new profession. The next day I headed back to Jersey.

Do You Believe In Miracles?

I spent the next few weeks traveling back and forth. I'd spend a week up North and then return to the South to take care of pending issues at the house. With one license under my belt, I was off and running toward the next, the toughest of them all, my Series 6.

Pops was very weak, but able to get around a little better

as the days passed. He was regaining his appetite and that was the best sign of all. I kept him company in the house while Mom worked and he shared more of himself than he ever had with me. We talked about his hell-raising days in the Navy and he retold the whole story of how my mother and he met. He also surprised me one day by taking me outside to teach me how to ride his motorcycle. He would never do that while I was playing professional sports. I'd asked several times but he just wouldn't do it. Now he felt it was time. Leaning against the car out front, Pops gave me instructions. In my first attempt I nearly ran into a parked car but got control of it in time. I'm sure he had second thoughts about what he was doing then, but he taught me anyway. Before long, I took my first solo trip around the block. When I returned I found him smiling ear to ear. A week later, I returned to Atlanta.

In mid-July I called my parents to get the word on all the tests. Pops' MRI had been done and tumor samples had been sent out so they could figure out exactly what we were dealing with. When Mom answered, I heard something strange in her voice. She hurried off, claiming she wanted to put my father on. When he picked up he said something I never expected – according to the specialist in charge of his case his tumor was NOT cancerous! In fact he never thought it was cancer in the first place; it had been my father's surgeon who insisted it was. To satisfy all parties they ran three separate tests. All three came back negative! While they wanted to run some more tests, they agreed that chemotherapy and radiation were now unnecessary. It was a miracle.

We didn't want to celebrate a victory too soon, but it was hard not to. When I hung up the phone I dropped to my knees right where I was standing and gave thanks for the miracle I was witness to. There was only one Person or Being responsible for something like this. And I thanked Him wholeheartedly.

Further tests revealed what the specialist thought all along. They had removed enough of the tumor the first time, so there wouldn't be another surgery for now. Plenty of observation would ensure they were correct, but Pops was given a clean bill of health. Now he was to work on getting his strength back, his body having been through a considerable amount. That would take time, but it looked like we were going to have more of that than we thought! We could *LIVE* with that.

Relationship Woes

Whatever I was going through, I always seemed to be trying to do it on my own. It was my own fault; I never asked for help or let anyone know what I might be facing. That's just a defense mechanism that comes with playing professional sports and living my whole life on the go, I guess. When things got tough or muddled I buried my head in the sand and blocked out the world. Those actions have always come with consequences.

Developing a relationship with Eddie after all the years that had passed was difficult. Our grand reunion over a year ago should have developed into much more than it had by now. Different circumstances kept us from getting closer, my participation in the XFL being one of them. I promised him I was going to be around, but I broke my promise- not because I didn't want to, but I allowed something else to hold priority at the time. I beat myself up sometimes, telling myself I might have been selfish in some of my decisions, but that is all hindsight, looking back. Part of reality was that I never got a lot of help from Lee. Rightfully so, she was very protective when it came to Eddie; he had experienced a great deal in his youth. My absence, combined with Lee's deteriorated marriage to Teddy, had to leave scars. But one thing she never did was take any responsibility for why things were the way they were to begin with. In conversation it always seemed like I was the villain. I knew better than to ask her the question that always burned in the pit of my stomach, "Do you feel any responsibility for turning me away all those years ago? I could have been a father if you had given me a chance."

Now I was honestly trying to be a part of my son's life, but it was never easy. When I tried to talk to him on the phone he rarely had much to say. It wasn't his fault because he *was* talking to a stranger, after all. I'd ask questions and he'd provide short answers. Sometimes I felt he would rather be doing anything in the world besides talking to me. When I sent gifts or money outside of my obligations, I never got a call or thank-you note to let me know that anything was received. Not needed, it would have been so appreciated by me. The real kick in the teeth came when I left a message on his birthday over the Christmas holiday before I left for XFL camp and my call went unreturned. A lot of that had to do with his mother. Lee sometimes played the role of victim herself. In that way, she could never be held fully responsible for anything. I wanted to be near Eddie, but I had obligations. That's not easily explained to a child- especially one who may already feel somewhat abandoned. Any suggestion of a trip out to see me fell upon ears that didn't "think it was a good idea." Lee always felt and stated that she had to be along because he needed her so much. I didn't necessarily think that was the case. He was between ten and eleven years old now and should have been allowed some solo time. Things weren't working out the way I had planned them or intended for them to be. I felt I could just never get over the hump when it came to my son. And when my father got sick, everything else became a second thought. My first priority was to be there for my family, no matter what the cost.

And, except for family, I was failing all relationship tests. Randy had been in Atlanta for over a year and a half when I finally finished in the XFL. Yet, we were no closer than when she lived in other states. In fact, during much of that year we were not even speaking. Our last breakup came right in the middle of my Bolts season. She was always patiently waiting for me to slow down and give her the relationship she desired, but I always seemed to have something else going on. It was a recurring theme. Randy made it clear that one of the only reasons for her coming to Atlanta was to be near me. And now I was back out on the road commuting for a one-day stay back in town weekly. In the middle of one of my drives from Birmingham to Atlanta, conversing on the cell phone, she told me she was thinking about dating someone else. That infuriated me. She was supposed to sit around and wait for me, right? The fact that I was never there, not always 100% truthful, dated when we were apart, and never gave her the commitment she needed and deserved was no reason for her to wonder if she was missing out on finding the man with whom she was really meant to spend the rest of her life! Ignorantly, I told her that if she wanted to find someone else, or already had for that matter, she should go ahead. She had my blessings! The argument that ensued while I drove like a madman down Interstate 20 was one of our classics and the last conversation we had for months. Later, when my father was sick, I wanted nothing more than to call her and cry on her shoulder; she was one of my best friends when I gave her the chance. My male pride wouldn't let me be the one to call her out of the blue, though. I didn't need her or anybody else. I could handle everything on my own. That is the way it has always been done; why change now?

I prepared for and passed my Series 6 exam in the middle of August. With my father's health improving it was easier both to concentrate and to move quickly to obtain my licenses. Way ahead of schedule, I really looked forward to starting my new career. By the beginning of September I had already scheduled my next exam, Series 63, Wednesday September 12, 2001.

One afternoon a week before that date I was just about to run out of the house when my telephone rang; it was my dad's mom whom I have always affectionately called "Mom Mom". Already out the door when I heard the phone ring, I ran back in and saw that it was her number on the phone. I let the voice mail pick up so I could call her back as I didn't want her to pay for the call. Usually, we talked once a week, me calling her as I did my other grandmother. When I redialed she picked up the phone and was surprised to hear my voice; she was just leaving me a message to let me know she was thinking about me. My little heart fluttered. We had a lovely conversation wherein I told her that I was actually supposed to be in New Jersey that week but that my plans had changed.

Kevin had wanted me to attend a training session in Secaucus, New Jersey but it conflicted with my Series 63 exam so he rescheduled for later in the month, now just two weeks away. I told her when I came up I was going to extend the trip past training and take her to our favorite restaurant. Finally, she told me how much she loved me. I hung up thankful and reflecting about how I surely loved my "Mom Mom"! The following Sunday morning, before eight o'clock I got a call from my mother. Mom Mom passed away suddenly late Saturday night, September 9, 2001. Our conversation the previous Wednesday was the last time I would ever talk to her.

September 11, 2001

Though I was so thankful for that last chance to let Mom Mom know how much I loved her, the pain of her loss was excruciating. I found it hard to eat or sleep over the next couple of days and could almost care less about my Series 63 exam on Wednesday morning. Too late to cancel, I purchased a flight out in the afternoon, post exam, to attend the Friday services. I was sitting at my computer in the office upstairs with the small television muted when the show I was watching was interrupted shortly after 8:46 a.m. The image on the television was horrific. A plane had slammed into the North Tower of the World Trade Center Buildings! My first thought was, "This is a terrible accident!" Turning up the volume, I watched out of the corner of my eye as I returned to studying. When I caught sight of the second plane slamming into the South Tower at 9:03, I knew this was no accident. Seconds later my telephone rang. It was Eric on the other line, checking in with me as we always did now, wanting to know if I saw what was going on. He worked in a high-rise in downtown Atlanta and had just gotten word to get out of there. The only hesitation he had was to call me before he vacated pronto.

Everything felt in complete chaos. I hung up with Eric and called my mother and father in New Jersey, wanting to hear they were okay. My father, still not fully recovered and now dealing with our family loss, picked up the phone on the first ring. My mother was already on her way home from the college and I was happy to hear that they were fine. Putting aside all plans for the day, I stayed on the phone with Pops until Mom got home.

Later that night I called New Jersey again as the nation tried to make sense out of the tragedy. I felt my father's pain through the phone. I couldn't even imagine what he was going through. Just a few months ago Mom Mom was worrying about my father. And just as he was getting better, out of nowhere, we lost her. My father shared the same bond with his mother as I do with both of my parents. The mere thought of losing them makes me sick. What he must've been feeling is indescribable. And as we tried to put all things into prospective, he made a statement I'll never forget. He said, "As much as my heart grieves for the families of the innocent victims in the terrorist attack, it's hard to look past my own pain." And I felt helpless to do anything to ease that pain.

My next dilemma was a big one. The terrorist attacks had shut down every airport in the nation and there was no word on when they would re-open. I had an exam to take the next morning and then, somehow, get to New Jersey to mourn with my family, as we honored and laid Mom Mom to rest. I ran into roadblocks that night as I tried to come up with a plan. The entire nation was crippled without air travel and every train was booked from Atlanta out. It wasn't until the early morning, after being up all night cramming for my exam, that I found a solution to my problem. After taking and passing my test in the morning I hopped an old familiar mode of transportation, bus. I departed from downtown Atlanta at three in the afternoon destined for a small city in southern Virginia. There I would jump a train up to Trenton, New Jersey, where I could join my family to mourn our loss as the nation did the same for all those lost in the terrorist attacks. The entire trip took well over 24 hours and it was every bit as horrible as you can imagine. Unfortunately, Irv, unable to pull off the cross-country journey on such short notice, missed the funeral services. Nobody felt worse about that than he, but it was a circumstance that couldn't be helped. On Friday, September 14th, we laid Mom Mom to rest. My father (how he did it I'll never know) serenaded her with a beautiful saxophone piece while standing next to her casket during the church service. She always loved to hear him play and it was one of his favorite things to do for her. His last song for her was most special of all.

First Flight

I was one of the first people to board a plane out of Newark, New Jersey when the airports re-opened on Sunday. I took the train up from Trenton and a cab to the terminal. It was like a ghost town. Arriving at the airport three hours before my flight, I expected major security delays but literally walked from the curb outside directly to the ticket counter. I was checked in, bags and all, in a matter of minutes. At the security check I went through almost more quickly than that because there was virtually no one there. The atmosphere in the terminal was eerie. In my mind, every person I looked at could be a potential terrorist. I wasn't alone in my thinking. I'm sure I caught the attention of nervous passengers as they pondered my intentions as well. The full-size jet was at ten percent capacity when we pulled away from our gate. I said a prayer before we took off with one thought; if anybody *looked* suspicious I was swinging first and asking questions later. I had never been so anxious to get off a plane in my life. Taking off, I experienced quite a surreal moment as we flew directly over Ground Zero. I could see the still smoldering ashes; knowing that human beings lay in the remains nauseated me. I said a silent prayer for those lost and those left behind to suffer the loss. Two hours later we landed safely in Atlanta. I wanted to kiss the ground when we disembarked.

Three weeks later, after another re-schedule for obvious reasons, I flew back into Newark to attend my MetLife training. When I returned to the South after my seven days of schooling I was fully accredited. Hired by Kevin, I joined MetLife as a Financial Services Representative.

Going from helmets and shoulder pads to suits and ties is not the easiest transition in the world. In fact, it was very intimidating as I began my new career. Shortly after accepting my new position, I traveled with Kevin to the corporate office in

Charlotte, North Carolina for the 'last quarter' meetings. I struggled to feel comfortable in the midst of successful people with years of business experience. The rookie on the team, I almost felt like an imposter. All the things I had accomplished on two different athletic fields didn't mean a thing in this new corporate world. I had confidence that I could adapt; it was just going to take time to learn the ropes.

As 2001 came to an end, I endeavored to settle into my new life. I had seemingly made the transition to a new phase and I was moderately happy. I got up each morning, made my way cross-town to my office and began the task of building a clientele, something proving tougher than anticipated. Times of frustration combined with small successes along the way as I learned something new each day. Kevin was very good with tutoring, his office door always open to me, and we had training sessions each week.

Personally, I felt empty. On the outside it looked like I had everything anybody would ever want in life. My big house was filled with hanging jerseys and all types of sports memorabilia scattered around and I enjoyed a good job and many close friends to keep me company. On the inside I was just missing that spark.

My relationship with Eddie, who lived in Utah, was almost back to square one. Lee was in a new relationship and back to her old tricks. Now that she had someone in her life it might be better if I just went away again. I felt she was always trying to get back at me for something I had done to her, not my son. She claimed to have Eddie's best interest at heart but refused owning up to her past actions. Everything was on my shoulders.

When I called her in September to inform her that my grandmother had passed, I asked that she give my father a call because it would mean a lot to hear from her and Eddie. My parents had kept in touch with her through the years even when I hadn't, sending Christmas and birthday presents to all of her kids not just their grandson. She didn't owe me anything, but *they* deserved a simple call offering condolences. They never heard a word from her. That really upset me. I was nearing the end of my rope in dealing with the whole situation. I didn't want to think like that, but maybe it would be better if I just let them live and be happy. All I seemed to do was get in the way and complicate things. I knew, actually, that the only person being hurt needlessly was my son. I didn't want to do that.

To lift my spirits I planned a big New Year's Eve party at the house – all of my friends invited. I even picked up the phone after months of separation and called Randy to invite her and whomever she wanted to bring. This was going to be the bash to start my new year off right.

That party was a huge success. I brought everybody that was in my life at that time together. Some met for the first time; others had known each other through me for years. Eric met Randy, Nate was there, both old neighbors from my old apartment complex plus new ones in my subdivision attended, and even Kevin brought his wife and friends. We ate, drank, played pool, threw darts and celebrated the coming of the New Year like there wasn't going to be a tomorrow. Somewhere in that night Randy and I got caught in the emotions of the holiday and began to talk. At the stroke of midnight we kissed and a flame was lit. Over the next few months we began seeing each other all the time again and our relationship looked like it was heading in a direction where we really might make it this time. I tried to give her everything I hadn't to this point, mainly more affection and open lines of communication with more honesty. I felt like I was filling a big hole in my life and that empty feeling was going away.

Under The Knife

As athletes, we carry our scars and wounds way past our last game on the field. I've met some of the old time football players, from the days before they used to wear helmets, and to hear how they live with different levels and degrees of pain in the later stages of their lives makes me hurt just thinking about it. Crippling arthritis, fingers permanently disfigured and the constant reminder of a bad limp are just some reminders they live with for the rest of their existences.

With all of the abuse I put my body through, I still consider myself fortunate to walk away from the game with only limited amounts of pain and few negative conditions. One thing that did finally catch up with me in April 2002 was my damaged left knee. It got to the point where I couldn't walk up or down a flight of stairs without holding on to the rail because the knee might give out. And it was constantly locking up. I couldn't keep it in a bent position for long or it would pop when straightened, loud enough to be heard across a noisy room, the pain piercing. This was something I had to get looked at and taken care of. As active as I was still trying to be, working out, playing basketball, bowling or whatever, I wasn't going to last long like this.

Through the NFL I was referred to a local sports medicine doctor in my area and after an MRI he didn't tell me anything I didn't already know. I needed surgery to take care of what was going on in there so I scheduled my operation for a week later in the middle of the month.

I had told my parents that I might need to go under the knife and when I got confirmation I called them to let them know that I couldn't escape it. Immediately, my mother wanted to fly down to Atlanta but I didn't want her to worry herself. She was almost insisting, but it seemed unnecessary to me. Randy was here and I had plenty of other people that could help out if needed.

She reluctantly agreed and didn't make a fuss after that. When we hung up I started to think, she really wanted to be here. When we were talking I felt like she thought I might not be able to handle things alone here in the house, but that wasn't it. She just wanted to be by my side. Both my brother and I had a surgery apiece under our belts; my shoulder in 1992 and Irv's knee in 1997. I was in Jersey with Mom and Pops for my first, but Mom had flown to Irv in New Orleans for his. And all she wanted now was to be a mother to her little boy. It wasn't five minutes later that I was back on the phone telling her I had rethought the idea and that it would be great to have her come down and take care of me. I felt her smile over the phone. She flew in on a Thursday and took me in for my operation on Friday morning, staying until the beginning of the next week.

My knee was in pretty bad shape but I was lucky to escape a big cut, just as I previously had with my shoulder; the surgeon was able to take care of me through arthroscopic surgery. Inside:

– My MCL was buried under a ton of scar tissue that had to be cleaned up. The ruptured ligament was curled up on opposite sides and there wasn't a reason to reconnect it after all the years it had been separated.

– My kneecap was being pulled out of socket to the inside because of a weak stabilizing muscle on the outer edge. The popping sound I heard when it was bent for a long time was the cap popping back into place. To correct that he had to pull and stitch the outer muscle in order to keep the kneecap from coming out and having to lodge its way back in.

– I had very little cartilage left. What was there they had to shave and clean up and that left me with a great deal of bone-on-bone grinding in the knee. I was walking and running around without any shock absorbers.

– The grinding resulted in numerous bone fragments that had to be removed.

– The early stages of arthritis had begun to set in behind the kneecap. The surgeon tried to smooth out some rough edges in order to make it a more comfortable fit in there.

When I saw my doctor after surgery he explained everything to me and considered me lucky considering what I had been doing to myself over the years. He warned that if I didn't start taking it easier I would be seeing him or another doctor again in about five years or so but then for a total knee replacement. I had to cut out running on hard surfaces and give up pounding activities such as basketball. He said it, but I did not hear it. I knew I would try to be a little smarter, but there was no way I was giving up some of my favorite things; I'm way too young to be shutting it down. I may have to accept consequences down the road, but that is just another sacrifice one makes for the life one leads.

Mom drove me back to the house and through the rest of the weekend she, along with Randy, took turns trying to baby me. Eric was also there, for comic relief. I tried to resist at first, always having been the one taking care of others, but eventually I gave in as they pampered me through the first few painful days. I began rehabilitating the knee a week after surgery and keep my fingers crossed to this day that it will hold up. I could never even dream to be near 100% again, for the rest of my life, but I'll settle for as many minimum-pain days as I can get.

Time waits for no one; life goes on. I had been employed by MetLife around six months in April after my knee surgery and I seemed to be getting the hang of things. I did have concerns over the direction I was heading with the company, though. When hired I was under the assumption that part of my mission as a member of a predominantly African-American firm was to help out in the community. I understood I was present to help people plan for their futures. Instead, after I'd been there a while I was urged to redirect my efforts – to look back, toward the world of sports and all the money floating around there. That put me in an awkward position. I was uncomfortable approaching old teammates and acquaintances I knew from that time in my life, asking them about their personal financial situations. To satisfy the wishes of the company I began doing it, though. That is when I began to lose faith in what I was doing. Chasing athletes around, trying to convince them to allow me to manage their money was not something I wanted. It reminded me of several conversations I had had about my own money when I still played. I couldn't stand pushy investors who didn't understand the word no and I didn't want to turn into one of them now. Yet, that's exactly the direction my career could take. While that was weighing on my mind heavily, it was to be the least of my worries. I was about to make a terrible mistake.

Things had again gotten very serious between Randy and me. It was May 2002 and I was considering proposing to her after all this time. I really did love her. She had been patient and continued to love me even when I made it difficult. I wanted to do the right thing by her after all we had been through together. One night of indiscretion was about to cost me her trust for life.

One thing I did through our entire relationship was keep friends of the opposite sex. While I considered that okay for me, it was not all right for her to do so. That is just the twisted way men think sometimes and I was as guilty as the next. I trusted her because she rarely gave me anything to question. I, on the other hand, gave her plenty to think about from time to time. Calls from women all across the country, sometimes late at night, were something with which she was forced to deal. In most cases it was innocent. I kept in contact with female friends dating all the way back to grammar school and I let her know that. But every now and then an awkward call came from someone I used to see and that was a guaranteed all-night argument possibly leading to another breakup. This time around I had put all of that aside; I didn't want to put her through it any more or go through it myself. I was really trying to do the right thing!

Randy usually spent two or three nights a week at my house. Because of where I lived and where she worked it was a tough commute for her, so I didn't always ask her to come out to see me. And I spent significant time at her condo to try and even it all out.

One night I got a call from a friend I'd known for over a year. I had met her at a charity basketball game I played in back in January of 2000 when the Super Bowl was in Atlanta. Hitting it off in a friendly way, we exchanged numbers that night and talked every now and then on the phone. There wasn't a physical attraction on my part but she let me know from time to time that she found me quite appetizing. I hadn't talked to her for months. Her call was to inform me that she was moving back to the West Coast to be near her family in California. Everything was packed in the back of a U-Haul and she was pulling out of town the next morning before rush-hour traffic. When she asked me if she could come crash at my house for the night since she had already moved out of her place, I should have said NO, but I didn't.

She didn't even get to my house until midnight. After a short chat, I showed her the guest bedroom. Somewhere in the middle of the night I got a knock on my bedroom door. I wish I had simply pretended not to hear it, but, once again, I didn't. I knew there was probably a specific reason she wanted into my room and I actually didn't want any part of it, but I let her in anyway. I fell victim to the temptation of the flesh. As I lay in my bed she started something that I should have stopped. Instead, I went along. If I could take it all back I would have, but the deed was done. I'd cheated on Randy and felt like the pig that I was. When I woke up the next morning my company was already gone. It was the last time I saw or heard from her, but the repercussions for the act I allowed to take place were looming.

Randy and I spent the following weekend together around my house having a great time and talking about our future together. In the midst of it, I was feeling extremely guilty. It wasn't the first time I'd ever slept with a woman while seeing another, but it was the first time I did it when in love and talking about living the rest of my life with one of the two. Near the end of the day we were upstairs putting things away in the bedroom when she looked into the drawer where I kept condoms. I didn't know how many were in there; I don't count. The only time I pay attention is when I'm low and it's time to go to the drugstore. She obviously did know and must have been keeping a running tab. I nearly choked on the spit in my mouth when she asked me about the missing one. Where was it anyway? One of the first rules I learned from my extreme player days early in my career was to deny any charge. Don't care if you get caught with your hand in the cookie jar and crumbs all over your face and in your lap- you don't know what they're talking about, it wasn't you. I took that path. She knew I was lying, just like I did, and it wasn't long before I was chasing her out the door, trying to get her to listen to me. That wasn't going to happen though. This time I'd hurt her like I had never before and she was going. And she didn't want anything to do with me ANY MORE.

For weeks I pleaded and begged over the phone, trying to explain my actions, but there wasn't much I could say that she wanted to hear. One of the things I had long known about Randy was the pain she had suffered as a teenager when her parents separated because of infidelity. I forced her to relive that even more directly. I hated myself for hurting someone that meant so much to me. But there was nothing I could do about it now. She was gone and I was left to deal with the consequences.

It was hard to look at myself in the mirror for a long time. If not for Eric, who had become my best friend in the world in less than a year, I could've just given up on everything. As I said before, from the outside it looked like I was leading the perfect life. As far as everybody else was concerned, Randy and I simply decided things weren't working between us. Eric was the only person I confided in about what had happened in my relationship. He got 100% truth and my friendship with him was such that we talked several times daily. First thing in the morning one of us would call the other and we'd talk and laugh about nothing. Then, in the middle of the day we'd catch up again and we usually talked yet again near the end of the day! Between all of that, if anything ever happened, didn't matter whether it was something serious, a good joke, or just to vent, we caught up with each other.

When everything happened with Randy I told him what I'd done and he didn't judge, only told me that all things happen for a reason. And he believed that the two of us would get back together. He felt that we were meant to be together and it made him sad to see us apart because I looked so happy when I was with her. I didn't know anybody could see that, but he knew me that well.

My life took on a stagnant feel. Nothing seemed to make me happy. I began to pull away from the outside world. If I wasn't at my office or looking for new business, going through the motions of work as I became more and more disenfranchised from it, I was sitting around my house feeling sorry for myself.

Things could have gone on like that for a very long time,

but one last go around with Randy was around the bend. Believe it or not, she wanted to give me a second chance. We were determined to make this relationship work or get it out of our systems if it killed us. Through the process I would both give up things I had worked very hard for and lose some of my identity.

Randy tried to move on but something kept telling her I was the man she was supposed to spend the rest of her life with. I didn't try to contact her while we were apart, respecting her stated wishes, because I knew how I had violated her trust. Out of town over the 4th of July holiday, visiting her family in the Midwest, Randy gave me a call because her father wanted to say hello to me. She had never told her family what I'd done. She didn't want them to think badly about me. Her father in the background as we conversed, Randy pretended all was well between us. On the other end, I told her a thousand times how sorry I was for betraying her trust and how much she was missed.

Randy missed me as well. When she came back into town after the holiday she called and we began speaking again. Things were never the same after my indiscretion, but we tried to fit that square peg into the round hole anyway. Randy, obviously, would never trust me again no matter what I did. And I walked on eggshells for the rest of our relationship together because of what I'd done. The first thing we started talking about when we restarted our relationship was my house. Before the incident she was willing to sacrifice the commute and one day consider moving in with me as we got closer to marriage. Now she didn't even want to step foot through the front door. If we were going to be together it wasn't going to be in my house ever. She made that very clear and I realized I had brought it all on myself so I suggested putting it on the market. By late July the sign was out in the front yard.

Randy also had a laundry list of things she didn't like about our relationship. All those were to change as well. I understood most of them but she was a little excessive. She wasn't at all shy about letting me know <u>EVERYTHING</u> she didn't like about me. I almost wanted to ask her how she could love me, as she seemed not to *like* anything about me, but I kept my mouth shut. I was on a short leash. I felt I was giving up my manhood. I had my own list, as any healthy couple should have balance and input from both sides, but I was the guilty party. My opinions didn't matter. At least, I wasn't going to voice them because I had no right at the time, so I thought. This was our relationship for now and when my house sold at the end of September it was to be how we lived together after I moved in with her.

We had done so much damage to a relationship that had started out so innocently six years ago that it was only a matter of time before it hemorrhaged. Neither of us wanted to face what we had said so many times and would say again over the next several months: "This just isn't working." Chasing love will make you do crazy things. Before I knew it, all my belongings were in storage, and I was living with my girlfriend at the start of October 2002. Initially we were happy, but that didn't last long. And, yet another terrible tragedy was waiting in the darkness. When this one hit, it sent me into a downward spiral.

A Piece Of My Heart

It was only a week and a half after my move to Randy's condo. A little voice in my head kept telling me to call my grandmother. Normally, I rarely let more than a week pass without talking to her. With all my heart I loved both of my grandmothers, but had a special bond with Grandma. When I was younger I spent more time with Grandma than Mom Mom as she used to take care of Irv and me when we were little. I remember Mom taking us to Trenton when were little so we could spend every Saturday with her. While Mom and my aunts went shopping, Irv and I sat on the couch, next to Grandma in her favorite chair, and watch Monster and Kung-Fu Theaters. She made hot tea for us and coffee for herself and we all sat and watched our shows. And when she 'needed' something from the corner store, she gave us money to go up for her. She always gave us a little extra so we could get some snack cakes, penny candy and sodas. After our excursion we'd all sit together and eat our treats.

Later, as I grew up, I was my Grandma's angel. She was the reason I avoided much trouble in life. I would just as soon jump off a building than disappoint that woman. I remember when I started getting tattoos as a grown man I didn't even want her to know about those. I always wanted her to think of me as her "Little Eddie" as she always called me. No matter how old I got, whether I was calling from across the country or sitting in her living room, whenever I heard her voice I felt like I was five years old. In recent years my favorite thing to do when I went back to New Jersey was to stop off at our favorite barbecue place around the corner from Grandma's apartment where she lived independently in a seniors building. I'd buy some ribs, mashed potatoes and rolls and go sit with her while we watched her favorite television programs, "The Price is Right" and "The Young and the Restless".

The last time I saw Grandma was over the summer when I went back for a visit. My cousin, LaToya, was having a house-warming party and Grandma sat in a chair in the living room. I looked up one time to find her just staring at me and smiling. I got up and went over to her and kissed her and then asked her to do something she hated, take a picture with me. I was about the only person she would ever do it for. I gave my camera to someone and they flashed as she gave a reluctant smile. The last time I had talked to her was a few days before I moved in with Randy. I had gotten so caught up with everything that I missed our weekly chat. I was now a few days late and that little voice reminded me to pick up the phone but I kept replying, "It's too late, I'll call tomorrow". I waited one day too long.

Late on a Thursday night, October 10, Randy in bed beside me, I called Mom and Pops at the house in New Jersey. Even though it was well past the time they were ever out of the house, I kept getting their answering machine. I worried that something was wrong. It was almost midnight now. After about the fourth try, my phone rang. It was Mom. Assuming she was at home, I didn't take notice from where she was calling. I told her I had just been trying to reach her. Her voice sounded sad and the second she told me she was calling from Grandma's, I knew something was wrong. I didn't want to believe the words telling me my grandmother had passed away in her apartment, the victim of a heart attack. My father was soon on the phone trying to console me as my mother stepped away to be with other family. I cried a river of tears that night, walking the streets alone until the early hours of the morning. I didn't want to be around anyone; I felt as bad as I had ever in my life. That tiny voice in my head, telling me to call Grandma, was trying to give me an opportunity to talk to her before she left, but I hadn't listened. I felt I had let her down. In the back of my mind I knew my grandmother never doubted how much I loved her – I was the apple of her eye, I could see that myself. It was just hard letting go without being able to say good-bye. The following week we laid my grandmother to rest and I spoke at her funeral. Just like the song says, "It's so hard to say good-bye."

When I got back from my grandmother's funeral I went through a state of depression and turned away from the world. First, I quit my job with MetLife. I hadn't been happy there for months. Having worked hard to make a new career, I got no joy out of what I was doing. Maybe work isn't supposed to be fun, but you should at least like what you are doing. Otherwise why do it? I felt similar disdain when I walked away from professional baseball.

'Things' never improved around the condo either. Instead of Randy and I coming together, we grew further apart under the same roof. And I knew the reason. She wanted the BIG commitment – MARRIAGE! It seemed like her friends were getting married. Every time we turned around we were attending another wedding. That bothered her and I could tell. We were in a catch-22, though. While she thought marriage would help us get past a lot of problems and put an end to the constant arguing, I wanted the arguing and bickering to stop before I even thought about it.

I talked to friends, telling them I was going to get the ring because it was time, but something always interrupted the process. Another fight, usually about something stupid, would have us at each other's throats; peace rarely resided in our house. Randy never believed I ever thought about marrying her, but I did. A major hurdle to overcome was her constant distrust, but I was to blame for that. And because of that issue I stopped doing *anything*. I didn't visit friends and rarely talked to anyone on the phone. I felt I was constantly looking over my shoulder, but I wanted to make Randy comfortable. I tried to mold myself into *exactly* what she wanted me to be. The problem was I was losing my identity along the way.

We lived like this for months, into the middle of 2003. Recruited by an old Falcon teammate, I had taken a job with a new financial firm, which dealt primarily with teachers and their financial futures. The job kept me on the road a lot – not such a bad thing sometimes. That seemed the only time we didn't

argue. I made a lot of mistakes as we tried to keep the relationship afloat and so did she. We honestly loved each other, but just
couldn't make it in the end. We tried counseling, reading books
and even watching "Dr. Phil". But it just wasn't meant for the two
of us. In the end, we were both still in love with the person we
met from 1996 but not willing to accept each other for becoming
different people as the years passed. All the time apart never
allowed either of us to get to know the other as we evolved into
who we were today. Shortly after my 34th birthday, June 2003, I
moved out of Randy's condo. Our relationship was definitely
over. Living together had brought that point home. We both
needed to move on. And we both saw that.

I felt I still had a future in Atlanta but needed to get away
for a bit, so I planned a trip to see Irv for the beginning of July.
As he had been trying to get me out to the desert for a while, this
would be the perfect time. We could both use each other a little
right now. Some of my friends in Atlanta worried that I would
go away and not come back, but I assured them my heart was
still in the South. I just needed to get away for a while.

Another devastating blow fell on June 25, 2003 when I
lost Eric at the age of 39. Eric Dixon was the best friend I had in
this world outside of family. My father always told me, "If you
are lucky in this life, you will be able to count four or five people
that you can call Best Friend." I was fortunate to be able to count
Nate, Calvin and Doug on that list but Eric had risen to an even
higher level. He used to joke with me that it was like we were
separated at birth and shared part of the same brain. When I was
down, he always seemed to call. I didn't even have to tell him
anything was wrong; he'd just have me laughing by the end of
the conversation. And I know I did the same for him. I shared
everything with him and he never judged me. During the period
after I cheated on Randy, Eric was about the only person that

came to the house. He came all the way from the West Side to keep me company when I went through those depressed periods. He had also befriended Randy.

The last time I saw Eric was on my birthday, June 5th. Randy had put together a dinner for me with some of my friends, Eric included, of course, but I could tell by talking to him during the day that he might not make it out that evening. Eric had a weight issue and additional health problems and lately he'd been complaining about always being tired. He wasn't getting out as much lately and I wasn't seeing him as often but continued talking to him several times a day. Because of my birthday I didn't go out of town that week for work. So, on my day off I went over to see him at his office at the Georgia Department of Revenue. That was something I did all the time. I'd stop in, he'd introduce me to all the people in the building, and we'd hang out for a bit. People thought he and I were crazy the way we'd break out in a fit of laughter sometimes in the big open office or out in front of the building. He was incredibly fun to be around and one of the best people I will ever know in my life.

Two weeks after I last saw him I flew up to New Jersey for LaToya's wedding. While there, I talked to Eric every day. My trip to Arizona upcoming, Eric joked that I was going to go out there and forget about coming back to Atlanta. When I flew back to Atlanta on the 24th the first person I talked to was Eric. We planned to do something the upcoming weekend. The next day, Wednesday, I got my usual morning call from him to discuss the antics going on around his office. He sounded as normal as any day I had ever spoken to him, laughing his big laugh. I had begun to prepare for my several week Arizona trip, and had a lot of running around and tying up of loose ends to do so I spent all day driving around town and talked to Eric two more times before evening.

In my storage unit looking for a couple of items I wanted to take to Arizona, my cell phone rang at around 6:45. Had it had been just about anybody else I wouldn't have answered the phone. My hands were full and I wanted to finish up so I could get out of there. Eric was at his parents' house sitting with his mom in her kitchen and getting ready to head home. He asked what I was doing and when I told him I was at the storage unit he said he'd let me go. He didn't call for any important reason he said, just had something he wanted to tell me. Before he hung up I told him to call me once he got home as I wanted to know what his little bit of info was. I was sure it was going to be some funny story about something or someone at work and I sure could use a good laugh right now; it had been a long day. He promised he would and hung up. That was the last time I ever talked to my friend.

That night, back where I was staying, I got busy, so it slipped my mind that I hadn't heard from Eric. The next morning when I got up I called him as I jumped in my truck to go to take care of some paperwork for a few of my clients. I was taking an extended vacation while the schools were out for the summer and had a lot to get done so I could enjoy myself out in the desert without having to deal with a lot of business. The message I left him when his voice mail picked up was stupid. We had this thing from a movie we both liked. Instead of leaving a normal message after the beep I just yelled, "Message!" into the phone. That meant, "Call me back when you get this, you know who it is." When evening came after a busy day and I hadn't heard from Eric all day, I should have been worried but I didn't think anything of the fact that I hadn't heard from him. I assumed he had gotten busy with the day, even though it was odd because we simply didn't go days without talking. I never would have expected what I was about to find out Friday morning.

When I woke up I still wasn't alarmed that I hadn't talked to Eric. Looking at the clock and seeing it was about 7:30, I knew he would already be in his office. First in the building most days because he hated traffic, Eric beat everybody to the punch by getting in as early as 6:00. One of the things we joked about most was his road rage. When I dialed his number and someone other than him picked up, I knew immediately that something was wrong. When his co-worker realized it was me, she explained how they had been looking for my number to get in touch with me. She hated to be the one to have to give me the news, but Eric had passed away on Wednesday night from a sudden heart attack.

I didn't believe her. She had to be playing some horrible joke. My friend could not be gone. Composing myself, I quickly called Eric's mother. I was about to lose it all over again as I heard her voice on the phone and she told me how my friend died.

Eric left her house shortly after our conversation. His mother watched him walk down the stairs, then waved from the window as she always did when he backed out of the driveway. A mile down the road he stopped for gas and had a heart attack in the parking lot of the convenience store. An ambulance rushed him to the hospital while he drifted in and out of consciousness. Before the doctors could do anything for him, his heart simply exploded.

Called by hospital staff, Eric's mom was under the assumption that he had a traffic accident, but was not seriously hurt. When she got there they would not let her see him until another family member arrived. That is when she knew something was wrong.

I broke down for days after that. Why did things like this have to happen to such good people? Eric and his family were some of the nicest people I had ever known; they were family to me. Not too long ago their concerns were directed toward his father as he battled some ailments. I remember cheering Eric up as he talked about his father's health concerns. We had just met when I went through the ordeal with my father two years prior. Now they were grieving his loss. It just didn't seem fair. I turned to drinking for a couple of days, trying to drown the sorrow and ease the pain, but I knew that wasn't the solution to the problem I had to face. I had to be there for Eric's family; they were the ones suffering most. On July 3rd Eric was laid to rest. Once again, I found myself in front of a large group of mourners, giving a speech about the loss of someone we all loved.

Life isn't supposed to be this tough. Some say that God will never give more than you can handle, but it seemed He sure laid it on the Dixon family. Two days after burying Eric, I flew out to Arizona. And exactly six weeks later I had to fly back to attend the funeral of Eric's oldest and closest sister. She died in a one-car accident on her way home from work heading to their parents' house. Walking into the same funeral home to view her body, attending the same church for her funeral services and walking by the unsettled earth where Eric was buried on the way to her gravesite was enough to convince me that it was time to move on in my life. Any thoughts of returning to the South were gone. I didn't care who or what was left behind, it was time to look ahead in a new direction.

Where Now?

Time marches on; it doesn't wait for anyone! As life has unfolded I have seen the view from every angle. I've been on the top and the bottom of the heap. And through it all I've had out-standing people in my life. They've been by my side to enjoy the good times as well as the bad. And I've learned many valuable lessons that will hopefully help carry me through the rest of my life. Nobody is promised tomorrow, but I sure plan on spending my todays loving the people that mean so much to me.

Mom and Pop

My mother and father have had enough to deal with in their lifetime already. They were successful in raising two knuckle-headed boys, without giving into the urge to kill us from time to time, and they should probably get medals for that. While my father's alcohol abuse threatened to destroy our family and their marriage, they stayed committed and fought through the tough times. On September 21, 2003 they celebrated their 35th wedding anniversary! They are both healthy, happy and more in love today than they were all those years ago. My mother is still at the college and my father still runs boilers on a partially-retired basis now. And they still live in the house in Browns Mills.

On November 14, 2003 another milestone was accomplished as my father celebrated his eleventh year of sobriety. 'One Day At A Time' he has managed to keep his life clean and on track.

Irv

After retiring from the NFL before the 2000 season my brother never looked back. He purchased a home in the northern suburbs of Phoenix, Arizona and began opening businesses. His relationship with his son is the most important thing in his life. Having been at odds from time to time with little Irv's mother, through the courts they have worked things out. They share custody and the little man started his first year of school, kindergarten, after celebrating his fifth birthday in August 2003.

Eddie

This is the most difficult part of my life, the area I have yet to get a firm grasp on even after all these years. I still don't have a relationship with my son. I love and miss him. Lee remarried in 2002 and felt I was only hurting my son by attempting to be in his life. Sad to say, I have almost given up hope that we will ever get things right between us. My one wish is that someday he will seek me out when he is ready to really get to know me. I only hope that his image of me is not too distorted due to my years of absence and his only hearing one side of the story. My mother has always said that it will happen when it is meant to be. I believe she is right and when the time is right we will be together.

Randy

After ending our relationship in June 2003, Randy and I have tried to remain friends. When Eric passed away she was front and center to give me the support I needed. I couldn't have gotten through the week leading up to the funeral without her.

Initially, reconnecting was tough because we still had deep feelings for one another and recognized the temptation to give our relationship another shot. We actually took a huge step away from each other for a while so as to avoid another mistake. The truth of the matter has finally sunk in: as much as we loved each other we just weren't meant to spend the rest of our lives together. She has moved on and I am happy for her. Still in the Atlanta area, she is doing well for herself. I know she will one day find what she was looking for in me. And I wish her nothing but the best because she deserves it.

EZ

The choppy waters have threatened to throw me out of the boat, but I'm trying to settle in for a smoother ride with calmer waters (hopefully!) ahead. The move to Arizona has become a permanent one for now. It was tough leaving Atlanta because of the many fond memories, but the time to move on had come. And the attraction of being near my brother at this stage in our lives is a major factor. After years of separation, the two of us caught in our careers, we finally have been able to spend quality time together. And it has been a blessing for both of us. We really needed each other for different reasons and God brought us back together.

Irv and I have gotten involved with schools throughout the valley, speaking to and mentoring students, as we both have done throughout our respective careers. We both believe strongly that children are our future. With so much negativity and so many obstacles before them, it is important we provide a positive message. When we speak to them, it is not about being athletes, although that is what first attracts their attention. We stress the importance of being accountable and responsible in making important, life-shaping decisions. When I see the light go on behind their eyes it is very gratifying personally, like hitting a homerun. And I realize my own significance.

I have also taken steps toward getting back to my first love, baseball. Additionally, I spend some free time instructing youngsters in the art of hitting a baseball. Passing on knowledge is another important aspect of helping the next generation.

Personally, I am at peace now because God has allowed me to accept the fact that there are some things that are just not in my control. I put my life in His hands. In His time all things will be revealed. I have learned many valuable lessons along the long road that has been my incredible journey. The key is to put the knowledge that I have acquired to use rather than making the same mistakes over and over, as I have sometimes done before.

If I'm ever going to find true love that will last, I must open my heart. I cannot be the big mystery or riddle that no one can ever 'solve'. Honesty is vital. There can be no secrets. And as far as my relationship with my son, I am going to take my mother's advice. I want to be there and I have to let him know that. As he matures, he will be able to decide how we proceed. It is my job to let him know that I am here though, waiting to cross the bridge when the time is right for the two of us. One day our need for each other will be enough to conquer all the problems that have existed and God will let us know when that is.

As I walk off into the sunset I realize the journey of life isn't over until you take that last breath. Every day is the next one in the rest of my life. In the past I've been up, down, and sometimes kicked around, but I'm still standing. It seems like I've lived two lifetimes already in a quick 35 years, the latest birthday celebrated June 5, 2004, but there is still an awful lot to do. And you can bet I'm going to be doing it EZ. Rest assured, you haven't heard the last from me yet!

Ed and Grandmom Miles - Thanksgiving 2001

*Eric Dixon
and Ed
Deceember 31, 2001*

Irv Sr. and Jr. – 2002

Ed and Parents
Super Bowl Week – Miami

■ **HE'S MY BROTHER.** The Smith brothers, Irv (82) and Ed (47), walk off the field together at the end of the last April minicamp workout. Irv is the projected starter at tight end, while Ed is battling for the backup role. Ed was claimed off waivers from Atlanta. After eight seasons in minor league baseball, including the 1995 season with the Canton Indians, Ed turned to pro football in 1996. In 1998, he helped the Fal-

Eddie and Friends, March 2000

Edward Smith

Little Eddie

Georgia Home (2001)

Nate Miller

Ed and Dad

Ed and Parents after game - 1998

Doug Glanville, Paul Torres and Ed – Orlando Cubs 1994

Ed and High School Coaches – 1999

▲ *Super Bowl Shoes and Helmet*

Super Bowl Ring
▶

Michael Jordan Baseball shoes

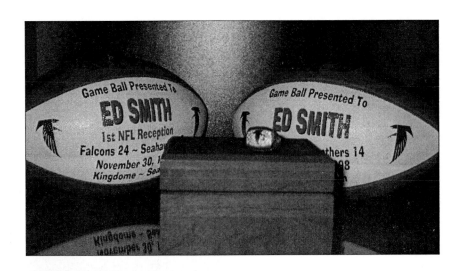

Bolts' Helmet

Hanging Jersey

Edward and Patricia Smith
Wedding Day
September 21, 1968

Dear Mr. Smith,

    I am a huge fan of yours and really enjoy watching you play on television. I try to see you play whenever games are televised, but one day would like to see you play in person. I was wondering if you might autograph these cards to me for my collection of XFL items. Thanks for your time, and good luck to you the rest of the season and in years to come.

        Your fan, Kurt

Ed,
   I've become a big
fan of the XFL + the
Bolts' are my favorite
team. I think you're
an awesome player for
them - a lot of fun to
watch!! It would mean
a lot if I could have
my card signed by you.
Thank you + good luck
winning it all with
Birmingham
        Your fan + thank you
      Ty

DATE

PAGE #

3-26-01

Dear Mr. Smith,
   Hello, I hope this note finds
all well with you. We are big
Bolts fan. You are a great
tight end. We are coming
to the game Saturday!
Will you please autograph
the enclosed cards?
I thank you for your time.

       Your fans
   Brett, Renee, & Ashley
      Sams

Dear Ed,

Hello, my name is Pat Gruber. I hope that this letter of mine finds you well and in good spirits. I am a big fan of yours and was hoping you could please autograph my trading card for me. I would very much appreciate it.

Thanks,

Pat

Dear Mr. Smith:
I greatly appreciate your XFL career and the enjoyment I've been fortunate to have in watching your games on TV. Thanks for being an inspiration to folks like me who want to make it big in this world. Please sign the enclosed card & return in S.A.S.E. at your discretion.

Sincerely,

William Taylor

Dear Mr. Ed Smith,

My name is Jon Boswell. I'm 16 years old and I would first like to congragulate you on all of your career success. Not too many people have played in the minors, NFl and you must be the only one w/ XFL experience! You are a true athlete! I'm writing to you to ask if you could please autograph my enclosed baseball card of you? It would be greatly appricated! Thank you in advance for your time and kindness and I wish you all the best in everything you do in the future!

Your fan

Jon Boswell

KAY JONES

Dear Mr. Smith:

My sons are great X FL fans. They also collect autographs. I know my sons would love to have your autograph. If you would be so kind as to sign the cards enclosed. I would be so very grateful.

I know my sons would appreciate having a autograph from you. I thank you for your time.

Sincerely
Kay Jones

Edward Smith